# Behavioral Economics: When Psychology and Economics Collide

Scott Huettel, Ph.D.

THE
GREAT
COURSES

PUBLISHED BY:

THE GREAT COURSES
Corporate Headquarters
4840 Westfields Boulevard, Suite 500
Chantilly, Virginia 20151-2299
Phone: 1-800-832-2412
Fax: 703-378-3819
www.thegreatcourses.com


Copyright © The Teaching Company, 2014


Printed in the United States of America

This book is in copyright. All rights reserved.

Without limiting the rights under copyright reserved above,
no part of this publication may be reproduced, stored in
or introduced into a retrieval system, or transmitted,
in any form, or by any means
(electronic, mechanical, photocopying, recording, or otherwise),
without the prior written permission of
The Teaching Company.

## Scott Huettel, Ph.D.
Jerry G. and Patricia Crawford Hubbard
Professor of Psychology and Neuroscience
Duke University

Professor Scott Huettel is the Jerry G. and Patricia Crawford Hubbard Professor in the Department of Psychology and Neuroscience at Duke University, where he has taught since 2002. He graduated with honors from The University of Texas at Austin, with a B.A. in Liberal Arts Honors and Psychology. Professor Huettel received his Ph.D. from Duke University in Experimental Psychology and completed a postdoctoral fellowship in functional brain imaging and decision science at Duke University Medical Center. He has appointments in a number of interdisciplinary units at Duke, including secondary appointments in the departments of Psychiatry and Neurobiology. In addition, he is the founding Director of the Duke Center for Interdisciplinary Decision Science (D-CIDES), which brings together faculty and students from across campus for interdisciplinary research and educational programs. Professor Huettel is a recipient of the Dean's Award for Excellence in Mentoring from the Duke University Graduate School and has been recognized as one of the top five percent of undergraduate instructors at Duke.

Professor Huettel is a leading researcher at the intersection of behavioral economics and neuroscience. His laboratory uses a combination of behavioral, genetic, physiological, and neuroscience techniques to discover the neural mechanisms that underlie higher cognition, with a focus on economic and social decision making. Much of his research—which includes collaborations with neuroscientists, psychologists, behavioral economists, and business and medical faculty—falls within the emerging interdiscipline of neuroeconomics. He is also a Past President of the Society for Neuroeconomics.

Professor Huettel is the author of more than 100 scientific publications, including articles in *Science, Nature Neuroscience, Nature Reviews*

*Neuroscience, Neuron, Psychological Science*, and other top journals in several fields. His research has been featured in many media outlets, including CNN, *Newsweek*, *Money* magazine, and NPR's *Science Friday*. Professor Huettel is the lead author of a primary textbook in neuroscience, *Functional Magnetic Resonance Imaging*, and is a coeditor of the textbook *Principles of Cognitive Neuroscience*. ∎

# Table of Contents

## INTRODUCTION

Professor Biography ................................................................. i
Course Scope ........................................................................... 1

## LECTURE GUIDES

**LECTURE 1**
What Is a Good Decision? ....................................................... 4

**LECTURE 2**
The Rise of *Behavioral* Economics ...................................... 23

**LECTURE 3**
Reference Dependence—It's All Relative ............................. 42

**LECTURE 4**
Reference Dependence—Economic Implications ............... 60

**LECTURE 5**
Range Effects—Changing the Scale ..................................... 79

**LECTURE 6**
Probability Weighting .............................................................. 98

**LECTURE 7**
Risk—The Known Unknowns ................................................ 117

**LECTURE 8**
Ambiguity—The Unknown Unknowns .................................. 136

**LECTURE 9**
Temporal Discounting—Now or Later? ................................ 155

**LECTURE 10**
Comparison—Apples and Oranges ...................................... 174

# Table of Contents

**LECTURE 11**
Bounded Rationality—Knowing Your Limits ................................. 192

**LECTURE 12**
Heuristics and Biases ..................................................................... 211

**LECTURE 13**
Randomness and Patterns ............................................................. 230

**LECTURE 14**
How Much Evidence Do We Need? ................................................ 249

**LECTURE 15**
The Value of Experience ................................................................. 268

**LECTURE 16**
Medical Decision Making ................................................................ 287

**LECTURE 17**
Social Decisions—Competition and Coordination ......................... 306

**LECTURE 18**
Group Decision Making—The Vox Populi ....................................... 325

**LECTURE 19**
Giving and Helping—Why Altruism? ............................................... 344

**LECTURE 20**
Cooperation by Individuals and in Societies .................................. 363

**LECTURE 21**
When Incentives Backfire ............................................................... 382

**LECTURE 22**
Precommitment—Setting Rationality Aside ................................... 401

**LECTURE 23**
Framing—Moving to a Different Perspective ................................. 420

# Table of Contents

**LECTURE 24**
Interventions, Nudges, and Decisions ............................................. 439

## SUPPLEMENTAL MATERIAL

Bibliography ................................................................................... 459

# Behavioral Economics:
# When Psychology and Economics Collide

**Scope**:

We all face difficult decisions: which new car to purchase, where to go to college, whether to take that dream vacation now or save more for retirement. Traditional economic models of decision making assume that people make those decisions in what is often called a rational manner—they weigh the costs and benefits of different outcomes, evaluate the future with patience and foresight, and acquire the appropriate information to make a good decision. These models have been extraordinarily powerful for predicting large-scale economic phenomena in a wide range of settings: how consumers respond to price changes, how voters react to new information, and many others.

Traditional economic models work extremely well—except when they don't. In some situations, people make decisions that seem to violate the foundational assumptions of rational choice models. Sometimes monetary incentives decrease people's likelihood to take an action, and sometimes additional choice options lead people to make worse decisions. Over the past half-century, decision scientists have identified anomalies, or biases, in people's behavior that can't readily be explained with traditional economic models. This research has sparked a new field of inquiry now called behavioral economics that integrates economics and psychology—and, recently, neuroscience—toward the goal of better explaining real-world decision making.

This course will provide a systematic introduction to the rapidly changing field of behavioral economics. It will consider how behavioral economics adopts traits from its parent disciplines of economics and psychology but combines them into a new approach for studying decision making. It will explore a remarkable range of counterintuitive and sometimes even paradoxical aspects of human behavior, often revealing that our decisions are based on completely unexpected factors. It won't, however, lose track of the underlying science. Each topic remains in close contact with the research that experts in the field pursue, and each topic builds to concrete recommendations so that you can understand why we have these biases, what purposes they serve, and how you can turn them to your advantage.

This course begins by exploring the history of behavioral economics, starting with the first recognition that concepts from psychology could actually contribute to the understanding of meaningful economic decisions. It will cover some of the foundational principles of behavioral economics, as encapsulated in the seminal work of pioneers like Daniel Kahneman and Amos Tversky, who created prospect theory. To understand those foundational principles, you will work your way from basic properties of how our brains work, through the psychology of motivation, all the way to our consumer choices in the real world. In addition, you will explore the key motivators for our decisions—factors like probability, risk, reward, and the passage of time—and how we integrate those factors to reach decisions.

The decision process, however, begins well before the moment of choice. So, you will consider what happens before decisions get made by looking at how people acquire information, strategize about the decision process, and simplify complex decisions to something more manageable. You will step back in time to consider the discoveries of Herbert Simon, who developed the idea of bounded rationality, and you will step forward to the latest research on how people use their emotions to shortcut complex decision making. You will explore the nature of randomness, why we see patterns that aren't there, the mistakes we make even when trying to be impartial, and when our experiences aren't necessarily a good guide. In addition, you will explore some underappreciated consequences of our decisions—why we might overvalue things and undervalue experiences and how our sense of self factors into our medical decisions.

You will explore how groups make decisions. Often, a group can reach accurate judgments and make excellent decisions, especially when that group's members are diverse and independent. However, small changes to how groups are formed and how they communicate can make groups much worse than the individuals therein. You will consider prosocial decisions like charitable giving and cooperation, each of which arises in ways that aren't predicted by traditional economic models but are predictable from new models that incorporate people's sense of fairness, personal identity, and social norms. In addition, you will learn some really remarkable ways in which economic incentives actually undermine good behaviors, particularly when people have social motivations for their actions.

Finally, this course will describe the ways you can use the tools of behavioral economics to make better decisions. The focus will be on two tools that work for a wide range of real-world situations: precommitting to a course of action and changing the frame of a decision problem. These tools—like behavioral economics itself—have attracted interest from government agencies, corporations, and other institutions. Interventions based on behavioral economics hold promise for shaping decision making at a societal level, from how people save for retirement to whether people make healthy eating decisions. However, like much of science, those interventions can lead to resistance or can even backfire, raising important ethical issues.

Through this course, you will gain a better sense of how you make decisions and what steps you can take to make better decisions. You will learn about your limitations and your biases. You will see how you, like everyone else, is an imperfect, short-sighted, and emotional decision maker. However, you will also see how those same biases can help you make very good decisions—when you apply the right tool to the right decision. You will learn how to turn your limitations into strengths. ■

# What Is a Good Decision?
## Lecture 1

Throughout this course, you will be introduced to tools for improving the process of decision making—the information you acquire and the strategies you adopt. While it's difficult, or maybe impossible, to eliminate your biases, you can use these tools to put yourself in situations where you'll make better decisions—where your biases aren't weaknesses, but strengths. This course explores many aspects of the decision-making process. You will learn how people deal with the different factors that shape their choices: from the value of rewards to the pain of loss, from probability and risk to time itself.

**Rational Choice Models**

- Traditional approaches to economic decision making invoke the so-called rational choice model, which is a framework for understanding and often formally modeling social and economic behavior. But what does it mean?

- The term "rational" carries a lot of baggage and leads to many misconceptions. A first misconception is that the word "rational" means the same thing in everyday conversation as it does to behavioral economists and other decision scientists. When we describe one of our friends as rational, we often want to imply that they are dispassionate, logical, thoughtful, and in control of their actions.

- However, to a decision scientist, "rational" means "consistency with some model." Rational decisions are not necessarily dispassionate, nor well reasoned, nor selfish. They aren't even necessarily good decisions, from others' perspectives. They simply are consistent.

- Consistency seems like a pretty straightforward criterion. A rational decision maker should always prefer better things to worse things—more money to less. That decision maker should be able to assess which choices lead to more desirable outcomes; in the language of economics, they should anticipate how much subjective value, or utility, would come from their choices. In addition, they should reliably make choices that maximize their expected utility. We should be able to take the past decisions of a rational decision maker and insert them into a mathematical model to predict their future decisions.

- Conversely, someone whose preferences are inconsistent and capricious would hardly be a "rational" decision maker. Furthermore, consistency shouldn't just apply to consumer purchases; it should apply to all of behavior.

- A second misconception is that a rational decision maker must be completely selfish. Rational choice models do not assume anything about what a decision maker prefers; they only state that those preferences consistently lead to choices. So, it may be rational to give to charity, to volunteer your time to help others, or to make sacrifices for the greater good. All of those actions are consistent with traditional economic models—assuming that someone derives utility not only from their own outcomes, but also from the outcomes experienced by others.

- A third misconception is that rationality refers to the decision process. Rational does not mean that a decision was generated by a conscious or logical or reasoned process. Instead, rationality refers to the outcome of decisions. Rational choice models are sometimes called "as if" models, meaning that choice behavior can be described "as if" someone followed a rational process—regardless of the underlying thoughts, beliefs, or computations.

- There are many different models of rational choice, each developed to explain different phenomena within microeconomics, consumer behavior, or decision science. Despite their diversity, these models tend to be built on a few simple foundations: When making decisions, we should exhibit consistent preferences that follow mathematical rules; we should prefer better things to worse things;

and we should take actions to obtain the things we most prefer, in order to maximize overall utility.

**Incentives**

- The great virtue of rational choice models is simplicity. Their assumptions are so basic that they almost seem tautological. People want more money, not less. Of course, this must be true—right? This simple statement lies at the core of traditional models. If it were incorrect, as unlikely as that might sound, then rationality itself would fall into question.

- The assumption that people want more money, not less, implies that people should be motivated by the opportunity to obtain more money. That is, money should be an incentive that can shape their behavior. We know that's true in many circumstances, such as the labor market or consumer responses to sale prices.

- Reward occurs when an external incentive disrupts our internal motivation for some behavior, such as paying people to give blood. It's one of the most striking findings in behavioral economics, because it calls into question that most basic assumption of rational choice models: that people want more money, rather than less.

- On the contrary, in many real-world situations, money can actually serve as a disincentive for behavior. This phenomenon is known to economists as reward undermining. It illustrates one of the deepest themes in this course—that traditional rational choice models explain most aspects of decision making but fail in very specific circumstances.

- Money is usually a very powerful incentive. Structuring monetary incentives the right way can have very positive effects. If the government wants to encourage people to save for retirement, it can create tax breaks on retirement savings. If a company wants to encourage its employees to quit smoking, it offers discounts on insurance copayments for nonsmokers.

- These sorts of incentives do work, usually in exactly the ways predicted by rational choice models. When the utility of the incentive becomes sufficiently great, people start behaving in a way that is good for themselves and good for society. Creating and tracking the effects of such incentives represents a major thrust of microeconomics—both in academic research and institutional policy.

**Sometimes monetary incentives work as motivation for people, but—surprisingly—sometimes they do not work.**

- But monetary incentives don't always work. They fail when they undermine our sense of moral duty; they fail when they crowd out other sources of motivation. Incentives—and rational choice models, more generally—work some of the time and fail some of the time.

- The failures of rational choice models aren't random. They aren't just anomalies that can be dismissed, rare events that can be explained away. Rational choice models fail to account for real-world behavior for specific reasons—reasons rooted in our psychology, biology, and environment. Rational choice models fail, and we can know why.

## *Deal or No Deal*

- Economists who analyzed the decisions of *Deal or No Deal* contestants found something surprising. As the game progressed, contestants tended to become more and more risk seeking, almost regardless of what happened. Contestants who were unlucky kept chasing after what little money was left. Contestants who were lucky stayed in the game in search of the largest prizes.

- All of the sounds, lights, and excitement of the game show push the contestants to become more risk seeking than they probably would be in everyday life.

- *Deal or No Deal* contestants make decisions about real money. They are motivated by large amounts of money; one contestant won a prize worth more than four million dollars. We might expect that they would make good, cautious decisions, but they often don't.

**Constraints**
- Do people make good, cautious decisions when the stakes get large—including buying cars, selecting a mortgage, and saving for retirement? Do they attend to the details, knowing how much more is on the line? The same biases found in the small decisions in the grocery store or laboratory also appear in the biggest decisions of our lives.

- We don't have special machinery that we can suddenly turn on when we face a big decision. We're stuck with the same brain circuits that helped our ancestors forage for food and track down prey—but never evolved to compare fixed- and adjustable-rate mortgages. We use what we have, even if we occasionally end up losing.

- Throughout this course, two fundamental types of limitations on our decision making will be emphasized. The first involves constraints on our cognitive abilities. Much as we might hate to admit it, there are limits on our intellectual capacities. We can't know everything, remember everything, and compute everything. Some people work well with numbers and data and can do complex calculations in their head. Other people have more difficulty with numbers and adopt different strategies for making decisions. But none of us is a supercomputer. There are some types of thinking that we do extremely well and other types that we do very poorly.

- We don't process information in absolute terms, for example, but in relative terms—by comparison to a point of reference. Even though a silver medal is objectively better than a bronze medal, after they win, Olympic bronze medalists tend to be happier than silver medalists. That's because they adopt different reference points: The bronze medalists think that they did well enough to earn a medal, while the silver medalists think that they didn't do well enough to earn a gold medal.

- Our brains are set up to use reference points; it's a way of simplifying the decision process. Using reference points does help in many circumstances, but if we adopt the wrong reference point, we lose perspective on what really matters.

- The second type of limitation is that we do not have unlimited time to make decisions. Real-world decision makers don't always have the luxury of waiting until all of the information is collected.

- Time constraints affect our economic decisions. When deciding whether to purchase a home, time is both your friend and enemy. Acting slowly gives you more time to gain information and deliberate on this largest of all purchases. But acting slowly also carries opportunity costs: Someone else may put in an offer, or interest rates may increase.

- These two limitations—cognitive abilities and time constraints—prevent humans from being the ideal rational decision makers posited by traditional economics. We cannot make optimal decisions that always lead to the best outcome, even if we wanted to.

- But we can recognize these limitations and try to optimize the decision process. The economist/psychologist Herbert Simon introduced the idea of bounded rationality, or rationality within limits. Simon contended that the key challenges for real-world decision making were in acquiring the right information, in simplifying the decision process, and in adopting strategies for decision making.

- We can't overcome these challenges by becoming even more analytic and deliberative in our decisions. Instead, we adopt rules called heuristics that allow us to prioritize some information over other, that simplify complex decisions into something manageable, and that give us strategies that can be implemented quickly and with little effort. Those heuristics help us improve our odds of making a good decision, even in the face of our limitations. But, like us, they're not optimal; they're just good enough, most of the time.

## Suggested Reading

Kahneman, *Thinking, Fast and Slow*.

## Questions to Consider

1. What sorts of decisions seem most difficult, and what features of those decisions make them seem so challenging?

2. What limitations of our biology—including limitations on how we think—might change how we approach complex decisions?

# What Is a Good Decision?
## Lecture 1—Transcript

Every day each of us makes innumerable decisions. As we go through our daily lives—driving, responding to e-mail, talking with friends—we have to constantly decide how to respond to new situations. And, frankly, most of the time our decisions are very good. Think about how many times you have avoided accidents while driving, or how many times you've had conversations where you didn't say the wrong thing. We are all very good decision makers in most real-world situations.

But why do some sorts of decisions seem so difficult? Why do intelligent, competent people find decisions about their investments or their healthcare so challenging? And, most importantly, how can we improve the decisions that we make? Understanding why people make the decisions they do is the core goal of the new field of "behavioral economics".

Consider these three real-world illustrations of why studying decision making can be so challenging:

Imagine a cancer patient who is given the choice between two surgical treatments. Each treatment has the same chance of curing the patient's cancer; in fact, the only difference is that some of the patients who might die from the first surgery would survive the second surgery but have severe but manageable complications. Most patients in this situation, however, choose the first surgery with the higher chance of death. Why is this?

Now consider a second scenario: A central concept in economics is that incentives matter. People will purchase more of a product when its price decreases, they work harder when they are paid more money. But, in some cases incentives actually backfire, as blood drive organizers have discovered. In many cases, offering people monetary payment for each pint of blood donated actually decreases their willingness to donate. Why would paying people to donate blood discourage them from donating?

Or consider this situation: Three Olympic medalists walk to the medal stand. They are the very top in the entire world in their sport. When they step on the podia, the gold medalist turns around and beams in triumph. The third-place bronze medalist smiles broadly. But, the second-place silver medalist manages only a weak smile and has disappointed eyes. Event after event, the same pattern occurs: The gold and bronze medalists are ecstatic, while the silver medalists are dejected. There's a paradox here—everyone would agree that a silver medal is better than a bronze medal, so why is the bronze medalist happier?

Each of these examples runs counter to our intuitions. We should choose a surgical treatment because it leads to better outcomes, not worse outcomes. Monetary incentives should make us more likely, not less likely, to support something. And, doing better—in sports, work, or our personal lives—should make us happier than doing less well.

Intuition, it turns out, is usually a very poor guide for understanding real-world behavior. Over the coming lectures, we'll consider these and many other examples in which people behave in ways that just don't make sense, at least at first. But as we dig deeper and look more closely at people's behavior, you'll start to see common features of decision making that seem like mistakes, but they recur over and over in a range of different settings. Examining behavior provides you with clues about the processes of decision making, and as you better understand behavior, then your intuitions will start to change.

Although this is not a traditional economics course, we will begin from the perspective of traditional economics.

Traditional approaches to economic decision making invoke the so-called rational choice model. This is a framework for understanding and often formally modeling social and economic behavior. But what does it mean? The term "rational" carries so much baggage, and leads to so many misconceptions, that I want to unpack what is typically assumed by a rational choice model.

A first misconception is that the word "rational" means the same thing in everyday conversation as it does to behavioral economists and other decision scientists.

When we describe one of our friends as rational, we often want to imply that they are dispassionate, logical, thoughtful, and in control of their actions. Book and film characters like the detective Sherlock Holmes or the *Star Trek* character Mr. Spock seem prototypically rational: They deductively reason through complex problems to arrive at a solution, without ever being burdened by unwanted emotion.

"Rational" to a decision scientist doesn't mean that. It means consistency with some model. Rational decisions are not necessarily dispassionate, nor well reasoned, nor selfish. They aren't even necessarily good decisions, from others' perspectives. They simply are consistent.

Consistency seems like a pretty straightforward criterion. A rational decision maker should always prefer better things to worse things, more money to less. That decision maker should be able to assess which choices lead to more desirable outcomes—in the language of economics, they should anticipate how much subjective value or utility that would come from their choices. And, they should reliably make choices that maximize their expected utility. We should be able to take the past decisions of a rational decision maker and insert them into a mathematical model to predict their future decisions.

Conversely, someone whose preferences are inconsistent and capricious would hardly be a rational decision maker. And, consistency shouldn't apply to consumer purchases alone; it should apply to all of behavior.

Imagine that you are the cancer patient I mentioned just a moment ago. You must choose one of two surgical procedures to treat your life-threatening medical condition. The first procedure has only two possible outcomes: It completely cures the cancer 80 percent of the time, but there's a 20-percent chance that you'll die during the surgery. The second procedure is generally similar but has more potential outcomes: Again, there's an 80-percent chance of being completely cured, and there's only a 16-percent chance of dying during the surgery. But, 4 percent of the time the surgery will result in a cure with some major complication, like severe scarring or recurring diarrhea.

Now, if you're like most people, when people are presented with these two types of surgery, you'll choose the first procedure: the one with the higher chance of death, but no scary complications. But, when asked which is better for someone else—death or scarring, or death or diarrhea—would say you prefer living with the complication over dying. Most people voluntarily choose something they say is objectively worse over something objectively better.

This bias arises for several reasons that we'll cover in this course, most notably that people treat rare and vivid outcomes as more likely than they really are. So, if one hears that there is an objective 1-percent chance of recurring diarrhea, then that 1 percent seems subjectively like about 5 percent, leading to overweighting of small probabilities and inconsistencies in our choices.

A second misconception is that a rational decision maker must be completely selfish. Rational choice models do not assume anything about what a decision maker prefers, they only state that those preferences consistently lead to choices. So, it may be rational to give to charity, to volunteer your time to help others, or to make sacrifices for the greater good. All of those actions are consistent with traditional economic models assuming that someone derives utility not only from their own outcomes but also from the outcomes experienced by others.

A third misconception is that rationality refers to the decision process. Rational does not mean that a decision was generated by a logical or conscious or reasoned process. Instead, rationality refers to the outcome of decisions. Rational choice models are sometimes called "as if" models, meaning that choice behavior can be described "as if" someone followed a rational process regardless of the underlying thoughts, beliefs, or computations. Rational decisions don't require the intellect of a Sherlock Holmes or the calmness of a Mr. Spock. In fact, later in this course we'll consider situations where the decisions of animals seem to follow rational choice models often better than humans.

So there are many different models of rational choice, each developed to explain different phenomena within microeconomics, consumer behavior, or decision science. Despite their diversity, these models tend to be built on a few simple foundations. When making decisions, we should exhibit consistent preferences that follow mathematical rules, like transitivity. We should prefer better things to worse things, more money to less. And, we should take actions to obtain the things we most prefer in order to maximize overall utility.

Now the great virtue of rational choice models is simplicity. Their assumptions are so basic that they almost seem tautological. People want more money, not less. Of course this must be true, right?

Let's examine this single assumption: People want more money, not less. This simple statement lies at the core of traditional models. If it were incorrect, as unlikely as that might sound, then rationality itself would fall into question.

The assumption that people want more money, not less implies that people should be motivated by the opportunity to obtain more money. That is, money should be an incentive that can shape their behavior. We know that's true in many circumstances, like the labor market or consumer responses to sale prices.

So, let's consider a very simple sort of incentive. Suppose that you are a volunteer leader in the local Red Cross or another charitable organization. You're coordinating a blood donation drive in your community. In previous years, the blood drive has gone reasonably well, with about 1,000 pints donated each time. That's a pretty impressive number, given that people weren't paid anything for donating and they didn't directly benefit from their donations. You set up your tent in the park at the center of town. You fly the normal banner over the front of the tent: "Blood Drive—Donate Today!" it reads. But this year, you have a simple plan to increase donations. You add a second sign reading simply "10 dollars per pint!" Now, in addition to all of the normal reasons to donate (helping others, feeling good about oneself) there's also the motivation of earning a little extra money.

Let's pause and break this situation down to its essence. You took the same decision situation as before, and you added a monetary incentive. People want more money, not less. A traditional rational choice model makes a simple prediction: The utility of donating blood should increase, and thus more people should donate.

So, what happens? You walk around a mostly empty tent, puzzled. The number of people donating blood goes down dramatically. Only about half as many people donate, even though they now have an explicit monetary incentive for donating. So, the next year you drop the monetary incentive and stop paying people for giving blood and the number of donations increases back to a normal level.

This phenomenon is known to economists as "reward undermining." Reward occurs when an external incentive disrupts our internal motivation for some behavior, like paying people to give blood. It's one of the most striking findings in behavioral economics, because it calls into question that most basic assumption of rational choice models: that people want more money, rather than less. On the contrary, in many real-world situations, money can actually serve as a disincentive for behavior.

We'll talk much more about reward undermining later in this course. But I wanted to introduce it here because it illustrates one of the deepest themes in this course: that traditional rational choice models explain most aspects of decision making, but fail in very specific circumstances.

Money is usually a very powerful incentive. Structuring monetary incentives the right way can have very positive effects. If the government wants to encourage people to save for retirement, it can create tax breaks on retirement savings. If a company wants to encourage its employees to quit smoking, it offers discounts on insurance co-payments for non-smokers.

These sorts of incentives do work, usually in exactly the ways predicted by rational choice models. When the utility of the incentive becomes sufficiently great, people start behaving in a way that is good for themselves and good for society. Creating and tracking the effects of such incentives represents a major thrust of microeconomics, both in academic research and institutional policy. But monetary incentives don't always work. They fail when they undermine our sense of moral duty, they fail when they crowd out other sources of motivation.

Incentives (and rational choice models, more generally) work some of the time, and fail some of the time. Here's the important point: The failures of rational choice models aren't random. They aren't just anomalies that can be dismissed, rare events that can be explained away. Rational choice models fail to account for real-world behavior for specific reasons, reasons rooted in our psychology, in our biology, and in our environment. Rational choice models fail, and we can know why.

Now, there are many reasons to dismiss the previous example of reward undermining. The monetary incentive was very small, only 10 dollars, and it might be the case that people aren't really motivated by small amounts of money. We'll talk more about how the amount of money influences decisions in later lectures.

But, for now, I want to shift to some much bigger incentives. Let me introduce you to Frank, who is one of the world's two worst contestants on the television game show *Deal or No Deal*. This game show is one of the most popular in television history, versions of it have been created in about 75 different countries, all with the same basic format.

Frank is a contestant on the Dutch version of the show. He opens the game by staring at a large set of numbered briefcases, 26 in all, each containing a different monetary prize. Frank knows what prizes there are; the smallest amount is one euro cent, while the largest amount is five million euros, which at that time was more than six million dollars. Frank does not know what prize is in what briefcase, however. He chooses one briefcase, and that case is set aside for him, unopened. Then, the real game starts.

On each round of the game, Frank will open a predetermined number of briefcases to learn more about what's not in his briefcase. The game show host will then offer some fixed amount of money in trade for Frank's briefcase, and Frank must then decide whether or not to accept that offer.

Frank begins by selecting six briefcases. Five of those briefcases contain small amounts of money, but one has the second-largest prize. The host offers Frank 17,000 euros in trade for his briefcase. Should Frank accept that deal?

There actually isn't a right answer. Because of the way that the prize values are distributed, about half of the briefcases are worth less than 17,000 euros and about half are worth more. So there's a pretty good chance that Frank would trade up by accepting the deal. But, Frank needs to consider how much money is in each briefcase. Because the list of prizes is known, and every prize is equally likely to be in his briefcase, the expected value of his briefcase is just the average of the remaining prizes. After that first round that expected value is more than 300,000 euros. So Frank wisely says, "No deal."

The second round of the game doesn't go as well. Frank opens five more briefcases. To his chagrin, case after case contains a large amount of money. He's lost the chance to win most of the large prizes in the game, and his expected value plummets to only 64,000 euros. The host offers him even less, only 8,000 euros, and Frank again says, "No deal."

You might be wondering why the offers seem so unfair. Frank is only being offered one-eighth of what his briefcase's expected value. There's a simple reason: The offers are purposefully unfair at the beginning of the game, so that contestants keep playing and the drama builds.

The game progresses and Frank's luck improves. By the sixth round of the game, there are only five briefcases remaining, and one of them holds 500,000 euros. Frank's expected value is back up to a little more than 100,000 euros. The host offers him 75,000 euros for his briefcase. Now, imagine that you are Frank. Your emotions have been on a rollercoaster for the past few minutes. You have the chance to walk away with a large amount of money, guaranteed. If you keep playing you could win the large prize, or you could leave with almost nothing. What do you do?

To many people, the answer seems obvious: Take the deal. The offer is enough money to change one's life, and it's guaranteed. So why take a risk? But Frank, being Frank, says, "No deal."

On the very next round, Frank opens another briefcase and stares in disbelief as the prize of 500,000 euros leaves the game. All of the large, life-changing prizes are now gone. In shock, Frank keeps going until the final round. Only two prizes are left: 10,000 euros and 10 euros. The host offers Frank 6,000 euros for his briefcase. That's 20 percent better than his expected value. Now, I'm not a financial advisor, but if anyone ever gives you a choice between a sure $6,000 or an even chance to win $10,000, take the sure money.

The host offers Frank more than his expected value because they want him to take the offer. They don't want him to walk away a loser; that's depressing to viewers and bad for ratings. Frank says, "No deal." He opens his briefcase to reveal 10 euros. He turned down enough money to change his life, and ended up with a single small bill to put in his wallet.

It is hard to explain Frank's decisions using a rational choice model. Turning down an offer that is more than expected value is not just unwise, it is inefficient. Even if he's an extremely risk-seeking person, he could have taken the sure money and then gone to a nearby casino, where he could have gambled at much better odds. Nor was this an especially complex decision. At the end, there were only two prizes remaining, it was easy to recognize that six is more than half of 10.

The economists who analyzed the decisions of Frank and other *Deal or No Deal* contestants found something surprising. As the game progressed, contestants tended to become more and more risk seeking, almost regardless of what happened. Contestants who were unlucky, like Frank, kept chasing after what little money was left. Contestants who were lucky stayed in the game in search of the largest prizes. All of the sounds, lights, and excitement of the game show push the contestants to become more risk seeking than they probably would be in everyday life.

*Deal or No Deal* contestants make decisions about real money. They aren't motivated by $10, like in the blood donation example from earlier. They are motivated by much larger amounts; one contestant won a prize worth more than four million dollars. We might expect that they would make good, cautious decisions, but they often don't.

Oh, and by the way, I mentioned that Frank was one of the two worst *Deal-or-NoDeal* contestants in history. There's one other contestant who ended up much like Frank when he played on the U.S. version of that game show, and you'll meet him in a very different context in a later lecture.

What happens for other sorts of large, real-world economic decisions? Buying cars, selecting a mortgage, saving for retirement? Do people make good, cautious decisions when the stakes get large? Do they attend to the details, knowing how much more is on the line? You know the answers. The same biases found in the small decisions in the grocery store or laboratory also appear in the biggest decisions of our lives.

We don't have special machinery that we can suddenly turn on when we face a big decision. We're stuck with the same brain circuits that helped our ancestors forage for food and track down prey, but never evolved to compare fixed- and adjustable-rate mortgages. We use what we have, even if we occasionally will end up like Frank.

Throughout this course, I'll emphasize two fundamental types of limitations on our decision making.

The first involves constraints on our cognitive abilities. Much as we might hate to admit it, there are limits on our intellectual capacities. We can't know everything, remember everything, compute everything. Some people work well with numbers and data and can do complex calculations in their head. Other people have more difficulty with numbers and adopt different strategies for making decisions. But none of us is a supercomputer; there are some types of thinking that we do extremely well, and other types that we do very poorly.

We don't process information in absolute terms, for example, but in relative terms, by comparison to a point of reference. Even though a silver medal is objectively better than a bronze medal, after they win Olympic bronze medalists tend to be happier than silver medalists. That's because they adopt different reference points. The bronze medalists think, "I did well enough to earn a medal," while the silver medalists think, "I didn't do enough to earn gold."

Our brains are set up to use reference points, that's a way of simplifying the decision process. And, using reference points does help in many circumstances, as we'll see in future lectures. But if we adopt the wrong reference point, we lose perspective on what really matters.

The second type of limitation is that we do not have unlimited time to make decisions. Put yourself in the place of a distant ancestor, walking through grassland. Out of the corner of your eye you see a flash of movement, a glint of sunlight, and you react. You immediately run for safety, just eluding a predator's clutches. Each of us exists because some of our ancestors made decisions rapidly and quickly, avoiding a predator, defusing a violent situation, steering away from a car crash in the road ahead. Real-world decision makers don't always have the luxury of waiting, waiting until all of the information is collected.

Time constraints affect our economic decisions as well. When deciding whether to purchase a home, time is both your friend and enemy. Acting slowly gives you more time to gain information and deliberate on this largest of all purchases. But acting slowly also carries opportunity costs, someone else may put in an offer, or interest rates may increase.

These two limitations, cognitive abilities and time constraints, prevent us humans from being the ideal rational decision makers posited by traditional economics. We cannot make optimal decisions that always lead to the best outcome, even if we wanted to.

But we can recognize these limitations and try to optimize the decision process. The economist–psychologist Herbert Simon introduced the idea of "bounded rationality," or rationality within limits. Simon contended that the key challenges for real-world decision making were in acquiring the right information, in simplifying the decision process, and in adopting strategies for decision making.

We can't overcome these challenges by becoming even more analytic and deliberative in our decisions. Instead, we adopt rules called heuristics that allow us to prioritize some information over other, that simplify complex decisions into something manageable, and that give us strategies that can implemented quickly and with little effort. Those heuristics help us improve our odds of making a good decision, even in the face of our limitations. But, like us, they're not optimal, they're just good enough, most of the time.

Over the two-dozen lectures of this course, we will explore many aspects of the decision-making process. We'll see how people deal with the different factors that shape our choices: from the value of rewards to the pain of loss, from probability and risk to time itself. We'll investigate what makes medical decisions difficult, why we sacrifice of ourselves to help others, and how emotions shape our decisions for both better and worse. And, we'll see over and over that people make decisions that seem like mistakes, inefficient, inconsistent, and unwanted mistakes.

Our mistakes seem like anomalies in an otherwise rational process of decision making. Our biases are often surprising and counterintuitive, and it is easy to just dismiss them as odd features of human nature. But they aren't oddities, they are clues. They point to the deeper general principles that govern decision making, that show we aren't rational decision makers. And, you'll start to recognize the limitations of your own thinking.

Knowing your limitations won't make them just go away; they are too deeply rooted in your biology. As I'll emphasize throughout the course, it is very difficult to change the basic mechanisms of decision-making. But that shouldn't be a depressing thought, it should be liberating. We are real people, with real limitations, making our way through a constantly changing world. We don't need to be perfectly rational. We just need to be good enough.

Throughout this course, I'll give you tools for improving the process of decision making, the information you acquire and the strategies you adopt. While it's difficult or maybe impossible to eliminate your biases, you can use those tools to put yourself in situations where you'll make better decisions, where your biases aren't weaknesses, but strengths. In the next lecture, we'll start to understand how decision scientists capture the biases in our decision making by exploring the fundamentals of behavioral economics.

# The Rise of *Behavioral* Economics
## Lecture 2

We don't need science to tell us that we aren't rational decision makers, at least in the way assumed by traditional economic models. We only need a moment of introspection, and we'll recognize our own limitations. But we do need science to help us understand those limitations and identify ways of overcoming our limitations—and becoming better decision makers. In this lecture, you will start to understand how decision scientists capture the biases in our decision making by exploring the fundamentals of behavioral economics.

**Traditional Models**

- In Milan, Italy, in the middle of the 16th century lived a physician named Girolamo Cardano. He is most famous today not for his medical virtues—which were considerable—but for one of his vices. He was a pathological gambler. Like the typical pathological gambler, he lost more than he won, but his losses inspired him to invent the mathematics of probability.

- Cardano's masterwork, *A Book on Games of Chance*, introduces probability as a way of thinking about gambling. If a gambler throws a six-sided die, the probability of rolling a five is one in six. Probability is thus defined as the number of desired outcomes divided by the number of possible outcomes. This definition can be applied to sets of outcomes as well: There are four distinct ways of getting a total of five when rolling two dice, out of 36 possible combinations. That means that the probability of rolling five on two dice is four in 36, or one in nine.

- By multiplying the amount that could be won by the probability of winning, the gambler could calculate what came to be called the expected value of a risky choice. Expected value is one of the landmark concepts in all of decision science—as well as in statistics and economics, more broadly. It provides a simple rule for decision making: Choose whatever option maximizes expected value.

- However, expected value has its limitations. For example, take the simplest sort of gamble: betting on the outcome of a single flip of a coin. Suppose that your friend pulls out a coin and offers you a bet: If it lands heads, then you'll win 10 dollars, but if it lands tails, then you'll pay your friend five dollars. The expected value is clearly in the bettor's favor: A 10-dollar gain is twice as much as a five-dollar loss. And, indeed, most people are willing to take this bet.

- But what happens if the stakes are increased? If the coin lands heads, then your friend will pay you 10,000 dollars; if the coin lands tails, then you will pay your friend 5,000 dollars. Do you take that bet? Expected value argues that you should take that bet; it's still very much in your favor. But many people would decline this bet.

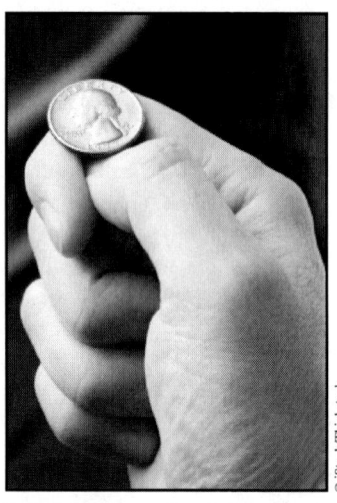

**Coin tosses are the simplest sort of gamble.**

- The mathematician and physicist Daniel Bernoulli, writing in the middle of the 18th century, used problems like this to argue that expected value did not account for people's real decisions—for two reasons. First, people placed different values on a good, like money, depending on their desires and circumstances. Second, a given amount of money was more important to people who had very little than to people who had very much. So the chance of a large gain might not be attractive, if we risk a large loss.

- Bernoulli argued that expected value needed to be replaced by a new concept, which we now call expected utility. Economics defines "utility" as the subjective value that is placed on some good or action.

- Over the next few centuries, economists developed models that assumed that people act to maximize their expected utility. Two people might make different choices because they prefer different goods, or one might be risk averse while the other is willing to tolerate risk, but each choice is assumed to maximize one's own utility. These are the so-called rational choice models. They assume that, in order to maximize utility, people have consistent preferences and make decisions that express those preferences.

- By the mid-20$^{th}$ century, rational choice models dominated economics—not only because those models could be built up from basic axioms and mathematical operations, but also because rational choice models were undeniably effective. Economists and other social scientists used them to explain market behavior; how companies developed incentives for their workers; how consumers responded to changes in prices; and even questions seemingly outside economics, such as how people vote or why countries go to war.

- But, in some ways, the very power of rational choice models had a blinding effect on the social sciences. When people's real-world decisions deviated from what was predicted by those models, then the behavior was questioned, not the models. Deviations from the models were often seen as unimportant anomalies—oddities of human behavior that were explained away or simply dismissed. But there have been clear examples that question the core assumptions of rational choice models.

## New Themes in Economics
- In the early 1960s, an economist named Vernon Smith was questioning some of the core assumptions of rational choice models, particularly as it applied to buying and selling within markets. To

Smith, some of those assumptions didn't make sense. For example, a common assumption was that people have complete information about the qualities of goods to be traded, the rules of exchange, and everything else. Complete information was thought to be necessary so that markets reach equilibrium—the steady state in which buyers and sellers are matched and exchange freely, with no shortages and no surpluses.

- But people don't have complete information; they don't know everything about the decision situation. And even if they did know everything, there's no guarantee that they would use that information efficiently.

- So, Smith created markets in a laboratory. He could control what information people had and the rules of their interactions, and then he could observe what happened. He found something remarkable: Even though people didn't have full information, and weren't necessarily rational in their behavior, his markets reached equilibrium anyway. Therefore, one didn't need rational individuals to explain rational market behavior.

- This sort of research—simulation of markets within a laboratory—can be called experimental economics. The key object of study for experimental economics is market performance, how markets behave given what individuals know and value. And, in that domain, experimental economics has been very successful.

- But there was a second new direction for research that began in the 1960s. Around the same time as Smith's early experiments, some economists and psychologists began to study individuals' choices in other contexts besides competitive markets, to better understand the biases and anomalies in decision making. This new enterprise became known as behavioral economics.

**Behavioral Economics**
- Behavioral economics applies experimental methods from psychology and other social sciences to problems in economics.

Importantly, it begins with observations about real-world behavior and then constructs models that can explain that behavior. That's the opposite approach from traditional economics, which began with rational choice models and then applied those models to real-world behavior.

- Behavioral economics combines methods from economics and psychology. These are both very large fields of science, so not all psychologists nor will all economists think the same way. But in general, research psychologists think about processes. They are interested in the processes of perception, attention, memory, and decision making that shape how we think and what we do. In contrast, research economists think about outcomes—how does a change in one variable influence another? Psychological concepts might be useful in explaining those outcomes, but that's not what's critical.

- A behavioral economist would likely be interested in both processes *and* outcomes: Why people choose something is as important as what they choose. So, the behavioral economist needs to set up experiments that reliably evoke specific psychological processes as well as specific decisions.

## Experimental Methods

- Behavioral economics experiments are planned with three principles in mind. First, experiments must be incentive compatible. That is, the participants should have some incentive to reveal their true preferences. This is usually accomplished by paying people for their choices.

- The easiest way to maximize incentive compatibility is to pay people for all of their choices. But if an experiment involves dozens or hundreds of decisions, paying people for every choice gets expensive quickly. So, a common procedure is to select one or a few choices—randomly from all of the choices made—and then pay someone for only those few choices. This ensures that the participant treats every choice as if it were being paid, while keeping the total payment to something manageable.

- The second principle of behavioral economics experiments is no deception. When participants come to the laboratory for an experiment, they know that they're in an experiment, so there's always the concern that they'll behave differently in the experimental setting than they would in the outside world. So, we tell people the truth: We tell them the sorts of decisions that they will make, what they might be paid, and how they will be paid.

- The third and final principle of behavioral economics experiments is no external influences. An external influence is anything other than the decision itself. To determine how people will actually behave in the real world based on how they behave during the experiment, external influences need to be eliminated.

## Prospect Theory

- Behavioral economics integrates experimental methods from psychology and economics and applies those methods to better understand how we make decisions. That simple description covers a very wide range of research, and across many disparate sorts of decisions, there are some common features that can help us think about many different decisions.

- By the late 1970s, experiments in the nascent field of behavioral economics had revealed many different anomalies in decision making—ways in which people's decisions didn't quite match what was predicted by rational choice models. These anomalies were compelling, often striking, but they were easy to dismiss. There wasn't any sort of underlying theory that could explain why people were biased, why they made good decisions in one context but bad decisions in another.

- However, in 1979, a paper was published in one of the most prestigious economics journals by psychologists Daniel Kahneman and Amos Tversky that had experimental data that showed biases in how people made decisions between monetary gambles—what Kahneman and Tversky called prospects because they were potential future gains and losses. These were the same sorts of simple choices that engaged Cardano and Bernoulli centuries before.

- Kahneman and Tversky's theory, called prospect theory, uses two concepts—probability weighting and reference dependence—to explain what people value. Probability weighting means that people treat some changes in probability as more important than others. Reference dependence means, simply, that people make decisions based on the perceived changes from some reference point.

## Suggested Reading

Camerer, "Prospect Theory in the Wild."

Kahneman and Tversky, "Prospect Theory."

## Questions to Consider

1. Why might behavioral economics be viewed with suspicion by at least some mainstream economists?

2. Why do behavioral economics experiments need to use real incentives, and why might people's decisions change depending on whether incentives are real or hypothetical?

# The Rise of *Behavioral* Economics
## Lecture 2—Transcript

We know that our decisions are imperfect. We give in to temptation, we shy away from risk, and we are inconsistent both in our preferences and our planning. We don't need science to tell us we aren't rational decision makers, at least in the way assumed by traditional economic models. We only need a moment of introspection, and we'll recognize our own limitations.

But we do need science to help us understand those limitations. And we do need science to help us identify ways of overcoming our limitations and becoming better decision makers.

Let's begin our exploration of the science by going back to Renaissance Italy, to the town of Milan in the middle of the 16th century. In Milan lived a physician named Girolamo Cardano. Cardano was not just any physician, he was one of the most famous physicians of his time. Royal families and even the Pope would consult with him about their ailments.

But, Cardano is most famous today not for his medical virtues, which were considerable, but for one of his vices. He was a gambler. Today, we'd call him a pathological gambler. In his own autobiography he admitted to being devoted to table games and dice, playing every day, and even drawing comfort from his gambling. Like the typical pathological gambler, he lost more than he won, but his losses inspired him to do something that was anything but typical: He invented the mathematics of probability.

Cardano's masterwork, *A Book on Games of Chance*, introduces probability as a way of thinking about gambling. If a gambler throws a six-sided die, the probability of rolling a 5 is 1 in 6. Probability is thus defined as the number of desired outcomes divided by the number of possible outcomes. This definition can be applied to sets of outcomes as well: There are four distinct ways of getting a total of 5 when rolling two dice, out of 36 possible combinations. That means that the probability of rolling 5 on two dice is 4 in 36, or 1 in 9.

Knowing such probabilities gave Cardano, and other informed gamblers, a mathematical cheat sheet that helped them in their betting. At that time, the odds associated with different games of chance were not as standardized as they are now. So, savvy gamblers could identify bets that were in their favor. If a gambling house paid 10 times your bet for rolling a 5 on two dice, then a gambler could expect to gain 10 units for every 9 units lost betting. The gambler would expect to make money with this bet, at least over the long run.

By multiplying the amount that could be won by the probability of winning, the gambler could calculate what came to be called the expected value of a risky choice. Expected value is one of the landmark concepts in all of decision science, as well as in statistics and economics, more broadly. It provides a simple rule for decision making: Choose whatever option maximizes expected value.

But, expected value has its limitations. Let's take the simplest sort of gamble: betting on the outcome of a single flip of a coin. Suppose that I pull out a coin and offer you a bet: If it lands heads I'll pay you $10, if it lands tails you'll pay me $5. Cardano would have leaped across a table to make this bet. The expected value is clearly in the bettor's favor—a $10 gain is twice as much as a $5 loss. And, indeed, most people are willing to take this bet.

But what happens if I increase the stakes? If the coin lands heads, I'll pay you $10,000; if the coin lands tails, you'll pay me $5,000. Do you take that bet? Expected value argues that you should take that bet; it's still very much in your favor. But many people would decline this bet, even though it's a better investment than anything that you or I will see in our lifetimes.

The mathematician and physicist Daniel Bernoulli, writing in the middle of the 18$^{th}$ century, used problems like this to argue that expected value did not account for people's real decisions, for two reasons. First, people placed different values on a good, like money, depending on their desires and circumstances. And, second, a given amount of money was more important to people who had very little than to people who had very much. So the chance of a large gain might not be attractive, if we risk a large loss.

Bernoulli argued that expected value needed to be replaced by a new concept, which we now call expected utility. Economics defines utility as the subjective value that is placed on some good or action. Over the next couple of centuries, economists developed models that assumed that people act to maximize their expected utility. Two people might make different choices because they prefer different goods—one prefers apples, and the other ice cream. Or, one might be risk averse while the other is willing to tolerate risk. But, each choice is assumed to maximize one's own utility.

These are the so-called rational choice models I introduced in the first lecture. They assume that, in order to maximize utility, people have consistent preferences and make decisions that express those preferences.

By the mid-20th century, rational choice models dominated economics, not only because those models could be built up from basic axioms and mathematical operations but also because rational choice models were undeniably effective. Economists and other social scientists used them to explain market behavior, how companies developed incentives for their workers, how consumers responded to changes in prices, and even questions seemingly outside economics like how people vote or why countries go to war.

But, in some ways, the very power of rational choice models had a blinding effect on the social sciences. When people's real-world decisions deviated from what was predicted by those models, then the behavior was questioned, not the models. Deviations from the models were often seen as unimportant anomalies—oddities of human behavior that were explained away or simply dismissed. But there have been clear examples that question the core assumptions of rational choice models. Let me give you two, one historical and one modern.

One of the first and clearest challenges to rational choice models, particularly to the idea of expected utility, came from the economist Maurice Allais in 1953. Now, Allais was an economist's economist, not some interloper from another field. He would later win a Nobel Prize for his work on how markets can be structured to be maximally efficient, including work on monetary supply and demand. But, Allais was also interested in rationality and in particular how psychological factors might influence people's choices.

He proposed a simple experiment that has come to be known as the Allais paradox. To make this paradox tangible, let's suppose that you are a contestant on a game show. You walk onto the stage and in front of you are two large, covered urns, each filled with 100 balls. On each ball is written a dollar amount. The host blindfolds you while explaining that you'll get to reach into one urn and pull out one ball to determine your prize.

The host goes on to explain the prizes that you might win. In the urn to your left, there are 33 balls that are worth $2,500, 66 balls that are worth $2,400, and one ball that is worth nothing. So, you have a 99 in 100 chance of winning something in that urn. In the urn to your right, all of the balls are worth $2,400. Which urn do you choose?

Most people choose the urn on the right in scenarios like this first one. Even though the expected value of the urn on the left is higher, because of all those balls worth $2,500, they're afraid of that 1 in 100 chance of getting nothing.

But, let's suppose you walk onto the stage and the host describes a different scenario. Now, the left urn has 33 balls that are worth $2,500, and 67 that are worth nothing. The right urn has 34 balls that are worth $2,400, and 66 that are worth nothing. Most people choose the urn on the left in scenarios like this second one; the difference between 34 balls and 33 balls doesn't seem like a big deal, so they go for the urn with the larger potential reward.

So, in the Allais paradox, people choose the right urn in the first scenario but the left urn in the second scenario. These two scenarios might have sounded different, but they actually involve exactly the same tradeoff. The left urn has 33 balls that are worth $100 more than their counterparts in the right urn, but that urn also has one extra ball that's worth nothing. Everything else is common across the two urns, and rational choice models assume that you should make your decision based on the differences between your options.

But the differences in small probabilities (0 percent versus 1 percent) matter a lot more to us than differences in intermediate probabilities (33 percent versus 34 percent). This phenomenon is called probability weighting, and it pervades our behavior in many sorts of risky decisions, from the willingness to purchase lottery tickets at infinitesimal odds, to the bias toward cures and away from prevention in medical decision making.

Let me move to a more recent example that challenges rational choice models. For this example, imagine that you are a cab driver in New York City. Within each day's 12-hour shift, you can work as much or as little as you like. But some days will be better than others—on rainy days, for example, the demand for cabs is much greater than on sunny days.

Rational choice models make a prediction familiar to any labor economist. Temporary increases in wages should lead to longer working hours, while temporary decreases in wages should lead to shorter working hours. If you are a cabdriver, you should work longer on rainy days where you are earning more, but less on sunny days where you are earning less.

But, would you do that? Suppose that you are four hours into your shift, and you've been busy with high-dollar fares the entire time. You've already earned as much as you typically earn in an entire day. Do you keep driving throughout the shift, or do you leave for home early, satisfied that you've made your day's target?

Economists analyzed exactly this situation, and found that New York cabdrivers work less when they are earning more per hour, and work more when earning less per hour. Does this matter for their incomes? Yes. If the same drivers had simply worked longer hours on good days and shorter hours on bad days, like would have been predicted by rational choice models, they would have earned 10 percent more for the same hours of work.

So, why do the cab drivers behave this way? The likely answer is that they show something called reference dependence; they have a goal for each day's earnings, and they are satisfied if they earn more than that goal and disappointed if they earn less. So, they work until they've earned more than their reference point, and then they stop. By thinking about each day in terms of a target reference point, the cab drivers ensure that they earn their desired pay, even if they aren't efficiently allocating their time in the way predicted by economics.

Rational choice models, despite their mathematical elegance, couldn't explain real-world economic behaviors. To some economists, that meant that a different approach was needed, an approach that drew inferences based on careful observation of real-world behavior. Of course, psychologists, political scientists, and anthropologists had been observing real-world behavior all along. So, what was different about this new approach? Let's pick up our history in the early 1960s, and find out.

At that time, an economist named Vernon Smith was questioning some of the core assumptions of rational choice models, particularly as it applied to buying and selling within markets. To Smith, some of the assumptions didn't make sense. For example, a common assumption was that people have complete information about the qualities of goods to be traded, the rules of exchange, and everything else. Complete information was thought to be necessary so that markets reach an equilibrium, the steady state in which buyers and sellers are matched and exchange freely, with no shortages and no surpluses.

But people don't have complete information. They don't know everything about the decision situation, and even if they did know everything, there's no guarantee that they would use that information efficiently. So, Smith created markets in a laboratory. He could control what information people had and the rules of their interactions, and then he could observe what happened. He found something remarkable: even though people didn't have full information, and weren't necessarily rational in their behavior, his markets reached equilibria anyway. So, one didn't need rational individuals to explain rational market behavior.

This sort of research, simulation of markets within a laboratory, can be called experimental economics. Now, the key object of study for experimental economics is market performance, how markets behave given what individuals know and value. And, in that domain, experimental economics has been very successful, as seen in the Nobel Prize awarded to Vernon Smith in 2002.

But there was a second new direction for research that began in the 1960s. Around the same time as Smith's early experiments, some economists and psychologists began to study individuals' choices in other contexts beside competitive markets, to better understand the biases and anomalies in decision making. This new enterprise became known as behavioral economics.

Behavioral economics applies experimental methods from psychology and other social sciences to problems in economics. Importantly, it begins with observations about real-world behavior and then constructs models that can explain that behavior. That's the opposite approach from traditional economics, which begins with rational choice models and then applies those models to real-world behavior.

Remember, the term "rational" (and its opposite, "irrational") are often misinterpreted. Rational doesn't necessarily imply thoughtful, well-reasoned, or even good decisions. It just means consistent with some model. And, that some decisions seem irrational doesn't mean that all of economics is called into question. It means that some specific aspect of economic theory—some assumption made about what people value—can sometimes be incorrect.

I emphasize this point because it is very easy to become enamored with behavioral economics. Learning about the biases that shape our decisions can change the way you think, causing you to see irrationality everywhere. But most of the time, we make pretty good decisions. Most of the time, the traditional approaches in economics work just fine. But, most of the time isn't all of the time. That's the key point. By understanding how people make decisions, we can predict when traditional economic approaches work and when they won't.

Now, back to behavioral economics. I've mentioned that it combines methods from economics and psychology. Psychologists and economists don't always think alike. These are both very large fields of science, and so not all psychologists nor all economists will think the same way. So, consider what I am about to say as a necessary simplification.

Research psychologists think about processes. They are interested in the processes of perception, attention, memory, and decision making that shape how we think and what we do. In contrast, research economists think about outcomes—how does a change in one variable influence another? Psychological concepts might be useful in explaining those outcomes, but that's not what's critical.

A behavioral economist would likely be interested in both processes and outcomes: Why people choose something is as important as what they choose. So, the behavioral economist needs to set up experiments that reliably evoke specific psychological processes as well as specific decisions. Let's see how those experiments work.

Behavioral economics experiments aren't quite as simple as you might think, especially if you've read about those experiments in popular books or the news media. Setting up an experiment requires careful planning, so that what the experiment reveals about the processes and outcomes is as specific as possible. Accordingly, behavioral economics experiments are planned with three principles in mind.

First, experiments must be incentive compatible. That is, the participants should have some incentive to reveal their true preferences; this is usually accomplished by paying people for their choices. For example, we can give people a choice between sure and risky options: say, between a sure $20 and a coin-flip's chance to win $50. The amounts need to be large enough to matter, and as you might imagine, there is considerable debate as to how large is large enough.

Now, the easiest way to maximize incentive compatibility is to pay people for all of their choices. So, if you chose the safe option in that example, you'd receive $20. If you chose the risky option, then we'd really flip a coin, and you might walk away with $50 or you might walk away with nothing.

But if an experiment involves dozens or hundreds of decisions, paying people for every choice gets expensive quickly. So, a common procedure is to select one or a few choices, randomly from all of the choices a person makes, and then pay someone for only those few choices. This ensures that the participant treats every choice as if it were being paid, while keeping the total payment to something manageable.

The second principle of behavioral economics experiments is no deception. When participants come to the laboratory for an experiment, well, they know that they're in an experiment. So, there's always the concern that they'll behave differently in the experimental setting than they would in the outside world.

When we bring people to our laboratories for experiments, they often initially suspect that we are deceiving them. They've read about psychological experiments that involve subliminal priming or that involve a social interaction that wasn't with another real participant but with a confederate of the experimenter. So they start speculating about the true nature of the experiment. We don't want that. That makes our experiments less effective.

So, we tell people the truth. Here are the sorts of decisions that you'll make. Here's what you might be paid, and here's how we'll pay you. And we tell people that we are telling them the truth; we tell them that we don't use deception. We've found, in my laboratory, that telling people that we want them to earn money can be reassuring. The experiments work better, and tell us more about real-world behavior, if people trust the experimenters.

The third and final principle of behavioral economics experiments is no external influences. What's an external influence? Anything other than the decision itself.

Suppose that you come to a laboratory for an experiment. When you arrive, you are told that the experiment is on altruism, how people give money to charitable causes, at no benefit to themselves. You are given an envelope with $50 in cash, and you are told that you can give some of that money to a local charity, say your town's literacy center. The experimenter stands there, holds out a donation box, and asks you to give whatever you decide to the charity.

Would that decision be free of outside influences? Of course not. You would surely feel some pressure to donate because of the presence of the experimenter. You might give $10 or $20 simply because you want to seem like a fair or generous person. To determine whether people will really give to charity in such experiments, we need to eliminate those sorts of external influences.

So, these are the three principles of behavioral economics research. First, decisions must be incentive compatible. Second, decisions must be free of any experimental deception. And, third, decisions must be free of any outside influences. These three principles allow us to be more confident in our experiments. We are more confident that our experiments manipulate the psychological process that we anticipated. And, we are more confident that our economic outcomes are meaningful. In a sense, adherence to these principles allows behavioral economics research to pass muster with both psychologists and economists, which isn't always an easy task.

So far, I've emphasized that behavioral economics is about behavior. Behavioral economics experiments observe real behavior—people making decisions that matter to them—and then use that behavior to better understand how people make decisions. But, in recent years, neuroscientists and economists working together have used the methods of behavioral economics to better understand how our brains make decisions. Research of this sort is often called neuroeconomics.

There are many misconceptions about neuroeconomics. Some neuroscientists think that neuroscience is poised to revolutionize economics. Some economists think that understanding the brain is simply irrelevant to answering economic questions. The truth, in my view, lies in between those extremes. Some of the time, understanding how our brains work can illuminate a complex issue, clarifying some paradox or building connections among seemingly diverse biases. So, throughout this course, I'll use selected examples from neuroscience as a way of helping you understand why we make decisions. But I'll do so with appropriate caution; we don't always need to understand our brains to understand ourselves.

So, behavioral economics integrates experimental methods from psychology and economics, and applies those methods to better understand how we make decisions. That simple description covers a very wide range of research: gambling with monetary rewards and risky choices, interpersonal interactions in economic games, consumer purchases, investment decisions, and even how patients and doctors make decisions about medical care. But, across all of those disparate sorts of decisions, there are some common features. There are some big ideas that can help us think about many different decisions.

By the late 1970s, experiments in the nascent field of behavioral economics had revealed many different anomalies in decision making, ways in which people's decisions didn't quite match what was predicted by rational choice models. These anomalies were compelling, often striking, but they were easy to dismiss. There wasn't any sort of underlying theory that could explain why people were biased, why we made good decisions in one context but bad decisions in another.

But in 1979 a paper was published by two psychologists, Daniel Kahneman and Amos Tversky, that couldn't be easily dismissed. It was published in *Econometrica*, one of the most prestigious journals in economics. It had experimental data that showed biases in how people made decisions between monetary gambles—what Kahneman and Tversky called prospects because they were potential future gains and losses. These were the same sorts of simple choices that engaged Cardano and Bernoulli centuries before. And, it had a theory.

Kahneman and Tversky's paper was called "Prospect Theory: An Analysis of Decisions Under Risk." This paper became one of the most influential and highly cited papers in the history of economics. Prospect Theory uses two concepts, probability weighting and reference dependence, to explain what people value.

Probability weighting means that people treat some changes in probability as more important than others. As shown by the example of the Allais paradox, people treat the difference between 0 percent and 1 percent as much more important than the difference between 33 percent and 34 percent, even though each has a similar effect on one's expected utility.

Reference dependence means, simply, that people make decisions based on the perceived changes from some reference point. In the example of the New York City cabdrivers, those cabdrivers didn't think about the rate at which they were earning money (which would have led them to work longer on good days). Instead, they used their typical day's earnings as a reference point, and they tended to quit when they reached that reference point.

For now, though, our brief history ends. In the next few lectures, we'll explore the basic elements of Prospect Theory in much more detail: what we value, how value changes according to our reference point, how our value changes according to the range of options we consider, and how probability influences our decisions. These basic elements serve as the building blocks for behavioral economics.

# Reference Dependence—It's All Relative
## Lecture 3

To understand many real-world decisions, we first need to understand why people value some things more than others. One possibility is that value comes from experienced or anticipated pleasure. But that isn't consistent with how our brain's reward system is set up—the key dopamine neurons aren't necessary for pleasure. Instead, these dopamine neurons respond in a way that encourages us to seek out new and better rewards. Our brain responds to new information about rewards, not necessarily to rewards themselves.

**Economic Value**

- Why do we choose something? Think about just how complicated even a simple decision, such as selecting a bag of tortilla chips, can be. Your normal snack preferences, your knowledge of different brands, your sense of nutritional value, and even the aesthetic quality of the packaging, among many other factors, all come together into some internal sense of value.

- That seemingly simple term, "value," lies at the heart of decision making. If we can understand how value is calculated, then we can understand the choices people make. In addition, we can learn more about how people's choices go awry—in day-to-day consumer choices, in long-term financial investments, and even in well-known medical disorders.

- Consider the term "value" from an abstract, economic point of view. One natural speculation is that positive value corresponds to pleasure—we purchase tortilla chips because they generate pleasure—whereas negative value corresponds to pain.

- In addition to pleasure, value is determined by how much we benefit from something. Many of the things that we value have clear benefits. Food provides nutrients, clothing protects us from the elements, our homes provide shelter, and even our social interactions have value through the well-being of our children, relatives, and friends. Some scientists extend this argument all the way to what is called adaptive fitness; they argue that value can be defined by the extent to which an action improves our chance of passing along our genes.

- Clearly, our decisions are influenced in some way by all of these sorts of tangible benefits. But it is easy to come up with counterexamples. Think of a recent trip to a restaurant. You might have paid a premium to eat a well-marbled steak, a plate of aged cheeses, or a tempting chocolate dessert. Going to that restaurant surely generated pleasure, but if anything, it provided fewer nutrients and had more deleterious effects on your health than much less expensive options—for example, cooking a fresh, simple meal at home.

- We can't explain what we value by either pleasure or benefits alone; they often trade off against each other. There are even cases where the value of a good can be completely detached from its benefits. An example is a rare designer handbag, which is valuable precisely because it is rare and exclusive, and thus, its demand actually increases with increasing price.

- In many situations, people spend too much money on things that have direct, tangible benefits, like material goods, and too little money on things that only lead to transient experiences, like vacations and social interactions.

## Neuroscience: Dopamine

- Neurons are the information-processing cells within the brain. There are about 100 billion neurons in your brain. Each neuron receives signals from other neurons, integrates those signals, and then forwards a new signal to another part of the brain.

- There are bumps and folds along the outer surfaces of the brain. The main bumpy, folded structure is the cerebrum (or cerebral cortex), which sits on top of a long stalk, whose bottom is the spinal cord and whose top is the brainstem.

- Different parts of the brainstem contribute to different aspects of bodily function. Some help regulate automatic processes like breathing, while others shape whether we are awake or drowsy, and still others play a role in emotions and feelings.

- The ventral tegmental area (VTA) is a tiny structure within the brainstem. There aren't many neurons in the VTA. Of the 100 billion neurons in the brain, only about half a million of those neurons are in the VTA. But those neurons are critical for our ability to make decisions.

- Within each neuron, signals travel electrically—that is, electrical currents travel along the membrane walls of the neuron. When one neuron sends signals to other neurons, those signals travel from the cell body at the center of the neuron down a long structure called an axon. If a thin electrical wire is inserted into the brain next to one of these neurons, then that wire can record those electrical signals and bring them to a computer.

- Sometimes the neuron only sends a few signals in a second; other times the neuron is much more active, and signals come out in rapid bursts. We call this the firing rate of the neuron.

- A dopamine neuron is a neuron that uses the chemical dopamine to communicate with other neurons. Each time an electrical signal moves along the neuron, it ends at a gap between neurons called a synapse and then triggers the release of the chemical dopamine. That dopamine is taken up by adjacent neurons, where it can in turn increase their activity.

- It had long been recognized that dopamine neurons—in the VTA and in other nearby structures—are critical for movement and actions. Degeneration of brainstem dopamine neurons has long been known to be a hallmark of Parkinson's disease, which can lead to an inability to control voluntary motor movements, rigidity, or uncontrollable tremors. More recently, however, neuroscientists began to recognize that dopamine neurons played an important role in how the brain determines value.

## Reward Prediction Error

- In the early 1990s, the neuroscientist Wolfram Schultz was exploring the function of VTA dopamine neurons in experiments with monkeys. By lowering a very thin wire into the VTA of a monkey, he could record the signals from one VTA neuron at a time while the monkey received rewards that it valued, such as juice.

- Schultz discovered that the same dopamine neuron increased its firing rate when the monkey received juice or received a warning signal about future juice but decreased its firing rate when the monkey didn't get the juice it was anticipating.

- These results point out the first fundamental property of dopamine neurons: They do not respond to rewards themselves but to the difference between expectation and reality. This concept is now known as reward prediction error.

- Unexpected positive events, like unexpected praise, increase the activity of our brain's dopamine system. Events that are worse than our expectations, like when we are expecting praise but don't receive any, decrease the activity of our brain's dopamine system.

## Wanting versus Liking

- Research on the association between dopamine and reward has led to a general conception that dopamine is the "pleasure chemical" in the brain. But does the activity of dopamine neurons really correspond to pleasure?

- Facial expressions associated with pleasure and with aversion are similar in rats, monkeys, humans, and many other mammals. Psychologist Kent Berridge and colleagues realized that they could rely on facial expressions to assess whether a rat found some juice pleasant or unpleasant. So, they ran the critical test to evaluate where dopamine neurons were associated with pleasure.

- They used a very selective neurotoxin that lesioned, or selectively damaged, neurons in part of the dopamine system in their rats. Without those neurons in good working function, the rats became aphagic, meaning that they wouldn't eat. More specifically, they wouldn't exert any effort to obtain food or even juice, even if they were hungry or thirsty. Without an intact dopamine system, these rats no longer *wanted* rewards like food or juice.

- However, they would still eat or drink if the food or juice was placed into their mouth. When these rats with damaged dopamine systems received something pleasurable, like sugar water, they leaned forward, made a round mouth, and licked their face and paws—exactly like neurologically normal rats. In other words, they liked sugar water.

- When the aphagic rats received a bitter solution, like lithium water, they gaped their mouth, protruded their tongue, and shook their head—again, exactly like neurologically normal rats. They disliked the bitter solution.

- So, if part of a rat's dopamine system is disabled, it will not walk across its cage to consume food, but it still shows normal hedonic responses to pleasant and unpleasant stimuli. These results are compelling evidence that dopamine neurons are not associated with experiences of pleasure, or *liking*, but for motivating animals to seek out rewards—what researchers call *wanting*.

- What causes liking, if not dopamine? Current research suggests that feelings of liking are associated with the activity of a different sort of neuron—one that uses opioids as neurotransmitters—but there's much more to be learned.

**Parkinson's and Pathological Gambling**

- Parkinson's disease is associated with the death of dopamine neurons. As the disease progresses—and more and more of those dopamine neurons die—it impairs movement, disrupts balance, and causes motor tremors. Parkinson's disease can't be cured, but its symptoms can be alleviated by drugs that replenish the brain's supply of dopamine and intensify the effects of dopamine in the brain.

- Based on the properties of dopamine neurons, side effects of those drugs might include amplifying the influence of unexpected changes in reward and increasing wanting, or reward-seeking behavior. If you have these two side effects, probably the worst place for you to go would be a casino.

- By the late 1990s, some neurologists were noticing that a few Parkinson's patients were also exhibiting uncontrollable pathological gambling; they would regularly go to casinos and

Pathological gambling has been discovered as a behavior that some Parkinson's patients have experienced as a result of the drugs taken to help alleviate symptoms of the disease.

spend much more than they should. But there wasn't any sort of general appreciation of this link. Many clinicians still thought of Parkinson's as a movement disorder and didn't appreciate the connections between dopamine and reward.

- However, in 2003, researchers at the Muhammad Ali Parkinson Research Center in Arizona conducted a comprehensive study and discovered that those patients who had been treated with the particular drugs that intensify the effects of dopamine had a greatly elevated rate of pathological gambling.

- Since this research, neurologists now recognize that some medications for Parkinson's disease can increase the risk of problem gambling, so they warn their patients of those risks and watch for signs of gambling or other compulsive behaviors.

### Suggested Reading

Rangel, Camerer, and Montague, "A Framework for Studying the Neurobiology of Value-Based Decision Making."

Zweig, *Your Money and Your Brain*.

### Questions to Consider

1. What is the difference between pleasure and motivation?

2. Under what circumstances could raising the price of a good increase its desirability?

# Reference Dependence—It's All Relative
## Lecture 3—Transcript

Why do we choose something? Suppose that you are walking through the supermarket, down a very familiar aisle: the snacks ... colorful, almost garish packages of chips and cookies fill the shelves. Most of the time you walk through this aisle quickly, without stopping, because you know your own weaknesses.

But this time, a bright blue unfamiliar package catches your attention. You stop and examine it, it's a new kind of tortilla chip, one marketed as spicy but still healthful. You turn the package over to read the nutritional information. Surprisingly, it's not too bad; the ingredients are natural, and even though it contains a lot of salt, there's not much sugar or fat. Plus, you haven't tried this brand of chips before, and so you could learn whether you like it. So, you place the chips in your basket and continue your shopping.

Why did you choose that bag of tortilla chips? Before you answer—assuming that you, like me, can relate to that hypothetical shopping trip—let's move from why to what. What was the choice being made? A traditional economist might describe the choice as between the tortilla chips and money, specifically their price. Of course, tortilla chips and money are two very different things. So, we'll have to compare them on some common scale for decision making, for which we use the shorthand of utility, as introduced in the last lecture. We derive positive utility (such as pleasure) from eating those tortilla chips, and that pleasure outweighs the negative utility (or pain) of giving up money.

There's a puzzle here, though. When we purchase something at the supermarket, we almost never consume it immediately. All of the benefits, whether through taste or nutrition, come much later, perhaps after hours or days. So, your choice must be based on something else, some internal sense, some anticipation about the future.

I want you to think for a moment about just how complicated even this sort of simple decision can be. Think about how much information you can bring to bear on this single consumer purchase. Your normal snack preferences, your knowledge of different brands, your sense of nutritional value, even the aesthetic quality of the packaging, those and many other factors come together into some internal sense of value.

That seemingly simple term, "value," lies at the heart of decision making. If we can understand how value is calculated, then we can understand the choices people make. And, we can learn more about how people's choices go awry, in day-to-day consumer choices, in long-term financial investments, and even in well-known medical disorders.

Let's begin by considering value from an abstract, economic point of view. One natural speculation is that positive value corresponds to pleasure—we purchase the tortilla chips because they generate pleasure—whereas negative value corresponds to pain. Indeed, we use the language of pleasure and pain all the time: We feel good about our decisions. The cost of that new car was painful, but worth it.

Linking value to pleasure and pain is an old idea. In the late 18th century, the English philosopher Jeremy Bentham composed an "Introduction to the Principles of Morals and Legislation," a spectacularly far-reaching work that explored everything from the nature of consciousness, to legal responsibility, to the fundamental motivators of our decisions.

He began with a simple declaration: "Nature has placed mankind under the governance of two sovereign masters, pain and pleasure. It is for them alone to point out what we ought to do, as well as to determine what we shall do. On the one hand the standard of right and wrong, on the other the chain of causes and effects, are fastened to their throne. They govern us in all we do, in all we say, in all we think: every effort we can make to throw off our subjection, will serve but to demonstrate and confirm it."

What forceful writing. "Two sovereign masters, pain and pleasure." "What we ought to do… what we shall do." Bentham seems to argue that not only do we value what gives us pleasure, but we should value pleasure—to paraphrase him bluntly, denying the pleasure principle only gets us in trouble. This thinking has served as the foundation of theories of utilitarianism, one of the major streams of moral philosophy in the succeeding centuries.

But, pleasure can't be the only thing that matters, and Bentham himself recognized that. About 30 years later, Bentham added a footnote to this section. He recognized that pleasure corresponds more to subjective states like happiness than to the underlying motivator for our actions.

So, what else besides pleasure could determine how much we value something? A second possibility is that value is determined by how much we benefit from something. Many of the things that we value have clear benefits. Food provides nutrients, clothing protects us from the elements, our homes provide shelter, even our social interactions have value through the wellbeing of our children, relatives, and friends. Some scientists extend this argument all the way to what is called adaptive fitness; they argue that value can be defined by the extent to which an action improves our chance of passing along our genes.

Clearly, our decisions are influenced in some way by all of these sorts of tangible benefits. But it is easy to come up with counterexamples. Think of a recent trip to a restaurant. You might have paid a premium to eat a well-marbled steak, a plate of aged cheeses, or a tempting chocolate dessert. Going to that restaurant surely generated pleasure, but if anything it provided fewer nutrients and had more deleterious effects on your health than much less expensive options, staying at home and cooking a simple meal with fresh produce, meats, and grain.

We can't explain what we value by either pleasure or benefits alone; they often trade off against each other. There are even cases where the value of a good can be completely detached from its benefits. Consider a rare designer handbag, of the sort worn by a Hollywood starlet to a high-visibility media event. That handbag may sell in luxury boutiques for tens of thousands of dollars, even though its features are objectively no better than those of a department-store $10 handbag. It is valuable precisely because it is rare and exclusive, and thus its demand actually increases with increasing price. This handbag is an example of a Veblen good, after the late 19th-century economist Thorstein Veblen.

And, a myopic focus on benefits can lose sight of life's true joys. A few years ago I took a family trip to the Great Smoky Mountains National Park. This park is one of America's natural treasures—almost a thousand square miles of hardwood forest, meadows, and valleys, laced throughout by streams that come down cold from the surrounding mountains. At one point during the trip, I was standing and shivering in one of those mountain streams, watching children splash about in the surrounding water. I was very cold, very wet, and very happy. I wouldn't trade the memory of that trip—and of those mountain streams—for anything, even though I'd be hard pressed to identify any benefit from standing knee deep in freezing water.

In many situations, people spend too much money on things that have direct, tangible benefits (like material goods) and too little money on things that only lead to transient experiences (like vacations and social interactions). We'll explore that paradox more deeply in a few lectures, but for now, it's important to note that both pleasure and tangible benefits matter, but they aren't the whole story.

So, if value isn't explained by pleasure nor by tangible benefits, what's left? To answer that question, we'll move from economics and to neuroscience. Since this will be our first extended discussion of concepts from neuroscience, I'd like to begin with something small: a single neuron inside the brain. Neurons are the information processing cells within the brain; there are something like 100 billion neurons in your brain. Each neuron receives signals from other neurons, integrates those signals, and then forwards the output to another part of the brain.

The location of the neuron we'll focus on is within the brainstem. Even if you aren't a neuroscientist or neurologist, you've seen images of the bumps and folds along the outer surfaces of the brain. That main bumpy, folded structure is the cerebrum (or cerebral cortex), which sits on top of a long stalk whose bottom is the spinal cord and whose top is the brainstem.

Different parts of the brainstem contribute to different aspects of bodily function. Some help regulate automatic processes like breathing, others shape whether we are awake or drowsy, and still others play a role in emotions and feelings. The neuron we care about is located in a tiny structure within the brainstem called the ventral tegmental area. That's a mouthful, so we'll refer to it by its abbreviation; ventral tegmental area, or VTA.

There aren't many neurons in the VTA. Of the 100 billion neurons in the brain, only about a half-million of those neurons are in the VTA. But those neurons are critical for our ability to make decisions.

Like all VTA neurons, our neuron contains the neurotransmitter dopamine. Since dopamine has become quite famous in the popular media, I want to take a quick digression and provide some sense of how neurons use dopamine and other neurotransmitters to communicate. The key idea is that within each neuron signals travel electrically; that is, electrical currents travel along the membrane walls of the neuron. When one neuron sends signals to other neurons, those signals travel from the cell body at the center of the neuron down a long wire called an axon. If a thin electrical wire is inserted into the brain next to one of these neurons, that wire can record those electrical signals and bring them to a computer.

The sound you're hearing right now is that electrical signal. Each of those clicks represents a single electrical signal moving along the neuron. You heard that sometimes the neuron is relatively quiet; it only sends a few signals in a second. Other times the neuron was much more active and signals came out in rapid bursts. We call this the firing rate of the neuron.

Earlier, I referred to a "dopamine neuron." That refers to the chemical this neuron uses to communicate with other neurons. Each time an electrical signal moves along this neuron, it ends at a gap between neurons called a synapse and then triggers the release of the chemical dopamine. That dopamine is taken up by adjacent neurons, where it can in turn increase their activity.

So, what does our dopamine neuron actually do? It had long been recognized that dopamine neurons, in the VTA and in other nearby structures, are critical for movement and actions. Degeneration of brainstem dopamine neurons has long been known to be a hallmark of Parkinson's disease, which can lead to an inability to control voluntary motor movements, rigidity, or uncontrollable tremors. But, more recently neuroscientists began to recognize that dopamine neurons played an important role in how the brain determines value.

In the early 1990s, the neuroscientist Wolfram Schultz was exploring the function of VTA dopamine neurons in experiments with monkeys. By lowering a very thin wire into the VTA of a monkey, he could record the signals from one VTA neuron at a time while the monkey received rewards that it valued. (I want to note that these wires are so thin that they don't damage the surrounding brain; in fact, by the year 2010 such wires were used to record similar signals in human Parkinson's patients who were undergoing electrical stimulation treatment.)

Monkeys really like juice, and so Schultz used a computer-driven apparatus to deliver fruit juice to a tube at the monkey's mouth. He began his experiments by sending fruit juice without advance warning, so that the monkey could not predict when its rewards would arrive. Each time the monkey received the fruit juice, Schultz observed a rapid increase in the firing rate of his dopamine neuron. Fruit juice, then firing, fruit juice, then firing, over and over. From this association, it would be very natural to conclude that this dopamine neuron fired because the monkey had just received the rewarding juice.

Then he changed the method slightly. He gave the monkey a warning, in the form of a short sound, about two seconds before the juice arrived. Over the next few minutes, something remarkable happened. The neuron stopped responding to the juice reward and began responding to the warning sound. I want to emphasize this key point: This neuron responded to juice only when it was unexpected.

Finally, he made one last change. He played the warning sound, but didn't deliver the juice thereafter. The neuron fired to the warning sound, but then actually decreased its firing rate at the time the juice should have been delivered.

Let me summarize this first experiment: The same dopamine neuron increased its firing rate when the monkey received juice or received a warning signal about future juice, but decreased its firing rate when the monkey didn't get the juice it was anticipating.

These results point out the first fundamental property of dopamine neurons: They do not respond to rewards themselves, but to the difference between expectation and reality. This concept is now known as "Reward Prediction Error."

Think about sometime that you received unexpected praise, say, a compliment from a friend at a party or from a colleague at work. How did you feel? That praise was probably very rewarding to you in large part because it was unexpected—you thought that you were having a normal conversation, and then the compliment arrived out of the blue. Unexpected positive events like that increase the activity of our brain's dopamine system.

But, suppose that you are expecting praise, say for your role on a project at work, and then a colleague simply thanks you without particular warmth or enthusiasm. How would you feel then? You'd probably feel disappointment; even though you received a bit of thanks, it was less effusive and heartfelt than you expected. Events that are worse than our expectations decrease the activity our brain's dopamine system. We'll return to how rewards relate to our expectations in the next lecture, when we talk about reference dependence.

Research on the association between dopamine and reward has led to a general conception that dopamine is the "pleasure chemical" in the brain. This association now permeates the popular media—major news outlets present stories with titles like "music releases the brain's pleasure chemical" and "addiction and the brain's pleasure pathway." But does the activity of dopamine neurons really correspond to pleasure?

Suppose that we revisited the experiment I just described, where monkeys were receiving squirts of fruit juice. How could we know if an animal receives pleasure from that juice? If a person were drinking the juice, then we could just ask them, and they could tell us, "Yes, this juice is tasty. It is a bit sweet, but still good." Obviously, we can't just ask a monkey or rat or any other animal in our experiments, and then listen to what it tells us.

So, pleasure had to be determined some other way. One of the great things about observing animals in experiments is that you get to know their tendencies pretty well. Some researchers, led by the psychologist Kent Berridge, knew that when rats received a squirt of juice, they tended to take on a standard sort of facial expression. They leaned forward, made a round mouth, and stuck their tongue out. You've seen this sort of expression before, it is the same expression that a young child makes when they taste something good. Rats, monkeys, humans, and many other mammals all show this same sort of facial expression when they like something.

Berridge and colleagues also noticed that when rats received something unpleasant, like juice tinted with a bitter additive, they made a different facial expression. They lean back, gape their mouth, and use their tongue to make a barrier across its opening.

You can simulate this yourself; just imagine that you lifted what you thought was a glass of cold, fresh water to your lips, took a sip, and then realized that it was actually vinegar. If you imagine tasting something unpleasant—not something disgusting or revolting—but unpleasant, then you'll likely generate a facial expression of dislike. Just as for expressions of pleasure, facial expressions associated with aversion are similar in rats, monkeys, humans, and many other mammals.

These researchers realized that they could rely on facial expressions to assess whether a rat found some juice pleasant or unpleasant. So, they ran the critical test to evaluate where dopamine neurons were associated with pleasure. They used a very selective neurotoxin that lesioned, or selectively damaged, neurons in part of the dopamine system in their rats. Without those neurons in good working function, the rats became aphagic, meaning they wouldn't eat. More specifically, they wouldn't exert any effort to obtain food or even juice. They wouldn't press levers in experiments, they wouldn't run through a maze, they wouldn't even walk across a room, even if they were hungry or thirsty. Without an intact dopamine system, these rats no longer wanted rewards like food or juice.

But, they would still eat or drink if the food or juice was placed into their mouth. So, what did these aphagic rats, those with the damaged dopamine system, do when they received something pleasurable, like sugar water?

They leaned forward, made a round mouth, and licked their face and paws ... exactly like neurologically normal rats. They liked the sugar water.

When the aphagic rats received a bitter solution, lithium water, they gaped their mouth, protruded their tongue, and shook their head, again exactly like neurologically normal rats. They disliked the bitter solution.

So, if part of a rat's dopamine system is disabled, it will not walk across its cage to consume food, but it still shows normal hedonic responses to pleasant and unpleasant stimuli. These results are compelling evidence that dopamine neurons are not associated with experiences of pleasure, or liking, but for motivating animals to seek out rewards, what researchers call wanting.

So, what causes liking, if not dopamine? Current research suggests that feelings of liking are associated with the activity of a different sort of neuron (one that uses opioids as neurotransmitters) but there's much more to be learned. The distinction between wanting and liking can be seen in several sorts of pathological decision making. Consider drug addiction. We now know that essentially all addictive drugs act on the brain's dopamine system in some way. Some addictive drugs cause dopamine neurons to fire more frequently, other drugs cause those neurons to release more dopamine when they fire, and still others cause dopamine to have greater effects on other neurons.

Take cocaine, for example. Normally, after a dopamine molecule is released by a neuron, it floats around and influences adjacent neurons until it is pumped back into the original dopamine neuron. But when cocaine is ingested, it prevents those "re-uptake pumps" from doing their job, so the rewarding effects of dopamine become more intense and long lasting. The feeling of wanting, especially for cocaine itself, becomes greatly increased.

When addiction becomes chronic, addicts may no longer experience pleasure from consuming their drug of choice, but their overactive dopamine system still pushes them to want more and more. Drugs become more valuable to addicts, even as they become less pleasurable.

So, I've described two features of these dopamine neurons. First, their firing isn't associated with rewards themselves but with changes in reward from expectations, or reward prediction error. And second, dopamine neurons aren't necessary for the pleasure associated with reward (or liking) but for the motivation to consume rewards (or wanting).

I want to now explore what happens when the dopamine system goes awry and see whether your intuitions have been changed by what you just learned.

Earlier I mentioned Parkinson's disease. As a reminder, Parkinson's disease is associated with the death of dopamine neurons. As the disease progresses and more and more of those dopamine neurons die, the disease impairs movement, disrupts balance, and causes motor tremors like trembling hands. Parkinson's disease can't be cured, but its symptoms can be alleviated by drugs, specifically drugs that replenish the brain's supply of dopamine and that intensify the effects of dopamine in the brain.

But, let's think for a moment about what side effects those drugs might cause, based on the two properties of dopamine neurons described earlier. First, they might amplify the influence of unexpected changes in reward; and second, they could increase wanting or reward-seeking behavior.

If you have these two side effects, probably the worst place for you to go would be a casino. All casino games involve rewards that arrive unexpectedly, and those unexpected rewards motivate people to keep playing just like unexpected squirts of juice motivate a monkey to perform an experimental task. In both cases, activity of dopamine neurons motivates reward-seeking behavior.

By the late 1990s, some neurologists were noticing that a few Parkinson's patients were also exhibiting uncontrollable pathological gambling—they would regularly go to casinos and spend much more than they should. But there wasn't any sort of general appreciation of this link; many clinicians still thought of Parkinson's as a movement disorder, and didn't appreciate the connections between dopamine and reward.

But in 2003 researchers at the Muhammad Ali Parkinson Research Center in Arizona conducted a comprehensive study. They examined the clinical histories of every patient that came through their clinic in a single year, and they found that those patients who had been treated with the particular drugs that intensify the effects of dopamine had a greatly elevated rate of pathological gambling.

These gambling problems often arose quickly. Within a few weeks of taking a new medication, some individuals who had never before gambled, or had only gambled infrequently and in moderation, reported uncontrollable urges to gamble, with resulting losses of tens of thousands of dollars. But, when their medication were stopped or decreased, the same individuals quickly returned to normal, with no desire to gamble.

Since this research, neurologists now recognize that some medications for Parkinson's disease can increase the risk of problem gambling, and so they warn their patients of those risks, and watch for signs of gambling or other compulsive behaviors.

Let's return to the idea of value, from the start of the lecture. To understand many real-world decisions, we need to first understand why people value some things more than others. One possibility is that value comes from experienced or anticipated pleasure, as introduced by Bentham. But that isn't consistent with how our brain's reward system is set up; the key dopamine neurons aren't necessary for pleasure.

Instead, these dopamine neurons respond in a way that encourages us to seek out new and better rewards. They increase their firing rate when a reward is better than our expectations, but they decrease their firing rate when a reward is worse than our expectations. And, they don't change their firing when our expectations are exactly met. Our brain responds to new information about rewards, not necessarily to rewards themselves.

As we'll see in the next lecture, these simple facts about how our brains work form the basis for one of the largest ideas in behavioral economics: reference dependence.

# Reference Dependence—Economic Implications
## Lecture 4

One of the cornerstones of behavioral economics is prospect theory, a descriptive model that attempts to explain what people will choose, not what they should choose. Prospect theory has two big ideas: reference dependence and probability weighting. In this lecture, you will explore the idea of reference dependence—what it means, why it is important, and what mechanisms create it, along with how it influences real-world decisions. Reference dependence can bias even our biggest decisions, shaping what we think about home purchases or retirement investing. However, reference dependence can also be one of the most powerful tools for making good decisions.

**Reward Prediction Error**

- Dopamine neurons in your brainstem respond to a range of rewards. Specifically, they change their rate of firing in a predictable manner: They increase their firing rate when rewards are better than expected but decrease their firing rate when rewards are worse than expected. In addition, if a reward is completely predictable—as when there was advance warning that the reward would be delivered—then the firing rate does not change at all.

- This is called the reward prediction error. The brain creates an expectation, or reference point, about what reward should be received at each point in time. When rewards are better than expected—or when the animal gains information about unexpected future rewards—then dopamine neurons increase their firing rate. If rewards are worse than expected, then dopamine neurons decrease their firing rate. Importantly, if some reward is exactly as expected, then firing rates do not change at all.

- Dopamine neurons do not respond to rewards themselves; they respond to whether a reward was better or worse than the current reference point—the reward prediction error.

## The Endowment Effect

- Reference dependence is one of the big ideas in behavioral economics. It leads to some of the most striking biases in our choice behavior—biases that we can learn to minimize in order to make better choices. One of the most famous biases is called the endowment effect. This bias has deep consequences for decision making.

- The endowment effect originally attracted the attention of economists because it helps to explain some puzzling features of market behavior, such as the fact that people don't trade goods as often as predicted by economic models.

- Suppose that when people ordered this course, half of them (randomly chosen) were sent a complimentary gift. You were one of the lucky ones. You received a mug with a *Behavioral Economics* logo on the side.

- A week goes by, and you unexpectedly have the opportunity to sell the mug. How much would someone have to pay for you to sell them that mug? Behavioral economists refer to this amount as your willingness-to-accept price. A typical amount in a laboratory experiment might be around 10 dollars; people are willing to accept 10 dollars in exchange for the mug they own.

- Now, suppose that you weren't one of the lucky ones. You didn't receive a free mug in the mail, and you don't know anything about that promotion. Instead, you just received an email offer to purchase the same *Behavioral Economics* mug. How much would you be willing to pay for that mug? In a typical laboratory experiment, people would be willing to pay about five dollars to purchase a mug.

- So, this hypothetical experiment would create two groups of people. The ones who received mugs would only be willing to sell them if they received 10 dollars or more. But the ones who didn't receive mugs would only be willing to buy them for five dollars or less. In other words, owning the mug shifts your reference point, so that your willingness-to-accept price becomes much greater than your willingness-to-pay price.

- A discrepancy between willingness to accept and willingness to pay leads to inefficient market behavior. Consider a good that is in limited supply, such as tickets to a basketball game. The market price for those tickets should depend on matching buyers with sellers. Over time, the tickets should end up in the hands of the people who find them most valuable.

- Suppose that there were 500 tickets available for a game and that 1,000 people wanted those tickets. If the tickets were first given out to 500 randomly chosen people, then market theory predicts that some of the people who didn't get the tickets would try to buy them from those who did and that the tickets would eventually end up in the hands of the 500 people who placed the greatest value on those tickets. But this doesn't happen.

- Duke University actually allocates basketball tickets to its students in this fashion: Students sign up for the option to buy tickets, which are then allocated by lottery. Students who entered one lottery for championship game tickets were interviewed beforehand. The median amount that students would be willing to pay to buy a ticket was 150 dollars, but the median price that people would be willing to accept to sell a ticket was 1,500 dollars.

- The random endowment changed the very way that these students thought about the basketball tickets. The students who won the ticket lottery described going to basketball games as an almost priceless experience. But the students who lost the lottery thought of the tickets as a consumer good.

- This ticket lottery provides a prototypical example of the endowment effect. Randomly giving some people a good—for example, basketball tickets—increased its subjective value by a factor of 10. Needless to say, these basketball tickets are not commonly traded on an open market. Sellers want far more money than the buyers are willing to pay.

- To an economist, the allocation of Duke basketball tickets is inefficient. The random distribution process leads to an enormous endowment effect, preventing the flow of tickets to those who valued them most beforehand. But the process does have its advantages. The lucky winners see their tickets as extraordinarily valuable, which increases attendance, the enthusiasm of the crowd, and the team's home-court advantage.

## Loss Aversion

- Reference dependence also contributes to a general bias toward loss aversion. People are more sensitive to economic losses than to economic gains. How much more sensitive? When we bring people into the laboratory for experiments, we ask them to make simple decisions about real gains and losses.

- We might ask them whether they would be willing to play a coin-flip game where if they flipped heads we pay them 20 dollars, but if they flip tails they pay us 15 dollars. Some people are willing to play that game, but most people aren't. When we improve the stakes to a gain of 20 dollars versus a loss of only five dollars, then almost everyone is willing to play the game.

- Across many experiments over many years, researchers have calculated the ratio of gains to losses at which people become willing to play this sort of coin-flip game. That ratio, which is called lambda, is typically a little less than two to one—that is, economic losses influence this simple decision approximately twice as much as economic gains. This is not a small bias, and almost everyone has it to some degree.

- Salespeople, marketers, and even political campaigns recognize the power of loss aversion for shaping your behavior. It results from a fundamental feature of how your brain works: reference dependence. By evaluating outcomes in terms of changes from

63

a reference point, your brain can use the same simple sort of computations in its decision making as it does in vision, hearing, and many other processes. Reference dependence provides a simple and flexible tool for functioning in a complex world. You can't just make reference dependence go away, even if you wanted to.

**Minimizing the Effects of Reference Dependence**

- One of the most powerful ways we can minimize the unwanted effects of reference dependence on our behavior, using it when it's helpful but not letting it guide us astray, is the simplest: shifting your point of reference. Suppose that you are considering whether to raise the deductible on your auto insurance. When thinking about insurance the usual way—in terms of protecting an asset like your car—you might be relatively conservative and want lower deductibles.

- But you can shift your point of reference and think of insurance differently: It is forfeiting a sure amount of money against an

**Consider separately the larger and smaller consequences of a decision. For example, would you separately buy custom floor mats if you weren't already buying a car?**

unlikely event. When people think about insurance as a necessary cost, people tend to be relatively risk tolerant and want higher deductibles. Shifting the reference point you use for a decision is one way to reframe the decision problem.

- A second useful approach is to consider separately the larger and smaller consequences of a decision. When making a very big decision, it is easy to lose perspective; against the total cost of a new car, spending extra on custom floor mats, for example, may not seem like a big deal. Ask yourself: If I already owned this car, would I pay 500 dollars for better floor mats? When you change your perspective, saving that 500 dollars may seem like a much better idea.

- Third, and finally, create hypothetical alternatives for your decision. Should you splurge on an extended family vacation this year? Of course, the vacation will be fun, and of course, the vacation will be expensive. By itself, it may be difficult to know whether the benefits are worth the costs. So, force an alternative point of reference: On what else would you spend the money? An alternative sort of vacation? A new car? Additional retirement savings? Very few economic decisions are made in complete isolation, and you can improve your chances of making good decisions by forcing yourself to create alternatives.

## Suggested Reading

Carmon and Ariely, "Focusing on the Forgone."

Lakshminaryanan, Chen, and Santos, "Endowment Effect in Capuchin Monkeys."

## Questions to Consider

1. In what ways might using reference points simplify our decisions?

2. What are real-world examples in which the endowment effect causes things we own to be overvalued?

# Reference Dependence—Economic Implications
## Lecture 4—Transcript

Welcome back. Previously, we talked about one of the cornerstones of behavioral economics, a descriptive model that attempts to explain what people will choose, not what they should choose. We call this model Prospect theory. Prospect theory has two big ideas: reference dependence and probability weighting. In today's lecture, I will explore the idea of reference dependence—what it means, why it is important, and what mechanisms create it—along with how it influences real-world decisions.

Traditional economic models assume that the value of money follows a pattern of diminishing marginal utility. That is, the difference between $0 and $1,000 seems subjectively much greater than the difference between $100,000 and $101,000. Marginal utility diminishes with each additional dollar you have. This concept makes intuitive sense—we all can imagine that a given amount of money is worth more to someone who has little, than to someone who has much. Utility, in traditional models, depends on absolute wealth.

Consider, for a moment, a simple thought problem. Suppose that you have just finished college, and you are about to sign your first employment contract with an up-and-coming Internet company. You are excited about the job, the work environment, and the benefits. Finally, after years with no assets, you are going to have a salary and receive a huge signing bonus. Now, let's suppose that the CEO of this company gives you a choice between two signing bonuses: You can either receive a sure $100,000—what a great company—or a signing bonus that is dependent on the flip of a coin. If the coin flips heads, you'll get $111,000; if the coin flips tails, you'll get only $90,000.

What do you choose? Choosing to flip the coin would earn new employees more money on average; the gain of $11,000 for heads is larger than the loss of $10,000 for tails. But you only get to flip the coin once, and you might be unlucky. This sort of decision is very hard for many people. Let me tweak the decision problem to make it much easier.

Suppose that the company instead offers you a fixed $100,000 startup, with no negotiation. You happily deposit the check in your new bank account and take a celebratory trip with a friend to Las Vegas. There, as part of a casino promotion, you have the opportunity to flip a single coin for a high-stakes gamble: If you flip heads you win $11,000, if you flip tails you lose $10,000. What do you choose?

When faced with this sort of decision, most people play it safe. The fear of losing $10,000 dramatically outweighs the possibility of winning $11,000. Of course, this second decision is mathematically equivalent to the first. In both cases, you choose between a safe option with a guaranteed amount of money and a risky option that could result in more or less money. So, why does the second decision seem easier?

The answer lies in reference dependence. Prospect theory proposed that people evaluate potential outcomes in terms of relative changes in wealth, not absolute wealth states. When faced with a risky decision, we think less about our bank account and more about whether we'll be better or worse off afterward. We end up being more risk-averse in our economic decisions than we should be, usually because we want to avoid losing money.

Reference points are common in our everyday lives. Consumers love sales—"20% off regular prices." From the perspective of our diminishing bank account, we don't save money when we buy something at 20 percent off. But, if we adopt the regular price as a reference point, getting something on sale can seem psychologically like saving. Marketers know this and use reference dependence to influence our purchasing decisions.

The concept of reference dependence will pervade this entire course. It is one of the most central ideas in behavioral economics, and we'll observe its influence in many, many sorts of decisions.

Imagine that you are walking along a country road on a dark night. There is a new moon overhead, so that the only light comes from the stars above. Your eyes adapt to the darkness and you see the road ahead, trees in the surrounding fields, and even the occasional bird in the cloudless sky. Ahead in the road you see a piece of white paper; it seems bright against the surrounding dark road. You walk over to the paper and pick it up.

Next, imagine that you were walking along that same road at midday. You squint for a moment, and then your vision adapts to the brightness. The sun's glare illuminates everything, the road and trees sparkle in the sunlight. Ahead in the road you see a piece of coal-black paper, and you walk over to pick it up.

We've all experienced these extremes. When we walk outside at night the world looks dark at first, but then our vision adapts. Similarly, when we walk outside into a sunny afternoon, the world looks very bright at first, but our eyes adjust.

We all see white paper in starlight as white and black paper in sunlight as black. But what we see doesn't correspond to the actual light coming off of those pieces of paper. The black piece of paper is actually reflecting more light into your eyes than the white paper. How much more? Not twice as much, not ten times as much, but about one million times as much. And it still looks black.

Your brain's visual system has to deal with an enormous range of light intensity. Bright sunlight and dark starlight differ by about eight orders of magnitude, or a hundred-million-fold difference in the number of photons reflected off an object. This dynamic range is much greater than that of neurons in our brain, which fire at rates of a few times per second to a few hundred times per second. This illustrates a fundamental problem of information processing: How can you represent information with sufficient range to accommodate big numbers, but with sufficient precision to resolve differences between small numbers?

Your visual system solves this problem in a remarkable way. It adjusts its point of reference based on the overall brightness. When the world is dark, the reference point decreases and tiny changes in absolute brightness increase the firing rate of neurons. But, when the world is bright, the reference point increases and much greater changes in absolute brightness are required to alter neurons' firing. These same principles apply to nearly every aspect of how your brain processes information, from your senses, to your motor system, and yes, to your decision making.

Let's consider the specific case of how your brain represents the utility of a reward. You've learned how dopamine neurons in your brainstem respond to a range of rewards. Specifically, they change their rate of firing in a predictable manner: They increase their firing rate when rewards are better than expected, but decrease their firing rate when rewards are worse than expected. And, if a reward is completely predictable, as when there was advance warning that the reward would be delivered, then the firing rate does not change at all.

Last time, we learned this was called the reward prediction error. The brain creates an expectation, or reference point, about what reward should be received at each point in time. When rewards are better than expected (or when the animal gains information about unexpected future rewards) then dopamine neurons increase their firing rate. If rewards are worse than expected, then dopamine neurons decrease their firing rate. Importantly, if some reward is exactly as expected, then firing rates do not change at all.

Let's move from the laboratory to the real world. Suppose that you are walking down the street, and you find an unused lottery ticket, like from a scratch-off game where you might win anything from a few dollars to a few hundred dollars. Your dopamine neurons would increase their firing in response to the unexpected reward.

Before you scratch off that lottery ticket, you don't know exactly how much it is worth. Your average expectation might be something like $2, the face value of the ticket. You scratch off that ticket and win $10. That would be better than your expectation, and your dopamine neurons would further increase their firing rate. But, suppose that you only won $1. Even though you won money, it would be less than your expectation, and the dopamine neurons would actually decrease their firing rate. I want to emphasis this one critical fact. Dopamine neurons do not respond to rewards themselves; they respond to whether a reward was better or worse than the current reference point, that's reward prediction error.

Let's move back into the domain of economic decision making. Online poker playing involves many, many risky decisions, some for small stakes and some for large stakes. Researchers have analyzed the outcomes of millions of games of online poker. They found something pretty remarkable: The poker players who won most often also lost the most money, overall. How can that be possible? The simple explanation is that those players tended to win games involving small amounts of money, but tended to lose games involving large amounts of money. The players who win most often are aggressive and stay in many hands, even if they don't have the best cards. Most of the time this seems like a good strategy because they discourage the other players from playing, and they can collect pots with relatively small amounts of money over and over. But some of the time, they'll play aggressively when they have a pretty good hand, but someone else turns out to have an even better hand. Then, they lose a very big pot of money.

But this raises another question: Why didn't these players learn from those large losses? The answer follows naturally from reference dependence. Dopamine neurons are very sensitive to whether you win or lose, but are less sensitive to how much you win or lose.

So, when a poker player wins $10 that is coded as a good event; the player's brain effectively motivates them to keep playing. Losing a very large amount of money, say $1,000, is coded as a bad event, but it doesn't seem 100 times worse than the good events. So, winning small amounts and losing big amounts is a great way to manipulate the activity of dopamine neurons, but also a quick path to bankruptcy. On a more positive note, very successful poker players lose most of the time, but when they lose they lose small amounts of money, and when they win, they win big.

So you can see why reference dependence is one of the big ideas in behavioral economics. It leads to some of the most striking biases in our choice behavior, biases that we can learn to minimize in order to make better choices. One of the most famous such biases is called the endowment effect. This bias has deep consequences for decision making.

I want you to imagine taking an apple and cutting off a small slice off of its side, giving a circle of fruit about an inch in diameter. How valuable is that slice of apple? Perhaps it isn't very valuable to you, but you aren't a capuchin monkey. Capuchins are small and very cute New World monkeys that really, really like apples. In an ingenious experiment, capuchin monkeys were trained to exchange coin-like tokens for treats like slices of apple. Their exchanges were price sensitive. A monkey might equally prefer apple slices and cereal cubes if both cost one token per piece, but if the price of cereal cubes dropped to one token per two cubes, then the monkey would choose the cheaper cereal cubes.

The monkeys were first endowed with one type of food, like apple slices, then given the chance to trade for another equally valued food, like cereal cubes. The monkeys only traded about 10 percent of the time; that is, they preferred whatever food they were randomly assigned. That's an endowment effect: The monkeys overvalue whatever they have, compared to what they could get.

Of course, there might be other explanations. The monkeys might not like to trade food at all, once they have it. So, the researchers ran the experiment again but now allowed the monkeys to trade their apple slices for the best treats of all, fruit rollups filled with marshmallow fluff. Now, the monkeys were willing to trade about 90 percent of the time. It isn't that the monkeys don't want to trade, they just showed the endowment effect and overvalued what they already had.

It is tempting to dismiss this example; after all, we humans are much smarter and better decision makers than a six-pound capuchin monkey. But we humans do the same thing. Suppose that I teach a class of 30 students. On the first day of class, I walk through the room carrying a bag containing school t-shirts and coffee mugs and I randomly give each student one of the two items. Then, immediately afterward, I announce, "I have some extra t-shirts and mugs in my bag. If you want to trade for the other item, just raise your hand." Only a few students, if any, will want to trade. It might be that I just got lucky—I happened to give coffee mugs to the students who like coffee mugs, and t-shirts to the students who like t-shirts. Or, it might be that students value items more after they've been given them. That's the endowment effect. The endowment effect originally attracted the attention of economists because it helps explain some puzzling features of market behavior, such as the fact that people don't trade goods as often as predicted by economic models.

Suppose that when people ordered this course, I ran a simple experiment. I sent half of them (randomly chosen) a complimentary gift. You were one of the lucky ones. You received a package, opened it up, and take out a mug. It has a spiffy Behavioral Economics logo on its side, is very useful for holding coffee or another beverage of your choice, but it is still just a mug.

A week goes by, and you unexpectedly have the opportunity to sell the mug. How much would someone have to pay for you sell them to that mug? Behavioral economists refer to this amount as your willingness-to-accept price for the mug. A typical amount in a laboratory experiment might be around $10. People are willing to accept $10 in exchange for the mug they own.

Suppose that you weren't one of the lucky ones. You didn't receive a free mug in the mail, and you don't know anything about that promotion. Instead, you just received an email offer to purchase the same Behavioral Economics mug. How much would you be willing to pay for that mug? In a typical laboratory experiment, people would be willing to pay about $5 to purchase a mug.

So, my hypothetical experiment would create two groups of people. The ones who received mugs would only be willing to sell them if they received $10 or more. But the ones who didn't receive mugs would only be willing buy them for $5 or less. In other words, owning the mug shifts your reference point, so that your willingness-to-accept price becomes much greater than your willingness-to-pay price.

A discrepancy between willingness-to-accept and willingness-to-pay leads to inefficient market behavior. Let's consider a good that is in limited supply, such as tickets to a basketball game. The market price for those tickets should depend on matching buyers with sellers. Over time, the tickets should end up in the hands of the people who find them most valuable. Suppose that there were 500 tickets available for a game, and 1,000 people wanted those tickets. If I first gave out the tickets to 500 randomly chosen people, then market theory predicts that some of the people who didn't get the tickets would try to buy them from those who did, and that the tickets would eventually end up in the hands of the 500 people who placed the greatest value on those tickets.

But this doesn't happen. Duke University actually allocates basketball tickets to its students in this fashion: Students sign up for the option to buy tickets that are then allocated by lottery. Students who entered one lottery for championship game tickets were interviewed beforehand. The median amount that students would be willing to pay to buy a ticket was $150, but the median price that people would be willing to accept to sell a ticket was a full $1,500. And the random endowment changed the very way these students thought about the basketball tickets. The students who won the ticket lottery described going to basketball games as an almost priceless experience, saying things like, "This is a once-in-a-lifetime opportunity." But the students who lost the lottery thought of the tickets as a consumer good, saying things like, "I could spend my money in many other ways." In a later lecture, we'll see why thinking about the tickets in terms of an experience versus as a consumer good turns out to have such strong effects on value.

This is a prototypic example of the endowment effect. Randomly giving some people a good—here, basketball tickets—increased its subjective value by a factor of 10. Needless to say, these basketball tickets are not commonly traded on an open market. Sellers want far more money than the buyers are willing to pay.

To an economist, the allocation of Duke basketball tickets is inefficient. The random distribution process leads to an enormous endowment effect, preventing the flow of tickets to those who valued them most beforehand. But the process does have its advantages. The lucky winners see their tickets as extraordinarily valuable, which increases attendance, the enthusiasm of the crowd, and the team's home-court advantage.

Reference dependence also contributes to a general bias toward loss aversion. At the beginning of this lecture, I stated that people are more sensitive to economic losses than to economic gains. How much more sensitive? When we bring people into the laboratory for experiments, we don't have them make decisions about thousands of dollars; we can't pay each participant that much. But we do ask them to make simple decisions about real gains and losses. We might ask them whether they would be willing to play a coin flip game where if they flipped heads we pay them $20, but if they flip tails they pay us $15. Some people are willing to play that game, but most people aren't. When we improve the stakes to a gain of $20 versus a loss of only $5, then almost everyone is willing to play the game.

Across many experiments over many years, researchers have calculated the ratio of gains to losses at which people become willing to play this sort of coin-flip game. That ratio, which is called lambda, is typically a little less than 2 to 1. That is, economic losses influence this simple decision approximately twice as much as economic gains.

This is not a small bias, and almost everyone has it to some degree. So, why aren't we paralyzed by loss aversion every time that we make a financial decision? Let me offer a few thought problems that illustrate the limits of loss aversion.

Suppose that you win a prize in a store raffle, say a new, highly desirable television. The box holding the television is torn, the television is perfectly fine, the damage is only to the box. Now, as you begin to walk out with your prize, the store offers to exchange your box for one in pristine condition. You wouldn't feel any loss aversion during that trade; even though you are giving up something of considerable value, you are exchanging it for something with exactly the same features.

Let's consider another thought problem. You have a gift certificate for a local clothing store. When you go shopping and walk to the cash register, do you feel loss aversion as you hand over the gift certificate? No, that's what gift certificates are for; they are intended to be exchanged for other goods. People do not typically feel loss aversion when they give up something that is supposed to be given up.

As a final thought problem, suppose that you are a car salesman. A prospective customer arrives at the dealership and shows interest in one of your new models. There's one major problem, however. That customer loves their existing car—it is still in good shape, it has required very little maintenance, and they still enjoy driving it. How could you minimize their potential loss aversion and sell them a new car?

One useful approach is to focus on what behavioral economists call "substitutability." Show them a car that shares many of the positive qualities of their existing car—something similarly stylish, maintenance free, and fun to drive—but also emphasize a small set of specific advantages, like extra horsepower or improved gas mileage. Discuss the trade-in process in detail; you want them to think about their existing car as an object for potential exchange. If they think about the process as a single transaction of upgrading their car, not as separate selling and buying transactions, then you have them right where you want them.

Salespeople, marketers, and even political campaigns recognize the power of loss aversion for shaping your behavior. It results from a fundamental feature of how your brain works: reference dependence. By evaluating outcomes in terms of changes from a reference point, your brain can use the same simple sort of computations in its decision making as it does in vision, hearing, and many other processes. Reference dependence provides a simple and flexible tool for functioning in a complex world. You can't just make reference dependence go away, even if you wanted to.

So, how can we minimize the unwanted effects of reference dependence on our behavior, using it when it's helpful, but not letting it guide us astray? Several strategies can help.

One of the most powerful is the simplest: shifting your point of reference. Suppose that you are considering whether to raise the deductible on your auto insurance. When thinking about insurance the usual way—in terms of protecting an asset like your car—you might be relatively conservative and want lower deductibles. But you can shift your point of reference and think of insurance differently: it is forfeiting a sure amount of money against an unlikely event. When people think about insurance as a necessary cost, they tend to be relatively risk-tolerant and want higher deductibles.

Shifting your reference point can even help you stay organized. When deciding whether to keep something (say, an old sweater) or donate it to charity, ask yourself, "What would I pay for this, if I didn't have it already?" If you wouldn't be willing to pay much, that may be a good indication that you should give it away. Shifting the reference point you use for a decision is one way to reframe the decision problem, and I'll talk much more about the effects of decision framing throughout the course.

A second useful approach is to consider separately the larger and smaller consequences of a decision. When making a very big decision, it is easy to lose perspective—against the total cost of a new car, spending extra on, say, custom floor mats may not seem like a big deal. Ask yourself: If I already owned this car, would I pay $500 for better floor mats? When you change your perspective, saving that $500 may seem like a much better idea.

Third, and finally, create hypothetical alternatives for your decision. Should you splurge on an extended family vacation this year? Of course, the vacation will be fun, and, of course, the vacation will be expensive. By itself it may be hard to know whether the benefits are worth the costs. So, force an alternative point of reference: On what else would you spend the money? A different sort of vacation? A new car? Additional retirement savings? Very few economic decisions are made in complete isolation, and you can improve your chances of making good decisions by forcing yourself to create alternatives.

Now you should have a deeper understanding of reference dependence, how it works in the brain and how it changes our processing of information. Reference dependence can bias even our biggest decisions, shaping what we think about home purchases or retirement investing. Yet, reference dependence can also be one of the most powerful tools for making good decisions. You may not be able to change yourself as a decision maker. But you can change your point of reference. By doing so, you may suddenly see your decision in a new light.

In the next lecture we'll learn another way that our decision making adjusts from one situation to another. That adjustment process, which leads to something called range effects, allows the same system to handle decisions both big and small.

# Range Effects—Changing the Scale
## Lecture 5

There are no big decisions. Regardless of whether you are buying a house or a cup of coffee, the processes that underlie your decision are similar. The same brain systems help you anticipate potential rewards, evaluate potential risks, and compare one option with another. You don't have any sort of special module in your brain that turns on for decisions that really matter—for those big decisions. In this lecture, you will learn about the adjustment process, which leads to something called range effects, that allows the same system to handle decisions both big and small.

**Range Effects**

- The range of some quantity is given by the span of its potential values. For example, fast-food prices vary over a small range (a few dollars); prices of jackets vary over a larger range (tens to hundreds of dollars); and televisions vary over an even larger range (hundreds to thousands of dollars).

- The basic principle of a range effect is as follows: Our sense of a meaningful difference in some quantity is inversely proportional to its range. If the typical price for an espresso and biscotti in your area is five dollars, when you see that a new coffee shop charges ten dollars for the same thing, you might walk out because the coffee is too expensive.

- If a typical price is five dollars, then each extra dollar represents 20 percent of that range—a huge effect. What matters is not the absolute change in price, but the relative change in price compared to the range.

- This phenomenon allows us to explain both sides of our paradox. The same five-dollar savings represents a large proportion of the range when we're purchasing coffee, a much smaller proportion when we're buying a jacket, and a tiny fraction when we're picking up a new television.

- Range effects are intimately related to the idea of reference dependence. Outcomes are good or bad not based on some absolute value, but on their relative value compared to some reference point. We reset our sense of value so that things better than the reference point are seen as good, and things worse than the reference point are seen as bad. Range effects involve changing the scale.

**Psychological Effects**

- Range effects may seem like yet another bias in our decision making, but they aren't specific to decision making. They affect what we perceive, how we move, and even what we remember. They arise because of a basic feature of our biology—how we're set up to deal with information across different scales.

- In the mid-19th century, Ernst Weber, one of the founders of psychology, was interested in range effects. One of his most famous experiments was also one of the most simple. He brought people into his laboratory and then had them lift one object and then another, and then he asked them to guess whether one was heavier. He found that the difference in weight needed to guess correctly was a constant proportion of the weight.

- For example, people could reliably distinguish a two-pound weight from a two-pound, one-ounce weight, but they couldn't tell the difference between a 20-pound weight and a 20-pound, one-ounce weight. At that larger range, the difference would need to be about a half of a pound or so to be noticeable. When lifting two objects, people can tell which one is heavier if they differ by about two or three percent in weight.

- This phenomenon has come to be known as Weber's law: The difference needed to discriminate two stimuli, what psychologists call a just noticeable difference, is a constant proportion of their magnitude.

- Weber's law seems to be practically universal. It holds for the weight of things we lift, the brightness of things we see, the loudness of things we hear, and even for our ability to represent numerical quantities. Just as a difference of five ounces matters much more when lifting 10-ounce weights than when lifting 10-pound weights, a difference of five dollars matters much more when spending 10 dollars than when spending 100 dollars.

- Weber's law captures the key feature of range effects. When we perceive, remember, or make decisions about small quantities, the range of potential values is small, and our judgments can be very precise. Small differences matter, when we're dealing with small ranges.

- But when we must deal with large quantities, there is a correspondingly larger range of potential values. That makes our judgments much less precise. We don't notice small differences against that backdrop. Once our range expands, differences need to be much larger to matter for our decisions.

### Neural Effects

- Why are range effects so ubiquitous? Our brains face the challenge of dealing both with very small quantities and with very large quantities. Visual perception has to work for dark starlight and for bright sunlight, and our decision making has to work for cups of coffee and for sports cars.

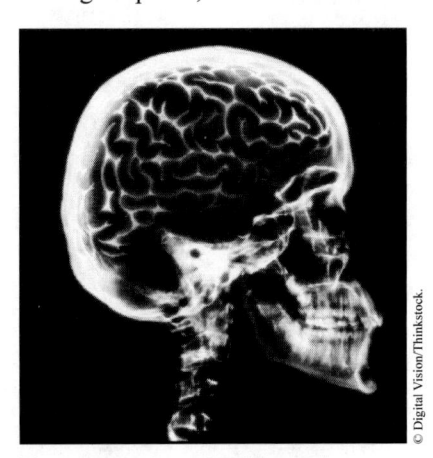

**The neurons in our brains send electrical signals to each other in order to make sense of the world.**

- So how do our brains represent things both small and large? Recall that the basic units of information processing in our brains are neurons—cells that communicate by sending electrical signals to each other. Most neurons can fire in a pretty limited range. They can fire electrical signals slowly, perhaps every second or so, or they can fire rapidly, perhaps 100 times per second.

- If you are outside at nighttime, neurons in your visual system can represent very dark objects by firing slowly—once a second—and represent very bright objects by firing rapidly—100 times a second. The brain's visual system is much, much more complex than this simplified example, but the basic principle holds.

- When you change from starlight to bright sunlight, there's about a million-fold change in the absolute intensity of the light. But your neurons can't suddenly start firing a million times per second; that's not biologically possible. They need to work within the same range as before, firing one time per second to 100 times per second. The same biological range needs to account for a much larger stimulus range.

- This idea is fundamental to everything we perceive—not just money, but everything else, too. Our brain adapts from processing small quantities to processing big quantities by changing the scale. That has a cost: When we move from small to big, we lose precision. A dollar seems meaningful for a cup of coffee, but it doesn't matter for a television. That's the essence of a range effect.

**Economic Decision Making**

- A meaningful difference in some quantity is inversely proportional to its range. Differences become less meaningful as quantities get bigger. This description of range effects sounds a lot like the idea of diminishing marginal utility for money. This idea, which is a bedrock concept in economics, was first articulated in the 18th century by Daniel Bernoulli.

- Diminishing marginal utility for money is a straightforward consequence of a much deeper phenomenon: Small differences don't seem meaningful when dealing with large amounts. Ten dollars matters more to someone who has almost nothing than to someone who is a millionaire many times over.

- There's a second implication of range effects, though—one that helps us understand a particularly thorny problem for behavioral economics. Suppose that your friend offers you a coin-flip gamble: If the coin lands on heads, your friend will give you 11 dollars, and if it's tails, you will give your friend 10 dollars. Some people will accept this offer, but most won't. Most people turn down gambles like this unless the potential gain is twice as big—or bigger—than the potential loss.

- The economist Matthew Rabin noted that if you turn down that gamble, it implies that the utility for the $11^{th}$ dollar above your current wealth state is considerably less than that of the $10^{th}$ dollar below your current wealth state. How much less? 10 divided by 11, or about 90 percent. Stated another way, turning down this gamble implies that the value of a dollar diminishes by 10 percent over a range of 21 dollars.

- If this were true—if the value of a dollar diminishes by 10 percent for every additional 11 dollars over what you have now—then very strange things would happen. The value of the $100^{th}$ dollar over what you have now would only be 42 cents. The value of the $500^{th}$ dollar over what you have now would only be about one cent. And the value of the $1,000^{th}$ dollar over what you have now would be only one-hundredth of one cent.

- This rate of diminishing marginal utility is a problem; it doesn't make sense. Money is worth less to us when we have more, but it's not the case that additional money would become essentially worthless if we had 1,000 dollars more than we have now.

- The problem arises because people shouldn't be risk averse over small stakes. The coin flip just described is a pretty good gamble— you should take it. And, if you are risk averse over small stakes, then you should be really, really risk averse over large stakes. You shouldn't turn down a coin-flip gamble—winning 11 dollars against losing 10 dollars—while also being willing to trust your retirement funds to the stock market.

- Why do people behave this way? Think about this phenomenon as a range effect. Suppose that we do recalibrate our value for money to fit the current range. We take the same scale and shrink it for small decisions and stretch it for big decisions. That implies that the value of money diminishes faster when we're dealing with small amounts—like the coin flip gambles—but much, much more slowly when we're dealing with large amounts—like our retirements.

- There are no big decisions. We use the same sort of processes to deal with quantities both large and small. But when we adapt to deal with large quantities, we lose precision in dealing with small quantities. That's the basic idea of a range effect. Our sense of a meaningful difference in some quantity is inversely proportional to its range.

**Minimizing Range Effects**

- We can take steps to avoid range effects—or at least minimize their unwanted influence on our decisions. First, begin with small decisions. If you begin with a decision involving large amounts of money, then you may lose the ability to make good decisions about smaller amounts of money. By beginning with smaller decisions, and moving up to bigger decisions later, you'll avoid losing perspective on small but still important decisions.

- Second, avoid undesirable options that exaggerate range effects. Considering a high-priced option when deciding among various options, even when you know it's out of your price range, will make differences in price seem less important. Marketers know this, so they ensure that there are high-priced alternatives in many decisions, even if they don't expect customers to choose them.

- Finally, force yourself to recalibrate. Don't lose perspective when making what seem like big decisions. In other words, don't think about seemingly big decisions in isolation. Instead, force yourself to think about how else you could use the money that you would save if you went with the less expensive option.

## Suggested Reading

Allon, Federgruen, and Pierson, "How Much Is a Reduction of Your Customers' Wait Worth?"

Rabin, "Risk Aversion and Expected-Utility Theory."

## Questions to Consider

1. How could marketers take advantage of range effects to push consumers toward a higher-priced item?

2. What strategies could you use to minimize those marketing techniques in your own decision making?

# Range Effects—Changing the Scale
## Lecture 5—Transcript

Have you ever faced a big decision? That seems like an easy question, right? You've probably bought a car or a house. You've may have decided whether to propose to your spouse or accept a proposal. You may have decided whether to quit your job, start a business, or go back to school. And, you may have decided how much to save for your retirement decades in your future or how much to draw from your retirement savings right now.

All of these seem like big decisions. They have large stakes. Buying a house is the largest financial transaction that most of us make. They have a long time horizon. When we invest in our education, or save for retirement, the benefits of our decision can be felt decades later. And, they all carry significant risk. Different choices send our lives down very different paths, as anyone who starts a new business recognizes acutely.

Let me ask you a second question. How did you make that big decision? Did you spend hundreds of hours listing the advantages and disadvantages of each option, determining the numerical weight of each of those factors, and using a mathematical formula to calculate which outcome led to greater expected utility? Probably not.

We do tend to spend a lot of time on what seem like big decisions, but that time is usually spent gathering information before the decision. If you are buying a home, you might spend most of your time touring potential homes, but when you enter a home that feels right, you don't spend hours calculating its expected utility. There's just too much information available in one of these big decisions for us to process it all. So people adopt simple rules that emphasize some information and ignore the rest. The big decision becomes much smaller.

This leads me to the simple message for today's lecture: There are no big decisions. Regardless of whether you are buying a house or a cup of coffee, the processes that underlie your decision are similar. The same brain systems help you anticipate potential rewards, evaluate potential risks, and compare one option with another. You don't have any sort of special module in your brain that turns on for decisions that really matter, for those big decisions.

This claim that there are no big decisions is purposefully provocative. I know that you can readily think of counterarguments. "How could buying a house be the same as a cup of coffee?" you might say. "I spent months researching and touring homes, and days agonizing over the final decision. It takes me one minute to buy my regular cup of coffee every morning."

I want to be clear, therefore, as to what I'm not claiming and what I am claiming. I am not claiming that all decisions are equally important. And, I'm not claiming that all decisions take equal amounts of time or evoke equal emotional responses. But, I am claiming that seemingly big decisions and seemingly small decisions share common processes. Big decisions are just small decisions on a larger scale, quite literally.

Let's start with a simple thought problem. Suppose that your favorite coffee shop is a little more than 15 minutes from your home, and your favorite espresso drink with biscotti costs $5—it's a good cup of coffee at a fair price. Now, suppose that another equally good coffee shop opens up only a minute or so from your home, and the same espresso drink with biscotti costs $10. It's twice the price as the other shop. So, here's the key question: Do you travel 15 minutes to purchase the $5 coffee, or spend $10 on coffee at a shop very near your home? In scenarios like this, most people report being willing to still travel 15 minutes to get the cheaper coffee. The difference between spending $5 and $10 seems pretty large.

Now, let me change the thought problem. Suppose that you want to purchase a jacket. It's available at a nearby store for $100, but you could also travel to a store 15 minutes away to get the same jacket for $95 dollars. What do you do? Most people would rather buy the jacket at the nearby store, saving time, rather than money.

Finally, let me change the scenario a third time. You are in the market for a television that costs $1,000 at a nearby store. You can drive 15 minutes farther to a second store and get the same television for $995, with all other factors equivalent. What do you do? This third thought problem seems easy.

We buy the television at the nearby store. Why travel somewhere to save such an insignificant amount?

All three problems contain the same simple tradeoff: spend 15 minutes more time to save $5. If that seems reasonable for coffee, it should seem reasonable for a jacket or television set. But we give up time for money when buying coffee, but we give up money for time when buying a television. What could explain this inconsistency? It isn't exactly a rational tradeoff between time and money.

In a clever study, researchers actually calculated how time and money do trade off when people go to fast-food restaurants. They measured how far people were willing to travel to go to those restaurants, they timed how long people waited in line in the restaurant drive-thrus, and they examined the prices people were willing to pay at different chains and locations.

The results of their analyses are frankly astonishing. Each additional second of average waiting time in the drive-thru lane is worth about 4 cents to the average consumer. If a fast-food restaurant takes one minute longer than its peers to serve customers, it needs to be about $2 cheaper in price to be competitive. One minute waiting is equal to $2.

Time is extraordinarily valuable to these fast-food customers; in fact, it's much more valuable than it should be. If one minute's wait translates to $2 in price, then that corresponds to $120 per hour, that's about 7 times that of the average wage in the area studied. Even the time driving to the restaurant was very valuable (it was a bit less than a third as valuable as time waiting at the restaurant, but that's still a rate much, much higher than the wages of most fast-food shoppers.

There's a paradox hidden here that I want to uncover. The thought problem suggested that money is more important than time for small purchases. People should be willing to trade off substantial travel time to save $5 on lunch, as confirmed by both experimental data and by the fact that restaurants advertise sales and special deals so heavily. But, the analysis of real-world fast-food shoppers suggests that those shoppers actually treat time as much more valuable than money; each minute is worth $2.

The solution to this paradox isn't found in standard economic models or current research in marketing. Instead, it actually comes from a very old idea in psychology, something tied closely to a basic property of brain function. Let me give this old idea name and form. It's called a range effect. The range of some quantity is given by the span of its potential values. For example, fast-food prices vary over a small range, a few dollars. Prices of jackets vary over a larger range, tens to hundreds of dollars. And televisions vary over an even larger range, hundreds to thousands of dollars.

Here's the basic principle of a range effect: our sense of a meaningful difference in some quantity is inversely proportional to its range. The intuition is pretty simple here. If the typical price for an espresso and biscotti in your area is $5, when you see that a new coffee shop charges $10 for the same thing you might walk out, muttering that the coffee here is way too expensive. If a typical price is $5, then each extra dollar represents 20 percent of that range, a huge effect. What matters is not the absolute change in price, but the relative change in price compared to the range.

This phenomenon allows us to explain both sides of our paradox. The same $5 savings represents a large proportion of the range when we're purchasing coffee, a much smaller proportion when we're buying a jacket, and a tiny fraction when we're picking up a new television.

And, the same idea applies to time. If we expect to wait in the drive-thru lane for only a minute or two, then that sets our expected range for waiting on the scale of minutes. A 3-minute wait at one chain may seem interminable, while a 30-second wait seems wonderful. The very speed of fast-food service exaggerates small differences in waiting time, making time much more valuable than money.

Range effects are intimately related to the idea of reference dependence discussed in the previous lecture. Outcomes are good or bad not based on some absolute value, but on their relative value compared to some reference point. We reset our sense of value so that things better than the reference point are seen as good, and things worse than the reference point are seen as bad.

Range effects involve changing the scale. It's as if we have a mental ruler that can be stretched or shrunk to accommodate the range of a given decision. When that ruler is stretched to a very large range, then a change needs to be really large to matter. But, when the ruler is shrunk to a small range, then a small change can seem very important.

Range effects may seem like yet another bias in our decision making, something curious and interesting, but ultimately not that important. But range effects aren't specific to decision making. They affect what we perceive, how we move, and even what we remember. They arise because of a basic feature of our biology: how we're set up to deal with information across different scales. So, I'd like to give you some insight into why we experience range effects.

Think back to an example from the previous lecture. Imagine that you are walking along a country road on a dark night. There is a new moon overhead, so that the only light comes from the stars above. Your eyes adapt to the darkness, and you see a piece of white paper on the road in front of you.

In the last lecture, I used this example to illustrate the idea of reference dependence. A white piece of paper still appears white when viewed outside during starlight, just as it does in bright afternoon sunlight. It doesn't appear white because of the absolute number of photons bouncing off the paper and hitting your retina; indeed, the absolute number is about a million times greater in sunlight compared to starlight. It appears white because it reflects relatively more photons than the surrounding dark road. That's reference dependence: Our experiences depend on relative changes compared to some reference point.

Let's think about what else happens when your reference point shifts. Suppose that in starlight that white paper is reflecting 10 photons per second onto a tiny patch of your retina. I'm making up numbers here, to keep the math simple, but it is true that in very dark conditions only a handful of photons hit a given part of your retina at a time. So, in starlight the range between darkness and lightness might correspond to only about 10 photons, so every photon matters.

But, when you go outside in bright sunlight, the white paper might reflect several million photons per second, and the range between darkness and lightness might now be a million photons. Now, a single photon doesn't matter. Instead, you might need a change of tens of thousands of photons per second in order to notice a change in the lightness of the paper. That's a range effect. This may still seem a little abstract, after all you can't see a photon and you can't count the number hitting your retina. So, let's move to a more concrete example.

In the mid-19th century, Ernst Weber, one of the founders of psychology, was interested in these sorts of range effects. One of his most famous experiments was also one of the most simple. He brought people into his laboratory and then had them lift one object and then another, and then he asked them to guess whether one was heavier. He found that difference in weight needed to guess correctly was a constant proportion of the weight.

For example, people could reliably distinguish a two-pound weight from a two-pound, one-ounce weight, but they couldn't tell the difference between a twenty-pound weight and a twenty-pound, one-ounce weight. At that larger range, the difference would need to be about a half-pound or so to be noticeable. When lifting two objects, people can tell which one is heavier if they differ by about 2 or 3 percent in weight. This phenomenon has come to be known as Weber's law: The difference needed to discriminate two stimuli, what psychologists call a just-noticeable difference, is a constant proportion of their magnitude.

You've probably experienced this yourself. If you were in the market for a new laptop computer, you may have lifted two different models and noticed that one was heavier than the other. That difference in weight was probably only a few ounces or maybe a pound, but it still seemed very meaningful. But if you lifted two chairs that differed in weight by a few ounces, you'd never be able to tell them apart.

Weber's law seems to be practically universal. It holds for the weight of things we lift, the brightness of things we see, the loudness of things we hear, and even for our ability to represent numerical quantities. Just as a difference of five ounces matters much more when lifting 10-ounce weights than when lifting 10-pound weights, a difference of $5 matters much more when spending $10 than when spending $100.

This simple rule, Weber's law, captures the key feature of range effects. When we perceive, remember, or make decisions about small quantities, the range of potential values is small, and our judgments can be very precise. Small differences matter, when we're dealing with small ranges. But when we must deal with large quantities, there is a correspondingly larger range of potential values. That makes our judgments much less precise. We don't notice small differences against that backdrop. Once our range expands, differences need to be much larger to matter for our decisions.

But why are these range effects so ubiquitous? To understand why, let's dig a bit deeper into our biology. Our brains face the challenge of dealing both with very small quantities and with very large quantities. Visual perception has to work for dark starlight and for bright sunlight, and our decision making has to work for cups of coffee and for sports cars.

So how do our brains represent things both small and large? Recall that the basic units of information processing in our brains are neurons: cells that communicate by sending electrical signals to each other. Neuroscientists say that a neuron fires each time it sends an electrical signal. Most neurons can fire in a pretty limited range, there's that word again. They can fire slowly, perhaps every second or so, or they can fire rapidly, perhaps 100 times per second.

If you are outside at nighttime, neurons in your visual system can represent very dark objects by firing slowly (once a second) and represent very bright objects by firing rapidly (100 times a second). I want to emphasize that the brain's visual system is much, much more complex than I'm implying in this simplified example, but the basic principle holds.

Remember that when you change from starlight to bright sunlight, there's something like a million-fold change in the absolute intensity of the light. But your neurons can't suddenly start firing a million times per second, that's not biologically possible. They need to work within the same range as before, firing one time per second to 100 times per second. The same biological range needs to account for a much larger stimulus range.

Let me emphasize this point, because it is fundamental to everything we perceive, not just money, but everything else too. Our brain adapts from processing small quantities to processing big quantities by changing the scale. That has a cost; when we move from small to big, we lose precision. A dollar seems meaningful for a cup of coffee, but it doesn't matter for a television. That's the essence of a range effect.

Let's turn back to economic decision making and explore the implications of range effects in some more depth. I want to highlight two such implications, one is straightforward, and the other is more subtle.

First, let's quickly revisit the definition of a range effect: a meaningful difference in some quantity is inversely proportional to its range. Differences become less meaningful as quantities get bigger. That sounds a lot like the idea of diminishing marginal utility for money. This idea, which is a bedrock concept in economics, was first articulated in the $18^{th}$ century by Daniel Bernoulli, who said, "The utility resulting from any small increase in wealth will be inversely proportionate to the quantity of goods previously possessed." So, diminishing marginal utility for money is a straightforward consequence of a much deeper phenomenon: small differences don't seem meaningful when dealing with large amounts. Ten dollars matters more to someone who has almost nothing than to someone who is a millionaire many times over.

There's a second implication of range effects, though, one that helps us understand a particularly thorny problem for behavioral economics. Recall the example of loss aversion from the previous lecture. Suppose that I offer you a coin-flip gamble: heads I give you $11, tails you give me $10. Some people will accept this offer, but most won't. Most people turn down gambles like this unless the potential gain is twice as big, or bigger, than the potential loss.

Let's think about what this implies, though, for the rate of diminishing marginal utility for money. The economist Matthew Rabin noted that if you turn down that gamble, it implies that the utility for the 11th dollar above your current wealth state is considerably less than that of the 10th dollar below your current wealth state. How much less? 10 divided by 11, or about 90 percent. Or, stated another way, turning down this gamble implies that the value of a dollar diminishes by 10 percent over a range of $21.

If this were true if the value of a dollar did diminish by 10 percent for every additional $11 over what you have now, then very strange things would happen. The value of the 100th dollar over what you have now would only be 42 cents. The value of the 500th dollar over what you have now would only be about one cent. And the value of the 1,000th dollar over what you have now would be only one-hundredth of one cent.

This rate of diminishing marginal utility is a problem—it doesn't make sense. Yes, money is worth less to us when we have more. But, no, it's not the case that additional money would become essentially worthless if we had $1,000 more than we have now. So, what's going on here?

The problem arises because people shouldn't be risk averse over small stakes. The coin flip I described was a pretty good gamble; you should take it. And, if you are risk averse over small stakes, then you should be really, really risk averse over large stakes. You shouldn't turn down a coin-flip gamble—winning $11 against losing $10—while also being willing to trust your retirement funds to the stock market.

Why do people behave this way? Let's think about this phenomenon as a range effect. Suppose that we do recalibrate our value for money to fit the current range. We take the same scale and shrink it for small decisions and stretch it for big decisions. That implies that the value of money diminishes faster when we're dealing with small amounts (like the coin-flip gambles) but much, much more slowly when we're dealing with large amounts (like our retirements).

Over and over again in this course, we'll encounter inconsistencies in people's decisions. They'll make a decision under one set of circumstances that doesn't make sense, given what they choose under other circumstances.

It's not reasonable to be risk averse when making decisions about a few dollars but close to risk neutral when investing our retirement portfolio.

Those inconsistencies start to make more sense when we think of people's decision making as adaptive. We don't just have one mental machine that processes all of our decisions the same way. We have a set of adaptive, flexible tools that we can bring to bear on a range of decisions, and we adjust those tools as needed. We can use the same tools to accommodate the magnitude needed for big decisions, and the precision needed for small decisions.

Therefore, there are no big decisions. We use the same sort of processes to deal with quantities both large and small. But when we adapt to deal with large quantities, we lose precision in dealing with small quantities. That's the basic idea of a range effect. Our sense of a meaningful difference in some quantity is inversely proportional to its range.

I've emphasized that range effects arise from basic principles by which our brains code information. But even though this behavioral economic phenomenon has a biological cause, it isn't inevitable. We can take steps to avoid range effects, or at least to minimize their unwanted influence on our decisions. Let me offer three specific recommendations.

First, begin with small decisions. If you begin with a decision involving large amounts of money, like whether to buy a car, then you may lose the ability to make good decisions about smaller amounts of money, say whether to purchase upgraded floor mats for that car. One hundred dollars might not seem that important after you've decided to spend tens of thousands of dollars, but that's still your money. By beginning with smaller decisions, and moving up to bigger decisions later, you'll avoid losing perspective on small but still important decisions.

Second, avoid undesirable options that exaggerate range effects. Suppose that you live in a large city and are looking for an apartment. You first tour a 1,000-square-foot apartment that's in the middle of your price range. Then you tour an 1,100-square-foot apartment; it's larger but somewhat more expensive. Then, on a whim, you tour a much larger 2,000-square-foot apartment, one that you know in advance you won't buy because it's located too far away from your place of work.

That last option is undesirable because of its location. So, in principle, it shouldn't affect your decision between the other two options. But it might. Touring that much larger apartment increases the range of apartment sizes that you've seen. So, the difference in size between the other two apartments will seem less meaningful.

The same principle holds for other factors, too. Considering a very high priced option will make differences in price seem less important. Marketers know this, and ensure that there are high priced alternatives in many decisions, even if they don't expect customers to choose them.

Finally, force yourself to recalibrate. Don't lose perspective when making what seem like big decisions. For many of us, the largest decisions we make involve purchases of cars and houses, for which the different options might vary by thousands, or tens of thousands, or hundreds of thousands. If you just consider those options in isolation, it's easy to be caught up in range effects.

So, don't think about these seemingly big decisions in isolation. Suppose that two cars differ in price by $5,000. Force yourself to think about how else you could use that money. Could it go toward a vacation? Membership at a gym? Recurring bills? All of the above?

By thinking about these smaller decisions, too, you'll regain some perspective. Perhaps the higher-priced option really is worth it to you. Or, perhaps you'd rather take the lower-priced option and have opportunities for many smaller rewards as well.

As a final thought, I'd like to emphasize that range effects are good for us. It's really quite remarkable that our decision making is so adaptive and flexible. We can deal both with the innumerable small decisions throughout each day, and with the rare larger decisions that shape the course of our lives for years to come.

In the next lecture, we'll move from a discussion of range effects and value to a discussion of probability. We'll learn why people find dealing with probabilities so challenging, and we'll explore some steps that can help us think about probabilities in a more natural manner.

# Probability Weighting
## Lecture 6

Why is it so difficult for us to judge the probability of events? And why do we fail to use probability information effectively even when it is given to us? To gain answers to these questions, you will need to explore the phenomenon of probability weighting, which describes the bias people show when working with probability. This phenomenon was, along with reference dependence, one of the two main advances in prospect theory—and, thus, probability weighting is one of the foundational concepts in behavioral economics.

**Probability**

- Probability is the likelihood that some defined event will occur. There are two common ways in which we describe something's probability. The first is in terms of percentages: There's an 80-percent chance of rain tomorrow. The second is in terms of frequency: Four out of five dentists recommend flossing daily.

- Probabilities are only meaningful to the extent that the events they describe are well defined. If you flip a fair coin, there is a 50-percent chance that it will land heads and a 50-percent chance that it will land tails. Those two events are exclusive—you can either flip heads or tails, but not both—and exhaustive, such that their two individual probabilities sum up to exactly 100 percent.

- Many other real-world events are similarly well defined. But many other sorts of events aren't well defined. Sometimes that's because of imprecision in the stated probabilities. An often frustrating example is weather forecasting. What is meant by a 50-percent chance of rain? The single probability of a 50-percent chance of rain could describe any of a very large set of potential events, only some of which might mean that you will need an umbrella.

- Behavioral economists refer to the way in which objective probabilities are transformed into subjective influences on a decision as probability weights. When we say that some factor "weighs heavily" on our decision, we mean that an objective difference in that factor has outsize influence compared to other factors. Probabilities that are overweighted are treated as more important than they should be, and probabilities that are underweighted are treated as less important than they should be.

- A rational decision maker should assign probability weights to different events in a manner that is both consistent and complete. Just as 50 percent is twice as likely as 25 percent objectively, consistency requires that 50 percent seem twice as likely as 25 percent subjectively so that twice as much weight is given to 50 percent in a decision. Completeness requires that the total probabilities for all possible events add up to 100 percent—not more and not less.

## The Availability Bias

- Research has shown that although the price that people are willing to pay for insurance *should* be proportional to their subjective probability of needing that insurance, those subjective probabilities are distorted and inconsistent.

- Why are our probability judgments so distorted? One thing you cannot do is rely on your personal experience. Instead, you have to estimate the probability of a very rare event by constructing scenarios in your mind about what might happen. If you bring to mind a vivid scenario about an event, it will seem more real and, thus, more probable. This phenomenon has been given several names, but it is typically called the availability bias.

- This seeming irrationality in our behavior isn't just a minor inconsistency, the sort of thing that shows up in laboratory experiments and breathless science journalism. It has real-world importance.

- Our biases will affect some sorts of probability judgments more than others. Crimes that are rare but very vivid are seen as more common than they really are—so that they can draw resources away from crimes that are more common but less vivid. In many cases, resources are devoted more to very rare and vivid social problems compared to more common problems.

**Probability Weighting**
- For each objective probability—from one percent to 100 percent—we want to know the subjective probability weight. When we make decisions, do we treat a one-percent chance just like one percent, or like something else?

- Events that could happen but aren't likely—low-probability events—can be defined as probabilities up to about 25 percent. Low-probability events tend to factor more into decisions than they should. That is, an event that has an objective one-percent chance of occurring could subjectively seem like it has a five-percent chance of occurring.

- We overestimate the likelihood of these low-probability events. In general, the smaller the probability, the more we overestimate its likelihood. For example, people who play the lottery are often optimistic about winning. However, the odds of a single ticket winning the largest, most popular U.S. lotteries are on the order of one in 175 million.

- The mathematics used to calculate the probability of lotteries in terms of time—along with the idea of expected value of a decision—were formally described in 1654 by the mathematician Blaise

**The odds of winning the lottery are not good, but people who play are optimistic.**

Pascal. The probability of a single ticket winning a Mega Millions lottery is almost identical to the probability of randomly choosing one single second from all the years, days, hours, and minutes since 1654 and picking the very second that you were born.

- But the overestimation of probabilities does not completely explain the popularity of lotteries. There are at least two other factors that contribute. One factor comes from the way our brains process rewards. The brain's dopamine system doesn't simply respond to rewards themselves; it responds to signals about future rewards, which can lead to anticipation of what could occur.

- The sense of possibility—the fantasies about what we can do with our winnings—can be very motivating, and it isn't necessarily irrational to spend one dollar on a ticket in order to have those feelings of anticipation.

- Also important are the social aspects of playing the lottery. People play in groups and discuss the upcoming jackpots with their neighbors, and those social factors can be powerful motivators.

- Events of intermediate probability, from about 25 percent to 75 percent, are those that might happen—or they might not. Within this range, the probability weighting function flattens out, meaning that a change in objective probability doesn't have that much subjective effect.

- For example, suppose that you go to your primary care physician and you are told that, because of your genetic profile, you have a five-percent probability of contracting a rare form of cancer in the next five years. There is a drug treatment that is expensive and has side effects, but it will eliminate any chance that you will develop this cancer, bringing your probability of cancer from five percent down to zero percent. Do you begin the drug treatment?

- When faced with this sort of scenario, people tend to be willing to undergo treatment; going from a five-percent chance to a zero-percent chance of cancer seems pretty dramatic. But suppose that your genetics indicate that you actually have a 60-percent probability of getting cancer but that the same drug treatment could reduce your probability down to 55 percent. You'll incur the same expense and face the same side effects for a change from 60 to 55 percent. Do you begin the drug treatment?

- This situation is much harder for most people. The difference between 60 and 55 percent seems pretty minor; it doesn't seem like the sort of change that would be worth taking on an expensive and painful course of treatment.

- Changes in probability in this medium-probability range are not irrelevant; they just have less subjective impact than at lower or higher probabilities. As a rough guide, within this middle range, for every two-percent change in objective probability there is slightly less than a one-percent change in subjective probability.

- High-probability events, which are above about 75 percent, should happen, even though there is a chance that they might not. Probabilities in this range are essentially the mirror image of medium-probability events: People underestimate the chances. An event that should happen with an objective 90-percent probability might seem subjectively like only a 75-percent chance, while an event that should happen with 99-percent probability might seem subjectively like about 95 percent.

- For many decisions, this implies that people become more conservative than they should when the odds are in their favor. In civil court cases, plaintiffs might settle for a lesser amount even though they have a very strong case; they underestimate their chances of winning. This influences our medical decision making as well; people often seek out unnecessary treatments to deal with a medical challenge that has a good prognosis.

- These three probabilities—low, medium, and high—combine into the probability weighting function of prospect theory. We overvalue low-probability events that could happen, undervalue high-probability events that should happen, and are largely indifferent to the probabilities of events in the middle. Our subjective sense of probability doesn't match the objective reality.

## Dealing with Probabilities

- Our judgments of probability are not accurate; they are systematically biased. They are biased because we don't have access to the true probabilities—we don't know whether we'll need insurance, for example. Instead, we estimate those probabilities when we need to. We construct stories about what could happen, based on our memories of past history and our reasoning about similar events.

- You can't eliminate these biases, but you can modify how you approach a decision, changing the very way in which you construct probabilities. The following are two tools for changing how you deal with probabilities.

- First, use the availability heuristic to your advantage. People tend to overestimate the likelihood of some event when it is relatively easy to create vivid stories. Therefore, if you want to reduce the chance that you'll be influenced too much by a rare event, think about the event in a way that makes it less vivid. Distance yourself from the event; imagine that you were advising someone else. By dampening our internal storyteller, we can improve the accuracy of our judgments for low- and high-probability events.

- To deal with medium-probability events, use a second tool: Think about probability in terms of frequency—for example, out of every 10 people who take this drug, two of them avoid a significant illness, and you might be one of them. By moving away from the abstract probabilities and emphasizing concrete individual cases, the frequency representation calls attention to the key fact: There are people who benefit from this course of treatment.

## Suggested Reading

Johnson, Hershey, Meszaros, and Kunreuther, "Framing, Probability Distortions, and Insurance Decisions."

Tversky and Fox, "Weighing Risk and Uncertainty."

## Questions to Consider

1. Under what circumstances are people most likely to purchase insurance, based on the phenomenon of probability weighting?

2. Why might people be less interested in taking steps to help prevent common medical conditions than to prevent uncommon medical conditions?

# Probability Weighting
## Lecture 6—Transcript

Welcome back. Today we're going to talk about probability, one of the factors that most affects our economic decision making. We all use it, sometimes without being aware we're using it, but are we using it well?

Probability seems like a simple concept: the likelihood that something will happen. How we should use probability in our decision making seems equally simple: If an outcome has 100-percent chance of occurring, we should treat that outcome as twice as important as one that has only a 50-percent chance, and four times as important as one that has a 25-percent chance, and 100 times as important as a 1-percent chance.

In essence, we should judge probabilities accurately and allow them to influence our decision making in a mathematically consistent manner. But, we don't. We show systematic biases in how we judge and use probabilities.

Why is it so difficult for us to judge the probability of events? And, why do we fail to use probability information effectively even when it is given to us? To gain answers to this questions, we'll need to explore the phenomenon of probability weighting, which describes the bias people show when working with probability. This phenomenon was, along with reference dependence, one of the two main advances in prospect theory, and thus probability weighting is one of the foundational concepts in behavioral economics.

Biases in probability judgments arise naturally, just from the statistics of the world around us. In fact, there is a specific probability weighting function that mathematically describes how people tend to convert objective information into a subjective sense of probability. These biases in the use of probability are endemic to every aspect of our decision making, from gambling to public policy to insurance, and many, many others. Now, that's a depressing thought.

But all is not lost. It turns out that there are worse and better ways to think about probability. The usual way is rife with bias and error, but by the end of this lecture, you'll understand some different ways of thinking about probability that may seem counterintuitive at first, but that lead to much more accurate, confident, and consistent decisions.

Let's begin by considering what we mean by probability. Probability is the likelihood that some defined event will occur. There are two common ways in which we describe something's probability. The first is in terms of percentages—there's an 80-percent chance of rain tomorrow. That's the way that seems most natural to people, and I'll use percentages in the bulk of this lecture. But there's a second way, in terms of frequency—saying something like 4 out of 5 dentists recommend flossing daily. Now frequency might seem like just a more complex way of stating a percentage, after all the two are mathematically equivalent. But, there are important differences between thinking in terms of percentages and thinking in terms of frequencies, and those differences will be important at the end.

Probabilities are only meaningful insofar as the events they describe are well defined. If you flip a fair coin, there is a 50-percent chance that it will land heads, and a 50-percent chance that it will land tails. Those two events are exclusive—you can either flip heads or tails, but not both—and exhaustive such that their two individual probabilities sum up to exactly 100 percent. Many other real-world events are similarly well defined. In a two-person political race, like many U.S. presidential elections, we may not know the true probabilities for candidate A or candidate B, but we know that only one of them will be elected and we know that no one else will be elected.

But many other sorts of events aren't well defined. Sometimes that's because of imprecision in the stated probabilities. An often-frustrating example is weather forecasting. What is meant by a 50-percent chance of rain tomorrow? Does that mean a 50-percent chance for rain somewhere and sometime in your local area? A 50-percent chance at every location and at every time in your local area? Or, most importantly, should you or should you not buy a ticket for tomorrow's baseball game at the outdoor stadium?

It is easy to make fun of weather predictions—and as someone who studies probability and decision making, I'd like to set the record straight. There is a hidden precision in weather forecasting. If the U.S. National Weather Service states that there is a 60-percent chance of rain tomorrow in, say,

Durham County, North Carolina, that percentage reflects the average chance across every location in Durham County of receiving rain at any point in time tomorrow.

That number may be precise, but what it means still isn't completely well defined. The single probability of 50-percent chance of rain could describe any of a very large set of potential events, only some of which might dampen your experience at the baseball game. But for now, let's consider decision situations in which the probabilities of different potential outcomes can be known or estimated with precision. How then should you use those probabilities in your decisions?

Behavioral economists refer to the way in which objective probabilities are transformed into subjective influences on a decision as "probability weights." This term may seem like jargon, but it actually maps on well to our intuitions. When we say that some factor "weighs heavily" on our decision, we mean that an objective difference in that factor has outsize influence compared to other factors. "Probability weighting" just means the same thing; probabilities that are overweighted are treated as more important than they should be, and probabilities that are underweighted are treated as less important than they should be.

A rational decision maker should assign probability weights to different events in a manner that is both consistent and complete. Just as 50 percent is twice as likely as 25 percent objectively, consistency requires that 50 percent seem twice as likely as 25 percent subjectively, so that twice as much weight is given to 50 percent in a decision. Completeness requires that the total probabilities for all possible events add up to 100 percent, not more and not less.

These may seem so obvious that they aren't even worth discussing. After all, who could be so silly as to think that there could be, say, a 40-percent chance of heads and also a 40-percent chance of tails? Or, that there could be a 200-percent chance of dying from some disease? However, even these simple rules are regularly violated.

Let's consider the example of purchasing life insurance. There are many sorts of life insurance products available, some are very complex and combine both insurance and investments, while others are much simpler. The most simple sort is typically called term life insurance; one pays a defined premium for a defined amount of insurance for a defined term of time. Most of the time, people purchase yearly and renewable term life insurance because of the general peace-of-mind it provides, but sometimes people purchase much shorter policies for specific reasons.

Suppose that you are about to step on a plane to fly to Bangkok, Thailand. You know that terrorism is a potential source of danger to travelers to Thailand. You are offered a flight insurance policy that will provide $100,000 worth of life insurance in case of your death due to terrorism. You can buy separate policies for the flight from your home airport to Bangkok, and for the flight from the Bangkok airport back home. How much would you pay for this coverage?

Let's think about this for a moment. There is some probability of a terrorist attack during your flights. The probability is pretty small, but it is there. So, you should be willing to pay some amount. But, how much would you pay for the flight out there? How much for the flight back?

I've adapted this scenario and taken its wording from a real experiment conducted by the behavioral economist Eric Johnson and his colleagues. They ran the original experiment on MBA students at their business school who were scheduled to travel to Bangkok for an educational program. At that time, there had been a recent U.S. State Department advisory about potential terrorist attacks in Bangkok, so the possibility of terrorism was vividly on the mind of those students.

When they gave participants a scenario similar to the one I gave you, participants reported that they were willing to pay about $14 for insurance on the flight to Bangkok and $19 for insurance on the way back, or $33 in total. But, that wasn't the only scenario that they tested.

They gave another group of participants a similar story but told them that they could buy one policy that covered both flights. Of course, an insurance policy that covers both flights should cost exactly as much as the sum of two policies, one for each flight, so this group should be willing to pay about $33, like the first group. The price that this second group was willing to pay for whole-flight insurance: only $14.

But that's not even the whole story. The researchers gave yet another group of participants the same basic story, and then told that group that they could buy travel insurance that would cover any terrorist act during the entire trip— the flight out there, the time on the ground, and the flight back. Of course, coverage for the entire trip should be more valuable than coverage for any of its parts, by itself. But the price that these participants were willing to pay for whole-trip coverage was only $7.

People were willing to pay almost three times as much for an insurance policy that only covered their return flight than for a policy that covered both their outgoing and return flights, as well as their entire time on the ground.

This and many other experiments show that although the price that people are willing to pay for insurance should be proportional to their subjective probability of needing that insurance, those subjective probabilities are distorted and inconsistent. As we just saw, people are willing to pay more than twice as much for insurance that covers one flight than for insurance that covers their entire trip.

Why are our probability judgments so distorted? Let me turn that question around, and ask it to you in a different way. How would you form a probability judgment for something like "term life insurance during a flight to Thailand"?

One thing you cannot do is rely on your personal experience. I'll go out on a limb and say that you've never died while on a flight to Thailand. Instead, you have to estimate the probability of a very rare event by constructing scenarios in your mind about what might happen. If you bring to mind a vivid scenario about an event, it will seem more real and thus more probable. This phenomenon has been given several names, but it is typically called the availability bias.

In the flight insurance example earlier, thinking about each flight independently forces people to think not only about what might happen on each flight but also about possible differences between their two flights. Bringing past events to mind, they might think that flights to the United States are more dangerous than flights away from the United States, and those vivid scenarios serve to increase the subjective probability of a terrorist event.

But when considering insurance for your entire trip, you'll think about spending time in your hotel, meeting colleagues and friends, touring local sights, and eating at restaurants. Those time periods don't lend themselves to creating a vivid scenario about terrorism, at least not to the degree of the flights themselves. So, you don't bring risky events to mind, and your subjective probability seems low.

We'll consider the availability bias again later in this course, when I introduce the key cognitive heuristics people use to simplify complex decisions. For now, though, I want to emphasize that this seeming irrationality in our behavior isn't just a minor inconsistency, the sort of thing that shows up in laboratory experiments and breathless science journalism. It has real-world importance.

Consider the national debates about crime, its prevention, and our justice system. Surveys of American adults have consistently shown that people think that crime is a serious problem in the United States, and, most importantly for today's lecture, that crime rates are on the rise. Since the late 1980s, almost every year a substantial majority of Americans have reported that they thought there was more crime than a year ago.

Whether crime is a serious problem is a matter of opinion, but whether crime rates are on the rise is a matter of data. And, the data indicate that crime rates dropped dramatically. Since the 1980s, per capita rates both of violent crime and of property crime have dropped in half in the United States, and this is part of a much, much longer gradual decrease in crime rates over the decades and centuries. Stated simply, people subjective estimates of crime rates are disconnected from the objective rates of crime. What causes this disconnect?

Ask yourself this question: Is there more crime in my area now than, say, 20 years ago? Then think for a moment about how you answered that question. You may have brought to mind recent crimes you've heard about on the news or from friends: a burglary or other property crime, or even some violent crime like a murder or kidnapping. Almost certainly, some such crime case was featured in the news this week. News agencies know that frightening crimes like a child being kidnapped by a stranger and held for ransom will capture the public's attention, so they focus on those cases when they arise.

But these very vivid crimes are also very rare. For instance, each year only about 100 to 150 children in the United Sates are abducted in stereotypical kidnappings, that is, taken away by a stranger who has malicious intent. Such crimes seem more common because we can readily bring them to mind, from memorable cases from the past, from current news, or even from our own instructions to our kids when we warn them about strangers.

You might argue that overestimating crime rates might be a good thing. Crime is clearly a problem even at the current lower rates, and fear of crime helps mobilize people, law enforcement, and governmental agencies toward taking action. But, I want to re-emphasize that our biases will affect some sorts of probability judgments more than others. So, crimes that are rare but very vivid are seen as more common than they really are, so that they can draw resources away from crimes that are more common but less vivid. For example, familial kidnapping is far more common than stranger kidnapping; poor security at bus stations is a more common problem than poor security at airports. A similar sort of logic can be applied to many sorts of social problems. In many cases, resources are devoted more to very rare and vivid problems compared to more common problems.

I've talked so far about subjective probability judgments of rare events, but it's now time to expand this judgment to events of all probabilities.

We want to know for each objective probability—1 percent, 2 percent, 3 percent, all the way to 100 percent—what is the subjective probability weight. When we make decisions, do we treat a one percent chance just like one percent or like something else?

For simplicity's sake, I want to first break down that entire range of probability into three categories—low probability, medium probability, and high probability—which I'll call "could," "might," and "should."

Let's begin with low-probability, events that could happen, but aren't likely. I'll define this range as probabilities up to about 25 percent. As I discussed previously in the contexts of insurance purchases and crime rates, low probability events tend to factor more into decisions than they should. That is, an event that has an objective 1-percent chance of occurring could subjectively seem like it has a 5-percent chance of occurring. An event that has an objective 10-percent chance could seem like it has a 20-percent chance.

We overestimate the likelihood of these low-probability events. In general, the smaller the probability, the more we overestimate its likelihood. Before any very large lottery drawing, there will be quotes from prospective players, usually taking an optimistic tone. "You can't win if you don't play." "Somebody will win, it might as well be me." Of course the odds of a single ticket winning the largest, most popular U.S. lotteries are on the order of 1 in 175 million.

It is hard to think about such long odds of winning. The numbers are so large that they are hard to make tangible without comparison to something else. So, let's think about this in terms of time. The mathematics used to calculate the probability of lotteries like this, along with the idea of expected value of a decision, were formally described in 1654 by the mathematician Blaise Pascal. Believe it or not, the probability of a single ticket winning a Mega Millions lottery is almost identical to the probability of randomly choosing one single second from all the years, days, hours, and minutes since 1654 and then picking the very second that you were born.

Does overestimation of probabilities explain the popularity of lotteries? Not completely. There are at least two other factors that contribute. One factor comes from the way our brains process rewards. As discussed in an earlier lecture, the brain's dopamine system doesn't simply respond to rewards themselves; it responds to signals about future rewards, which can lead to anticipation of what could occur. The sense of possibility, the fantasies about what we can do with our winnings, can be very motivating, and it isn't necessarily irrational to spend $1 on a ticket in order to have those feelings of anticipation. Also important are the social aspects of playing the lottery. People play in groups and discuss the upcoming jackpots with their neighbors, and those social factors can be powerful motivators.

Let's move from these low-probability events to events of intermediate probability, from about 25 percent to 75 percent. I'll refer to these as "might" events—they might happen or they might not. Within the might range, the probability weighting function flattens out, meaning that a change in objective probability doesn't have that much subjective effect.

Let me illustrate this with a thought problem. Suppose that you go to your primary care physician and you are told that, because of your genetic profile, you have a 5-percent probability of contracting a rare form of cancer in the next five years. There is a drug treatment that is completely effective; it is expensive and has side effects, but it will eliminate any chance that you will develop this cancer. It will take your probability of cancer from 5 percent down to 0 percent. Do you begin the drug treatment? When faced with this sort of scenario, people tend to be willing to undergo treatment—going from 5 percent to 0 percent chance of cancer seems pretty dramatic.

Let's modify this thought problem. Suppose that your genetics indicate that you actually have a 60-percent probability of getting cancer, but that the same drug treatment could reduce your probability down to 55 percent. You'll incur the same expense and face the same side effects, for a change from 60 percent to 55 percent. Do you begin the drug treatment?

This situation is much harder for most people. The difference between 60 percent and 55 percent seems pretty minor —that doesn't seem like the sort of change that would be worth taking on an expensive and painful course of treatment. People might say, "I might get cancer, or I might not, regardless, so I don't need to ruin my quality of life in the meantime."

I don't want to imply that changes in probability are irrelevant in the might range, just that they have less subjective impact than at lower or higher probability events. As a rough guide, within this middle range, for every two-percent change in objective probability there is slightly less than a one-percent change in subjective probability.

Finally, let's consider high probability events, those with probabilities above about 75 percent. Such events should happen, even though there is a chance that they might not. Should events are essentially the mirror image of might events: People underestimate the chances. An even that should happen with an objective 90-percent probability might seem subjectively like only a 75-percent chance, while an event that should happen with 99-percent probability might seem subjectively like about 95 percent.

For many decisions, this implies that people become more conservative than they should when the odds are in their favor. In civil court cases, plantiffs might settle for a lesser amount even though they have a very strong case; they underestimate their chances of winning. Gamblers who bet on horse races tend to, in the aggregate, bet too much on low-probability longshots and too little on high-probability favorites. And, as we'll see much later in this course, this influences our medical decision making as well—people often seek out unnecessary treatments to deal with a medical challenge that has a good prognosis.

These three parts—could, might, and should—combine into the probability weighting function of prospect theory. We overvalue low-probability events that could happen, we undervalue high-probability events that should happen, and we are largely indifferent to the probabilities of events in the middle. Our subjective sense of probability doesn't match the objective reality.

Our judgments of probability are not accurate, but are systematically biased. They are biased because we don't have access to the true probabilities; we don't know whether we'll need insurance, we don't know the probability of violent crime in our area. We can't just look up those probabilities from some database in our brains. Instead, we estimate those probabilities when we need to. We construct stories about what could happen, based on our memories of past history and our reasoning about similar events.

Can we eliminate these biases? No. These biases don't disappear once we know about them. You can't suddenly start seeing 45 percent and 55 percent as very different in probability, or start thinking about a 99-percent chance of success without being concerned about that 1-percent chance of failure. But what you can do is modify how you approach a decision, changing the very way in which you construct probabilities. Let me give you two tools for changing how you deal with probabilities.

First, use the availability heuristic to your advantage. Remember that I stated that people tend to overestimate the likelihood of some event when it is relatively easy to create vivid stories. So, if you want to reduce the chance that you'll be influenced too much by a rare event, think about the event in a way that makes it less vivid. Distance yourself from that event; imagine that you were advising someone else. What would you tell them? Would you advise your friend to buy insurance for his smartphone, or would he be better served by passing, given the high cost of insurance and the low probability of needing replacement? Would you tell your friend to avoid a camping trip in the woods because of a very rare chance of an undetected tick bite?

By dampening down our internal storyteller, we can improve the accuracy of our judgments for low- and high-probability events. But what about that large range in the middle, events that might happen, or they might not. The problem for those events is not inaccuracy, per se, but an insensitivity to changes in probability. What could make someone think that the difference between 45 percent and 50 percent matters?

To deal with might events, use a second tool: Think about probability in terms of frequency. Throughout this lecture, I've purposefully described every example in terms of percentages, like 10 percent. But probability can also be represented in terms of frequency, like 1 in 10. So, let's rephrase the sorts of examples from earlier in the lecture. Suppose that in people who take drug X, the risk of a significant illness following influenza exposure decreases from 60 percent to 40 percent. Based on what I described previously, even this large change in objective probability doesn't have a major influence on our subjective probability weight, and many people might fail to take this beneficial drug.

Let's change this example from percentages to frequencies, stating it a different way. "Of every 10 people who take drug X, two of them avoid a significant illness. You could be one of those two." By moving away from the abstract probabilities and emphasizing concrete individual cases, the frequency representation calls attention to the key fact: there are people who benefit from this course of treatment.

Note that neither of these tools (manipulating the availability heuristic or representing probabilities as frequencies) requires any sort of complex mental arithmetic or a deep understanding of probability theory. And, neither always works; for example, some events are just so vivid or so difficult to estimate that your probability judgments are likely to be inaccurate regardless. But by knowing your bias, and by thinking about probabilities in a different way, you just might improve your odds.

In the next lecture, we'll take this basic building block of probability and combine it with value. We'll consider what happens when people have to trade off probabilities of better and worse outcomes and more certain events, as we explore one of the deepest and most important concepts in behavioral economics: risk.

# Risk—The Known Unknowns
## Lecture 7

In this lecture, you will consider what happens when people have to trade off probabilities of better and worse outcomes and more certain events as you explore one of the deepest and most important concepts in behavioral economics: risk. We can't eliminate risk, and we shouldn't avoid risk. However, with the right approach and the right mindset, we can manage risk. In this lecture, you will learn the importance of seeking a healthier attitude toward risk.

**What Is Risk?**
- In an economic context, a decision involves risk when it can lead to more than one outcome, when those outcomes have different values, and when the probabilities of those outcomes are known or can be estimated.

- This economic definition doesn't exactly match all of the ways in which we use risk in daily conversation. For example, we describe real-world behaviors as risky if we might get hurt doing them—like skydiving—and we describe our investments as risky when we might lose money—like purchasing stocks. However, a decision can be risky even if nothing really bad can happen.

- Risk is also different from ambiguity. A decision involves risk when the probabilities of its outcomes are known or can be estimated. We know, for example, the probabilities of flipping heads or tails. We can estimate the probabilities of getting lower and higher interest rates based on recent fluctuations in mortgage rates. When we can't know or estimate the probabilities of an outcome, then the decision is said to involve not risk but ambiguity.

**Risk Aversion**
- For many sorts of economic decisions, we can describe people's choices as being risk averse, risk neutral, or risk seeking. Most

common are risk-averse choices; that is, where people prefer a safe option over a risky option with equal expected value.

- A utility function determines how much subjective value we get from different amounts of an objective quantity, like money. It was recognized long before the advent of behavioral economics that people's subjective value for money—and most other things—showed diminishing marginal utility.

- In traditional models, this was described in terms of wealth states: A dollar is worth more to someone who has nothing than to someone who has a million dollars already. Prospect theory moved away from wealth states but kept the idea of diminishing marginal utility: The difference between gaining one dollar and two dollars is more than the difference between gaining 1,000 dollars and 1,001 dollars. This sort of utility function leads to risk aversion—at least as a broad principle.

- Which would you rather have: a sure 1,000 dollars or a coin-flip gamble between zero dollars and 2,001 dollars? Intuitively, this seems like an easy choice to most people: Take the sure 1,000 dollars. But why is that choice so easy? It's not because the 1,000 dollars is a better choice, at least by expectation; if anything, you'd expect to earn very slightly more, on average, by choosing the risk option.

- This is an easy choice because of diminishing marginal utility. The subjective difference between zero and 1,000 dollars seems much larger to us than the subjective difference between 1,000 and 2,001 dollars—so we choose the safer option and avoid the chance of getting zero dollars. Therefore, provided that someone shows diminishing marginal utility for money, he or she will be naturally risk averse.

- This is only part of the story. People are often risk averse when making small decisions, such as those involving a few tens of dollars. Even slight risk aversion over such small stakes implies massive risk aversion over large stakes, as shown by the economist

Matthew Rabin. We can't explain real-world risk aversion just by diminishing marginal utility.

- To see what else might be needed, let's return to loss aversion, which means that economic losses influence our decisions more than economic gains—on average, about twice as much. This phenomenon affects the way people think about risky decisions. If people think about risky options as involving losses and gains, from the reference point of the safe option, their subjective sense of potential loss can readily outweigh their sense of potential gain.

**Risk Seeking**
- Risk-seeking behavior is often inefficient. If someone is truly risk seeking over monetary gains, then he or she can be exploited. He or she will be willing to take bad bet after bad bet, much like the pathological gambler who can't walk away from the table.

- But what about monetary losses? Do people tend to be risk averse or risk seeking when faced with decisions that involve risky losses versus sure losses? This is a much harder question. A moment's intuition might suggest that if people are more averse to losses than to gains, then they might be even more risk averse for decisions involving losses.

- Consider this question from a behavioral economics perspective. Prospect theory proposed that people have diminishing marginal utility for both gains and losses. That is, the difference between losing zero dollars and losing 100 dollars might be pretty bad, but the difference between losing 1,000 dollars and losing 1,100 dollars isn't anywhere near as great.

- So, what does this fact mean for decisions involving risk? People tend to be risk averse when making decisions about potential gains, but people tend to be risk seeking when making decisions about potential losses.

### How Do People Think about Risk?

- Are our risk attitudes a stable personality trait, like extroversion, that shapes all of our choices? The decision scientist Elke Weber and her colleagues explored this question by asking participants questions about how often they engaged in different sorts of risk-taking behaviors. The questions involved investment behaviors, recreational behaviors, social behaviors, gambling behaviors, health-related behaviors, and ethical behaviors.

- If attitudes toward risk represent a stable personality trait, then people who frequently engaged in one type of risky behavior would be more likely to engage in the other types of risky behavior. But that's not what Weber found.

- Instead, these different risky behaviors formed separate categories that were not strongly correlated. Knowing that someone is risk averse in his or her investments, for example, doesn't tell you much about whether he or she is averse to risky social behaviors or to risky recreational activities.

- Why aren't these different risky behaviors related? You might not engage in a risky behavior because you are intrinsically risk averse, or it might be because you don't perceive any benefit from an activity or because you overestimate the risk of something negative happening as a result.

- When Weber and colleagues asked their participants about perceived benefits and perceived risks of each activity, they found that perceived benefit and perceived risk explained most of the differences between categories. So, someone who is risk averse in their investments but risk seeking in their recreation might overestimate the probability of a market crash, while deriving more benefit than other people from extreme sports.

- There are two key findings from this research. First, there's essentially no such thing as a purely risk-averse or risk-seeking individual; the same person can have very different tendencies for different types of decisions. Second, differences in how we each approach risk in different aspects of our lives are driven by our perceptions—of how much benefit we'll gain and of the probability of a bad outcome.

**Managing Risk**

- Risk isn't necessarily bad. Investors who minimize risk earn less money, on average, than those who are willing to take on risk. So, our goal shouldn't be to avoid risk, but to manage it. There are two basic rules that you can follow in order to manage risk. The first is simple: Diversify.

- The Nobel Laureate economist Harry Markowitz developed an elegant approach to managing investment risk. His central idea was that an optimal portfolio should contain assets that are not correlated—that do not tend to move together over time. New investments won't reduce the risk of a portfolio if they are largely correlated with existing investments, so it doesn't necessarily improve your portfolio's diversity when you buy into a new hot stock or take on yet another large-cap mutual fund.

- For the sorts of investments most people make, this approach prioritizes one type of investments: broad mutual funds that reflect the overall performance of the larger financial markets. That doesn't mean such investments are the only reasonable strategy for retirement, but there are indeed very strong reasons to value investment diversity when trying to manage risk.

- The second rule is also simple: Avoid regret. In other words, you should think about risk a bit differently—so that bad outcomes don't lead to regret. It's often good to regret our mistakes so that we learn and make better choices next time. But that regret does us little good when investing. Because high-reward investments tend also to be of high risk, it is good if we can dampen down our feelings of regret when necessary.

- One effective approach for doing this comes not from behavioral economics but from clinical psychology. Psychologists have long been interested in strategies that help people dampen down their emotional reactions; such reappraisal strategies can be very helpful when dealing with adverse events that are outside one's own control.

  **The goal of investors is to manage their risk—not to avoid it. On average, those who minimize risk earn less money than those who take on risk.**

- Researchers have explored a particular strategy called thinking like a trader. To do this, think of yourself as a dispassionate observer of your own investment portfolio. Each of your investments is part of a larger whole, and any one of your investments might go up or might go down on any day.

- Expand your time horizons: Don't think about the day's or month's market results, but instead about your prudent, well-considered approach toward managing risk. Each decision you make is part of your larger strategy. It isn't even meaningful to regret one decision or one day's market fluctuation by itself. The larger strategy and long-term results are what matter.

### Suggested Reading

Bernstein, *Against the Gods*.

Reyna and Farley, "Risk and Rationality in Adolescent Decision Making."

## Questions to Consider

1. Why is diversification an effective tool for minimizing risk?

2. What is the difference between risk aversion and loss aversion?

# Risk—The Known Unknowns
## Lecture 7—Transcript

No object is more associated with the concept of risk than a coin. The coin has become the ultimate arbiter of chance: When the team captains come to midfield before the start of each Super Bowl, the crowd quiets momentarily as the referee tosses a large coin into the air, and then half the crowd will erupt in cheering because their favored team wins the toss. The game hasn't even started and already luck is on their side. The connection between coin flips and risk is so ubiquitous that we even refer to an event whose outcomes are equally likely as a "toss up."

Coin flips present a pretty straightforward sort of risk. There are only two outcomes, those outcomes are equally likely, and most importantly, we know that the process of flipping the coin is random. What happened on the last coin flip has no bearing on what happens on this coin flip.

Let's see what happens in a simple laboratory experiment. Suppose that you are given a choice between a safe option and a risky option. The safe option is a sure $1, there's no risk there; if you choose the safe option you'll get exactly one dollar. The risky option leads to a coin flip; if the coin lands heads you'll receive $2.50, but if the coin lands tails you'll receive nothing. Returning to a concept from an earlier lecture, the expected value of the risky option is $1.25; the average of the two equally likely outcomes. So, what should you choose, the safe or the risky option?

If you are playing this game once, there is no right answer. Yes, the risky option has a higher expected value, but its outcomes are more variable, and so what you choose could depend on your tolerance for risk. But, suppose that you play this game 20 times, one after another. If you chose the risky option every time, you'd usually do better than someone who chose the safe option every time, and you'd often do much better. More than a quarter of the time you'd earn an extra $10, not bad for taking on a little risk.

Let me tell you what happened when two groups of participants played this game. Participants in group 1 had what you might consider a pathological response to risk. They started off choosing the risky option, but as the game progressed they systematically moved toward the safe option. Even more strikingly, their behavior was influenced by regret over bad outcomes; if they chose the risky option and lost, then they became much more likely to switch over immediately to the safe option. This first group earned about $20 on average, right about what would be expected for choosing the safe option every time.

Participants in group 2 had what you might consider a healthy attitude toward risk. They started off choosing the risky option, and kept choosing it even if the coin flips started going against them. Their behavior stayed pretty consistent over the course of the experiment, and they were rewarded for their good choices, earning about $25 on average.

Interestingly, the first group (those with a seemingly pathological response to risk) were neurologically normal individuals recruited from advertisements in the local community. That is, people like you and me tend to show regret and risk-aversion, and they don't earn as much money as they should.

The second group (those with a healthy approach to risk) were individuals who had significant brain damage. They typically had experienced a stroke or tumor within a region at the base of the frontal lobes called the orbitofrontal cortex. And, they didn't show normal regret.

Why would this particular type of major brain damage help people to deal better with risk? It wasn't because of brain damage, in general. There was another group of people in the same study with damage to different regions of the brain, and that third group was just as bad at the task as the neurologically normal individuals. So, something about regret provides an important clue for understanding decision making under risk.

In an economic context, a decision involves risk when it can lead to more than one outcome, when those outcomes have different values, and when the probabilities of those outcomes are known or can be estimated. So, the example of the coin-flip gamble involves risk because there are two outcomes, one outcome leads to more money than the other, and the probabilities of those outcomes are known.

This economic definition doesn't exactly match all of the ways in which we use risk in daily conversation. For example, we describe real-world behaviors as risky if we might get hurt doing them, like sky diving, and we describe our investments as risky when we might lose money, like purchasing stocks. But, a decision can be risky even if nothing really bad can happen. Suppose that you are about to purchase a home, and are deciding whether to lock in a particular interest rate for your mortgage. You can lock in a low interest rate now, or you could wait to see if a better rate appears in the coming weeks. Your rate might be pretty good regardless, but you still face a choice between a safer option or a riskier one.

Risk is also different from ambiguity. I said that a decision involves risk when the probabilities of its outcomes are known or can be estimated. We know, for example, the probabilities of flipping heads or tails. We can estimate the probabilities of getting lower and higher interest rates based on recent fluctuations in mortgage rates. When we can't know or estimate the probabilities of an outcome, then the decision is said to involve not risk but ambiguity. Many interesting real-world decisions are thought to involve ambiguity, but that's a topic for the next lecture.

For many sorts of economic decisions, we can describe people's choices as being risk-averse, risk-neutral, or risk-seeking. Most common are risk-averse choices; that is, where people prefer a safe option over a risky option with equal expected value. To understand why, let's return to the idea of a utility function.

A utility function determines how much subjective value we get from different amounts of an objective quantity, like money. It was recognized long before the advent of behavioral economics that people's subjective value for money, and most other things, showed diminishing marginal utility. In traditional models, this was described in terms of wealth states: A dollar is worth more to someone who has nothing than to someone who has a million dollars already. Prospect theory moved away from wealth states but kept the idea of diminishing marginal utility: The difference between gaining $1 and $2 is more than the difference between gaining $1,000 and $1,001.

This sort of utility function leads to risk aversion, at least as a broad principle. To understand why, consider this schematic example. Which would you rather have: a sure $1,000 or a coin flip gamble between $0 and $2,001? Intuitively, this seems like an easy choice to most people: take the sure $1,000. But why is that choice so easy? Not because the $1,000 is a better choice, at least by expectation; if anything, you'd expect to earn very slightly more, on average, by choosing the risky option. This is an easy choice because of diminishing marginal utility. The subjective difference between $0 and $1,000 seems much larger to us than the subjective difference between $1,000 and $2,001, so we choose the safer option and avoid the chance of getting $0.

So, provided that someone shows diminishing marginal utility for money, then they will be naturally risk averse. I want to offer a quick disclaimer here. What I'm describing is part of the story, but it isn't the whole story. As described in the previous lectures, people are often risk-averse when making small decisions, such as those involving a few tens of dollars. Even slight risk aversion over such small stakes implies massive risk aversion over large stakes, as shown by the economist Matthew Rabin. We can't explain real-world risk aversion just by diminishing marginal utility.

To see what else might be needed, let's return to an idea from an earlier lecture: loss aversion. As a reminder, loss aversion means that economic losses influence our decisions more than economic gains, on average, about twice as much. This phenomenon affects the way people think about risky decisions. If people think about risky options as involving losses and gains, at least from the reference point of the safe option, their subjective sense of potential loss can readily outweigh their sense of potential gain.

So far, I've emphasized risk aversion and haven't given any examples of risk-seeking behavior. Part of that is because risk-seeking is often inefficient. Back in the first lecture, we talked about Frank, one of the two worst-ever Deal-or-No Deal contestants. He turned down a sure 6,000 euro for a 50/50 chance at 10,000 euros. If Frank had just taken the sure 6,000 euros and left the studio, he could have walked to a roulette table at a local casino and placed 5,000 euros on black, which is basically a coin-flip bet. He'd still get to gamble, but he'd walk away with something in his pocket, regardless. His risk seeking was inefficient.

If someone is truly risk-seeking over monetary gains, then they can be exploited. They'll be willing to take bad bet after bad bet, much like the pathological gambler who can't walk away from the table. But what about monetary losses? Do people tend to be risk-averse or risk-seeking when faced with decisions that involve risky losses versus sure losses? This is a much harder question. A moment's intuition might suggest that if people are more averse to losses than to gains, then they might be even more risk averse for decisions involving losses.

Let's consider this question from a behavioral economics perspective. Prospect theory proposed that people have diminishing marginal utility for both gains and losses. That is, the difference between losing $0 and losing $100 might be pretty bad, but the difference between losing $1,000 and losing $1,100 isn't anywhere near as great.

So, what does this fact mean for decisions involving risk? Let's reverse an example from earlier. Suppose I bring you into my laboratory and give you the following choice between a safe option and a risky option: You pay me $1,000 or else we'll flip a coin. Heads you pay me $2,000, tails you pay me nothing. Obviously we can't extort money from our participants in this way. But we can run experiments with this general flavor and see what people do. If there is diminishing marginal utility for losses, then the $2,000 loss shouldn't seem twice as bad as a sure $1,000 loss—it's worse, to be sure, but it isn't twice as bad. So, in this example, most people would be willing to flip that coin.

People tend to be risk-averse when making decisions about potential gains, but people tend to be risk-seeking when making decisions about potential losses.

So far my examples have all been about economic risk, and obviously the term "risk" is applied to many things other than financial decisions. When we describe one of our friends as risk averse, we usually don't mean to imply that we've looked at their portfolio and seen a preponderance of bonds over stocks. Instead, we mean that they don't like to try new things, they are afraid of physical challenges, or they are happy with their current state.

This raises an obvious question: Are our risk attitudes a stable personality trait, like extraversion, that shapes all of our choices? The answer might seem obviously "yes"; we can readily bring to mind stereotypes of stodgy bankers who invest conservatively, dress conservatively, and surely never bungee-jumped in their life. But, those stereotypes are hardly data.

The decision scientist Elke Weber and her colleagues explored this question by asking participants questions about how often they engaged in different sorts of risk-taking behaviors. Some were investment behaviors, like "investing 5 percent of your annual income in a very speculative stock." Others were recreational behaviors, like "piloting your own small plane." Others involved social behaviors like "approaching your boss to ask for a raise." And still others involved gambling, health-related, or ethical behaviors.

If attitudes toward risk represent a stable personality trait, then people who frequently engaged in one type of risky behavior would be more likely to engage in the other types of risky behavior. But that's not what Weber found. Instead, these different risky behaviors formed separate categories that were not strongly correlated. Knowing that someone is risk averse in their investments, for example, doesn't tell you much about whether they are averse to risky social behaviors, or to risky recreational activities.

So, why aren't these different risky behaviors related? I want you to think about why you might not engage in a risky behavior, say piloting your own small plane. It might be because you are intrinsically risk-averse. Or, it might be because you don't perceive any benefit from learning to pilot a plane. Or, it might be because you overestimate the risk of crashing.

When Weber and colleagues asked their participants about perceived benefits and perceived risks of each activity, they found that perceived benefit and perceived risk explained most of the differences between categories. So, someone who is risk-averse in their investments but risk-seeking in their recreation might overestimate the probability of a market crash, while deriving more benefit that other people from extreme sports.

So, there are two key findings from this research. First, there's essentially no such thing as a purely risk-averse or risk-seeking individual; the same person can have very different tendencies for different types of decisions. Second, differences in how we each approach risk in different aspects of our lives are driven by our perceptions, of how much benefit we'll gain and of the probability of a bad outcome.

This might seem like a rather academic point. Why should we care about whether or not someone is intrinsically risk-averse or risk-seeking? But understanding risky behavior isn't just a puzzle for decision scientists, it is critical for solving the single greatest source of problems in our society: adolescents.

Many of you have known adolescents. You may even have been an adolescent yourself, at some time. And so, you may recognize all of the problems associated with the teenage years of life: auto accidents, rates of drug abuse, sexual experimentation, violence, social isolation, bullying, and many others.

Adolescents are notorious for engaging in risky behaviors in a variety of domains. Some can be self-destructive, like those just mentioned. But other risky behaviors lead to personal growth: reaching out to new friends, building a self-identity, and becoming willing to test out new ideas in new settings. For bad and good, when people leave childhood and move toward adulthood they start taking risks.

The usual stereotype about adolescents is that they are irrationally risk seeking: They engage in behaviors like driving under the influence of alcohol because they don't understand the consequences of their behavior, they underestimate their chances of an accident, and they are so myopically optimistic that they think bad things can't happen to them.

That stereotype doesn't fit with what we now know about adolescent decision making. Adolescents are more likely to engage in risky behaviors, to be sure, but they don't engage in such behaviors for the stereotypical reasons. Adolescents are about as accurate as adults in estimating the probabilities of bad outcomes, and they aren't any more optimistic than adults in thinking that bad outcomes can't happen to them.

What leads to risk-taking behavior, then? Work by the psychologist Valerie Reyna has shown that, when thinking about a risky behavior like driving drunk, adolescents tend to overvalue the positive consequences like social interactions with friends. But they undervalue the negative consequences like an auto accident. In short, the potential benefits of a decision matter more than the potential costs.

Let me emphasize this point. Adolescents engage more in risky behaviors not because they are unable to understand risk but because they think the benefits outweigh the costs. Your average teenager—the one that causes a parent to shake her head in disbelief several times a day—isn't necessarily any worse of a decision maker than your average adult. Instead, that teenager sees the consequences of their decisions in a different light.

This perspective means that some of the interventions typically used to shape adolescent decision making might be misguided. Teaching teenagers about the risks associated with their decisions might not help. They already know the potential outcomes and their probabilities pretty well. We probably shouldn't try to train adolescents to be better decision makers.

So what can we do to improve the decisions of adolescents? There's no easy solution, but I want to foreshadow one possibility, something we'll consider more deeply at the very end of this course. It's called pre-commitment. Essentially, it would be better for all of us if many adolescents, much of the time, weren't even in situations where they could make tough decisions. As an example of an institutional pre-commitment, in many locations, adolescents are not legally allowed to drive with other adolescents as passengers. Following such laws reduces the chances that an adolescent will enter into a situation where social pressures lead to a bad decision.

That said, we don't necessarily want to teach our children to avoid all risks, they could miss out on many of the most important and formative experiences of our lifetimes: becoming independent, meeting a first love. Risk isn't necessarily bad. Investors who minimize risk earn less money, on average, then those investors who are willing to take on risk. So, our goal shouldn't be to avoid risk, but to manage it. How should we manage risk?

There are two basic rules. The first is simple: diversify.

Let's think about the example of a middle-class investor who saves for retirement using a 401k account that contains a portfolio of investments. The 401k-mechanism has become extraordinarily popular among both employees and employers alike. Employees like it because it provides them with some control over their retirement savings, while they get the benefits of a tax-deferred account. Employers like it because it reduces their risk. They aren't on the hook for an unknown amount of future payments, as was traditionally the case for pensions and other defined benefits plans.

When economists conducted a comprehensive survey of the investments held in the retirement savings accounts of employees in the 20 largest 401k plans, they found something concerning. On average, these employees held almost half of their retirement savings in the stock of a single company: their own employer. In many cases, employees can invest in their own company's stock at a substantial discount, and that makes it good to purchase that stock in the first place. But there are two very good reasons to sell company stock as soon as possible, which for most employees of large firms is immediately.

First, the price of a single stock fluctuates much more than that of the broader stock markets, in the case of these employees' company stocks, more than twice that of the benchmark S&P 500. Such fluctuations are especially bad for people nearing retirement age, but people actually held more company stock the closer they were to retirement. Second, the price of your company's stock is correlated, at least partially, with your own job security. So, a colossal disaster, product failure, or scandal could cost you not only your monthly paycheck now but also most of your savings for the future, as unfortunately experienced by employees in well-publicized company meltdowns like that of Enron in 2001.

In essence, using your own company's stock as a cornerstone of your retirement planning introduces an unwanted correlation between your income and your retirement savings. That increases the risk of your financial portfolio—some event out of your control, like the fraud of a top executive, could have a catastrophic effect on your finances.

The Nobel Laureate economist Harry Markowitz developed an elegant approach to managing investment risk. His central idea was that an optimal portfolio should contain assets that are not correlated, that do not tend to move together over time. New investments won't reduce the risk of a portfolio if they are largely correlated with existing investments, so it doesn't necessarily improve your portfolio's diversity when you buy into a new hot stock or take on yet another large-cap mutual fund.

For the sorts of investments most people make, this approach prioritizes one type of investments: broad mutual funds that reflect the overall performance of the larger financial markets. That doesn't mean such investments are the only reasonable strategy for retirement, but there are indeed very strong reasons to value investment diversity when trying to manage risk.

The second rule is also simple: avoid regret. This rule seems either meaningless or impossible. We all have regrets, even despite our best intentions. What I mean here is that you should think about risk a bit differently, so that bad outcomes don't lead to regret.

Let's think back to the coin-flip game from the beginning of the lecture. In that game, neurologically normal people showed regret whenever their risky choice led to a bad outcome; they tended to retreat immediately to safety, costing them money in the long run. The people with damage to their orbitofrontal cortex didn't show regret, they didn't move to a lower-value safe option, and they made more money overall. So, would you (or your stockbroker) be better off with orbitofrontal brain damage?

Of course not. Losing feelings of regret would be catastrophic in many real-world decisions. It's often good to regret our mistakes so that we learn and make better choices next time. But that regret does us little good when investing. Because high-reward investments tend also to be of high risk, it is good if we can dampen down our feelings of regret when necessary.

One effective approach for doing this comes not from behavioral economics but from clinical psychology. Psychologists have long been interested in strategies that help people dampen down their emotional reactions; such reappraisal strategies can be very helpful when dealing with adverse events that are outside one's own control. So, researchers have explored a particular strategy called "thinking like a trader." To do this, think of yourself as a dispassionate observer of your own investment portfolio. Each of your investments is part of a larger whole, and any one of your investments might go up or might go down on any day.

Expand your time horizons: Don't think about the day's or month's market results, but instead about your prudent, well-considered approach toward managing risk. Each decision you make is part of your larger strategy. It isn't even meaningful to regret one decision or one day's market fluctuation by itself. The larger strategy and the long-term results are what matters.

By expanding your time horizons, and perhaps by not checking your stocks as often, you'll be much better off. I can't promise that you'll make better investments. That's a much more complex process than could be covered in any lecture. But what is reasonable is to seek a more healthy attitude toward risk.

Even these simple steps, seeking diversity and avoiding regret, can be surprisingly difficult to follow, and they can even conflict with each other.

The financial writer Jason Zweig tells a wonderful anecdote about an interview he conducted with Harry Markowitz, the same Harry Markowitz who invented optimal portfolio theory. He asked Markowitz whether and how he followed his own mathematical formulae in constructing his own investment portfolio. Markowitz gave a very thoughtful answer. No, he didn't. He said that "Instead, I visualized my grief if the stock market went way up and I wasn't in it, or if it went way down and I was completely in it. My intention was to minimize my future regret."

Dealing with risk was hard for Harry Markowitz. It is hard for the rest of us as well. We can't eliminate risk and we shouldn't avoid risk. But, with the right approach and the right mindset, we can manage risk. In the next lecture, we'll learn about something much harder to manage: decisions where we don't know the probabilities, where we can't estimate the risks. Those decisions involve ambiguity.

# Ambiguity—The Unknown Unknowns
## Lecture 8

Decisions when faced with missing information, or ambiguity, can be some of the most difficult to make. You know that a good decision could be made with the right information, but you just don't have it. In this lecture, you will learn about three sorts of situations that lead to ambiguity aversion: hidden information, asymmetric knowledge, and unfamiliar contexts. In all three situations, we tend to avoid choice options where information is missing and where we feel less competent. And, in all three situations, the presence of ambiguity means that we treat the decisions differently than if there was only risk.

### Risk versus Ambiguity

- In his book *Risk, Uncertainty, and Profit*, economist Frank Knight's key insight is that there are two distinct types of uncertainty. Measurable uncertainty—decision where the probabilities of potential outcomes are known or could be estimated—was called risk.

- There was another type of unmeasurable uncertainty. He argued that there are decisions that we know could lead to different outcomes, but for which we do not know the probabilities and, importantly, cannot estimate those outcome probabilities. We don't know—and cannot readily estimate—what we don't know. Knight referred to this second type of decision as involving uncertainty, and economists sometimes call it Knightian uncertainty. It is also referred to as ambiguity.

- When Knight advanced his idea that there were two distinct forms of uncertainty, he did so based not on data but on his own intuitions. The idea of unmeasurable uncertainty made sense to Knight—and helped his arguments—but he didn't have any evidence that it actually existed.

- That evidence didn't come until 1961, through the efforts of a doctoral student in economics named Daniel Ellsberg, who sought to identify the circumstances under which people might behave as if influenced by ambiguity instead of just risk. He developed a thought problem that has since become known as the Ellsberg paradox, which is paraphrased as follows.

- Suppose that you are walking through your state fair toward a prize redemption station. You've just won two tickets that each give you some chance to win large prizes. You walk up to the barker running the station. He looks at you, smiles, and explains how his game works.

- He points to a large opaque urn in front of him. The urn has a hole in the top through which you can reach, but you can't see anything inside. "In this urn," he says, "are 90 Ping-Pong balls. Thirty of those balls are painted red, and the rest are either black or yellow—I can't tell you how many of each."

- Then he says, "For your first ticket, you get to call out a color and reach into the urn. If you pull out the color you just called, then you'll receive 100 dollars. What color do you call?" If you are like most people, you'd call out "red." You'd rather go with the known probability of one in three instead of some unknown probability for the other colors. Suppose for a moment that you didn't play this game right away, but instead waited to let the barker explain what you could win with your other ticket.

- "For your second ticket, I'll make the game even better for you: Yellow balls are automatic winners. So, you just have to call out either 'red' or 'black' and then reach into the urn. If you pull out the color you just called or you pull out a yellow ball, then you'll receive 100 dollars. What color do you call?"

- If you call out "red," you'll win with any of the red and yellow balls; you know that there's at least 30 such balls, but you don't know exactly how many. However, if you call out "black," you know that black plus yellow gives you 60 potential winners out of 90 balls. So, if you are like most people, you'll call out "black."

- Let's distill these two decisions to their essence. You know that there are 30 red balls and 60 black or yellow balls, with unknown probabilities of each. In both cases, you are given a meaningful incentive to choose the color that seems most likely. If you think that there are more red balls than black balls, then you should pick red in both cases.

- If you think that there are more black balls than red balls, then you should pick black in both cases. No matter what, though, you shouldn't switch your choices. But almost everyone does—and that's the Ellsberg paradox. The reason people switch their choices in these two decisions—going from red to black—is because of ambiguity aversion: People don't want to bet on situations in which the probabilities are unknown.

## Evoking Ambiguity Aversion: Hidden Information

- Consider a simple economic decision. Suppose that you could pay money to play a simple coin-flip game: If the coin is heads, you win 100 dollars, and if it's tails, you win nothing. How much would you pay to play that game?

- This decision involves just risk, not ambiguity. You know the outcomes and their probabilities. So, your willingness to pay depends just on your risk aversion in this gamble. If you are risk neutral, you'd pay the expected value of the game, which is 50 dollars, but if you are slightly risk averse, like most people, then you might pay a bit less—maybe 45 dollars.

- Let's introduce ambiguity into this decision. We can replace the flip of a coin with a draw from an Ellsberg urn with 100 balls, some of which say "win 100 dollars" and some of which say "win nothing," but you don't know the probabilities. Let's assume for the moment that the urn—like the coin—is fair. There could be anywhere from zero to 100 winning balls in that urn, with equal probabilities of any number. This is what statisticians call a uniform probability distribution. You just don't know what that number is.

- How much would you pay to play this second game? When people play games like this in a laboratory, they aren't willing to pay 50 dollars, even though that's the expected value of this second game, too. They aren't even willing to pay as much as they would for the similar coin flip. Instead, the average willingness to pay is much lower, perhaps 25 dollars or even less. People don't treat this second situation—where the probabilities are unknown—as just another risky decision. Something's different about the decision when ambiguity is involved.

- Research shows that our brains recognize when we don't have all of the available information about probability—the unknown unknowns—and our brains construct rules that help us work around that missing information. That constructive process isn't necessary for risky decisions—the known unknowns.

## Evoking Ambiguity Aversion: Asymmetric Knowledge

- The second situation that leads to ambiguity aversion is asymmetric knowledge, which means that one of the parties in some transaction knows something that the other parties do not. You've experienced this if you've ever haggled about the price of a handcrafted artwork, sought a second opinion about a medical procedure, or tried to buy a used car.

- Similar asymmetries arise in any situation where knowledge relevant to some decision is possessed by one person, but not others. We don't like asymmetric knowledge. We don't like the ambiguity it creates, and we want to withdraw from the decision, walking off of the used car lot and away from a potentially untrustworthy partner.

- One common example of an asymmetric knowledge situation is purchasing insurance. Insurance exists as a consumer product for two key reasons. The first reason is that the odds are in the insurer's favor. The insurer can estimate the risks associated with a particular sort of insurance policy. This allows the insurer to set the premiums sufficiently high so that people who purchase a specific sort of insurance pay in more through their premiums, on average, than the insurers have to pay out in claims.

- So, why would any rational person buy insurance? The answer comes from the second reason: Policyholders are more risk averse than insurers. Each of us who owns insurance of some form is at least somewhat risk averse. We don't want to face the catastrophic consequences of a severe illness or a complete loss of our home or car, so we are willing to pay more for our insurance policy than its expected cost to the insurer. The insurer spreads out its risk over many, many policyholders, so it can be close to risk neutral and still make money.

**Insurers estimate the risks associated with an insurance policy. They can remain close to being risk neutral by speading out their risk over many policyholders.**

- When thinking about insurance as just involving risk, the decisions of the insurers to decline any coverage just doesn't make sense. But, insurance involves more than risk, as shown in an elegant study by the economist Nathaniel Hendren, who realized that applications for health insurance policies involve information that is asymmetric—but not in the usual way. For health insurance, the policy applicant has considerable information that just isn't available to the insurer.

- Hendren's key insight was that insurance markets fail for high-risk individuals because those individuals know something about their health that the insurers do not. Faced with that private information, the insurers become ambiguity averse, leading to a market that is worse off for individuals, insurers, and the public interest alike.

## Evoking Ambiguity Aversion: Unfamiliar Contexts

- The third and final way ambiguity influences decisions is unfamiliar contexts. We prefer to make decisions by drawing conclusions from our own knowledge, as imperfect and probabilistic as it may be. Even if that knowledge isn't sufficient to help us make a good decision, it still seems better than the ambiguity associated with an unfamiliar context.

## Minimizing the Effects of Ambiguity

- Our aversion to ambiguity is often well justified; ambiguity arises in some of the most difficult decision problems we face. There is a two-step approach that can help us think about ambiguity, if not always deal with it.

- In a first step, ask yourself, what information is missing? If you cannot identify any missing information, then the situation may simply involve risk, and you can make the decision using any of the tools discussed throughout this course.

- However, if there is some missing information, then the situation likely involves ambiguity, and you should proceed to a second question: How could I get the missing information? Identify a path, if possible, for converting your decision from ambiguity to risk. But, in some cases, despite your best efforts, you won't get all of the information you need.

## Important Terms

Knight, *Risk, Uncertainty, and Profit*.

Post, Van den Assem, Baltussen, and Thaler, "Deal or No Deal?"

## Questions to Consider

1. What is ambiguity, and how is it different from risk?

2. Why might people be so averse to ambiguity in their decisions?

# Ambiguity—The Unknown Unknowns
## Lecture 8—Transcript

Donald Rumsfeld was one of the more controversial U.S. cabinet members of the past few decades. He served terms as the Secretary of Defense in both the 1970s and 2000s, becoming the civilian administrative leader of the U.S. military in several wars and many smaller conflicts. During those turbulent times, there were many opportunities for controversy, many difficult decisions that Rumsfeld had to justify to a skeptical public.

But Rumsfeld won't be remembered just for controversial decisions themselves. He'll also be remembered for his manner of explaining those decisions, a way of speaking that was unique in recent politics. Unlike the typical political figure, one who speaks in declarative sound bites, Rumsfeld adopted an almost professorial tone. The most famous example occurred in a press conference in February 2002. Rumsfeld was pressed by a question about whether there was any evidence that Iraq had supplied terrorist organizations with weapons of mass destruction, or even that the Iraqi government had any link to those terrorist groups.

He began his answer in typical politician-speak: "Reports that say that something hasn't happened are always interesting to me, because as we know … ." And then, he suddenly said something remarkable: "There are known knowns; there are things we know we know. We also know there are known unknowns; that is to say, we know there are some things we do not know. But there are also unknown unknowns, the ones we don't know we don't know."

What an amazing quote! Here we have one of the most powerful political figures in the country, describing perhaps the most controversial issue in American politics at that time, and he begins to lecture on the nature of uncertainty.

Let's unpack his quote into three parts.

First, "There are known knowns ... [the] things we know we know." That one is straightforward. Known knowns are certain events, those for which we can confidently predict what would happen.

Second, "There are known unknowns"; things we know we don't know. Knowledge that we know we don't have— that sounds like risk. We don't know what's going to happen when we bet on a roulette table or move our money from bonds to stocks, but we know that we don't know. That sort of uncertainty can be managed using strategies like those from the last lecture.

Ok, now to the third and key part, there are "unknown unknowns, the ones we don't know we don't know." What could that mean? By definition, an unknown unknown isn't risky because we don't know and can't estimate the probabilities. It is something else, but what? We'll consider exactly what this could mean in today's lecture.

As an epilogue, Donald Rumsfeld was pilloried in the media for this quote. A British group even recognized him with its annual Foot in the Mouth award, and several online sites reorganized his statement into a sort of political free-verse poetry. But, in the end it became a defining quotation for him. He even used an excerpt as the title of his autobiography: *Known and Unknown*.

Let's move back in time to the year 1921. The United States had recently exited World War I and was suffering through a brief but acute economic depression. Economics, as a field at that time, had the great challenge of balancing two disparate sets of goals. It sought the elegance and mathematical clarity of the hard sciences, like physics. But it also sought to be applicable to real-world policies and institutions, like other social sciences. The economist Frank Knight sought to bring these two goals together, at least conceptually, in his book *Risk, Uncertainty, and Profit*.

Knight's key insight was that there are actually two distinct types of uncertainty. Measurable uncertainty—decision where the probabilities of potential outcomes are known or could be estimated—was called risk. That's the same definition used in the previous lecture. But there was another type of unmeasurable uncertainty. He argued that there are decisions that we know could lead to different outcomes, but for which we do not know the probabilities and, importantly, cannot estimate those outcome probabilities. We don't know, and cannot readily estimate, what we don't know. Knight referred to this second type of decision as involving uncertainty, and economists sometimes call it Knightian uncertainty. But, we're going to call it ambiguity.

So, let's consider this distinction between risk and ambiguity. When Knight advanced his idea that there were two distinct forms of uncertainty, he did so based not on data but on his own intuitions. The idea of unmeasurable uncertainty made sense to Knight, and helped his arguments, but he didn't have any evidence that it actually existed.

That evidence didn't come until 1961, through the efforts of a doctoral student in Economics named Daniel Ellsberg. That name, Daniel Ellsberg, may sound familiar to some of you, particularly those who have interests in war, politics, and American history. Ellsberg wasn't exactly the typical academic economist. In the work that led to his Ph.D. dissertation, Ellsberg sought to identify the circumstances under which people might behave as if influenced by ambiguity instead of just risk. He developed a thought problem that has since become known as the Ellsberg Paradox. I'll paraphrase this paradox in the following example.

Suppose that you are walking through your state fair toward a prize redemption station. You've just won two tickets that each give you some chance to win large prizes. You walk up to the barker running the station. He looks at you, smiles, and explains how his game works.

He points to a large opaque urn in front of him. The urn has a hole in the top through which you can reach, but you can't see anything inside. "In this urn," he says, "are 90 Ping-Pong balls. Thirty of those balls are painted red, and the rest are either black or yellow. I can't tell you how many of each. For your first ticket, you get to call out a color and reach into the urn. If you pull out the color you just called, then you'll receive $100. What color do you call?"

What color would you call? There are 30 red balls and 60 other balls that are either black or yellow, with unknown probability. There could be 30 black and 30 yellow, 10 black and 50 yellow, 59 black and one yellow, or any other combination. You just can't know. So, what would you call? If you are like most people, you'd call out "red." You'd rather go with the known probability of 1 in 3, instead of some unknown probability for the other colors.

Let's suppose for a moment that you didn't play this game right away, but instead waited to let the barker explain what you could win with your other ticket. "For your second ticket, I'll make the game even better for you. Yellow balls are automatic winners. So, you just have to call out either 'red' or 'black" and then reach into the urn. If you pull out the color you just called or you pull out a yellow ball, then you'll receive $100. What color do you call?"

So, what would you call now? If you call out "red," you'll win with any of the red and yellow balls; you know that there's at least 30 such balls, but you don't know exactly how many. But, if you call out "black," you know that black plus yellow gives you 60 potential winners out of 90 balls. So, if you are like most people, you'll call out "black."

Let's distill these two decisions to their essence. You know that there are 30 red balls and 60 black or yellow balls, with unknown probabilities of each. In both cases, you are given a meaningful incentive to choose the color that seems most likely. If you think that there are more red balls than black balls, then you should pick red in both cases. If you think that there are more black balls than red balls, then you should pick black in both cases.

No matter what, though, you shouldn't switch your choices. But almost everyone does, and that's the Ellsberg Paradox. The reason why people switch their choices in these two decisions, going from red to black, is because of ambiguity aversion. People don't want to bet on situations in which the probabilities are unknown.

I am using the term "ambiguity aversion" in a descriptive sense here. There's a debate within economics as to whether people are really averse to ambiguity, per se, or instead are using simple heuristics to hedge against uncertainty. For example, one might expect that the carnival barker has more information than you and that when he offers you a bet with unknown odds, those odds aren't likely to be in your favor. Resolving that debate is far beyond the scope of this discussion. We'll stick to ambiguity aversion as a term that describes people's behavior, but as you'll see, people show the same behavior in several different situations, some of which are consistent with a simple heuristic and some of which aren't.

So, who was Daniel Ellsberg? Following his academic work on uncertainty, which explored examples of hidden information, like this one, during the 1960s he moved to the Pentagon and eventually the State Department, where he applied his research to problems in military decision making, like the potential decision to start a nuclear war. In 1968, Ellsberg helped prepare a 7,000-page document that summarized U.S. decision making in Vietnam, including the many lessons that were being learned as the war went worse and worse for U.S. troops.

In 1969 Ellsberg learned that those lessons were being ignored by the current administration, and he began covertly photocopying and distributing that enormous history of Vietnam-era decision making, first to members of Congress, and then to the major newspapers of the day. Those leaked documents became known as the Pentagon Papers. So, Daniel Ellsberg, the academic researcher who set the stage for how we think about decision making under ambiguity is now chiefly famous for his role in shaping the public narrative about the Vietnam War, perhaps the single conflict with the most unknown unknowns in U.S. history.

Now, I want to describe three circumstances that evoke ambiguity aversion. The first is that of hidden information.

Let's consider a simple economic decision. Suppose that you could pay money to play a simple coin-flip game: heads you win $100, tails you win nothing. How much would you pay to play that game?

By now you recognize that this decision involves just risk, not ambiguity. You know the outcomes and their probabilities. So, your willingness to pay depends just on your risk aversion in this gamble. If you are risk neutral, you'd pay the expected value of the game, which is $50. But, if you are slightly risk-averse, like most people, then you might pay a bit less, say $45.

But, we can introduce ambiguity into this decision. We can replace the flip of a coin with a draw from an Ellsberg urn with 100 balls, some of which say "win $100" and some of which say "win nothing," but you don't know the probabilities. Let's assume for the moment that the urn, like the coin, is fair. There could be anywhere from 0 to 100 winning balls in that urn, with equal probabilities of any number. This is what statisticians call a uniform probability distribution. You just don't know what that number is.

How much would you pay to play this second game? When people play games like this in a laboratory they aren't willing to pay $50, even though that's the expected value of this second game, too. They aren't even willing to pay as much as they would for the similar coin flip. Instead, the average willingness to pay is much lower, perhaps $25 or even less. People don't treat this second situation, where the probabilities are unknown, as just another risky decision. Something's different about the decision when ambiguity is involved.

A few years ago, my colleagues and I explored decisions of this sort using an approach that combined behavioral economics with neuroscience. We examined participants' brains while they made either risky decisions with known probabilities or ambiguous decisions with hidden, unknown probabilities. We found systematic brain differences between risk and ambiguity.

In particular, decisions involving ambiguity evoked more activation in the brain's prefrontal cortex, which has been frequently associated with setting up rules for behavior, and that activation predicted how much ambiguity would affect people's decisions. Subsequent research has shown that this brain response was specific to situations where some true probability was known to be hidden, like in the Ellsberg Paradox, and is not there in situations of complete ignorance.

In essence, our brains recognize when we don't have all of the available information about probability, the unknown unknowns, and our brains construct rules that help us work around that missing information. That constructive process isn't necessary for risky decisions, the known unknowns.

Let's move to the second situation that leads to ambiguity aversion: asymmetric knowledge. By asymmetric knowledge, I mean that one of the parties in some transaction knows something that the other parties do not. You've experienced this if you've ever haggled about the price of a handcrafted artwork, sought a second opinion about a medical procedure, or tried to buy a used car.

When you step onto the used car lot, you and the salesperson aren't playing on a level field. The salesperson knows the history of the vehicle, including relevant facts like its repair history. You don't. The salesperson knows about any tricks the dealership uses to make its cars seem more attractive than they really are. You don't. And, the salesperson knows the local market conditions, including typical selling prices for similar vehicles. You don't, unless you've really done your homework.

Similar asymmetries arise in any situation where knowledge relevant to some decision is possessed by one person, but not others. We don't like asymmetric knowledge. We don't like the ambiguity it creates, and we want to withdraw from the decision, walking off of the used car lot and away from a potentially untrustworthy partner.

One common example of an asymmetric knowledge situation is purchasing insurance. Think for a moment about why insurance exists, at least as a consumer product. Insurance exists for two key reasons. The first reason is that the odds are in the insurer's favor. The insurer can estimate the risks associated with a particular sort of insurance policy. This allows them to set the premiums sufficiently high so that people who purchase a specific sort of insurance pay in more through their premiums, on average, than the insurers have to pay out in claims.

So, why would any rational person buy insurance? The answer comes from the second reason: Policyholders are more risk-averse than insurers. Each of us who owns insurance of some form is at least somewhat risk-averse. We don't want to face the catastrophic consequences of a severe illness or a complete loss of our home or car, and so we are willing to pay more for our insurance policy than its expected cost to the insurer. The insurer spreads out its risk over many, many policyholders, so it can be close to risk-neutral and still make money.

As a quick digression, psychological factors push many people to purchase insurance for the wrong reasons. Insuring a relatively inexpensive consumer electronics product, such as a smartphone, is rarely a good idea. Yes, it is easy to imagine circumstances in which we might need that insurance, but no, the loss of a smartphone would rarely be financially catastrophic. Given the substantial markups and many limits on electronics insurance policies, most people would be better served passing on the policy and just self-insuring and saving the money.

Conversely, flood insurance has historically been heavily subsidized by the U.S. federal government. Even though flood insurance is often expensive, its expense typically underestimates the true cost of insuring very expensive real estate against a rare natural disaster. And, the loss of a home would be a truly catastrophic event for which few people could self-insure. But only a small minority of people for whom flood insurance is optional actually purchase that insurance.

People often see insurance as important protection against relatively common and moderately costly losses, like when buying insurance against the loss of one's smartphone, or when setting a low deductible on one's auto insurance. But that attitude gets the goal of having insurance exactly wrong. We don't buy insurance to mitigate probability, but to mitigate risk. Common events like dropped smartphones and minor fender benders aren't worth insuring against because the odds aren't in our favor. But rare and catastrophic events, like threats to our health or loss of our homes, are surely worth insurance. Even though the odds still aren't in our favor, we are better served by a known small loss than a rare and catastrophic loss.

So far, I've still talked about insurance as a sort of risk, but there's a really remarkable way in which insurance moves into the domain of ambiguity. Historically, insurance markets in the United States determined how much a given person should pay based on a sense of shared risk. If you and I both applied for an insurance policy, and neither of us has a particularly salient pre-existing condition, then each of us might be treated similarly by the insurer. By insuring a large enough group of people—some of whom were very healthy and others of whom required much more medical care—an insurer could spread out its risk across enough people that its costs could be statistically estimated.

Let's suppose that someone who has a pre-existing condition, say a recent stroke, applies for medical insurance. If there is a true market for insurance, then it stands to reason that this person should pay more for their insurance than someone with no such condition. So, they should be able to buy insurance but pay a higher price. Here's the key problem: insurers often wouldn't even offer them a policy. Why not? Insurers are acutely sensitive both to risk-adjusted pricing and to making as much money as possible. Why would they not just offer a policy at a higher rate, so as to not turn away a potentially high-revenue customer?

When thinking about insurance as just involving risk, the decisions of the insurers to decline any coverage just doesn't make sense. But, insurance involves more than risk, as shown in an elegant study by the economist Nathaniel Hendren. Hendren realized that applications for health insurance policies involve information that is asymmetric, but not in the usual way. For health insurance, the policy applicant has considerable information that just isn't available to the insurer.

A stroke, for example, can lead to completely divergent outcomes. Some people recover quickly and almost fully, others are completely incapacitated, and the majority of people have some degree of residual impairment that isn't always evident at first examination. The key point to recognize is that the people who have suffered a stroke usually know their condition, and the potential need for additional care, better than the insurers.

Suppose, then, that an insurer decided to offer a policy to a particular group of high-risk patients, say those having suffered a stroke, at a significantly higher price, double the normal rates. Who would purchase this very expensive insurance? The relatively healthy individuals with a good prognosis might decide to forgo insurance; it would be too expensive for what they would get out of it. Instead, the insurance would be purchased by those individuals who know that they are in bad shape and likely to need much more care.

There's no way out of this problem, at least from the insurer's perspective. If they charged triple the normal rate for insurance, then only those people who think they are likely to need much, much more care than typical are likely to buy insurance. Hendren's key insight was that insurance markets fail for high-risk individuals because those individuals know something about their health that the insurers do not. Faced with that private information, the insurers become ambiguity-averse, leading to a market that is worse off for individuals, insurers, and the public interest alike.

For my third and final example of how ambiguity influences decisions, we'll consider decision making in unfamiliar contexts.

Suppose that I offer you $1,000 for predicting the weather on July 4th of next year, and I'll even give you your choice of two questions. Question A: Will the high temperature in New York City on July 4 be more or less than 85 degrees Fahrenheit? Question B: Will the high temperature in Baku, Azerbaijan, be more or less than 85 degrees Fahrenheit?

Which question would you choose to answer, A or B? When faced with questions like this one, people show a strong tendency to make predictions about something familiar, which for a majority of U.S. residents, at least, would be New York City. So, they'd rather guess about New York's temperature, even if they aren't sure about which way to guess.

I want to emphasize that our bias toward the familiar doesn't depend on actually knowing the answer to the question. Eighty-five degrees is approximately the median high temperature in New York City on that date, and none of us can predict whether next year's temperature would be higher or lower than that average. So, our guesses aren't likely to be any better on a coin flip or any better than a complete guess in an unfamiliar context.

Suppose that I then told you that 85 degrees was also approximately the median high temperature in Baku, Azerbaijan, on that date. You'd probably still have a strong bias toward answering the question about New York City, even though the two questions are well-matched in terms of both temperature and probability. But why?

We prefer to make decisions by drawing conclusions from our own knowledge, as imperfect and probabilistic as it may be. Even if that knowledge isn't sufficient to help us make a good decision, as in the case of the weather prediction task I just described, it still seems better than the ambiguity associated with an unfamiliar context.

I've just described three sorts of situations that lead to ambiguity aversion: hidden information, asymmetric knowledge, and unfamiliar contexts. In all three situations, we tend to avoid choice options where information is missing and where we feel less competent. And, in all three situations, the presence of ambiguity means that we treat the decisions differently than if there was only risk.

So how can we minimize the effects of ambiguity on our decisions? There's no easy answer here. Our aversion to ambiguity is often well-justified; ambiguity arises in some of the most difficult decision problems we face. I'll suggest a two-step approach that can help us think about ambiguity, if not always deal with it.

In a first step, ask yourself "What information is missing? Is there something that I should know before making this decision?" If you cannot identify any missing information, then the situation may simply involve risk, and you can make the decision using any of the tools discussed throughout this course.

But, if there is some missing information, then the situation likely involves ambiguity, and you should proceed to a second question: "How could I get the missing information?" Identify a path, if possible, for converting your decision from ambiguity to risk. Perhaps you are bidding on a new home and you realize that the seller has information about the home's quality that you lack. Seek disclosure of that information, to minimize the asymmetry in knowledge between you and the seller. But, in some cases, despite your best efforts, you still won't get all of the information you need. Decisions when faced with missing information, or ambiguity, can be some of the most difficult to make. You know that a good decision could be made with the right information, but you just don't have it.

Donald Rumsfeld, after making that distinction between known unknowns and unknown unknowns, continued by saying: "And if one looks throughout the history of our country and other free countries, it is the latter category [unknown unknowns] that tend to be the difficult ones." Decisions often aren't hard because of what we know. They are hard because of what we don't know.

In the next lecture, we'll move from decisions about probability, risk, and ambiguity to decision about time—should we spend now or save for the future? Such decisions present a particularly challenging form of uncertainty, one that we all face when dieting, investing in our education, or saving for retirement.

# Temporal Discounting—Now or Later?
## Lecture 9

This lecture moves from decisions about probability, risk, and ambiguity to decisions about time: Should we spend now, or save for the future? Such decisions present a particularly challenging form of uncertainty, one that we all face when dieting, investing in our education, or saving for retirement. In this lecture, you will learn about why decisions involving time are so challenging and how we can make better decisions about our future.

**Temporal Discounting**

- To an economist, the term "discounting" means a reduction in value. Therefore, "temporal discounting" means a reduction in value because of the anticipated passage of time.

- Suppose that you walk into a behavioral economics laboratory to do an experiment on temporal discounting for money. The experimenter gives you a choice between two options that differ in their reward value and timing, and you just report what you prefer. Which would you rather have: 100 dollars today or 110 dollars in six months?

- In laboratory experiments, most people prefer receiving 100 dollars today—the smaller, sooner reward. This implies that the value of money diminishes over time; we'd rather have less now than more later. Let's change the question. Which would you rather have: 20 dollars today or 200 dollars in one month? Now, most people choose 200 dollars in one month; they pick the larger, later reward.

- In the laboratory, we can ask people a series of these questions, systematically varying the reward values and timing, and then estimate a mathematical function, called the temporal discounting function, that describes how time influences the subjective value of money.

- When we measure people's temporal discounting in the laboratory, the most obvious result is that people vary tremendously in their patience. Some people discount money very slowly, such that they have equal value for 48 dollars now and 50 dollars in six months. Others discount very, very rapidly. They have equal value for 20 dollars now and 50 dollars in just one month.

- Behavioral economists have argued that people engage in a sort of mental accounting for their financial decisions—they assign decisions to different mental accounts and apply different rules to each account. The retirement savings and the money earned in the laboratory reflect two different mental accounts.

- It would be much more efficient for us to apply the same rules across all such accounts so that we aren't too impulsive in one setting and too patient in another. However, that turns out to be very difficult.

**Why We Discount**

- There are at least three explanations for why rewards are worth less in the future than they are in the present. First, delayed outcomes can also be risky outcomes. Waiting to receive a reward carries risks. The promise of a future reward might not be kept. Our personal circumstances might change—we might step in front of a bus tomorrow, or we might win the lottery. The longer the delay, the greater the risk and, thus, the less a future reward should be worth. However, we can't explain away temporal discounting as just a natural response to risk.

- A second explanation is more psychological: Temporal discounting arises from temptation. People tend to discount primary rewards like food and juice much more rapidly than money. Moreover, people who find a particular type of reward especially tempting—like those who report loving candy, chocolate, or chips—show faster discounting for that reward than other similar rewards. However, temptation doesn't explain why we show such high discounting for money, especially when we don't desperately need that money right now.

- There is a third explanation that is a bit subtler than the other two. Think of, for example, a 25-year-old single male in the United States who is just beginning to save for retirement. Every dollar saved for retirement is taken away from his 25-year-old self—that money is not available for whatever activities he values right now. Instead, it is aside for the as-yet-unknown desires of his 65-year-old self.

- Perhaps his 65-year-old self will like to travel, or will want to support charitable causes, or will need long-term medical care. He doesn't know—and cannot know—what his 65-year-old self will use the money for. He just knows that it is a good idea to reserve some of his current money for his future self.

## Preference Reversals

- The first of three key anomalies in temporal discounting behavior is preference reversals, which are flips in preference from one reward to another as time passes. Consider the following choice. Which would you prefer: 100 dollars now or 105 dollars a week from now? Many people find this to be a pretty easy choice; they'd rather have the smaller but sooner 100 dollars.

- Let's change the dates. Which do you prefer: 100 dollars in 52 weeks or 105 dollars in 53 weeks? Now, this seems like a very easy choice to almost everyone: They'd rather have the larger, later 105 dollars.

- These two situations only differ because of the passage of time: The second scenario just happens one year later than the first. However, people choose differently in the two situations, choosing the smaller, sooner reward when it is near but the larger, later reward when it is distant.

- Think about what that implies about people's preferences. Someone who prefers 105 dollars in 53 weeks would have to wait, and wait, for their reward to be delivered. Then, after a year had passed, they would then be in exactly the situation of the first question, and they'd now prefer to get the 100 dollars now instead of waiting another week. Their preferences would reverse, just because of the passage of time.

- Preference reversals like this imply that people discount rewards faster when they are near in time. Thus, they aren't consistent with the constant discounting of an exponential function. But they are consistent with the rapid short-term discounting of a hyperbolic function. There is a consensus that temporal discounting should follow an exponential function, but that it actually follows a hyperbolic function, in most settings. So, we may want to be rational, but we're really impulsive.

**Sequence Effects**
- A second anomaly in intertemporal choice is that of sequence effects. By itself, temporal discounting implies that we should want to receive good outcomes as soon as possible, when they are most valuable to us. Often, that is true, but there are specific situations in which we'd instead prefer to wait for a good outcome.

- Suppose that you have won gift certificates for dinners at three local restaurants. You're familiar with all three. One is basically a no-frills English pub. The second is the fanciest Italian restaurant in town. The third is a casual French bistro that is intermediate in price and quality. Over the next three weekends, you can dine at these three restaurants in any order you choose. Which do you pick for your first weekend? Second? Third?

- There's no right answer, and people may have personal reasons for picking these in any order. However, people do show a strong general tendency for an ascending sequence of quality: They'd first go to the pub, then to the casual bistro, and then finally to the fancy restaurant. Temporal discounting can't explain this effect, because the most valuable option is saved for last.

- Why do people save the best option for last? People want to have that feeling of anticipation, which is an extremely powerful motivator for our decisions. Anticipated gains lead people to purchase lottery tickets that have astronomically low chances of winning. Anticipated regret pushes people away from risky investments, even when those investments are strongly in our interest. Feelings of anticipation can override the normal decrease in value that comes with temporal discounting.

**Dread**
- Finally, there's dread, that feeling you get when you know that something bad will happen. You know it's coming, it's going to be unpleasant, you can't avoid it, and you just want it over with. Even though dread seems more like a feeling than an object for scientific study, behavioral economists and neuroscientists have sought to understand its causes. One approach in the laboratory involves the delivery of moderate electric shocks.

- If you were in one of these experiments, the researchers would bring you into the laboratory, sit you down in a comfortable chair, and then attach an electric lead to your forearm. They'd then give you a set of calibration shocks to determine your maximum pain tolerance—the strongest shock you can bear. Then, they'd give you choices between pairs of shocks that differ in their strength and timing—for example, between 10 percent and 90 percent of your maximum pain tolerance and with delays between one and 30 seconds.

- You might think that people would want to put off the aversive shocks as long as possible. Or, at the least, they'd just choose whatever option gives them the least pain overall. But that's not what happens. Many people actually prefer to get a larger shock immediately instead of waiting a long time for a smaller shock. Such behavior runs exactly opposite to standard temporal discounting models.

- The neuroeconomist Greg Berns used functional MRI to examine brain responses while people were awaiting these sorts of delayed shocks. He found that while people waited for the upcoming shocks, those people who showed the most dread also showed an anticipatory response in brain regions that process pain; it was as if their brains simulated the upcoming negative experience. That waiting period—that feeling of dread—is itself aversive. People actually find the experience of dread sufficiently aversive that they are willing to take their lumps now so that they don't have to wait, and dread, any longer.

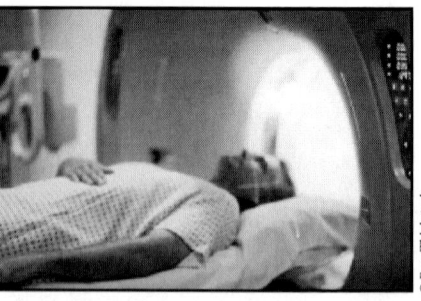

**Functional magnetic resonance imaging (fMRI) measures changes in blood flow in the brain.**

## Making Better Intertemporal Decisions

- There are surprisingly simple things that we can do to make better intertemporal decisions. The first of these is straightforward: Expand your time horizon. Don't think about consequences as occurring at a single moment or day, but as unfolding over a long window of time. By expanding your time horizon, you'll be more accurate in how you envision an uncertain future.

- A second rule requires a little more work: Change your reference point. Think not about delay, but acceleration. When the same decision is framed as an acceleration—giving up money to get a reward sooner—people tend to become much more patient. They don't want to give up some of their reward in order to receive it sooner. This phenomenon, which is called asymmetric discounting, provides a pretty simple tool for making more patient decisions. Just use the most patient outcome as a reference point, and frame the sooner option as being a sacrifice, not a gain.

- The final rule requires the most effort, but it is potentially the most helpful: Think about your future self. Don't just acknowledge that you have a future or that you'll have expenses later that you don't have now. Think about your future self as a person and consider that future self's needs, as explicitly as you can.

## Suggested Reading

Kirby and Herrnstein, "Preference Reversals Due to Myopic Discounting of Delayed Reward."

Weber, et al, "Asymmetric Discounting in Intertemporal Choice."

## Questions to Consider

1. What are preference reversals in temporal discounting, and why do they occur?

2. What strategies are effective for increasing the patience of our intertemporal decisions?

# Temporal Discounting—Now or Later?
## Lecture 9—Transcript

Are you saving enough money for your retirement? You've probably asked yourself this question before. Depending on how close you are to your planned retirement date, you might ask yourself this question almost every day. And, if you are already retired, you've surely considered whether your current income and lifetime savings are enough to maintain your desired lifestyle.

If you are like most working-age U.S. adults, you'll express cautious optimism about your retirement. Perhaps you haven't saved as much as you would have liked, but you know that you are partially covered by Social Security income. You plan to save more and more as your retirement date nears. Besides, you don't think that you'll need all that much in retirement; your normal monthly expenses will go down. You just want enough for the occasional vacation or dinner with friends.

Unfortunately that cautious optimism is often unwarranted. Based on comprehensive national surveys, approximately half of all American households are projected to fall 10 percent or more below the income needed to maintain their lifestyle. Most current retirees report that they haven't saved enough—about half of all households report essentially no savings, aside from home equity—meaning that Social Security provides the primary source of retirement support. And, the people who are most likely to have significant expenses during retirement, those with ongoing health challenges, report the least savings.

Why don't people save enough for retirement? In some cases, personal circumstances prevent the accumulation of significant wealth. Chronic health conditions, care for disabled children, or other lifetime financial demands can make saving difficult or impossible. But problems with retirement savings are pervasive in our society. Even among people who have a relatively high household income and have remained healthy, a substantial minority still haven't saved enough to maintain their standard of living.

To understand why people fail to save for retirement (even when they know that they should) will require stepping back from this specific problem. The decision to save for one's retirement is a prototypic example of what we call intertemporal choice, in that we sacrifice the ability to spend a smaller amount of money now, under the idea that our money will grow and thus we can spend a larger amount of money later. In today's lecture, we'll talk about why decisions involving time are so challenging and how we can make better decisions about our future.

I'll begin by introducing the idea of temporal discounting. To an economist, the term "discounting" means a reduction in value. So, "temporal discounting" means a reduction in value because of the anticipated passage of time.

Let's suppose that you walk into a behavioral economics laboratory to do an experiment on temporal discounting for money. The experimenter gives you a choice between two options that differ in their reward value and timing, and you just report what you prefer. So, which would you rather have, $100 today or $110 in six months? In laboratory experiments, most people prefer receiving $100 today, that's the smaller, sooner reward. This implies that the value of money diminishes over time—we'd rather have less now than more later.

Let's change the question. Which would you rather have, $20 today or $200 in one month? Now, most people choose $200 in one month; they pick the larger, later reward.

In the laboratory, we can ask people a series of these questions, systematically varying the reward values and timing, and then estimate a mathematical function, called the temporal discounting function, that describes how time influences the subjective value of money.

So, what do we get if we measure people's temporal discounting in the laboratory? The most obvious result is that people vary tremendously in their patience. Some people discount money very slowly, such that they have equal value for $48 now and $50 in six months. Others discount very, very rapidly. They have equal value for $20 now and $50 in one month.

Temporal discounting isn't restricted to money or even to humans. A very wide variety of animals show temporal discounting of one form or another. Rodents (like squirrels) and birds (like scrub jays) exhibit caching behavior. They put aside food in hidden caches during times of plenty, and then return to those caches when times are lean, often days, weeks, or even months later. In effect, those animals are engaging in a form of temporal discounting, spending effort to acquire food now, so that they have sustenance later.

Caching behavior represents a relatively extreme case, and most of the time animals don't show this level of patience. Researchers have tested many animals' temporal discounting rates using laboratory procedures analogous to those for humans. For example, a researcher might give a rat a choice between a small squirt of juice now and a large squirt of juice later. By varying the juice amounts and timing that researcher could map out the rat's temporal discounting for juice, just like was done with humans for money.

When tested in procedures like this, non-human animals show very fast discounting for rewards like food and juice. Pigeons and rats discount such rewards following only a few seconds, while monkeys and apes discount over tens of seconds to minutes. Such differences make sense based on what we know about the brains of these different animals; the brain of a chimpanzee, for example, is considerably more developed than that of a pigeon, and thus it isn't surprising that the chimpanzee can remain patient for a minute or two, while the pigeon is only patient for a few seconds.

But, let's think for a moment about just how long people show discounting. When did you first start saving for retirement? For many people, the answer to that question is "in my 20s." Assuming a plan to retire around age 65 or later, that implies that people often delay monetary rewards for 40 years or more, or something like 20 million minutes, compared to two or three minutes for a chimpanzee.

This difference probably reflects the special nature of money more than anything special about us humans. You see, we can test humans using procedures similar to those for monkeys and chimps, using non-monetary rewards like squirts of juice or viewing photographs of attractive faces. When we test humans for those sorts of rewards, then their discount rates turn out to be pretty similar to those of our primate relatives—people aren't willing to wait more than some seconds to minutes to view a more attractive image or to get a larger squirt of juice.

So, there seems to be something special about money. And, we're not even consistent in our attitudes toward money itself. Let's return to that example of a very patient person I mentioned earlier, someone who is indifferent between $48 now and $50 in six months. That may indeed seem pretty patient in isolation; this person is willing to wait six months just to gain $2. But, let's think about this not as a one-shot decision but as a potential investment. This decision is equivalent to an investment with an effective rate of return of about 8.5 percent per year, roughly similar to the average annual return for the broad stock market over the past 50 years. And, unlike the stock market, this decision is risk-free.

Let's consider another example. If you report that you would rather have $100 now than $110 in one month, then you are turning down a risk-free investment with a 185-percent annual return. I can't guarantee much of my investing advice, but I can guarantee this: that's far better than any risk-free investment that you or I will ever be offered.

Behavioral economists have argued that people engage in a sort of mental accounting for their financial decisions. They assign decisions to different mental accounts, and apply different rules to each account. So the same person who has some of her retirement savings locked into long-term treasury bonds that return two percent per year can come into the laboratory and turn down a guaranteed return of almost 200 percent per year. The retirement savings and the money earned in the laboratory reflect two different mental accounts.

It would be much more efficient for us to apply the same rules across all such accounts, so that we aren't too impulsive in one setting and too patient in another. But, that turns out to be very difficult, at least, without the sorts of tools I'll provide at the end of the lecture.

So far, I've described what temporal discounting is, but let's now move to the question of why we discount. There are at least three explanations for why rewards are worth less in the future than they are in the present.

First, delayed outcomes can also be risky outcomes. We've already talked about the idea of a risk premium—we require a higher expected return to invest in something risky, like the stock market, than something safe like a money market account. Waiting to receive a reward also carries risks. The promise of a future reward might not be kept. Our personal circumstances might change—we might step in front of a bus tomorrow, or we might win the lottery. The longer the delay, the greater the risk, and thus the less a future reward should be worth.

Explaining temporal discounting in terms of risk makes intuitive sense. But, it doesn't explain everything. As one piece of evidence against this explanation, people's attitudes toward risk and their attitudes toward delay are only weakly correlated. Someone who is very risk-averse might also be very patient in their temporal decisions, even though being patient should carry more risk. Likewise, when people are faced with large decisions, say those involving thousands of dollars, they become more risk-averse but also more patient. So, we can't explain away temporal discounting as just a natural response to risk.

A second explanation is more psychological: Temporal discounting arises from temptation. I mentioned that people tend to discount primary rewards like food and juice much more rapidly than money. Moreover, people who find a particular type of reward especially tempting (like those people who report loving candy, chocolate, or chips) show faster discounting for that reward than other similar rewards. And, addicts show very, very rapid discounting for drug-related rewards: They value drugs when they can be obtained right now and quickly discount the value for future drugs to almost nothing.

That temptation also plays a role in temporal discounting also seems intuitive. We've all felt the lure of some tempting reward like a piece of cake, and it's easy to see how that temptation can cause us to overvalue the present at the expense of the future. But, it also can't explain all aspects of temporal discounting. Temptation doesn't explain why we show such high discounting for money, especially when we don't desperately need that money right now.

And, even after controlling for the relative temptation associated with different sorts of rewards, statistical analyses reveal that there's still something left over, a more general sort of impulsiveness or patience that extends across all of our decisions. This means that temptation, at least by itself, can't explain temporal discounting.

There is a third explanation, though, and it's a bit more subtle than the other two. Think of a 25-year-old, say a single male in the United States, who is just beginning to save for retirement. Every dollar saved for retirement is taken away from his 25-year-old self; that money is not available for dinners out with friends, for buying running shoes, for purchasing books to read, or for whatever other activities he values right now. Instead, it is aside for the as-yet-unknown desires of his 65-year-old self.

Perhaps his 65-year-old self will like to travel, or will want to support charitable causes, or will need long-term medical care. He doesn't know and cannot know what his 65-year-old self will use the money for. He just knows that it is a good idea to reserve some of his current money for his future self.

I emphasize this third perspective because it can guide toward specific steps that help us resist temptation, become more patient, and yes even save more for retirement. So, let's keep this perspective in mind for the next few minutes, while I introduce some of the key anomalies in temporal discounting behavior.

The first is preference reversals, flips in preference from one reward to another as time passes. Imagine two hypothetical decision makers, Elizabeth and Henry, each of whom is about average in terms of their overall patience. They differ, however, in how they think about time.

To Elizabeth, the value of money decreases with a constant proportion over time. One hundred dollars now might keep 90 percent of its value over one month, 90 percent of what's left over the second month, 90 percent of what's left over the third month, and so forth. The first month is no different from the fourth month—time is time is time. Elizabeth's temporal discounting function for $100 would look like a smooth curve that starts high and then loses 10 percent of its current value each month. The mathematical term for such a curve is an exponential function.

Henry approaches money differently. To him, the present matters much more than the future. So, $100 now might only be worth about $75 after a one-month delay, and only $60 after two months. But future times don't matter as much to Henry. He doesn't really care much about the difference between 11 months or 12 months or between 12 months and 13 months. Henry's temporal discounting function for $100 would decline much more sharply than Elizabeth's, at first, but then would flatten out thereafter. The mathematical term for this curve is a hyperbolic function.

There's been an impressive amount of research trying to fit these, and other curves, to people's temporal discount functions. While some details remain unsettled, there is a consensus that temporal discounting should follow an exponential function, but that it does follow a hyperbolic function, in most settings. To illustrate this consensus, let's consider the following choice. Which would you prefer: $100 now or $105 a week from now? Many people find this a pretty easy choice, they'd rather have the smaller but sooner $100. Now, let's change the dates. Which do you prefer: $100 in 52 weeks or $105 in 53 weeks? Now, this seems like a very easy choice to almost everyone: They'd rather have the larger, later $105.

Now these two situations only differ because of the passage of time; the second scenario just happens one year later than the first. But, people choose differently in the two situations, choosing the smaller sooner reward when it is near, but the larger later when it is distant. Think about what that implies about people's preferences. Someone who prefers $105 in 53 weeks would have to wait, and wait, and wait for their reward to be delivered. Then, after a year had passed, they would then be in exactly the situation of the first question, and they'd now prefer to get the $100 now instead of waiting another week. Their preferences would reverse, just because of the passage of time.

Preference reversals like this imply that people discount rewards faster when they are near in time. Thus, they aren't consistent with the constant discounting of an exponential function. But they are consistent with the rapid short-term discounting of a hyperbolic function. So, we may want to be rational like Elizabeth, but we're really impulsive like Henry.

A second anomaly in intertemporal choice is that of sequence effects. By itself, temporal discounting implies that we should want to receive good outcomes as soon as possible, when they are most valuable to us. And, often that is true. We'd rather have money now instead of later, we indulge with the slice of cake even though we'll need to exercise more later. But, there are specific situations in which we'd instead prefer to wait for a good outcome.

Suppose that you have won gift certificates for dinners at three local restaurants. You're familiar with all three. One is basically a no-frills English pub—it's inexpensive, has good food and drink, but is more like comfort food than a fancy meal. The second is the fanciest Italian restaurant in town, a real splurge in all regards. And the third is a casual French bistro—it's intermediate in price and quality, clearly better than the pub, and clearly worse than the fancy Italian restaurant. Over the next three weekends, you can dine at these three restaurants in any order you choose. Which do you pick for your first weekend? Second? Third?

There's obviously no right answer here, and people may have personal reasons for picking these in any order. But, people do show a strong general tendency for an ascending sequence of quality: they'd first go to the pub, then the casual bistro, and then finally the fancy restaurant. Temporal discounting can't explain this effect, since the most valuable option is saved for last.

So why do people save the best option for last? A good guide might come from your intuitions about what you'd do. When reflecting on this decision, you might have had thoughts like, "I'll save the fancy restaurant until the end, so that I can look forward to it." That is, you wanted to have that feeling of anticipation.

Anticipation is an extremely powerful motivator for our decisions. Anticipated gains lead people to purchase lottery tickets that have astronomically low chances of winning. Anticipated regret pushes people away from risky investments, even when those investments are strongly in our interest. And, feelings of anticipation can override the normal decrease in value that comes with temporal discounting.

Finally, there's dread, that feeling you get when you know that something bad will happen. You know it's coming, it's going to be unpleasant, you can't avoid it, and you just want it over with. For many people, an effective way to elicit dread is to think about an unpleasant upcoming experience, say that you'll have to give a speech to a large audience. Even though dread seems more like a feeling than an object for scientific study, behavioral economists and neuroscientists have sought to understand its causes. One approach in the laboratory involves the delivery of moderate electric shocks.

If you were in one of these experiments, the researchers would bring you into the laboratory, sit you down in a comfortable chair, and then attach an electric lead to your forearm. They'd then give you a set of calibration shocks to determine your maximum pain tolerance, the strongest shock you can bear. Then, they'd give you choices between pairs of shocks that differ in their strength and timing, say between 10 percent and 90 percent of your maximum pain tolerance, and with delays between 1 and 30 seconds.

Now, this might sound like an unpleasant sort of experiment to be in, and it is. Participants find these shocks very aversive. Even though they are being paid for being in the study, they still want to minimize their discomfort throughout. So you might think that people would want to put off the aversive shocks as long as possible. Or, at the least, they'd just choose whatever option gives them the least pain, overall. But, that's not what happens. Many people actually prefer to get a larger shock immediately instead of waiting a long time for a smaller shock. Such behavior runs exactly opposite that of standard temporal discounting models.

The neuroeconomist Greg Berns used functional MRI to examine brain responses while people were awaiting these sorts of delayed shocks. He found that while people waited for the upcoming shocks, those people who showed the most dread also showed an anticipatory response in brain regions that process pain; it was as if their brains simulated the upcoming negative experience. That waiting period, that feeling of dread, is itself aversive. People actually find the experience of dread sufficiently aversive that they are willing to take their lumps now, so that they don't have to wait (and dread) any longer.

Because of all these phenomena—temporal discounting, preference reversals, sequence effects, and dread—choices that involve time seem very hard. And, that's true most of the time. We do make mistakes, we are inefficient, we are impatient in the face of temptation. It's a wonder that any of us have adequately planned for next year's expenses, much less our distant retirements.

But there are surprisingly simple things that we can do to make better intertemporal decisions. The first of these is straightforward: Expand your time horizon. Don't think about consequences as occurring at a single moment or day, but as unfolding over a long window of time.

This is particularly important for long-term decisions like saving for retirement. In one study, researchers gave different information to two groups of employees who were planning their retirement. One group viewed a distribution of annual returns for bond funds and for stock funds, and most people allocated their retirement funds to bonds. You can imagine why—the stock funds were far more variable year-to-year than the bond funds.

But, the other group of employees saw estimated 30-year returns for the same bond funds and stock funds, and 90 percent of them allocated their retirement money to stocks. Over a 30-year period, which is much closer to the normal working lifetime, the variability associated with stocks washes out and the overall returns are much higher. By expanding your time horizon, you'll be more accurate in how you envision an uncertain future.

A second rule requires a little more work (but only a little): Change your reference point. Think not about delay, but acceleration. Suppose that you have a choice between a $50 gift certificate that you can spend today or a $75 gift certificate that you can spend in three months. The natural reference point for that decision is today. People naturally think about the second reward as being delayed from the present—you are giving up the opportunity for reward over that period of delay.

But you can change your reference point. Let me break apart that same decision and present it in a different manner. First, you receive a $75 gift certificate that you can spend in three months. It's yours if you want it. But, you also have the option to sacrifice $25 of that gift certificate, leaving $50, if you would like to spend the gift certificate today. Do you want to make that sacrifice?

When the same decision is framed as an acceleration (giving up money to get a reward sooner) people tend to become much more patient. They don't want to give up some of their reward in order to receive it sooner. This phenomenon, which is called asymmetric discounting, provides a pretty simple tool for making more patient decisions. Just use the most patient outcome as a reference point and frame the sooner option as being a sacrifice, not a gain.

The final rule requires the most effort, but it is potentially the most helpful. Think about your future self. I don't mean that you should just acknowledge that you have a future, or that you should remember that you'll have expenses later that you don't have now. No, I mean something much more literal. Think about your future self as a person and consider that future self's needs, as explicitly as you can.

If you are, say, 40 years old and planning for retirement, you may find this difficult and even aversive. You still think of yourself of young and vibrant, and you don't know what sorts of activities your retirement age self will seek out. Suppose you receive a windfall inheritance. How do you weigh, say, the purchase of a used sports car against a contribution to your retirement savings?

At a minimum, make the tradeoffs between the present and future very explicit: "Let's see, I can either spend that $30,000 now, investing $0 in my retirement. Or, I can spend $0 now and have about $100,000 to spend in retirement, assuming a relatively conservative investment." It turns out that just thinking about those zeros—"investing $0 in my retirement"—makes people more patient.

But, ideally, you should think about your future self. Try to bring to mind what your future self might enjoy. It's easy to do that for your current self, so you'll have to work extra hard to make things fair for your future self. What activities might you like? Where could you go? What different hobbies might you explore? Whom could you help, and how?

Construct a story for your future self, it doesn't have to be perfect. Just think about your future self as a person. And, think about the moral responsibility to do right by your future self. After all, there's no one on whom your future depends more than you.

In the next lecture, we'll begin exploring the tradeoff process in more detail, how we can compare one option to another, and move from indecision to a concrete decision.

# Comparison—Apples and Oranges
## Lecture 10

There is now strong evidence that value isn't something we just look up from some internal table. Our brains construct subjective value when we make decisions—and even when we are just going through our daily activities. Value isn't something stable, intrinsic, or immutable. In this lecture, you will explore how people create and compare the subjective values of different options in order to make a decision. Specifically, you will consider two big ideas: constructed preferences and common currency.

**Constructed Preferences**

- The idea of constructed preferences contends that subjective value is something we create as needed. This idea hasn't always been well accepted in economics, but it is consistent with what psychologists now think about how memory works.

- The idea of constructed preferences can be applied to any decision situation, no matter how simple. This idea contends that we don't necessarily have intrinsic preferences that determine our choices of different goods—for example, that an apple is worth more than a dollar. Instead, we figure out what's important to us by working through the decision problem.

- This idea has been heretical to some economists; they think that people have stable and consistent preferences and that people have enough sense of their own preferences that they can look them up as needed. But this idea is consistent with how cognitive scientists now think about memory. Memories aren't looked up and processed as integrated wholes, but constructed from disparate elements at the time of retrieval.

- There are two decision biases. The first is called the decoy effect, which arises when the introduction of an unchosen option shifts what we value—specifically, biasing us toward an option that seems objectively better than the decoy. Marketers often use decoy effects, if not always as part of a conscious plan. In addition, some political scientists have argued that decoy effects can influence elections. For example, the introduction of a third-party candidate can shift undecided voters toward one of the two major-party candidates.

- The second decision bias is called the compromise effect. In situations where there are no objectively better or worse options, people tend to compromise. They tend to pick the intermediate choice that seems like a compromise between the extremes.

- Compromise is not always in our interest. When we compromise, we don't get to take advantage of the extremes. It might actually be a good idea to pick the best-located hotel room, the cheapest bottle of wine, or the most reliable car. And, if we consistently compromise, we can be exploited. A restaurant owner can make an expensive bottle of wine's price seem more reasonable by adding a rare and even-more-expensive bottle to the wine list.

- Constructed preferences lead to biases like preference reversals, decoy effects, and compromise effects—so why do we construct value, if it leads to so many mistakes? Why aren't our preferences more consistent and stable, so that we can look them up when needed?

- There are two answers to these questions. The first answer is that these biases actually help us make decisions. You are faced with a difficult choice between two or more similar items. Those items have different advantages and disadvantages, but it is often difficult to know what's really important.

- So, if there's an option that you won't regret—either because it is clearly better than some other option or because it is a good compromise—you can choose it and get on with the rest of your life. None of these biases overrides all other factors that motivate your decision; instead, they tend to push you one way or the other when you are faced with a particularly difficult choice.

- The second answer is a bit more complicated: Our preferences are constructed because that's how our brains have to work. We don't always know what factors are going to be relevant to a decision, in part because we have to value such dissimilar things—we weigh time versus effort, we trade money for food. To do this, we have to construct a common currency for value.

**Common Currency**
- The economist-turned-neuroscientist Antonio Rangel, working with the marketing scientist Hilke Plassmann, has used simple decisions to understand how the brain computes value. If you were a participant in one of their experiments, you'd fast for part of the day and then come to the research laboratory—hungry.

- You'd then lie down in an fMRI scanner and view a series of familiar brand-name snacks. When each snack appeared on the screen, you'd indicate how much you'd be willing to pay for it. When the experiment ended, you'd stay in the laboratory even hungrier than before. The researchers then would choose one snack, randomly, and sell it to you for the price you were willing to pay.

- Rangel, Plassmann, and their colleagues found that a particular brain region's activation tracked how much people were willing to pay for each snack. We call that region the medial orbitofrontal cortex, an area that receives input from dopamine neurons.

- The activation of this region was greater for snacks for which people would pay three dollars than for two-dollar snacks, greater for snacks for which people would pay two dollars than for one-dollar snacks, and so on. Importantly, the activation was independent of the specific objects on which people were bidding. Two different people might prefer completely different snacks, but they would both show increased activation to the specific snacks that they found most valuable.

- Rangel, Plassmann, and others have shown that the activation of the medial orbitofrontal cortex tracks other sorts of willingness to pay, such as how much people will pay for physical goods like wine or electronics, or how much people will pay to avoid eating something unpleasant.

- These results are consistent with the idea that the medial orbitofrontal cortex represents a common currency for subjective value—how much something is worth to us regardless of what it is. Our brains use that common currency to make decisions between different sorts of goods. Even if our brains process food using one pathway and money using another, those different pathways each feed into the medial orbitofrontal cortex so that different goods can be compared on the same scale.

## Integrating Construction and Common Currency

- Subsequent research has explored whether the construction of subjective value is a relatively automatic process—whether this brain region constructs value signals even in the absence of explicit choice.

- If we show people physical goods like food or electronics in an experiment, we only get a sense of their anticipated value; the actual experienced value comes later when people consume or use the good. So, research has been conducted that looks at decisions about viewing faces.

- Human faces are perhaps the single most universally motivating visual stimulus. We love looking at faces of our family and friends, and even of people unfamiliar to us. Researchers took advantage of this bias in a two-part neuroscience experiment.

- In the first part, each participant just passively viewed faces of varying attractiveness and passively received monetary rewards. They didn't have to do anything. From this, we could examine how the brain responds to the experience of more versus less attractive faces and the experience of better versus worse monetary rewards.

When people see electronics, for example, the anticipated value of the electronics can be estimated, but when people actually use electronics, the experienced value can be determined.

- Then, in the second part, the same participant made active decisions to spend some of the money he or she had just earned in order to view attractive faces. From this, we could determine how much money they were willing to pay in order to see an attractive face.

- If subjective value is being constructed automatically, then we should be able to use brain signals generated while people look at attractive faces to predict their later decisions about different attractive faces.

- That's exactly the brain signal we found in the medial orbitofrontal cortex—the same brain region that was thought to represent a common currency across different rewards. If someone was willing to pay a lot to view attractive faces, then the brain response in that region was much greater for faces than money. But if someone would rather keep his or her money, then the brain response was greater for money than faces.

**Active Construction**
- Despite the additional time and energy required, constructed preferences provide an enormous advantage over something more static: They are extraordinarily flexible. What we prefer and, in turn, what we choose can change depending on the current context in which we are making decisions. When our mood shifts or when we enter a new environment, we start to prioritize new features of a complex decision, and our preferences change as well.

- This scientific background leads to specific advice for decision making. In particular, your value for something is constructed based on the questions you are asking. So, ask different questions. If you are trying to decide between two similar items, step back and ask yourself how much you'd be willing to pay for one of them. Then, ask how much you'd be willing to pay for the other. You might come to a different decision—or have different insight about your decision—by thinking about items independently rather than by only thinking about them in comparison with each other.

- If you are making a decision among a set of options, ask yourself how your decision might change if one or more of those options were just unavailable. Rule something out, for the moment, and see if your preferences shift. Are you compromising for compromise's sake? Are you influenced by an irrelevant decoy?

- You don't always know what's important to you. So, use these processes of active construction to your advantage. Use them to simulate a slightly different sort of decision problem so that you can learn more about your own preferences—whether you are valuing the right things or whether you are fixating on some minor aspect of the decision. This construction process is critical because we don't have perfect knowledge about the world, about goods we could purchase, or even about our own preferences.

## Suggested Reading

Huber, Payne, and Puto, "Adding Asymmetrically Dominated Alternatives."

Payne, Bettman, and Johnson, *The Adaptive Decision Maker*.

## Questions to Consider

1. How could restaurant owners use the decoy effect to increase purchases of a high-margin item on their menu?

2. What is meant by a "common currency" for decision making?

# Comparison—Apples and Oranges
## Lecture 10—Transcript

Walk through any Las Vegas casino today, and you'll see computer video screens everywhere. Every casino floor is covered with computers: video poker machines, video slot machines, even video simulations of table games like blackjack. Each one of these games seeks to capture your attention with brilliant colors, engaging animations, and a host of cues that signal money and prizes. Their sounds merge into a cacophonous symphony of computerized noise.

But, if you had walked through Las Vegas casino floors in March 1969, you would have found only one computer, off by itself on a balcony in the Four Queens casino. There stood a large cabinet containing a PDP-7 minicomputer, an attached and much smaller video screen, and a gaming table. Like other tables in this casino, this one displayed a roulette wheel, but sitting on the table was a computer keyboard that allowed casino patrons to gamble electronically, as part of a remarkable experiment.

This experiment was run by the psychologists Sarah Lichtenstein and Paul Slovic, who wanted to test a peculiar phenomenon they had identified in their laboratory. They had found that the subjective value participants assigned to some economic gamble, like the spin of a $5 roulette wheel, seemed to depend on how the gamble was presented. Such variability didn't make sense to economists, who thought that value was something more fundamental and invariant. To economists, someone's answer to a question about value shouldn't change based on how they were questioned, any more than the price of a pan in an old Sears and Roebuck catalog should change each time someone flipped to that page.

Lichtenstein and Slovic knew that economists would be more accepting of their results if real money was involved, so they brought a mini-laboratory to the casino and recruited real casino patrons to play gambling games for real money. At the beginning of each game, the player walked up to the computer and chose their stakes, from 5 cents to 25 cents per chip (remember, this was 1969). Then, they players played two games.

In the first game, which I'll call the choosing game, the players were shown pairs of bets that were matched for expected value: in each pair, one of the bets had a higher probability of winning, while the other was associated with larger potential rewards. The player chose one of the two bets, and then a casino employee who was serving as the dealer spun the roulette wheel to resolve the bets.

In the second game, which I'll call the pricing game, the players were just shown one bet at a time, say, a 75% chance of winning 10 chips and a 25% chance of losing 2 chips. They then indicated at what price they'd be willing to sell the bet back to the dealer, and give up the chance to play. So, they might think, "a 75% chance of winning 10, a 25% chance of losing 2 … hmm, that's pretty good … I'll give it back to you for 5 chips." These games went on for as much as several hours, and some people won or lost as much as $80 (again, remember that this was 1969, so 80 dollars was quite a lot of money).

Now, I want to establish some intuitions about how people should play these two different games. In the choosing game, the players just indicate whether they'd choose gamble A or gamble B, gamble C or gamble D, and so on. If they choose A over B, then that implies that A must be the more valuable gamble, and it should command a higher price in the pricing game. In short, each player's choices should line up with their prices. But they don't. The players often chose a high-probability gamble over a high-reward gamble, but then later in the experiment sold the high-reward gamble for the greater price. Their preferences often reversed, depending on what question was being asked.

Over the next several decades, psychologists and economists conducted study after study of what we now call preference reversals. The psychologists showed repeatedly that people reversed their preferences depending on whether they were choosing or pricing. In general, people were more likely to choose gambles with the highest probability of winning, but people also reported that gambles with the highest magnitude of winning should command higher prices. Economists tried what they could to make these preference reversals go away, with relatively little success. Subjective value depends on the way we ask the question.

In today's lecture, we'll explore how people create and compare the subjective values of different options in order to make a decision. We'll consider two big ideas today: constructed preferences and a common currency.

The idea of constructed preferences contends that subjective value is something we create as needed. This idea hasn't always been well accepted in economics, but it is consistent with what psychologists now think about how memory works. Let's explore this concept and its implications for decision making.

To understand what this idea means, and what it's not, it's worth thinking in terms of an analogy. Suppose that you are trying to sell your car. You take the car to a large used-car lot on the edge of town, one that is part of a national chain. The salesperson writes down the make and model of your car, looks at the current mileage, walks around the car to check for damage, and then reads a note from a mechanic giving your car a clean bill of health. Then, she goes to a computer, types in that information, and looks up the price.

To this company, the value of your car is given by a listing in some database. If all the necessary information is available, then that value can be looked up, and it doesn't change based on the time of day, the mood of the salesperson, how you are dressed, or any other subjective factor.

Suppose that you had instead tried to sell your car yourself through an online advertisement. An interested buyer comes to your house to see the car. He walks around the car, asks you about a scratch on a door, opens the hood to look at the engine, and then steps back and just stares at the car. He looks at you, looks at the car again, and then makes an offer.

To this buyer, the value of the car wasn't in some database ahead of time. It didn't even exist until he met with you and saw the car. At that point, he combined his own financial constraints, his judgment about the quality of the car, and even his sense of your savvy as a negotiator, all feeding into his offer. If he had been in a better mood, or if your house wasn't quite as nice, then perhaps he would have offered more money. In this case, the value of the car wasn't looked up, it was constructed.

Stepping away from this specific analogy, the idea of constructed preferences can be applied to any decision situation, no matter how simple. This idea contends that we don't necessarily have intrinsic preferences that determine our choices of different goods – say, that an apple is worth more than a dollar. Instead, we figure out what's important to us by working through the decision problem.

This idea has been heretical to some economists; they think that people have stable and consistent preferences, and that people have enough sense of their own preferences that they can look them up as needed. But it's consistent with how cognitive scientists now think about memory. Try to remember an event from your recent past, say eating breakfast earlier today. Perhaps you remember the place you were sitting. Perhaps you remember the taste of the food, the smell of your coffee. Perhaps you remember what you were doing—reading, talking, relaxing. When we bring our memory of breakfast to mind, it seems like we are reliving an event from our past, as if we looked up that memory in some database and then pressed play on an internal movie.

We now know that memories aren't accessed that way. Memories aren't looked up and processed as integrated wholes, but are constructed from disparate elements at the time of retrieval. Different components of memories (sights, sounds, smells) aren't even stored together in our brains. Instead, they are stored in different parts of the brain, according to what sort of information they contain, and then only integrated when an associated memory is brought to mind. And, when memories are brought to mind, they are most flexible and likely to change.

Our preferences are like our memories. They are often constructed at the moment of a decision. They don't use all possible information, but emphasize what we think is most important in that moment. And, the very act of construction makes them susceptible to change.

So, let's consider some implications of the idea of constructed preferences. I'll introduce two decision biases. The first is called the decoy effect.

Suppose that you are in the market for a wine refrigerator. I don't mean a fancy wine storage closet with multiple cooling zones and custom racking. I mean a simple refrigerator dedicated to holding bottles of wine. I picked this because it's a relatively simple product, one that basically varies on two key features: size and price. Let's also suppose that each of these features matters for your decision: larger is better than smaller, and less expensive is better than more expensive.

You walk into an appliance store and you see two models on display. Model A only holds 24 bottles of wine and costs $100, while model B holds 36 bottles of wine but costs $150. So, your choice is between a smaller, cheaper model A and a larger, more expensive model B. How do you make that decision?

What you should do seems clear. You should look at each model, determine its value, and choose the one with the greatest value relative to its price. Your choice should be determined only by your intrinsic preferences and by information about model A and model B. But, we don't always do what we should.

While you are thinking about your options, you suddenly notice a third model, C. It holds 30 bottles of wine and costs $175. It's objectively worse than model B, in that it is smaller and more expensive. So, it should be irrelevant to your decision between models A and B. But it's not.

Model C, in this example, is what behavioral economists call a decoy. It is objectively worse than one of the other options in a choice set, so it shouldn't be chosen itself. But decoys shape the process of choice. Suddenly, the large but expensive model B seems like a really good deal. Thirty-six bottles for $150? That's much better than 30 bottles for $175. So, the introduction of the irrelevant decoy, the new model, C, which you would never choose, eliminates your indecision. You choose B, the option clearly better than the decoy, and you walk out of the store confident in your purchase.

In summary, the decoy effect arises when the introduction of an unchosen option shifts what we value, specifically, biasing us toward an option that seems objectively better than the decoy. Marketers often use decoy effects, if not always as part of a conscious plan. And, some political scientists have argued that decoy effects can influence elections; for example, the introduction of a third-party candidate can shift undecided voters toward one of the two major-party candidates.

Now I'll move to a second decision bias: the compromise effect. Let's suppose that you are planning an extended stay in an expensive city, say London. You are searching for an apartment to rent for the duration of your visit, but suitable apartments are scarce, and you only have three options. Option 1 is in an ideal location right in the city center, but it is very expensive, close to the limit of your budget. Option 2 is a few tube stops out from the heart of the city and moderately priced. And Option 3 is at the very end of a tube line in the suburbs but very inexpensive. Which do you choose?

You've probably been in a situation that has this basic flavor. Here, there are no objectively better or worse options. The different options progressively trade off location and cost. What people tend to do in such situations is compromise. They tend to pick the intermediate choice, the one that isn't the closest nor the farthest, not the cheapest nor most expensive. They pick the option that seems like a compromise between the extremes.

Compromise is not always in our interest. When we compromise we don't get to take advantage of the extremes. It might actually be a good idea to pick the best-located hotel room, the cheapest bottle of wine, or the most reliable car. And if we consistently compromise, we can be exploited. A restaurant owner can make an expensive bottle of wine's price seem more reasonable by adding a rare and even-more-expensive bottle to the wine list, as we learned in our discussion of range effects.

Constructed preferences lead to biases like preference reversals, decoy effects, and compromise effects. So, why do we construct value, if it leads to so many mistakes? Why aren't our preferences more consistent and stable, so that we can look them up when needed?

There are two answers to these questions. The first answer is that these biases actually help us make decisions. Think about the sorts of scenarios I've described in this lecture: You are faced with a difficult choice between two or more similar items; those items have different advantages and disadvantages, but it is often hard to know what's really important.

So, if there's an option that you won't regret—either because it is clearly better than some other option or because it is a good compromise—you can choose it and get on with the rest of your life. None of these biases overrides all other factors that motivate your decision, instead, they tend to push you one way or the other when you are faced with a particularly difficult choice.

The second answer is a bit more complicated: Our preferences are constructed because that's how our brains have to work. We don't always know what factors are going to be relevant to a decision, in part because we have to value such dissimilar things: We weigh time versus effort, we trade money for food. To do this, we have to construct a common currency for value. Let's see how our brains do that.

Think back to the last time you felt hungry. Perhaps you skipped breakfast or worked through dinner or had a day full of exercise. Now suppose that I had offered you one of your favorite snacks right at that moment, perhaps a bag of pretzels, some fruit, or a candy bar. How much would you have paid for that snack? That seems like a simple question, right? Maybe you'd pay a dollar, maybe a few dollars, maybe only a few cents. But, if you were hungry and you were offered a favorite food, you'd pay something.

The economist-turned-neuroscientist Antonio Rangel, working with the marketing scientist Hilke Plassmann, has used this sort of simple decision to understand how the brain computes value. If you were a participant in one of their experiments, you'd fast for part of the day and then come to the research laboratory hungry. You'd then lie down in an fMRI scanner and view a series of familiar brand-name snacks: crackers, chips, candy, and so forth. When each snack appeared on the screen, you'd indicate how much you'd be willing to pay for it. And, when the experiment ended, you'd stay in the laboratory even hungrier than before. The researchers then choose one snack, randomly, and sell it to you for the price you were willing to pay.

This is a clever approach—take hungry people and sell them snacks while measuring their brain function—but it rests on the assumption that people will tell the truth about their subjective value. Setting up the experiment the wrong way, in contrast, could give people incentives to lie; they might underbid their true price so that they don't have to pay as much.

So, I want to take a quick digression to explain how researchers give people an incentive to tell the truth. A common technique is to use something called a Becker-DeGroot-Marschak (or BDM) auction, named after the economists who developed it more than 50 years ago. It introduces an element of randomness into the transaction, in order to prevent people from trying to shade their true willingness to pay.

Suppose that you are hungry, and when you are given the opportunity to buy a favored snack, say an apple, you'd be willing to pay as much as $2 for that apple, but not willing to pay more. The goal of the BDM auction is to ensure that you have no incentive to say anything other than $2, when asked how much you'd be willing to pay.

The key trick introduced by this auction is to determine the actual selling price randomly. So, after you bid $2 for that apple, the experimenter determines a price using a random number generator, such as rolling a die. If that random price is less than or equal to your bid, then you pay the random price. So, if the die comes up $1 then you'd only pay one dollar. If the random price is more than your bid, like $4, then there's no transaction.

Determining the selling price using a random number generator removes any incentive for people to misrepresent their true price. If you had underbid and said you were only willing to pay $1 for the apple, you'd lose the opportunity to buy the apple for $2. If you had overbid and said that you were willing to pay $3, you might get stuck paying more than you intended. So, behavioral economists use this tool to ensure that people tell the truth.

Now, Rangel, Plassmann, and their colleagues gave people many choices of this sort, snack after snack after snack. They found that a particular brain region's activation tracked how much people were willing to pay for each snack. We call that region the medial orbitofrontal cortex. To locate this region in your brain, just touch a finger to your lower forehead, right between your eyebrows. Your finger is pointing back toward your brain's orbitofrontal cortex, which refers to the bottom of your frontal lobes, just above the orbits of your eyes. Medial just means the middle of this region, along the gap between the two hemispheres of your brain. This area receives input from those dopamine neurons that I introduced in earlier lectures.

When I say activation in this region tracked willingness-to-pay, I mean something very simple: The activation was greater for snacks for which people would pay $3 than for $2 snacks, greater for snacks for which people would pay $2 than for $1 snacks, and so on. And, importantly, the activation was independent of the specific snacks on which people were bidding. Two different people might prefer completely different snacks—one person loves chocolate, the other chips—but they would both show increased activation to the specific snacks that they found most valuable.

Rangel, Plassmann, and others have shown that the activation of the medial orbitofrontal cortex tracks other sorts of willingness-to-pay, such as how much people will pay for physical goods like wine or electronics, or how much people will pay to avoid eating something unpleasant. One experiment even showed that this region's activation predicted the degree to which someone's soft drink preferences were influenced by brand labels, like Coca-Cola versus Pepsi. When someone sees the label of their preferred soft drink while consuming it, there's more activation in this region compared to when they do it on a blind taste-test.

These results are consistent with the idea that this brain region (the medial orbitofrontal cortex) represents a common currency for subjective value, how much something is worth to us regardless of what it is. Our brains use that common currency to make decisions between different sorts of goods, choosing whether we'd rather keep our money or buy a snack, rather spend our money on a television or a vacation. Even if our brains process food using one pathway and money using another, those different pathways each feed into the medial orbitofrontal cortex, so that different goods can be compared on the same scale.

Subsequent research has explored whether the construction of subjective value is a relatively automatic process, such as whether this brain region constructs value signals, even in the absence of explicit choice.

My colleagues and I wanted to evaluate whether people construct subjective value automatically, but we didn't want to look at decisions about physical goods like food or electronics. If we show people those sorts of goods in an experiment, we only get a sense of their anticipated value—the actual experienced value comes later when people consume or use the good. So, we decided to look at decisions about viewing faces.

Human faces are perhaps the single most universally motivating visual stimulus. We love looking at faces of our family, our friends, even of people unfamiliar to us. Advertisers know this. Flip through any magazine and you'll see faces staring back at you on page after page. In many advertisements, a model's face will be more noticeable than the product that's being sold. We took advantage of this bias in a two-part neuroscience experiment.

In the first part, each participant just passively viewed faces of varying attractiveness and passively received monetary rewards. They didn't have to do anything, just lie back and look at faces and receive some money. From this, we could examine how the brain responds to the experience of more-versus-less attractive faces and the experience of better-versus-worse monetary rewards. Then, in the second part of the experiment, the same participant made active decisions to spend some of the money they had just earned in order to view more attractive faces. From this, we could determine how much money they were willing to pay in order to see an attractive face.

If subjective value is being constructed automatically, then we should be able to use brain signals generated while people look at attractive faces to predict their later decisions about different attractive faces. That's exactly the brain signal we found in the medial orbitofrontal cortex (the same brain region that was thought to represent a common currency across different rewards). If someone was willing to pay a lot to view attractive faces, then the brain response in that region was much greater for faces than money. But, if someone would rather keep their money, then the brain response was greater for money than faces.

In summary, there's now strong evidence that value isn't something we just look up from some internal table. Our brains construct subjective value when we make decisions, and even when we are just going through our daily activities. Value isn't something stable, intrinsic, or immutable. This might seem inefficient, why bother with all that processing each time we have to make a decision?

Despite the additional time and energy required, constructed preferences provide an enormous advantage over something more static: They are extraordinarily flexible. What we prefer and, in turn, what we choose, can change depending on the current context in which we are making decisions. When our mood shifts or we enter a new environment, we start to prioritize new features of a complex decision, and our preferences change as well.

This scientific background leads to specific advice for decision making. In particular, I've emphasized that your value for something is constructed based on the questions you are asking. So, ask different questions. If you are trying to decide between two similar items, step back and ask yourself how much you'd be willing to pay for one of them. Then ask how much you'd be willing to pay for the other. You might come to a different decision, or have different insight about your decision, by thinking about items independently rather than by only thinking about them in comparison with each other.

If you are making a decision among a set of options, ask yourself how your decision might change if one or more of those options were just unavailable. Rule something out for the moment, and see if your preferences shift. Are you compromising for compromise's sake? Are you influenced by an irrelevant decoy?

You don't always know what's important to you. So use these processes of active construction to your advantage. Use them to simulate a slightly different sort of decision problem, so that you can learn more about your own preferences, whether you are valuing the right things, or whether you are fixating on some minor aspect of the decision.

This construction process is critical because we don't have perfect knowledge about the world, about goods we could purchase, or even about our own preferences. In the next lecture we'll consider the limits on our own decision-making abilities through an exploration of bounded rationality.

# Bounded Rationality—Knowing Your Limits
## Lecture 11

For many relatively simple decisions, all of us follow a compensatory process—we trade off rewards against risks, effort against time. But for complex decisions, we find a simple rule that helps us make sense of a complex situation. The use of simple rules to help make good decisions most of the time has become one of the major themes in behavioral economics. It's called bounded rationality. Our decision-making process isn't "rational," under the traditional economic definition of the term. But taking into account our limitations, or bounds, our decisions can sometimes look very rational.

**Limited Computational Abilities**

- The first major contributor to bounded rationality is our own limited computational abilities. A complex, powerful brain is an extraordinarily expensive luxury, metabolically speaking. In a very real sense, our brains want to do as little computation as possible, while still making good decisions.

- Computational limitations are a feature—an advantage—of our brains. Even though the brain has extraordinary computational power, with approximately 100 billion neurons and at least 1,000 times that number of connections between neurons, all that power isn't enough to perceive everything, to remember everything, and to weigh every cost and every benefit in an optimal fashion.

- Our brains aren't designed to process everything; doing so would be much, much too expensive. So, they simplify—when they can. They preferentially focus on some information, and throw away other information, to keep energy costs as low as possible.

- Simplification isn't always a good idea. If we take a complex problem and throw away the wrong information—for example, ignoring interest rates when deciding to refinance our home—

then we'll make very bad decisions. So, the main challenge lies in knowing what information we should process and what we should ignore. Our brains solve this challenge in an ingenious way: They take advantage of the structure in the world around us.

**The World Is Structured**

- Structure refers to the stable, predictable properties of the world around us. There are two main ways in which our world is structured, and that structure encourages us to simplify complex situations.

- First, the world is stable. This stability provides an important advantage: It helps us minimize the sort of processing we do. Every time you blink, which happens thousands of times each day, the world around you disappears and then reappears—but you don't notice it. That's because your brain assumes that the world is the same before and after the blink. It doesn't need to remember everything.

- Second, changes in the world are predictable. When we get new information, that information helps us predict what is likely to happen next. When we see lightning, we predict thunder. This prediction tends to be accurate because there are natural physical laws by which lightning causes thunder, and we have enough experience to have learned that causal relationship.

- This idea of structure will help when thinking about real-world decision making. Our processes of decision making, just like processes of perception or memory, assume that we make decisions in a structured world. That's what they evolved for—decisions in our natural world. However, many of our decisions don't have the same sort of structure. The stock market, for example, is neither stable nor predictable, and the very processes that help us make decisions in the natural world may hurt us when we make investments.

## Bounded Rationality

- The concept of bounded rationality grew, in large part, out of the work of Herbert Simon, who was recognized with the Nobel Prize in Economics. He was trained as a political scientist, and he made major contributions to psychology, computer science, and many other fields. Throughout his career, Simon continually questioned the assumptions of rational choice models, and he sought not merely to reject those models, but to create something new in their place.

- In 1955, Simon set forth his ideas in a paper called "A Behavioral Model of Rational Choice." Simon used the word "behavioral" in much the same sense, well before behavioral economics became a field of its own. The two main features of Simon's bounded rationality are limited search and satisficing.

- If you decided to buy a car today, how many options would you have? 10? 100? 1,000? More? In the U.S. market alone, there are several dozen manufacturers, each with many models, and each of those models has a bewildering array of optional features for you to choose from. You can't possibly evaluate every possible car against every other car; you have neither the time nor the energy to do so.

- How can you make a good decision? Let's think about the search process. When decision scientists or psychologists talk about the word "search," they mean "exploring the set of options." We need some process for narrowing those overwhelming options to a manageable set. So, instead of considering as much information as possible, we try to limit our search. We focus on a particular

**When shopping for a new car, you could never weigh all of the models, colors, and features that exist against each other.**

category (sports cars), or a desired feature (fuel economy), or a preferred manufacturer. Doing so might limit our options down to only a handful of cars.

- Suppose that you've identified three models that seem like reasonable options. How do you pick one? A truly rational decision maker would approach the problem by listing every advantage and disadvantage and determining how those factors trade off against each other.

- Simon recognized that this approach was mathematically complex, time consuming, and likely to emphasize minor factors at the expense of what's really important. So, he proposed an alternative approach, which he called satisficing—a neologism that combines the words "satisfy" and "suffice." It's a complicated word that describes a common-sense idea: good enough.

- Suppose that you are trying to decide between three car models, and there are several features that are most important to you: performance, reliability, and fuel efficiency. For each feature that you are evaluating, Simon argued, you set up some aspiration level, and you judge each car model based on whether its feature is better or worse than your aspiration.

- So, for fuel efficiency, you might judge that more than 30 miles per gallon is "good enough." For performance, your aspiration level is more subjective; you want the car to feel both responsive and fun during your test drive.

- When you evaluate your three models, you find out that one satisfies your aspirations. It is "good enough" on every factor—fuel efficient, fun to drive, reliable—so you choose it, and you drive off the lot excited about your new purchase.

- This might have seemed like a perfectly reasonable way to purchase a car: Limit your search to a few models and then find something that is good enough on each feature that matters. In addition, it is reasonable; it doesn't require any complex computations or take an inordinate amount of time. But it isn't optimal. You can make mistakes.

- A limited search process will, most of the time, lead you to a set of good options. But it can miss the best option. Your search might be unnecessarily constrained by your own biases or by your limited knowledge. If you are looking only at sports cars, then you might never consider a car classified as a high-performance sedan, even if that car would otherwise be perfect for you.

- Satisficing has a critical limitation: Using an aspiration level throws away potentially important information. Suppose that you evaluated cars based on only two factors: gas mileage and reliability. For gas mileage, your aspiration level was 30 miles per gallon, and for reliability, your aspiration level was one of the top 10 most reliable cars, as listed in a major consumer magazine. You look at two cars, A and B. Car A meets both criteria while B only meets the reliability criterion. So, A is better, right? Not necessarily.

- Suppose car A gets 31 miles per gallon and is the 10th most reliable. It's clearly a good enough option, given your criteria. But car B gets 28 miles per gallon and is the single most reliable car. The difference between 31 miles per gallon and 28 miles per gallon probably isn't a big deal, but the difference between the first and 10th most reliable cars probably does matter. So, setting an aspiration level tends to exaggerate differences right around that aspiration level, while ignoring differences above or below.

- Satisficing isn't perfect. But it isn't supposed to be perfect, or optimal, or mistake-free. Instead, it's supposed to help us simplify complex decisions to something manageable—by limiting our search and by satisficing—so that we make a decision that's good enough.

- Satisficing can particularly help us when the world is structured in our favor, and we're more likely to use satisficing or another heuristic when we are overwhelmed, fatigued, or otherwise have impaired processing.

**Core Tension**

- Bounded rationality is an extraordinarily important idea. In some ways, it's at the very core of behavioral economics. We aren't omniscient, foresighted, and economically rational; we're just humans, simple and flawed, trying to make our way through a complex world. Bounded rationality argues that we won't make optimal decisions—but that we can make decisions that are good enough. So, embrace your limitations.

- Simplify as much as you can, but not too much. When you are making decisions about matters in the real world—about matters with which you are familiar, about matters that are stable and predictable—then simplifying can help you make much better decisions. It's often much better to try to identify the few most important factors in a decision rather than to spend energy and time identifying all factors that play into a decision.

- When the stakes are small or you are under time pressure or you just don't have much information, then a satisficing approach can help you make a decision that's good enough—and let you move on to more important decisions.

## Suggested Reading

Gigerenzer, Todd, and T. A. R. Group, *Simple Heuristics That Make Us Smart*.

Simon, *Models of Man*.

## Questions to Consider

1. How can using an aspiration level simplify our decisions? What problems could it introduce?

2. What are the parallels between the solution to the best-choice problem and human dating and marriage?

# Bounded Rationality—Knowing Your Limits
## Lecture 11—Transcript

Welcome back. In an earlier lecture, we discussed the often-misunderstood idea of rationality. Rational doesn't mean that our decisions are entirely based on reason, but that they are consistent; they weigh different potential outcomes in a manner that maximally reaches our goals. In this lecture, we're going to discuss how that model of rationality doesn't always match how we approach real-world decisions.

Benjamin Franklin, the American founding father and polymath, was famous for his aphorisms: simple rules for everyday life. Within the pages of *Poor Richard's Almanack*, he set forth proverbs that contained much wisdom in few words: "Lend money to an enemy and you will gain him, to a friend and you will lose him." "Necessity never made a good bargain." "Fish and visitors stink in three days."

At their core, proverbs are simplifications. They give us rough rules to follow, rules that seem like sound advice most of the time. "Lend money to an enemy and you will gain him, to a friend and you will lose him."

We can easily appreciate the wisdom in that simple statement. If we lend money to an enemy they'll appreciate our kindness, and start seeing us more favorably. We're no longer their enemy, but someone connected to them. But, when we lend money to a friend, there's a risk that that money will change our relationship; we're no longer just a friend but a partner in an economic transaction.

Benjamin Franklin was famous for these proverbs. Even though he was simultaneously one of the most famous statesmen and scientists of his time, we still think of him as the ultimate American pragmatist, someone whose simple rules for life helped innumerable people through complex decisions. But, ironically, Franklin didn't necessarily follow his own simple rules when he made decisions.

In the 1770s Franklin corresponded with the English scholar Joseph Priestley. Like Franklin, Priestley was a polymath who made seminal contributions to diverse fields. As a chemist, Priestley invented the method for infusing carbon dioxide into drinking water, creating soda water; as a philosopher, his writings set the stage for the development of utilitarianism. Priestley treated Franklin as a scientific mentor and continually sought out his advice.

In one 1772 letter to Priestley, Franklin explained his method for making complex decisions. Franklin first took a piece of paper and drew a line down the middle. He wrote "pro" at the top left of the paper and "con" at the top right. Then, over the next few days, each time he thought of a reason for or against the decision, he wrote that reason in the appropriate column. Once he thought that he had listed every reason that could influence his decision, he then estimated the weight that should be given to each reason.

If the weight of a pro reason was approximately equal to that of a con reason, then he drew lines through them, to cancel them out. He even allowed for differences in relative weight: if two of the pro reasons seemed equivalent to three of the con reasons, he'd cancel all of those out. Once he had cancelled everything out that he could, he'd look to see what side had something left, and he'd choose accordingly. What a remarkable process! He listed factors that could influence his decision, estimated their weights, and then effectively just added everything up in what he called a "prudential algebra."

Let's think for a moment about the two types of advice given by Benjamin Franklin. The first type is evident in this letter to Priestley. Franklin describes trying to obtain as much information as possible, and then trading off positive and negative factors against each other in a rational, almost mathematical manner. It's a prototypic example of what behavioral economists now call compensatory decision making: The advantages of a particular choice can trade off against, and compensate for, its disadvantages.

But, through the proverbs in *Poor Richard's Almanack*, Franklin provides advice of a very different type. He gives us simple rules that help make decisions. When we follow those rules, we aren't obtaining as much information as possible. We aren't adopting a complex algebraic strategy for weighing the pros and cons of our decision. By following the proverb, we'd make good decisions most of the time, while avoiding some obvious mistakes and without having to think too hard. These proverbs support what behavioral economists call heuristic decision making: following simple rules that usually lead to good decisions.

So far, this course has focused primarily on compensatory decision making. I've described different factors (like reward, probability, risk, and time) that feed into our decisions, and how we integrate those factors, consciously and subconsciously, to reach a decision. For many relatively simple decisions, all of us follow a compensatory process; we trade off rewards against risks, effort against time.

But, for complex decisions, we're not Benjamin Franklin. Few people ever adopt the sort of explicit calculus necessary for true compensatory decision making. Instead, we simplify. We find a simple rule that helps us make sense of a complex situation. The use of simple rules to help make good decisions most of the time has become one of the major themes in behavioral economics. It's called bounded rationality.

The term "bounded rationality" makes sense because our decision making process isn't rational, at least under the traditional economic definition. We aren't compensatory decision makers. We aren't consistent decision makers. And, we surely aren't optimal decision makers. We don't always choose the option that is best for us. We are, however, surprisingly good at taking complex situations and simplifying them into something manageable. Taking into account our limitations, or bounds, our decisions can sometimes look very rational.

Let me begin by introducing the first major contributor to bounded rationality: our own limited computational abilities. To understand how we are limited, we'll need to take a quick digression into neurobiology. Let's take a hypothetical average adult male in the United States. This man is about 5' 10" tall and weighs about 200 pounds. How much does his brain weigh?

This isn't something that we often think about, how much a brain weighs. So, the answer might not be obvious or even intuitive. In an average adult male, the brain weighs only about three to four pounds, or a little less than 2 percent of the total body weight.

Two percent? That's not much. But that man's brain uses up about 20 percent of his body's energy supply. From birth to death, day after day, that two percent of his body requires 20 percent of all the calories he consumes, and almost all of the human brain's energy needs go to support information processing. A complex, powerful brain is an extraordinarily expensive luxury, metabolically speaking.

What do I mean by expensive? Think about the primary challenges faced by your pre-modern ancestors: finding food, staying warm, avoiding predators. That 20 percent of the body's energy represents 20 percent of all the food found over the course of the year. Keeping that percentage as small as possible meant fewer risky hunts, greater resilience to times of scarcity, and fewer risks of daily life. So, in a very real sense, our brains want to do as little computation as possible, while still making good decisions.

I want to emphasize this point, because there's often misinformation in popular books and news stories about the brain. Computational limitations are a feature, an advantage of our brains. Even though the brain has extraordinary computational power—with approximately 100 billion neurons and at least 1,000 times that number of connections between neurons—all that power isn't enough to perceive everything, to remember everything, and to weigh every cost and every benefit in an optimal fashion.

Our brains aren't designed to process everything. Doing so would be much, much too expensive. So, they simplify when they can. They preferentially focus on some information, and throw away other information, to keep energy costs as low as possible.

Now, simplification isn't always a good idea. If we take a complex problem and throw away the wrong information, say, ignoring interest rates when deciding to refinance our home, then we'll make very bad decisions. So, the main challenge lies in knowing what information we should process and what we should ignore. Our brains solve this challenge in an ingenious way: they take advantage of the structure in the world around us.

What do I mean by structure? Structure refers to the stable, predictable properties of the world around us. Let me illustrate the two main ways in which our world is structured, and how that structure encourages us to simplify complex situations.

Imagine that you are walking alone down a well-trodden path through a dense hardwood forest. You hear a noise off to your left. You catch your breath and turn your head in the direction of the noise while you keep walking. Through the trees, you see something large walking parallel to your path, not more than 50 feet away. It's a deer, so you relax and watch as it disappears into the forest.

Now, think for a moment: What information actually entered your brain? That deer was 50 feet away and constantly passing behind tree after tree. Even though you never had an uninterrupted view of the deer's entire body, your visual system automatically assumes that you see the same deer each time it passes behind a tree.

Let's continue walking down the forest path. As you walk, you notice that the clouds above seem to be darkening. The wind picks up considerably, and the air starts to feel slightly damp. Then, you see a flash of lightning in the distance, and you brace yourself for what comes next: the sound of thunder. In this example, we can see the two main types of structure.

First, the world is stable. You see one deer walking behind tree after tree, because that's the simplest explanation. A deer doesn't teleport from location to location like an animation on a computer screen. You know it is still there, even as it moves out of view behind a tree.

This stability provides an important advantage; it helps us minimize the sort of processing we do. Close your eyes right now then open them again. Every time you blink, which happens thousands of times each day, the world around you disappears and then reappears, but you don't notice it. That's because you brain assumes that the world is the same before and after the blink. It doesn't need to remember everything.

Second, changes in the world are predictable. When we get new information, that information helps us predict what is likely to happen next. We see lightning, we predict thunder. This prediction tends to be accurate because there are natural physical laws by which lightning causes thunder, and we have enough experience to have learned that causal relationship.

I am emphasizing this idea of structure because it will help when thinking about real-world decision making. Our processes of decision making, just like processes of perception or memory, assume that we make decisions in a structured world. That's what they evolved for, decisions in our natural world. But, many of our decisions don't have the same sort of structure. The stock market, for example, is neither stable nor predictable, and the very processes that help us make decisions in the natural world may hurt us when we make investments.

So now, let's turn to the specific case of bounded rationality. This concept grew in large part out of the work of Herbert Simon. It is hard to characterize Herbert Simon and his work. He was clearly an economist—at least, he was recognized with the Nobel Prize in economics—but he was trained as a political scientist, and he made major contributions to psychology, computer science, and many other fields. Throughout his career, Simon continually questioned the assumptions of rational choice models, and he sought not merely to reject those models, but to create something new in their place.

In 1955, Simon set forth his ideas in a paper called "A Behavioral Model of Rational Choice." Notice that word "behavioral." Simon uses it, in much the same sense, well before behavioral economics becomes a field of its own. Let's look at the two main features of Simon's bounded rationality, limited search and satisficing, within a real-world example of a familiar and complex decision: buying a car.

If you decided to buy a car today, how many options would you have? 10? 100? 1,000? Probably more. In the U.S. market alone, there are several dozen manufacturers, each with many models, and each of those models has a bewildering array of optional features for you to choose from. You can't possibly evaluate every possible car against every other car. You have neither the time nor energy to do so.

So, how can you make a good decision? Let's think about the search process. When decision scientists or psychologists talk about search, they mean exploring the set of options. We need some process for narrowing those overwhelming options to a manageable set. So, instead of considering as much information as possible, we try to limit our search. We focus on a particular category (sports cars) or a desired feature (fuel economy) or a preferred manufacturer. Doing so might limit our options down to only a handful of cars.

Now suppose that you've identified three models that seem like reasonable options. How do you pick one? A truly rational decision maker would approach the problem much like Benjamin Franklin, listing every advantage and disadvantage and determining how those factors trade off against each other. Simon recognized that this approach was mathematically complex, time consuming, and likely to emphasize minor factors at the expense of what's really important. So, he proposed an alternative approach, which he called satisficing. Satisficing is a neologism that combines "satisfy" and "suffice." It's a complicated word that describes a common-sense idea: good enough.

Suppose that you are trying to decide between three car models, and there are several features that are most important to you: say, performance, reliability, and fuel efficiency. For each feature that you are evaluating, Simon argued, you set up some aspiration level, and you judge each car model based on whether its feature is better or worse than your aspiration. So, for fuel efficiency, you might judge that more than 30 miles per gallon is good enough. For performance, your aspiration level is more subjective. You want the car to feel both responsive and fun during your test drive, and so on.

When you evaluate your three models, you find out that one satisfies your aspirations. It is good enough on every factor (fuel efficient, fun to drive, and reliable) and so you choose it, and you drive off the lot excited about your new purchase. This might have seemed like a perfectly reasonable way to purchase a car: limit your search to a few models and then find something that is good enough on each feature that matters. And, it is reasonable; it didn't require any complex computations or take an inordinate amount of time. But it isn't optimal. You can make mistakes.

A limited search process will, most of the time, lead you to a set of good options. But it can miss the best option. Your search might be unnecessarily constrained by your own biases or by your limited knowledge. If you are looking only at sports cars, you might never consider a car classified as a high-performance sedan, even if that car would otherwise be perfect for you.

And, satisficing has a critical limitation: Using an aspiration level throws away potentially important information. Let's suppose for the moment that you evaluated cars based on only two factors: gas mileage and reliability. For gas mileage, your aspiration level was 30 miles per gallon, and for reliability your aspiration level was one of the top 10 most reliable cars, as listed in a major consumer magazine. You look at two cars, A and B. A meets both criteria, while B only meets the reliability criterion. So, A is better, right?

Not necessarily. Suppose car A gets 31 miles per gallon and is the 10th most reliable. It's clearly a good enough option, given your criteria. But car B gets 28 miles per gallon and is the single most reliable car. Now the difference between 31 miles per gallon and 28 miles per gallon probably isn't a big deal; in fact, as we'll see in a future lecture, it's much less important than it might seem. But, the difference between the 1st and 10th most reliable cars probably does matter. So, setting an aspiration level tends to exaggerate differences right around that aspiration level, while ignoring differences above or below.

So, satisficing isn't perfect. But it isn't supposed to be perfect, or optimal, or mistake free. Instead, it's supposed to help us simplify complex decisions to something manageable by limiting our search and by satisficing, so that we make a decision that's good enough.

Satisficing can particularly help us when the world is structured in our favor, and we're more likely to use satisficing or another heuristic when we are overwhelmed, fatigued, or otherwise have impaired processing.

For an example, let's stay in the domain of car purchases but move to Germany. There, customers of a major manufacturer can create a car to their exact specification. They log into a computer program and choose the interior color, exterior color, the steering wheel, even the type of rearview mirror and style of gearshift knob. There are 67 decisions in all, some involving a list of more than 50 possible options and others involving only a few options.

The manufacturer helps simplify the process by indicating a default option at the top of each list, and, incidentally, this default is almost always the cheapest option. Let me emphasize this: The manufacturer has structured the computer program so that its default options are usually in the consumer's interest.

The decision scientist Jonathan Levav and his colleagues worked with the manufacturer to vary the way the computer program presented these decisions. Some people began with relatively complex choices, others began with relatively simple choices, but they all faced the same choices, just in different orders.

Even though the order in which decisions are presented shouldn't influence real-world choices, especially for something as important as a car purchase, it does. People start off carefully considering each option—they spend more time and are less likely to choose the defaults. But, as they move through the computer program, they can't process all of the information, so they get faster and start picking the default option. And, does this matter? Yes. In one study of 450 real-world car buyers, the people who started off choosing expensive and complex features (interior and exterior colors and the engine) created cars that cost about 1,500 euros more on average, compared to people who ended by making those decisions.

So, as people make this series of choices, they move from a more analytic approach to decision making to a more heuristic approach, they become more and more likely to pick the default option. Those people who used the default recommendations for the expensive features ended with less expensive but still high-quality cars.

We also become more likely to use satisficing when we can't focus our attention on the important features of a decision. There's been quite a lot of work on the idea of unconscious decision making: that we might make better decisions by not consciously deliberating on our alternatives. This idea has been studied in a variety of domains from, yes, car purchases to apartment rentals to simple consumer choice.

Most experiments share a similar flavor. If you were a participant, you'd come into the laboratory, sit in front of a computer screen, and see a series of statements describing the features of two options. "Car A has good gas mileage." "Car B has 6 cup holders". Those features are presented in a long list, and some features would be more useful for your decision (like gas mileage) and some would be less useful (like the cup holders). One of the cars is objectively better than the other, based on the features presented.

After you saw all of the features in the list, then you'd either be given the opportunity to deliberate on your decision for some time, perhaps 15 minutes, or would be distracted from that decision by another task, such as solving crossword puzzles. Then, you'd get to indicate what option was better. The key finding is that when people are distracted, they are often more likely to choose the objectively better option. Conversely, active deliberation on the decision seems to lead to more mistakes.

The phenomenon of unconscious decision making has attracted both attention and criticism. On the one hand, it fits our intuitions; we often advise our friends to relax and think about something else before making a tough decision. But on the other hand, there's an ongoing debate about why this phenomenon might work, if it does.

Now let's approach this phenomenon from the lens of bounded rationality. Suppose that there were two cars, each with 12 features, and you saw each of those features one after another in a long list. You can't remember everything in that list, that's beyond the scope of most people's memory. So, what happens when you are distracted? You forget (and what you forget are the minor details) the unimportant factors, the cup holders. Forgetting can be a very good thing. If distraction causes us to lose the less relevant information, but still hold onto the most important features, then we might indeed make better decisions.

Bounded rationality is an extraordinarily important idea. In some ways it's at the very core of behavioral economics —we aren't omniscient, foresighted, and economically rational. We're just humans, simple and flawed, trying to make our way through a complex world. Bounded rationality argues that we won't make optimal decisions but that we can make decisions that are good enough. So, embrace your limitations!

Suppose that you are a hiring manager who needs to find the best candidate for an important position. It's hard enough to hire the best person, but let's make this problem even harder. Let's suppose that you are sitting at a table at a job fair. And, let's further suppose that there is a line of 1,000 people snaking away from your table. When each person steps up to the table, you need to interview them, and then make an up or down decision on the spot. Either hire them, or let them walk away, where they'll be hired to another job and lost to your company. What is the probability that you could hire the single best person out of that 1,000? And, how can you maximize your chances?

This is known as the best-choice problem, and it turns out to have a simple, elegant, and encouraging solution. You should interview and reject the first 367 people in line, and then choose the first person who is better than the best so far. Why is this? When you start interviewing people, you don't know what the best person might look like, so you should spend some of your time searching, determining the quality of candidates without choosing one. Then, when you have enough information, you can satisfice: pick the first candidate who is better than what you've seen so far.

This two-step process maximizes your chances of picking the best person. Why reject the first 367, not more, not fewer? That quantity is 1,000 divided by $e$, the fundamental mathematical constant. In fact, it gives you a 36.7 percent (or 1 over $e$) chance of finding that person. That seems pretty good.

As a final message, simplify as much as you can, but not too much. When you are making decisions about matters in the real world, about matters with which you are familiar, about matters that are stable and predictable, then simplifying can help you make much better decisions. It's often much better to try to identify the few most important factors in a decision, rather than to spend energy and time identifying all factors that play into a decision. And, when the stakes are small or you are under time pressure or you just don't have much information, then a satisficing approach can help you make a decision that's good enough, and let you move on to more important decisions.

Benjamin Franklin wasn't the only great thinker of the ages to make decisions by listing pros and cons. Charles Darwin did it, too, one time, when he was deciding to get married to Emma Wedgwood. He listed the pros (a constant companion, family life and conversation, children) and he listed the cons (a loss of freedom, financial pressures). The list was strongly weighted toward the more numerous negative consequences, and many of the positive outcomes were tinged with concern, such as the expense and anxiety of children. But, in the end, Darwin made a simple decision: He married Emma, and they remained happily married with 10 children for the rest of his days.

We aren't rational. We're boundedly rational. We use simple rules, called heuristics, because those rules help us make decisions that are good enough, most of the time. In the next lecture, we'll learn about some of the most common heuristics that influence our decision making and that can sometimes lead our decisions astray.

# Heuristics and Biases
## Lecture 12

Heuristics are often considered to be special cases of bounded rationality. Heuristics aren't weaknesses or failures in our decision making; they are tools that help us make good decisions most of the time. The key challenge lies in using the right tool in the right situation. This lecture will focus on four of the most important heuristics, each of which provides a tool for overcoming a particular sort of cognitive limitation: the familiarity heuristic, which involves memory; the anchoring heuristic, which involves valuation and reference points; the representativeness heuristic, which involves the estimation of probabilities; and the affect heuristic, which involves simulation of feelings and emotions.

**The Familiarity Heuristic**

- The familiarity heuristic means that we recognize something. The familiarity heuristic makes brand-name consumer products more desirable and violent crimes seem more common than they really are. Familiarity comes from the ease with which something is available to be brought to mind, and thus, it is sometimes called the availability heuristic.

- The decision scientist Gerd Gigerenzer has shown that being too familiar with what's being judged can actually undermine the benefits of familiarity. When making judgments like which city is larger or which author has sold more books, Gigerenzer and colleagues showed that the most accurate judgments would be made by someone who's only familiar with about 75 percent of the items being judged; that person would typically do better than someone who has at least heard of every item before.

- Familiarity provides such a powerful tool because of the structure in the world around us. If you ask casual sports fans to predict the winners of Wimbledon tennis matches, they often simply pick the player with whom they are familiar. These simple judgments of familiarity have been shown to be good predictors of who will win a match and even do slightly better than the actual player rankings.

- The familiarity heuristic is also connected to our judgments of probability. People tend to overestimate small probabilities but underestimate large probabilities. This can lead to a strange phenomenon called subadditivity, in which the total probability (which must be 100 percent) ends up less than the sum of the individual probabilities.

- The familiarity heuristic affects our economic decisions, too. People overvalue and are more likely to invest in the stocks of familiar companies. This can lead to very bad outcomes. In the extreme, investing one's retirement savings in one's own company stock carries a massive risk: For example, a catastrophic event that bankrupted the company could also eliminate all retirement savings.

- But there is other evidence from behavioral finance that investors whose portfolios have a bias toward familiar companies, such as those from one's own geographic area, obtain slightly higher returns than investors who show no familiarity bias. Familiarity involves the use of information, and that information might help some investors.

**The Anchoring Heuristic**

- The second heuristic is anchoring. This heuristic uses some initial estimate as an anchor to bias our subsequent judgments. We use anchoring when we are uncertain: We don't have all the information needed to make an accurate judgment, so we latch onto anything given to us.

- Does our galaxy contain more or fewer than 100,000 stars? How many stars are in the Milky Way Galaxy? This second question is not something for which you have personal experience. Even if you've seen the Milky Way, you've only seen a small fraction of its stars. And, unless you are an astronomy buff, you probably haven't encountered the answer recently, so you can't give an estimate based on explicit knowledge. Without personal experience or explicit knowledge, you need to find something on which you can base your estimate.

- The first question provided a number—100,000—which is an anchor. It seems like a big number, and if you're being asked about it, then you might infer that it's close to the right answer. So, when faced with a difficult judgment like determining how many stars are in the Milky Way, people often begin with any number given to them and then adjust their estimate upward or downward from that anchor. The anchor, like its nautical namesake, constrains how far a subsequent estimate can move.

- No one knows exactly, but the current best estimates are that there are several hundred billion stars in the Milky Way Galaxy. In this case, the anchor given was about one million times too low—so it typically leads to estimates that are likewise far too low. If you had been given a much larger anchor—Does our galaxy contain more or fewer than a *trillion* stars?—then the estimates would have been much, much higher.

**The Milky Way Galaxy consists of several hundred billion stars, one of which is Earth's Sun.**

- Marketers use anchoring when pricing goods that are rare, infrequently purchased, or difficult to value. Consider expensive furniture or jewelry at a specialty store. Often, these items will be displayed with a very high suggested retail price. That price might have no connection to reality; it doesn't represent the cost of manufacturing, consumer demand, or anything else meaningful. It's just an anchor. The store wants you to start with that suggested retail price and then negotiate downward. They know that providing a very high anchor increases customers' estimates of value and leads to higher eventual selling prices.

- It is important to emphasize that anchoring works even if there is no meaningful connection between the anchor and the subsequent estimates. In some laboratory experiments, researchers have generated anchors by asking people to spin a roulette wheel or to write down the last two digits of their social security number. Even when the anchor is generated in a completely random fashion, it still can influence behavior. Furthermore, anchoring influences real-world economic transactions, even those with extraordinarily large stakes.

## The Representativeness Heuristic

- The third heuristic is the representativeness heuristic, which helps us estimate probabilities through the following simple rule: Prototypic events are likely events.

- The following illustrates this heuristic; it is a description of a person named Rebecca. Think about what sort of job she might have.
    - Rebecca is intelligent, extroverted, and gregarious. From an early age, she always liked looking at the night sky and speculating about life on other planets. In school, she was always strong in math and science courses, although she was a good writer as well. As an adult, she loves going *fast*—running, riding horses, and even driving fast cars are all passions. She is willing to take risks, especially if they allow her to pursue her dreams. And, she's a good communicator, especially for things she feels passionate about.

- How likely is it that Rebecca is a teacher? An astronaut? A lawyer? A science writer?

- This example has been adapted from the work of Daniel Kahneman and Amos Tversky, two pioneering figures in behavioral economics. When people are given scenarios like this, they commonly report that Rebecca is most probably an astronaut—she seems like a prototypic astronaut. She's interested in science and math and has a love for the night sky and life on other planets. She's willing to take risks and is passionate about her work. Next most probable would be science writer; she loves science and is a good writer and communicator, after all. And least probable would be lawyer and teacher.

- Now, have you ever met an astronaut? Do you have an astronaut living on your street? At any one time, the United States has about 100 people whose current job description is "astronaut"—that's it. By comparison, there are several million teachers, more than a million lawyers, and thousands of science writers.

- Even if Rebecca seems most representative of an astronaut, there are so few astronauts that it is much more likely that she's a teacher or lawyer. There are surely many more science-oriented and risk-loving teachers and lawyers than there are astronauts.

- The representativeness heuristic fails here because these professions differ dramatically in their base rates. Teachers and lawyers are much, much more common than science writers and especially astronauts.

- So, why do we rely on representativeness when it leads to such obvious mistakes? This heuristic exists because it is a fast and simple guide to probability. Students with good grades are more likely to do well in medical school. The leading brand of toothpaste is a good product. Prototypes are often prototypes for a reason; they're often the best or most common member of some category.

- Representativeness fails when prototypes are rare—like astronauts—but succeeds when prototypes are common. That rule provides clear guidance: Be wary when representativeness points you toward some rare conclusion.

## The Affect Heuristic
- The final heuristic is that of the affect heuristic. To a psychologist, "affect" means the internal sense of emotion—what we feel, our

mood. The affect heuristic involves choosing one option over another based on their anticipated effects on our emotional state.

- Emotions don't always get in the way of our decisions; they can be extraordinarily useful. When we use the affect heuristic, we are simulating our future self—and what our future self might feel after we've made our decision. To the degree that our simulations are accurate, we can check out the consequences of our decisions before we even make them.

- Simulation is one of the most powerful tools we have for making good decisions. The neuroscientist Antonio Damasio recognized this in his somatic marker hypothesis. He argued that our brains store representations of our feelings and the associated body states, which he called somatic markers.

- For example, when we walk down an unfamiliar dark alley at night, our brains store the feeling of dread, the racing heartbeat, and the sense of alertness that accompany our risky action. The next time we approach a dark alley at night, our brains can bring to mind the stored somatic marker. We can simulate that feeling—of taking that risk—before we ever step foot down the alley, and then we can choose another path home.

- Simulation is a fast process. We don't have to consciously think about it; we just do it automatically. The affect heuristic often leads to good choices, in that we can anticipate and avoid decisions that would make us unhappy, regretful, or angry. However, it fails when negative consequences of our decisions are particularly easy to bring to mind or when we overestimate short-term mood at the expense of long-term satisfaction.

### Suggested Reading

Beggs and Graddy, "Anchoring Effects."

Tversky and Kahneman, "Judgment under Uncertainty."

## Questions to Consider

1. Why do people use heuristics, given the mistakes that can be made?

2. How can we use our emotions to improve our decisions?

# Heuristics and Biases
## Lecture 12—Transcript

It's easy to think that we humans are poor decision makers. If you read popular press books on decision making, you'll hear tale after tale about how we misuse probability, rely on the wrong information, and can be most confident when we are most wrong. You might find it a wonder that our species has survived this long. But, as I've stressed throughout this course, we aren't poor decision makers, at least for the sorts of decisions for which our species evolved. Yes, we all make mistakes, but those mistakes don't reveal our weaknesses but our strengths.

In today's lecture, I'll explore the topic that has received the most attention, and probably generated the most misinformation, in popular treatments of decision making: the use of heuristics.

As introduced in the previous lecture, heuristics are tools for optimizing the process of decision making. Heuristics change how we approach decisions by ignoring some available information (or prioritizing other information) so that decisions can be made faster, with less effort, or more accurately. For example, suppose that you were asked to guess the winner of this week's marquee football game, say, the Steelers are playing the Packers. If you were a football fan, you might have a ready answer based upon these teams' past history, their perceived strengths and weaknesses, and even knowledge about relevant statistics.

But let's also suppose that you aren't a football fan. You can't rely on any of that useful information, so you have to guess. You know about one of the players on the Steelers (he's famous, and always in funny commercials), so you pick the Steelers to win. This represents something that decision scientists call the familiarity heuristic. People think that familiar things are better: more valuable, more frequent, and in the case of sports, more likely to win.

Let's see how this decision fits the definition of a heuristic. Does it ignore some available information? Yes, almost all information that could be useful—who is favored in the game, who is the home team, and everything else—is simply ignored. Does it prioritize other information? Yes, the decision uses one fact: There's a famous player on the Steelers. Was the decision made faster, with less effort? Yes, it is fast and almost effortless to think, "I've heard of that player on the Steelers."

And last, was the decision accurate? Your task was to predict the winner of a football game. No one knows ahead of time which team will win, there's too much uncertainty involved. So, accuracy doesn't mean, "Does the heuristic make the right prediction?" Instead, we have to ask, "Does using the heuristic improve our chances of making the right prediction?" In this specific case, is familiarity a positive predictor of winning?

Let me hold off on answering that specific question for a few minutes. But for now, I can say that heuristics are almost always faster, almost always less effortful, and often but not always more accurate than other decision-making processes.

Heuristics are not necessarily irrational, at least not in the lay sense of that word. When we don't have much information toward a decision, using a heuristic may be our best approach. And, as I'll describe in several examples, heuristics often work well even when we do have lots of information.

Nor are heuristics necessarily emotional. Some heuristics involve emotion, but most do not, and one can make fast, low-effort decisions without ever feeling sadness or anger or any other emotion.

Heuristics are often considered to be special cases of bounded rationality. Recall that bounded rationality arises from the interaction of two factors: our own computational limitations and the existence of structure in the environment. Because of the many ways in which our computational abilities are limited and the many sorts of structure in the environment, many different sorts of heuristics have been identified.

I'll focus today on four of the most important heuristics, each of which provides a tool for overcoming a particular sort of cognitive limitation. These four heuristics are

- The familiarity heuristic, which involves memory;

- The anchoring heuristic, which involves valuation and reference points;

- The representativeness heuristic, which involves the estimation of probabilities; and

- The affect heuristic, which involves simulation of feelings and emotions.

Let's start with the familiarity heuristic. By familiarity, I specifically mean that we recognize something.

The familiarity heuristic makes brand-name consumer products more desirable, makes violent crimes seem more common than they really are, and made the casual football fan choose the Steelers over the Packers in our opening example. Familiarity comes from the ease with which something is available to be brought to mind, and thus it is sometimes called the availability heuristic.

In one study of familiarity, researchers in Germany tested German students on simple questions about the relative population of cities in the United States, questions like "Which is larger, Philadelphia or Lubbock, Texas?" They also tested them on cities in Germany: "Which is larger, Frankfurt or Essen?" Obviously, the German students knew much more about cities in Germany than about cities in the United States. But they actually got a higher proportion of questions correct when asked about the U.S. cities. How can that be possible?

To understand why, let's think for a moment about what familiarity means. Most of us are familiar with New York City, New York, but not with New Bern, North Carolina. We are familiar with the writing of Charles Dickens but not necessarily that of Crockett Johnson. And, we are familiar with elephants but not with pangolins.

What makes us more familiar with New York compared to New Bern? New York is populous, a world hub for commerce and information, and a constant presence in the news media. You've been exposed to New York City, in one way or another, thousands of times in your life. New Bern is a former capital of North Carolina and the birthplace of Pepsi Cola. It's a charming small town, but unless you've had a specific reason to go there, you may never have heard of it.

Let me emphasize this: Our sense of familiarity develops because of the structure in the world around us. Large cities tend to be culturally or economically significant, and they are more likely to be familiar.

So, let's think about those German students. When they were asked questions about cities in Germany, they were familiar with all of those cities, so familiarity wasn't a useful clue as to which one was larger. But when the same students were asked about U.S. cities, then suddenly their sense of familiarity became a good guide to population. "Which is larger: Philadelphia, Pennsylvania, or Lubbock, Texas?" That's an easy question for someone from Germany, the familiar city is the larger one. And familiarity turns out to be a wonderful guide for answering all sorts of similar questions.

"Which mammal lives longer: An elephant or a pangolin?" When researchers asked people questions like this one, people usually just chose the animal that was familiar to them, and they were right most of the time. We are more familiar with larger, longer-lived animals, and so our sense of familiarity again tracks something meaningful.

The decision scientist Gerd Gigerenzer has shown that being too familiar with what's being judged can actually undermine the benefits of familiarity. When making judgments analogous to the previous examples (which city is larger, which author sold more books) Gigerenzer and colleagues showed that the most accurate judgments would be made by someone who's only familiar with about 75 percent of the items being judged—that person would typically do better than someone who has at least heard of every item before.

Familiarity provides such a powerful tool because of the structure in the world around us. Let me give you another example. If you ask casual sports fans to predict the outcomes of Wimbledon tennis matches, they often simply pick the player with whom they are familiar. These simple judgments of familiarity have been shown to be good predictors of who will win a match, and even do slightly better than the actual player rankings.

The familiarity heuristic is also connected to our judgments of probability. Remember the key lesson from the lecture on probability: People tend to overestimate small probabilities, but underestimate large probabilities.

This can lead to a strange phenomenon called subadditivity. Think about a 50-year old man in the United States, we'll call him Stephen. Stephen has smoked for much of his adult life, although he is trying to quit. He's in generally good health despite a diet high in fatty foods and a largely sedentary lifestyle. He does have a family history of heart attack and stroke.

I give this sort of example in class and ask my students, "How likely is Stephen to die of a heart attack? Of stroke? Of heart disease? Of lung cancer? Of brain cancer? Of melanoma?" And of a few other diseases. A typical student might guess that Stephen has a 25-percent chance to die of a heart attack, a 15-percent chance of a stroke, a 30-percent chance of heart disease, a 25-percent chance of lung cancer, a 20-percent chance of brain cancer, and so on.

Then I ask the students to add up their probabilities. The students usually laugh because they've just estimated that Stephen has something like a 150-percent chance of dying from these different causes. The students can readily link Stephen's smoking to lung cancer, or his diet to heart disease. So, when they think about each cause of death in isolation, it's judged to be more likely it should be. That's subadditivity: The total probability (which must be 100 percent) ends up less than the sum of the individual probabilities.

The familiarity heuristic affects our economic decisions, too. People overvalue and are more likely to invest in the stocks of familiar companies. This can lead to very bad outcomes. In the extreme, investing one's retirement savings in one's own company stock carries a massive risk; for example, a catastrophic event that bankrupted the company could also eliminate all retirement savings.

But there is other evidence from behavioral finance that investors whose portfolios have a bias toward familiar companies, such as those from one's own geographic area, obtain slightly higher returns than investors who show no familiarity bias. Familiarity involves the use of information, and that information might help some investors.

Now, let me move to the second heuristic: anchoring. This heuristic uses some initial estimate as an anchor to bias our subsequent judgments. We use anchoring when we are uncertain. We don't have all the information needed to make an accurate judgment, so we latch onto anything given to us.

Think back to when you first saw the Milky Way. You were outside on a dark night, away from civilization, and you looked up and saw that fuzzy band of stars running across the night sky. You only saw a few hundred or maybe a few thousand of the brightest nearby stars, but our galaxy contains many more. Let me ask you a question. Does our galaxy contain more or fewer than one hundred thousand stars? Let me ask you a second question. How many stars are in the Milky Way galaxy?

Let's think about that question. When I ask you "How many stars are in the Milky Way galaxy," that's not something for which you have personal experience. Even if you've seen the Milky Way, you've only seen a small fraction of its stars. And, unless you are an astronomy buff, you probably haven't encountered the answer recently, so you can't give an estimate based on explicit knowledge. Without personal experience or explicit knowledge, you need to find something on which you can base your estimate.

The first question asked, "Does our galaxy contain more or fewer than one hundred thousand stars?" That number, 100,000, provides an anchor. It seems like a big number, and if I'm asking you about it, then you might infer that it's close to the right answer.

When faced with a difficult judgment like "How many stars in the Milky Way," people often begin with any number given to them, and then adjust their estimate upward or downward from that anchor. Someone who thinks that the number is larger than 100,000 might adjust upward, say to 500,000.

The key idea is that the anchor (like its nautical namesake) constrains how far a subsequent estimate can move.

So, what's the right answer here? No one knows exactly, but the current best estimates are that there are several hundred billion stars in the Milky Way galaxy. In this case, the anchor I gave you was about one million times too low, so it typically leads to estimates that are likewise far too low. If I had used a much larger anchor by asking "Does our galaxy contain more or fewer than a trillion stars," then the estimates would have been much, much higher.

Marketers use anchoring when pricing goods that are rare, infrequently purchased, or difficult to value. Consider expensive furniture or jewelry at a specialty store; often, these items will be displayed with a very high suggested retail price. That price might have no connection to reality whatsoever. It doesn't represent the cost of manufacturing, consumer demand, or anything else meaningful. It's just an anchor. The store wants you to start with that suggested retail price and then negotiate downward. They know that providing a very high anchor increases customers' estimates of value and leads to higher eventual selling prices.

It is important to emphasize that anchoring works even if there is no meaningful connection between the anchor and the subsequent estimates. In some laboratory experiments, researchers have generated anchors by asking people to spin a roulette wheel or to write down the last two digits of their social security number. Even when the anchor is generated in a completely random fashion, it still can influence behavior; for example, the people who write down large numbers are also willing to pay more for bottles of wine.

But, anchoring is far more than a party trick for behavioral economists. It influences real-world economic transactions, even those with extraordinarily large stakes. Consider the rarified world of fine art auctions. What is the value of Cezanne's *The Card Players*, or Munch's *The Scream*, or van Gogh's *Vase with 15 Sunflowers*? Each of these sold for tens or hundreds of millions of dollars. They are clearly valuable—each represents a one-of-a-kind masterwork by a great artist. But what sets their price? Why would one van Gogh sell for 40 million dollars and another for 80 million dollars?

Economists analyzed the sale prices of more than 15,000 paintings, all auctioned at major institutions in London and New York. They found that the price of a given painting reflected many factors specific to that painting: who painted it, its size, its medium, whether it was signed, among others. All of those factors make sense as contributors to the price of a painting.

But price also reflects the current market. If the current market for fine art is hot, then paintings will sell for more money. But if the market is cold, perhaps because of a down economy, then paintings will sell for less. The art market is notorious for boom and bust cycles. The average price for paintings within a category might double or halve within a year. So, whether the current market is hot or cold should also influence the selling price of a painting.

Now let's suppose that a painting first comes up for auction during a hot market, which inflates its selling price. So, what happens when it comes on the market again, in a few years? If that inflated selling price serves as an anchor for buyers (something that guides their subsequent willingness to pay) then the next sale price should be higher than predicted. The reverse would happen for paintings that were first sold in a cold market—they would command less at auction when sold again in a few years.

The data show that anchoring effects pervade art auctions. Once a price was established for a painting—regardless of whether that price was set during boom times or bust times—then that price influences how much people are willing to pay years later. So, if you are in the market for expensive fine art, look for pieces that were last sold years ago in a down market. Those pieces are likely to be systematically undervalued.

The third heuristic that I'll discuss is the representativeness heuristic. This heuristic helps us estimate probabilities through the following simple rule: prototypic events are likely events. To illustrate this heuristic, I'll describe a person, let's call her Rebecca, and you should think about what sort of job she might have. Here's a description: "Rebecca is intelligent, extroverted, and gregarious. From an early age, she always liked looking at the night sky and speculating about life on other planets. In school, she was always strong in math and science courses, although she was a good writer as well.

"As an adult, she loves going fast—running, riding horses, and even driving cars are all passions. She is willing to take risks, especially if they allow her to pursue her dreams. And, she's a good communicator, especially for things she feels passionate about."

So, how likely is it that Rebecca is a teacher? Just think of a rough percentage. An astronaut? A lawyer? A science writer?

I've adapted this example from the work of Daniel Kahneman and Amos Tversky, two pioneering figures in behavioral economics. When people hear scenarios like this, they commonly report that Rebecca is most probably an astronaut. She seems like a prototypic astronaut. She's interested in science and math, and has a love for the night sky and life on other planets. She's willing to take risks and passionate about her work. Next most probable would be science writer—she loves science and is a good writer and communicator, after all. And least probable would be lawyer and teacher.

Think for a moment. Have you ever met an astronaut? Do you have an astronaut living on your street? At any one time, the United States has about 100 people whose current job description is astronaut. That's it. By comparison, there are several million teachers, more than a million lawyers, and thousands of science writers. Even if Alice seems most representative of an astronaut, there are so few astronauts that it is much more likely that she's a teacher or lawyer—there are surely many more science-oriented and risk-loving teachers and lawyers than there are astronauts. The representativeness heuristic fails here because these professions differ dramatically in their base rates. Teachers and lawyers are much, much more common than science writers and especially astronauts.

Why do we rely on representativeness when it leads to such obvious mistakes? This heuristic exists because it is a fast and simple guide to probability. If it's a beautiful clear morning, it's unlikely to rain in the afternoon. Students with good grades are more likely to do well in medical school. The leading brand of toothpaste is a good product. Prototypes are often prototypes for a reason: They're often the best or most common member of some category.

Representativeness fails when prototypes are rare (like astronauts) but succeeds when prototypes are common. That rule provides clear guidance: be wary when representativeness points you toward some rare conclusion. To paraphrase the old saying to medical students, "When you hear hoofbeats behind you, expect horses not zebras."

The final heuristic I'll discuss is that of the affect heuristic. To a psychologist, affect means the internal sense of emotion, what we feel, our mood. The affect heuristic involves choosing one option over another based on their anticipated effects on our emotional state.

Suppose that you are deciding between two vacation destinations: a beachfront resort and a mountain cabin. You struggle with this decision. Both are great options and there isn't an obvious objective criterion that separates them.

When you think about the beachfront resort, you feel a sense of serenity. You imagine ocean breezes and drinks with umbrellas, and you feel calm. But, when you think of the mountain cabin, you imagine yourself standing there in the crisp, cool mountain air, and wishing you were on a tropical beach instead. So you choose the beach and have a great time on vacation.

Emotions don't always get in the way of our decisions. They can be extraordinarily useful. When use the affect heuristic, we are simulating our future self, and what our future self might feel after we've made our decision. To the degree that our simulations are accurate, we can check out the consequences of our decisions before we even make them. If I choose the beach, I'll feel serene. If I choose the mountains, I'll be cold and regretful.

Simulation is one of the most powerful tools we have for making good decisions. The neuroscientist Antonio Damasio recognized this in his somatic marker hypothesis. He argued that our brains store representations of our feelings and the associated body states, which he called somatic markers. (Somatic is a fancy way of saying body.)

For example, when we walk down an unfamiliar dark alley at night, our brains store the feeling of dread, the racing heartbeat, and the sense of alertness that accompany our risky action. Now, the next time we approach a dark alley at night, our brains can bring to mind the stored somatic marker. We can simulate that feeling (of taking that risk) before we ever step foot in the alley, and then we can choose another path home.

Simulation is a fast process. We don't have to consciously think: "How would I feel if?" We just do it automatically.

The affect heuristic often leads to good choices, in that we can anticipate and avoid decisions that would make us unhappy, regretful, or angry. But, it fails when negative consequences of our decisions are particularly easy to bring to mind or when we overestimate short-term mood at the expense of long-term satisfaction. We often procrastinate when faced with undesirable but necessary courses of action—such as selling a stock in which we've lost money—because we are influenced too much by the short-term pain of taking action.

I want to conclude by re-emphasizing the most important point of today's lecture: Heuristics aren't weaknesses or failures in our decision making, they are tools that help us make good decisions most of the time. The key challenge lies in using the right tool in the right situation.

Each of the heuristics I discussed works better in some situations than others. The familiarity heuristic helps us when we have only limited information toward a decision, but can actually be counterproductive when we have more detailed knowledge. The anchoring heuristic works best when past events are good predictors of the future, but it can bias our judgments when the past isn't like today. The representativeness heuristic is very useful in thinking about many sorts of common real-world categories, but less helpful for rare examples or atypical categories. And, the affect heuristic works well when our decisions have meaningful emotional consequences, but not as well when those emotional consequences are too salient or too fleeting.

So, how can we know whether using a heuristic might be helpful? How can we know when to step back and approach a decision more analytically? There's no simple answer to these questions. But, in the spirit of today's lecture, I can offer a simple rule that works most of the time: Heuristics perform best when making decisions about natural real-world events, particularly those for which we have prior experience.

By natural events I mean something that happens in the natural world, the sort of thing that our ancestors might have experienced in ancient times. Under this rule, heuristics are most useful for judgments about social situations, about our own personal reactions, or about things that we experience physically and tangibly.

Using a heuristic to choose a restaurant is likely to work out well. You have lots of experience choosing restaurants, and that past experience is likely to be a good guide for the future. Using a heuristic to choose the mutual funds for your retirement account may not be so successful.

In 2005 Bill Miller was probably the most celebrated mutual fund manager in the world. His flagship fund had beaten the S&P 500 for an amazing 15 years in a row, from 1991 until 2005. That's a pretty impressive streak, and the amount of money he managed grew dramatically with each passing year.

While his streak was ongoing, it attracted considerable interest from the financial community and the popular press. One article explained his success in simple terms: "To win spectacularly, you have to take risks." That's the representativeness heuristic in action. The most successful mutual fund managers, the ones who had the greatest returns, took the most risks. Does that imply that taking risks is good? That taking risks ensures future success?

Let's fast forward to 2011. Bill Miller's mutual fund was near the worst one percent of all funds in its class, and he stepped away (with much less fanfare) from leading the primary mutual fund in his company. His performance was a paradox: The same person who was at the top of the market for so many years, now was at the bottom.

In the next lecture, we'll examine what happens when people are faced with uncertain, random environments like in stock-picking, and we'll see if we can explain this paradox.

# Randomness and Patterns
## Lecture 13

People believe that they see patterns in all sorts of places, from the stock market to horoscopes. It's very easy to dismiss those beliefs as superstitions or foolishness and then to ignore the lessons they teach us. This lecture will show you what we can learn from studying them instead. We're naturally good at seeing patterns, even when they aren't really there, but if we seek the right evidence, we can learn what patterns are real and what aren't—and make better decisions as a result.

**What Is Randomness?**

- Randomness means that you can't predict the future from the past. A simple way to generate a random sequence is to flip a standard coin 20 times. You can diligently record the outcomes of the first 19 flips, looking for patterns in that sequence, but no amount of analysis will ever help you predict what will happen on the 20th flip. There will always be equal chances of a head and a tail. The process of flipping a coin leads to a sequence of events that is unpredictable.

- Suppose that you instead asked a friend to generate a sequence of 20 hypothetical coin flips—by writing them down without using a real coin. If you could study the first 19 flips in your friend's sequence, you could indeed improve your probability of guessing the 20th. This is a nonrandom process.

- It turns out that people show a particular bias when trying to behave randomly. They switch too much. They try to make short sequences of events seem random, and they introduce too many patterns that alternate between events. Look at the 19th flip. If your friend wrote tails, guess heads—or vice versa. Because your friend is human, and carries the same biases as the rest of us, looking at his or her past behavior can improve your predictions. Nonrandom processes are predictable, at least in principle.

- The idea of randomness is closely tied to the idea of information. A process that is completely random carries no information about the future, and it doesn't tell us anything that helps us make better decisions. However, a nonrandom process contains information; if we know what to look for, we can learn from that information and make better decisions in the future.

- Think about sequences of events in the natural environment. When we see lightning, we can predict that we'll soon hear thunder. When we drop a stone at the top of a hill, we can predict that it will roll downward. Events in the natural world are predictable because they were generated by nonrandom processes; the laws of physics bind different events together into meaningful sequences.

- Just because something is nonrandom, it doesn't mean that we know everything or can predict the future perfectly. Sometimes we see lightning, and then the thunder doesn't come. However, with careful observation of a nonrandom process, our predictions about the world around us get better over time.

- In every case that you can imagine, learning about patterns in nature—and in other people—made our ancestors more likely to survive and prosper. It's no wonder, then, that we've evolved to be really, really good at finding patterns. Our brains look for patterns automatically, without any conscious effort, and even if there's no pattern to be found.

- Patterns don't have to be in time. When we look at a mesa on Mars and see a face, that's because our brains are interpreting the collection of cliffs and plateaus as a face-like pattern. We're particularly good at seeing faces in almost anything.

- Your brain is constantly looking for structure out there in the world. It's looking for something that's predictable, that's meaningful, that it can use to guide behavior. When we see a predictable pattern and anticipate what will happen next, we can use simple rules like heuristics to help us not only avoid unnecessary processing but also make better decisions.

## ESP

- We've all experienced things that seem unexplainable; we're thinking about a friend with whom we haven't spoken in months, and then that friend calls us that very day. To present-day scientists, such experiences are just random coincidences. But in the first half of the 20$^{th}$ century, incidents like this were seen by some people as legitimate, scientific evidence of extrasensory perception (ESP).

- Probably the most famous proponent of ESP research was J. B. Rhine, a botanist who became fascinated with these phenomena. Rhine coined the term "ESP" because of his belief that people can perceive things without relying on the usual senses like sight or hearing.

- Over nearly a century of research, there's never been a single example of a person who can walk into a room, sit down at a table, and always guess cards at a rate greater than chance. Nor has anyone identified a plausible biological mechanism by which ESP could arise. A short-term pattern might just be chance, not evidence.

- As time has passed since Rhine's early studies, the evidence for ESP hasn't gotten any stronger. That's one of the hallmarks of a random process: We can't learn from it over time.

## Gambling

- Modern casinos know that people see patterns in random events, and they take full advantage. Consider the game of roulette. A small ball is spun around a numbered rotating wheel, and players bet on which number the ball will stop. From spin to spin, the outcome will be completely random. The wheel rotates so fast that even tiny changes in how the ball is spun have unpredictable effects.

- However, if you walk by a modern roulette table, you'll often see an electronic scoreboard that shows the outcomes of the last few spins. Players will check those scoreboards to look for patterns, and they will stay at the table and change their bets accordingly.

- It doesn't matter what they bet; the house advantage is the same regardless. So, why does the casino provide those scoreboards? To keep players at the table. The casino just wants them to see patterns and keep betting.

- With most types of gambling, you can't predict the future from the past. We see patterns in what's already happened—not what will happen. If the past doesn't predict the future, then looking for patterns can't help us.

**Hot-Hand Effects**

- Suppose that you are attending a basketball game. On one of the teams is LeBron James, one of the most talented athletes in professional sports. LeBron dribbles down the court and makes a jump shot, and a few minutes later, he makes his next shot. Then, a minute later, he makes a third shot in a row. What is the probability that his fourth shot will go in?

  **The hot-hand effect describes the notion that a basketball player seems to be on a "hot" streak.**

- LeBron is an outstanding player who makes about half of his shots. Given that he's made three shots in a row, does he now have a greater than 50-percent chance to make the fourth shot? Many people would say that LeBron has a "hot hand" and predict that his chances of making the next shot are considerably greater than normal.

- However, this nonrandom "hot-hand effect" does not stand up to scientific scrutiny. Research has shown that the probability of making a shot does not change, regardless of whether the previous shot was made or missed. In other words, the sequences of made and missed shots are essentially random.

- We think that there is a hot-hand effect because we can remember examples of players making four or five or more shots in a row; when one of our favorite players does that, we might leap out of our seat with excitement. Those are vivid memories. However, remember the representativeness heuristic from the previous lecture: We overestimate the probability of events that can be easily brought to mind.

**Generating Random Series**
- When an individual or corporation is suspected of financial fraud, a forensic accountant evaluates their financial records. In many cases, those financial records have been doctored; the perpetrator tries to destroy evidence by replacing the illicit transactions with random numbers representing seemingly innocuous transactions. How could one determine whether a set of transactions might be fraudulent?

- One surprising tool comes from the nature of randomness itself. In the 1930s, the physicist Frank Benford collected measurements of a wide range of phenomena: the populations of cities, the size of rivers, and even statistics of baseball players. For every measurement, he wrote down the first digit. For example, if the city had a population of 1,000, 10,000, or 1,000,000, he wrote down "1." He repeated this for thousands and thousands of data points and then plotted how often each numeral—from 1 to 9—came up as the first digit.

- We might expect that each numeral would be the first digit equally often, or about 11 percent of the time. Instead, Benford found that the numeral 1 was the most frequent (about 31 percent of the time), and each succeeding numeral was less and less frequent, with 9 only appearing as the first digit about 5 percent of the time. This relationship has become known as Benford's law.

- Benford's law has become a powerful tool for forensic accountants. When people create sets of random numbers, as when an embezzler seeks to cover his tracks, they try to use every numeral equally. But that attempt at randomness doesn't match the sort of randomness in real account balances, and thus, it can be detected.

- Benford's law illustrates the importance of thinking about the process that generates structure. If events come from some well-defined process, like the growth of money due to compounding interest, then knowledge about that process can help us make decisions. However, if we don't know or can't know the generative process, then patterns are unlikely to be helpful.

**Recommendations**

- First, know when patterns are likely to be meaningful—and when they aren't. We often think that we can predict the future based on the patterns of the past. We are inveterate predictors, but we keep trying to predict even when we shouldn't. We often get it exactly backward: The things that we think are random aren't, but the things that we think aren't random are.

- Second, don't think about a pattern without thinking about what *didn't* happen.

- Third, look for evidence that gets stronger as time passes. If a pattern is just due to randomness, then as time passes, it won't recur—the evidence won't get any stronger. However, if there's something real, then the pattern will become clearer and clearer.

## Suggested Reading

Gilovich, *How We Know What Isn't So*.

Gilovich, Vallone, and Tversky, "The Hot Hand in Basketball."

Taleb, *Fooled by Randomness*.

## Questions to Consider

1. Why does our brain constantly look for patterns in the environment?

2. What distinguishes patterns that are likely to be meaningful from those that are meaningless and random?

# Randomness and Patterns
## Lecture 13—Transcript

Welcome back. In the last lecture, we talked about how we use simple rules called heuristics to try to make sense of the world around us. Those heuristics work because our world is structured. It has regularities, patterns, and detecting those patterns can often help us make very good decisions. But sometimes the patterns we detect can lead us astray.

On July 31, 1976, the U.S. space agency NASA released a photograph of Mars. At that time, the Viking 1 orbiter was circling our planetary neighbor, snapping photographs of landforms to help identify a landing location for a space probe. Usually, its photos attracted little attention from the public. But this photograph drew people's attention. NASA's official photo caption said, "The picture shows eroded mesa-like landforms. The huge rock formation in the center, which resembles a human head, is formed by shadows giving the illusion of eyes, nose, and mouth." To a geologist, the image looks like an eroded mesa. But to all the rest of us, it looks strikingly like a human face.

Over the succeeding years, the face on Mars generated no end of controversy. To many people, it was a sign of an ancient alien civilization on another planet. Other people thought it had religious significance. And, still others considered it clear evidence of a conspiracy that reached into the highest levels of NASA.

The scientists argued that this image didn't show a face; it just showed a rock formation that had been shaped by random geological processes. But, that didn't stop the popular belief in a face on Mars, which continued for decades afterward. Why did so many people believe in an alien civilization on Mars? Why do people believe in astrology, extrasensory perception, and many other pseudosciences? Why are people readily taken in by financial scams that promise them impossible returns at minimal risk?

These may all sound like fringe beliefs to you—the sorts of ideas that other people believe in. I want to emphasize, though, that we all are susceptible to beliefs of this sort. We are set up to look for meaning, even when there's nothing but randomness.

So, let's begin with some simple definitions. What is randomness and why does it matter for decision making? Randomness means that you can't predict the future from the past. A simple way to generate a random sequence is to flip a standard coin 20 times. You can diligently record the outcomes of the first 19 flips, looking for patterns in that sequence, but no amount of analysis will ever help you predict what will happen on the 20$^{th}$ flip. There will always be equal chances of a head and a tail. The process of flipping a coin leads to a sequence of events that are unpredictable.

Let's now change from a random process to a non-random process. Suppose that you instead asked a friend to generate a sequence of 20 hypothetical coin flips by writing them down without using a real coin. If you could study the first 19 flips in your friend's sequence, you could indeed improve your probability of guessing the 20$^{th}$.

How? It turns out that people show a particular bias when trying to behave randomly. They switch too much. They try to make short sequences of events seem random, and they introduce too many patterns that alternate between events. Look at the 19$^{th}$ flip. If your friend wrote tails, guess heads, or vice versa. Because your friend is human and carries the same biases as the rest of us looking at their past behavior can improve your predictions. Non-random processes are predictable, at least in principle.

I emphasize this distinction because the idea of randomness is closely tied to the idea of information. A process that is completely random carries no information about the future, and it doesn't tell us anything that helps us make better decisions. But, a non-random process contains information. If we know what to look for, we can learn from that information and make better decisions in the future. So, what sorts of processes are random and what sorts of processes are non-random? That's the key question, and I'll only answer it halfway for now.

Think about sequences of events in the natural environment. When we see lightning, we can predict that we'll soon hear thunder. When we drop a stone at the top of a hill, we can predict that it will roll downward. Events in the natural world are predictable because they were generated by non-random processes; the laws of physics bind different events together into meaningful sequences.

Our interactions with other people are also non-random, even if it might sometimes seem otherwise. There's a history in all of our relationships. When we interact with someone, we might build trust or break it, we might send signals of friendship or hostility. Those different events create or break social connections. We even call good friends dependable, because we can predict how they'll behave toward us.

Just because something's non-random, that doesn't mean that we know everything or can predict the future perfectly. Sometimes we see lightning, and then the thunder doesn't come. But, with careful observation of a non-random process, our predictions about the world around us get better over time.

By anticipating the seasonal migrations of game, our ancestors became better hunters. By observing how different crops grew in different soils, they became better farmers. In every case that you can imagine, learning about patterns in nature, and in other people, made our ancestors more likely to survive and prosper. It's no wonder, then, that we've evolved to be really, really good at finding patterns. Our brains look for patterns automatically without any conscious effort, and even if there's no pattern to be found.

A few years ago, my colleagues and I did a simple experiment. We showed people a random sequence of circles and squares. Even though the sequence was completely random, people's brains were continually trying to find patterns in that sequence. As people started to perceive a pattern, say after seeing three squares in a row, the activity levels in the region of the brain called the prefrontal cortex would decrease with each successive event that fit that pattern. Essentially, the brain used less and less energy as events seemed more and more predictable. But, when something unexpected happened, suddenly the prefrontal cortex sprang into action to form a new prediction.

Patterns don't have to be in time. When we look at a mesa on Mars and see a face, that's because our brains are interpreting the collection of cliffs and plateaus as a face-like pattern. We're particularly good at seeing faces in almost anything—if you look around where you are right now, you might see a face in a pattern in wood, or in the front end of a car, or a computer monitor.

Your brain is constantly looking for structure out there in the world. It's looking for something that's predictable, that's meaningful, that it can use to guide behavior. When we see a predictable pattern and anticipate what will happen next, we can use simple rules like the heuristics I talked about in the previous lecture. That helps us not only avoid unnecessary processing but also make better decisions.

People believe that they see patterns in all sorts of places, from the stock market to horoscopes. It's very easy to dismiss those beliefs as superstitions or foolishness and then to ignore the lessons they teach us. Let's see what we can learn from studying them instead.

We've all experienced things that seem unexplainable—we're thinking about a friend with whom we haven't spoken in months, and then that friend calls us that very day. To present-day scientists, such experiences are just random coincidences. But in the first half of the 20$^{th}$ century, incidents like this were seen by some people as legitimate, scientific evidence of extrasensory perception, or ESP.

Probably the most famous proponent of ESP research was J. B. Rhine, a botanist who became fascinated with these phenomena. Rhine coined that term, ESP, because of his belief that people can perceive things without relying on the usual senses like sight or hearing. Rhine did try to apply scientific methods to the study of ESP. In fact, early in his career he became famous for debunking a Boston socialite who claimed to communicate with the dead. His skepticism enraged that socialite's famous supporters, one of whom was a British writer who accused Rhine of "colossal impertinence." In a colossal irony, that defender of ESP was none other than Sir Arthur Conan Doyle, the creator of the most rational character in literature, Sherlock Holmes.

As Rhine's career progressed, he decided that he needed a way to rigorously test ESP. So, in the 1930s, he created a deck of 25 cards, each with one of five simple shapes. To test for ESP, he would bring someone into his laboratory, shuffle the deck face-down, and then ask them to guess what shape would come next, one guess at a time for the 25 cards. Most people would guess about 5 out of the 25 correctly, that's close to chance. But occasionally someone would guess 10 correctly or 12 correctly or perhaps even more. Does that mean that person has ESP? Or did they just get lucky?

Well, when you looked more closely at Rhine's data, you'd notice that if someone did very well on one test—say, they guessed 12 out of 25 correctly—then they'd do less well on subsequent tests. If you looked at their data over hundreds of tests, their overall guessing rate would be very close to chance.

Even if one interprets Rhine's data in the most charitable way, the effects of ESP are vanishingly small, and inconsistent with both physics and biology. Yet, despite these concerns, Rhine believed in ESP throughout his entire life. So, why did he believe?

Think of all the times that he ran experiments. All the times that he watched someone guess four, five, six cards in a row. He probably observed more patterns that seemed to provide evidence for ESP than any other person in human history. But, here's the key idea: A short-term pattern might just be chance, not evidence. Over nearly a century of research, there's never been a single example of a person who can walk into a room, sit down at a table, and always guess cards at a rate greater than chance. Nor has anyone identified a plausible biological mechanism by which ESP could arise. As time has passed since Rhine's early studies, the evidence for ESP hasn't gotten any stronger. That's one of the hallmarks of a random process: We can't learn from it over time.

Let me move to a second example: gambling. Modern casinos know that people see patterns in random events, and they take full advantage. Consider the game of roulette. A small ball is spun around a numbered rotating wheel, and players bet on which number the ball will stop. From spin to spin, the outcome will be completely random. The wheel rotates so fast that even tiny changes in how the ball is spun have unpredictable effects.

But, if you walk by a modern roulette table, you'll often see an electronic scoreboard that shows the outcomes of the last few spins. Players will check those scoreboards to look for patterns and will stay at the table and change their bets accordingly. It doesn't matter what they bet, the house advantage is the same regardless. So, why does the casino provide those scoreboards? To keep players at the table. The casino just wants them to see patterns and keep betting.

Let's switch to baccarat, the game played by the highest of high-rollers. Baccarat resembles poker in some ways. One person is designated the player, and the house is called the banker. The player and banker are each dealt cards according to predetermined rules. Everyone else bets on whether the player or the banker will win the hand. It's a game of great dignity played slowly and dramatically for very large sums of money. Because of this drama, a variant of baccarat was the preferred game of James Bond.

Despite all of its ritual, the most common version of baccarat involves absolutely no strategy. The cards are dealt out according to fixed rules, and neither the player nor the banker can do anything to affect what happens. In its essence, the game is the same as betting on flips of a coin, all you can do is decide to bet "player" or to bet "banker" and then watch to see what happens.

So, what do high-roller baccarat bettors do? They track the pattern of the game over time. The casinos issue special cards on which the bettors can mark who wins each round, or a computer screen attached to the table shows the history of winners and losers. Those screens show that history in as many as five or more different graphical formats so that people can look for patterns. If the banker and player alternate winning, that generates an alternating pattern known as "ping pong." Other patterns are given evocative names that mirror their shape; a vertical line followed by a horizontal line is called "the dragon." But an alternating pattern, a repeating pattern, or anything else tells you nothing about what's going to happen next. In baccarat, like most gambling, you can't predict the future from the past.

Here's the key lesson: We see patterns in what's already happened, not what will happen. If the past doesn't predict the future, then looking for patterns can't help us.

Now, suppose that you are attending a basketball game. On one of the teams is LeBron James, one of the most talented athletes in professional sports. LeBron dribbles down the court and makes a jumpshot, then a few minutes later makes his next shot, then a minute later makes a third shot in a row. When he comes down the court the fourth time, he rises up to attempt a jumpshot, and your heart rises with him (or sinks, depending on whether you are rooting for his team).

Let's pause the game with Lebron in mid-air. What is the probability that this shot will go in? LeBron is an outstanding player who makes about half of his shots. Given that he's made three shots in a row, does he now have a greater than 50-percent chance to make the fourth shot? Many people answer yes. They say LeBron has the "hot hand," and they predict that his chances of making the next shot are considerably greater than normal.

But does this non-random "hot-hand effect" stand up to scientific scrutiny? More than two decades ago a team of researchers systematically tested a simple question: Are basketball players more likely to make a basket if their previous shot was successful? They examined data from the previous year's NBA season, tracking every shot taken by every player on one team. They also looked at data from their local college team. They even brought both collegiate and recreational players into the gym and had them take hundreds of shots.

The conclusion was clear and compelling: The probability of making a shot did not change, regardless of whether the previous shot was made or missed. Since that time, there have been hundreds of analyses of data from real-world basketball games as well as from other sports. The core conclusion of that first study has been corroborated repeatedly: The sequences of made and missed shots are essentially random.

Sports fans and players might find this conclusion unbelievable. Of course basketball players have a hot hand, we've seen it and remember it. We've seen our favorite players make shot after shot, where they can't miss. And, what about all of the other sports? A baseball player who hits homeruns on three consecutive at bats, a football quarterback who completes pass after pass, or a golfer whose every putt heads straight for the hole. How can some scientists claim that there isn't a hot-hand effect? Aren't our memories enough proof?

Our memories aren't proof. Actually, they're the problem. We think that there is a hot-hand effect because we can remember examples of players making four or five or more shots in a row; when one of our favorite players does that, we might leap out of our seat with excitement. Those are vivid memories. But, remember the representativeness heuristic from the previous lecture. We overestimate the probability of events that can be easily brought to mind.

Let me illustrate this concept a different way. Suppose Lebron James made 50 percent of his shots not because of his skill but because of a random process. Then we could imagine each game as a series of coin flips—if he took 20 shots in a game, there would be 20 flips of a coin. Every few games, the coin would come up the same way over and over again in a long streak, just by chance. We would remember that streak, and attribute it to a hot hand, even though the hot hand of the basketball player is no more real than the hot hand of the coin flipper.

So, does nothing matter? Is everything in a basketball game just random? Not exactly. The players believe in the hot-hand effect, too. So, players who make a few shots in a row will start shooting more and taking more difficult shots.

Ok, let's now restart the game. LeBron James releases his jumpshot, and it goes in. Thousands of fans rise in exultation. The announcer confidently exclaims that Lebron's shooting hand is on fire. Did LeBron make that shot because he had the hot hand? No, he made that shot because he is a good shooter, and a random process happened to go his way.

As a final example, let's move to the world of finance, specifically the world of forensic accounting. When an individual or corporation is suspected of a financial fraud, a forensic accountant evaluates their financial records. In many cases, those financial records have been doctored. The perpetrator tries to destroy evidence by replacing the illicit transactions with random numbers representing seemingly innocuous transactions. How could one determine whether a set of transactions might be fraudulent?

One surprising tool comes from the nature of randomness itself. In the 1930s the physicist Frank Benford collected measurements of a wide range of phenomena: the populations of cities, the size of rivers, even hitting statistics of baseball players. For every measurement, he wrote down the first digit. For example, if the city had a population of 1,000, 10,000, or one million he wrote down "1." If the population was 2,000, etc., he wrote down "2."

He repeated this for thousands and thousands of data points, and then plotted how often each numeral (from 1 to 9) came up as the first digit. We might expect that each numeral would be the first digit equally often, or about 11 percent of the time. But, that's not what Benford found. Instead, the numeral 1 was the most frequent (about 31 percent of the time) and each succeeding numeral was less and less frequent, with nine only appearing as the first digit about fiver percent of the time. This relationship has become known as Benford's law.

To understand Benford's law better, let's return to the financial domain. Consider a large investment bank that holds the retirement funds for thousands of investors. Those investors differ in innumerable ways: some are wealthier than others, some started investing earlier than others, and so forth. Benford's law predicts that more than six times as many accounts would begin with the digit 1 than would begin with the digit 9.

Why? Let's assume, for simplification, that the average account increases in value by about 10 percent per year. An account with $10,000 will take about seven years to double to $20,000. But, an account with $90,000 will grow to $100,000 in only slightly more than one year. The same principle holds regardless of whether the account has hundreds, thousands, or millions of dollars therein. Going from one to two requires doubling, but going from nine to one again requires only a little more than 10-percent gain. The same reasoning applies to the population of cities, the heights of mountains, or to almost anything else that can be measured.

Benford's law has become a powerful tool for forensic accountants. When people create sets of random numbers, as when an embezzler seeks to cover his tracks, they try to use every numeral equally—fraudulent balances tend to begin with 9 just as often as they begin with 1. But that attempt at randomness doesn't match the sort of randomness in real account balances, and thus it can be detected.

Benford's law illustrates the importance of thinking about the process that generates structure. If events come from some well-defined process, like the growth of money due to compounding interest, then knowledge about that process can help us make decisions. But, if we don't know or can't know the generative process, then patterns are unlikely to be helpful.

Let me summarize today's lecture in three short recommendations.

First, know when patterns are likely to be meaningful and when they aren't. We often think that we can predict the future based on the patterns of the past. We are inveterate predictors; we see patterns in the weather, in the outcomes of sporting events, in the fluctuations of the financial markets. But, we humans keep trying to predict even when we shouldn't. We often get it exactly backwards: The things that we think are random, aren't, but, the things that we think aren't random, are.

There are several rough guidelines that can help you know when patterns are likely to be the result of a random process. In general, if a pattern is very abstract, if it could arise because of many different reasons, and if experts disagree about what will happen next, then a pattern may be nothing more than randomness. You shouldn't use that pattern in your decision making.

When investing, it's very tempting to look for patterns in the fluctuations of market indices and stock prices. But it's difficult to time the markets from month-to-month, much less to find a meaningful signal in the day-to-day noise of the markets. Don't overestimate your own abilities, it's easy to see something that isn't really there.

Second, don't think about a pattern without thinking about what didn't happen. At the end of the previous lecture, I talked about Bill Miller, a mutual fund manager who became famous for beating the S&P 500 benchmark 15 years in a row and then stepped away from managing his firm's central fund 5 years later after that same fund became one of the very worst in its class. Did Bill Miller suddenly forget how to invest? Did his hot hand turn cold? No. Even this amazing streak seems to be just a pattern in randomness once you think about what didn't happen.

There are approximately 8,000 mutual funds available to U.S. investors. Suppose that whether a fund does better or worse than average is not based on the skill of the manager but on randomness, like flipping a coin each year to see whether the fund beats the market. Researchers have calculated the chance that any of those 8,000 funds would have had a 15-year winning streak sometime in the past few decades. That chance is 3 in 4. It might be that Bill Miller forgot how to invest. But a simpler explanation is that with so many funds to choose from there's bound to be some very long streaks, just by chance.

And, there's an interesting second act in the story of Bill Miller's investments. He subsequently co-managed a mutual fund that adopted a contrarian strategy. It sought out shares of companies whose stock prices had been hammered because of other investors' doubts about their future viability, despite good fundamentals in the present. As the stock market rebounded strongly in 2013, Bill Miller was featured in news stories again, this time because his new fund had the highest three-year returns in its class.

Third, and finally, look for evidence that gets stronger as time passes. If a pattern is just due to randomness, then as time passes it won't recur; the evidence won't get any stronger. But, if there's something real, then the pattern will get clearer and clearer.

Let's think back to the face on Mars. In the years after that first 1976 photo, the NASA leadership realized that people were curious. They wanted to know more about this spot on another planet that looked so human. By the late 1990s, a new spacecraft, the Mars Global Surveyor, was again flying around Mars snapping photographs. So, when the opportunity presented itself, NASA adjusted the course of that spacecraft very slightly so that it could take a photo of the same rocky mesa at much, much higher resolution than before. It was really an amazing photo, a view of another planet with resolution down to the meter level. And, it looks like a mesa. Not a face, not an alien civilization. Just rocky hills in the middle of a flat landscape.

We're naturally good at seeing patterns, even when they aren't really there. But, if we seek the right evidence, we can learn what patterns are real and what aren't, and we can make better decisions as a result.

In the next lecture, we'll explore the nature of evidence—what is it, how should we use it, and how much evidence do we need to make a good decision.

# How Much Evidence Do We Need?
## Lecture 14

In this lecture, you will learn about the nature of evidence. How should we incorporate evidence into our decisions and judgments, and in what ways do we make mistakes? We want to find evidence that supports our beliefs, that helps us make dramatic discoveries or win arguments. We're very good at seeking out that supporting evidence, and we're very good at developing counterarguments against evidence in which we don't believe. But we need to be skeptical—not just about others, but about ourselves. Sometimes, we just shouldn't believe our own eyes.

**What Is Evidence?**
- Information can be meaningful or meaningless. Meaningless information doesn't help us predict what will come next. When we make decisions, we only care about meaningful information—information that helps us make better decisions, that helps us decide on one course of action or another. We care about meaningful information, called evidence.

- It's ideal if we have a great deal of high-quality evidence supporting our decision. But that's not always the case. Sometimes we have only a little evidence, but it's of high quality; other times, we have a lot of evidence, but it's of low quality. Both of these are valuable for decisions. You want high-quality information, when you can get it, and you want lots of information, when you can get it, but you don't always have lots of high-quality information.

- When people have to decide between two options—one with a little high-quality evidence and the other with a lot of low-quality evidence—they often make systematic mistakes. In particular, people tend to overestimate the quality of evidence. And they underestimate the value of having lots of evidence, even if it's low quality.

## Evidence Quality

- People overestimate the likelihood of events that seem typical, familiar, or memorable. In large part, this overestimation happens because we are so good at inductive reasoning—drawing evidence from one example and applying that evidence for some more general judgment or decision. We see patterns and generalize from those patterns, as shown in the previous lecture on randomness.

- We're so good at drawing evidence from events, in fact, that we'll use that evidence even when it shouldn't apply. We're easily influenced by anecdotes and stories, even if those anecdotes shouldn't be relevant to our decision. Anecdotes and extreme events don't necessarily provide good evidence. Events can seem extreme *because* they are atypical and unrepresentative, in which case they shouldn't shape our decisions.

- When thinking about whether to accept a new job, don't just think about the ideal circumstances. Force yourself to think about what's typical, along with what could be extremely good or extremely bad. Considering a broader range of evidence can help you make better decisions.

## Confirmation Bias

- Another reason that people overestimate the quality of their evidence toward a decision is that people tend to seek out evidence that confirms their existing beliefs, instead of evidence that could refute those beliefs. That's called confirmation bias.

- We see echoes of confirmation bias in the popular media, in our conversations, and in ourselves. When people take a strongly held position—like on a political hot-button issue—they interpret new evidence in whatever way best fits their existing beliefs. So, new evidence tends to reinforce people's strongly held beliefs, even when that same evidence might be seen by a neutral party as challenging those same beliefs.

- Several factors contribute to the confirmation bias. One possibility is that people preferentially seek out streams of information that tend to support their prior beliefs. There's good evidence that this matters; for example, people prefer news programs that tend to share their political slant, not challenge it, and they avoid other potential sources of conflicting information.

- Another possibility is that when people see evidence against a strongly held position, they simply ignore it. That's usually not true, though. When shown two arguments—one confirming their beliefs, the other disconfirming—people tend to spend relatively little time reading and thinking about the confirming evidence. Instead, they spend their time looking at disconfirming evidence, not ignoring it.

- So, that leads to a third possibility: People actively reinterpret evidence that would otherwise argue against their belief. When they read an argument against their position, they don't just accept that argument. Instead, they start thinking about counterarguments.

**People tend to seek out evidence that confirms their existing beliefs, instead of evidence that could refute those beliefs.**

They internally generate new evidence in support of their prior belief, which in turn actually strengthens their original position.

- This gives us two main reasons for the confirmation bias: We prefer sources of evidence that tend to confirm our existing beliefs, and we counterargue disconfirming evidence, strengthening our original beliefs in the process.

- It's very difficult to eliminate the confirmation bias. None of us wants to be constantly challenged in our beliefs, and we all want to feel that our beliefs are rational and justified. All one can hope to do is minimize it as much as possible.

- There's one approach that helps—and it's not very difficult, if you are willing to try it. You just have to switch sides. You should force yourself to take the other position and present its case without counterargument.

- Do your best to identify the most reasonable and strongest arguments for that other position. The key is to avoid counterarguing for your existing beliefs. Instead, put yourself in the shoes of another person, a reasonable member who happens to take the other side. That'll disengage you from the desire to be consistent—from your own passions—and force you to think about the evidence from another perspective.

- Ideally, you want to think about alternatives to your prior beliefs as early as possible so that you aren't too biased in the evidence you acquire. However, it's still good practice for all of us to challenge our beliefs, even strongly held ones.

## Sample Size
- People tend to underestimate the value of having lots of evidence, even if that evidence is of low quality. In many cases, the amount of evidence is given by the statistical term "sample size," which describes how many data points have been measured.

- People often have a hard time interpreting information about sample size. It's not that they think sample size isn't important—we all know that more evidence is better than less evidence. Instead, the challenge for decision making comes when quality of evidence and sample size come into conflict.

- Suppose that your friend shows you two coins. You are told, truthfully, that one of the coins is weighted on one side so that it will flip that same side about two-thirds of the time. The other coin is just a normal, fair coin. You need to guess which is which.

- Your friend pulls one coin, chosen randomly, out of his or her pocket and flips it three times. It comes up heads each time. Your friend then pulls the other coin out of his or her pocket and flips it over and over. After a few minutes, the tally is 20 heads and 15 tails.

- When surveyed, most people guess that the first coin is the biased one; it always comes up heads. But even a fair coin will flip the same way three times in a row pretty often—about 25 percent of the time. The second coin has a much larger sample size, and it actually is slightly more likely to be the biased coin.

- For many sorts of decisions, there's a sort of diminishing returns for sample size. A good example comes from polling in nationwide elections. If you want to find out what candidate a majority of Americans prefers for president, for example, you don't need to survey millions of people. A survey of a few hundred to about a thousand people will provide a reasonably small margin for error—on the order of about four percent. Increasing the sample size beyond that point wouldn't make the poll much better.

- What matters most for polling is that the sample is representative. There shouldn't be any systematic bias in who participated. A large poll doesn't do any good if the people's opinions aren't independent from each other, as can happen if a poll samples too many people from one geographic area or from the same age range. It's usually better to have a sample of 500 people who are broadly representative of the population than a poll of 10,000 unrepresentative people.

- We often do better with more, low-quality evidence, but once sample size becomes large enough, then there are cases like polling for which quality becomes more important.

**Evidence Accumulation**
- We only have a few tantalizing hints about the process of evidence integration and why it sometimes goes awry, at least for complex real-world decisions. Those hints come from research on much simpler sorts of decisions—those only involving two known outcomes, with no uncertainty. The basic idea is that evidence is accumulated over time, and a decision is reached when the evidence reaches some criterion.

- The current best models assume that evidence accumulates continuously until we reach a decision. If the evidence seems to be very high quality, then the rate of accumulation is faster, and we decide more quickly, although we are also more prone to mistakes. If there's a lot of low-quality evidence, then the rate of accumulation is slower, and our decisions are slower but potentially more accurate.

- There's much more to be learned about this process. We don't yet know whether the very basic mechanisms that help explain fast, two-item choices are also used for much slower and more complex choices. And, it's not yet possible to explain all of the biases presented in this lecture.

- However, this very simple sort of model holds promise. It's consistent with how our neurons work, it's consistent with basic psychological experiments, and it's consistent with simple economic choices. So, there are good reason to believe that more complex decisions work in much the same way.

## Suggested Reading

Morewedge, Gilbert, and Wilson, "The Least Likely of Times."

Sheehan, "Venus Spokes."

## Questions to Consider

1. What trade-offs do we make when we wait for more evidence before making our decisions?

2. What is the confirmation bias, and how does it affect our decisions?

# How Much Evidence Do We Need?
## Lecture 14—Transcript

In the last lecture, we explored the distinction between randomness and evidence. We want to use evidence to make good decisions, but we often have a hard time knowing when to trust the evidence in front of us and when to be skeptical. Let me introduce you an amazing example of when not to trust the evidence we see.

In the late 19th century, one of the most famous astronomers in the world was an amateur, not professional, scientist. His name was Percival Lowell. Lowell was born into a very wealthy family in Boston. His wealth allowed him to pursue his intellectual passions, chiefly astronomy, and he combined a passion for science with a businessman's pragmatism.

At that time, astronomical observatories were typically located where people were, in large cities or in universities. Lowell decided to found an observatory on a mountainside in the middle of nowhere, near Flagstaff in what was then the Arizona territory. The sky there was dark and clear, and the new telescope he installed there was one of the largest refracting telescopes in the world. It could gather more light than almost any other.

In short time, Lowell and his observatory colleagues became world leaders in astronomy. They mapped the surface of Mars, identified many new asteroids, and even discovered tantalizing hints that sparked the search for what is now called the dwarf planet Pluto. Lowell was, by any measure, an exceptional scientist with a careful, keen eye.

But, Lowell ended his career in scientific disgrace. In 1896, Lowell published a map of the surface of Venus that showed a large dark spot slightly to the right of the center of the planet, as viewed from Earth. Radiating away from that spot were a set of spoke-like dark paths, each twisting and turning in a complicated pattern. Lowell interpreted what he saw as evidence for an alien civilization on Venus. The central spot was a massive capital city, and the spoke-like paths were roads and other structures that connected the capital to other communities throughout the planet.

Even at that time, this was a controversial, even extraordinary claim. Others looked into their telescopes (admittedly often smaller telescopes at worse sites for observing) and saw no cities, no canals. And, the idea that there was a civilization on Venus, that just seemed preposterous to most scientists of the day.

We now know, based on all of our modern observations of Venus, that there are no cities, no roads visible from space. In fact, through modern visible-light telescopes, Venus actually appears largely featureless; it's so bright and has such thick cloud cover that you can't see any surface details.

Percival Lowell—one of the most passionate, careful, and technologically sophisticated astronomers of his day—got it wrong. He made two mistakes. First, he placed too much trust in evidence that only he could see compared to what everyone else claimed. And, he should have been more skeptical given that it was at least somewhat unlikely that there would be an advanced civilization on our nearest planet.

In today's lecture, I'll discuss the nature of evidence. How should we incorporate evidence into our decisions and judgments, and in what ways do we make mistakes?

Let's begin with a brief consideration of information. That's one of those words that clearly means something to each of us, even if it is difficult to define. The engineer Claude Shannon is often considered the founder of information theory. After World War II, he was working on the mathematics of communication—how messages are transported from place to place. He defined information as, roughly, a reduction in uncertainty.

Suppose, for example, that a communication channel could send two possible signals, say, the dot and dash of Morse code. If someone was waiting for the first signal to arrive, they would have uncertainty about those two possibilities. Then, when the signal arrived, say, as a dash, then the two possible outcomes would be reduced to one. The reduction of two possibilities to one outcome is called a bit of information. Information reduces uncertainty.

Information can be meaningful or meaningless. When Shannon developed his theory of communication, he wasn't necessarily interested in meaningful communication, messages that tell somebody something. In fact, he explicitly stated that whether messages have meaning isn't relevant to the engineering problems of sending and receiving them.

But, when we make decisions, we only care about meaningful information. Suppose that you have an old, pre-digital television set hiding in your attic. When you turn on that set, and it doesn't receive any signal, it will show a speckled, flickering pattern. All the small pixels on the television will be flashing randomly.

Does the flickering pattern carry information? Yes. In fact, that random pattern carries much more information than any sort of real television signal. To help you think about this, imagine that the television was instead showing a tranquil beach scene, from a static camera pointing out toward the ocean as waves rolled slowly in. If you saw one frame of that beach video, you'd know a lot about the other frames. The beach and the ocean would tend to be in the same places from moment to moment. Only a little of the information in the video changes from frame to frame.

When the television only shows flickering noise, however, one frame of noise tells you nothing about the next frame. You'd need a lot more information to represent every pixel on every frame of the video. But, that information is meaningless; it doesn't help us predict what will come next.

For decision making, we care about information that helps us make better decisions, that helps us decide on one course of action or another. We care about meaningful information, which I'll call evidence. It's ideal if we have a great deal of high-quality evidence supporting our decision. But that's not always the case. Sometimes we have only a little evidence, but it's of high quality. And other times, we have a lot of evidence, but it's of low quality.

You can think of the pros and cons of these two possibilities in a single example. Suppose that you were trying to decide whether to go to a new downtown restaurant for dinner tomorrow. If you called a close friend who recently went to dinner there, you'd get one person's opinion, but that opinion would be very trustworthy. Or, you could look up reviews of that restaurant online. You might get many people's opinions, although each opinion wouldn't be that trustworthy, individually. Both of these are valuable for decisions. You want high-quality information, when you can get it. And you want lots of information, when you can get it. But you don't always have lots of high-quality information.

When people have to decide between two options, one with a little high-quality evidence and the other with a lot of low-quality evidence, they often make systematic mistakes. In particular, people tend to overestimate the quality of evidence. And, they underestimate the value of having lots of evidence, even if it's low quality.

Let's first see how people overestimate the quality of evidence.

When I talked about heuristics, I talked about how people overestimate the likelihood of events that seem typical, familiar, or memorable. In large part, this overestimation happens because we are so good at inductive reasoning: drawing evidence from one example and applying that evidence for some more general judgment or decision. We see patterns and generalize from those patterns, as I discussed in the last lecture on randomness. We're so good at drawing evidence from events, in fact, that we'll use that evidence even when it shouldn't apply.

Suppose that you're the CEO of a company that sells bicycles, and you're making the final decisions about the release of a new bicycle targeted toward male casual riders, people who tend to ride their bikes only a few hours per month. Your marketing team comes to your office with video testimonial from a rider who road-tested the new bicycle in a focus group. Before they show you the video they tell you that this rider is not typical of your target market segment, he rides every day.

Now, if you care about the quality of the evidence, you shouldn't let this video influence your decision too much. This rider isn't typical of the group you aren't targeting, so the evidence shouldn't be considered high quality. But, here's the surprising thing: people still use this evidence. In fact, in laboratory experiments that test these sorts of decisions, people are equally influenced by evidence regardless of its quality. In the example of the bicycle-firm CEO, it wouldn't matter whether the video was from a rider identified as outside the target market, identified as inside the target market, or from a rider whose typicality wasn't mentioned.

Of course, real-world marketers are very aware of who's likely to buy their products, and so they go to great trouble to collect data from consumers in those target market segments. But, the basic point still holds: We're easily influenced by anecdotes and stories, even if those anecdotes shouldn't be relevant to our decision.

Let me give you a simple task. Think about a time in your past that you spent on a plane, waiting for your flight to take off. If you've flown enough times in your life, you've probably had at least one memorable flight delay (that time when you sat on the plane as it taxied to the runway, then there was a mechanical problem, then they resolved the delay, then there was icing on the wings, then you had to wait for the de-icer, then there was another delay because of the weather, and so on). So, let me know ask you a question. How unpleasant is flying? Is a taking a flight something you look forward to, or something you dread?

There's no right answer here. Different people have different attitudes toward flying. But I want to explain what I've just done. When I asked you to think about a time that you've spent on a plane, what comes to mind most naturally are the vivid, unusual, and frankly rare events, like the delay that never ends. When people bring those rare and memorable events to mind, on average those events are seen as stronger evidence than they should be. After thinking about an extreme flight delay, people would be more likely to think that flying is pretty unpleasant.

But now suppose that you were instead asked to describe a typical flight from your past. You wouldn't bring to mind an extreme event, like an extensive flight delay. Instead, you'd probably think about some flight that went more-or-less as expected. If people are first asked to think about typical events from their past, then their judgments about the future aren't as clouded by extremes of emotion.

Anecdotes and extreme events don't necessarily provide good evidence. Events can seem extreme because they are atypical and unrepresentative, in which case they shouldn't shape our decisions. When thinking about whether to accept a new job, don't just think about the ideal circumstances, something like, "I'll be in line to be VP within five years, I'll get to travel on the annual company trip." Force yourself to think about what's typical, along with what could be extremely good or extremely bad. Considering a broader range of evidence can help you make better decisions.

There's another reason that people overestimate the quality of their evidence toward a decision: People tend to seek out evidence that confirms their existing beliefs, instead of evidence that could refute those beliefs. That's called confirmation bias. We see echoes of confirmation bias in the popular media, in our conversations, and in ourselves. When people take a strongly held position, like on a political hot-button issue, they interpret new evidence in whatever way best fits their existing beliefs. So, new evidence tends to reinforce people's strongly held beliefs, even when that same evidence might be seen by a neutral party as challenging those same beliefs.

In one study, research participants were presented arguments for and against a controversial issue, such as new taxes to support the local schools. Regardless of their own belief, they were asked to evaluate the arguments as objectively as possible, so that they could explain each argument to another person. And, after each argument was presented, they rated its strength.

As you might expect, people showed the confirmation bias. Arguments that confirmed their beliefs were rated as strong, while arguments that challenged their beliefs were rated as weak. But the experiment didn't stop there. The researchers also found that the confirmation bias was strongest in the people who had the most knowledge about politics, as measured by a separate test. That is, confirmation bias doesn't go away as people gain knowledge, it gets stronger.

Several factors contribute to the confirmation bias. One possibility is that people preferentially seek out streams of information that tend to support their prior beliefs. There's good evidence that this matters; for example, people prefer news programs that tend to share their political slant, not challenge it, and they avoid other potential sources of conflicting information.

Another possibility is that when people see evidence against a strongly held position, they simply ignore it. That's usually not true, though. When shown two arguments—one confirming their beliefs, the other disconfirming—people tend to spend relatively little time reading and thinking about the confirming evidence. Instead, they spend their time looking at disconfirming evidence, not ignoring it.

So, that leads to a third possibility: People actively reinterpret evidence that would otherwise argue against their belief. When they read an argument against their position, they don't just accept that argument. Instead, they start thinking about counterarguments. They internally generate new evidence in support of their prior belief, which in turn actually strengthens their original position. This gives us two main reasons for the confirmation bias: We prefer sources of evidence that tend to confirm our existing beliefs, and we counter-argue disconfirming evidence, strengthening our original beliefs in the process.

Now, it's very difficult to eliminate the confirmation bias. None of us wants to be constantly challenged in our beliefs, and we all want to feel that our beliefs are rational and justified. All one can hope to do is minimize it as much as possible. There's one approach that helps, and it's not very hard, if you are willing to try it. You just have to switch sides. By that I mean that you should force yourself to take the other position, and present its case without counterargument.

If you passionately believe that taxes should be raised to support the public schools, then force yourself to argue the virtues of reduced taxes as well as you can. You might argue that reduced taxes will lead to a stronger local economy, more local jobs, a more vibrant cultural scene, and eventually a larger tax base for those schools. Do your best to identify the most reasonable and strongest arguments for that other position.

The key here is to avoid counter-arguing for your existing beliefs. Instead, put yourself in the shoes of another person, a reasonable member of your community who happens to take the other side. That'll disengage you from the desire to be consistent, from your own passions, and force you think about the evidence from another perspective. Ideally, you want to think about alternatives to your prior beliefs as early as possible, so that you aren't too biased in the evidence you acquire. But, it's still good practice for all of us to challenge our beliefs, even strongly held ones.

Let's now move from the quality of evidence to the amount of evidence. I mentioned that people tend to underestimate the value of having lots of evidence, even if that evidence is of low quality. In many cases, the amount of evidence is given by the statistical term sample size, which describes how many data points have been measured. People often have a hard time interpreting information about sample size. It's not that they think sample size isn't important; we all know that more evidence is better than less evidence. Instead, the challenge for decision making comes when quality of evidence and sample size come into conflict.

Suppose that I have two coins. I tell you truthfully that one of the coins is weighted on one side so that it will flip that same side about two-thirds of the time. The other coin is just a normal fair coin. You need to guess which is which.

I pull one coin, chosen randomly, out of my pocket, and I flip it three times. It comes up heads each time. I pull the other coin out of my pocket and I flip it over and over. After a couple of minutes, the tally is 20 heads and 15 tails.

When surveyed, most people guess that the first coin is the biased one (it always comes up heads). But even a fair coin will flip the same way three times in a row pretty often, about 25 percent of the time. The second coin has a much larger sample size, and it actually is slightly more likely to be the biased coin.

I want to offer one important caveat, however. For many sorts of decisions, there's a sort of diminishing returns for sample size. A good example comes from polling in nationwide elections. Sometimes you'll see criticism of a national poll that takes the following form: They only surveyed 500 people. How can they draw conclusions about more than 300 million Americans?

If you want to find out what candidate a majority of Americans prefers for president, for example, you don't need to survey millions of people. A survey of a few hundred to about a thousand people will provide a reasonably small margin for error, on the order of about four percent. Increasing the sample size beyond that point wouldn't make the poll much better.

What matters most for polling is that the sample is representative. There shouldn't be any systematic bias in who participated. A large poll doesn't do any good if the people's opinions aren't independent from each other, as can happen if a poll samples too many people from one geographic area or from the same age range. It's usually better to have a sample of 500 people who are broadly representative of the population than a poll of 10,000 unrepresentative people. So, even though I'm emphasizing the counterintuitive point that we can often do better with more, low-quality evidence, once sample size gets large enough, then there are cases like polling for which quality becomes more important.

So far, I've told you that we integrate evidence to help us reach decisions and that we don't always integrate evidence the right way. But, I haven't yet told you how evidence integration actually works, how psychological or neurobiological processes take different sources of evidence and integrate them into a decision. There's a good reason I haven't told you this: We don't know.

We only have a few tantalizing hints about the process of evidence integration and why it sometimes goes awry, at least for the complex real-world decisions I've discussed in this lecture. Those hints come from research on much simpler sorts of decisions: those only involving two known outcomes, with no uncertainty. The basic idea is that evidence is accumulated over time, and a decision is reached when the evidence reaches some criterion.

Let me illustrate this with an analogy. Suppose that you are sitting at an intersection in a major city. You watch the crossing traffic flowing left and right. If you just glance at the street for a moment, you can't tell right away which direction had more traffic, to the left or to the right. But, after you watch for a few seconds, you might have a guess. And, after a minute or so, you can reach a judgment—left, there are definitely more cars going left.

Researchers have used experimental paradigms with this sort of flavor: A human participant or animal watches a display with moving dots, and their task is to decide whether more dots are going left or more dots are going right. For now, let's consider two conditions: one in which there are 5 percent more dots moving to the right, and the other in which there are 25 percent more dots moving to the right.

When researchers record activity in neurons thought to be involved with evidence integration, an interesting pattern emerges. In both of those conditions, 5 percent and 25 percent, the activity of the neuron increases over time. But it increases much faster in the 25-percent condition, where the evidence is stronger.

The neuron's activity increases continuously until it reaches some threshold value. It might take a bit more or less time to reach that threshold, depending on the quality of the evidence—it's faster when there's 25-percent bias than when there's 5-percent bias. But once it reaches the threshold the decision is made.

The current best models assume that evidence accumulates continuously until we reach a decision. If the evidence seems to be very high quality, then the rate of accumulation is faster, and we decide more quickly, although we are also more prone to mistakes. If there's a lot of low-quality evidence, then the rate of accumulation is slower, and our decisions are slower but potentially more accurate.

This basic model can be extended into simple consumer choices. Imagine that there are two competing products sitting side-by-side on a supermarket shelf. Your eyes flit back and forth between them, looking at one, then the other. With each eye movement, you bias the process of evidence accumulation toward the product you're currently viewing. Again, when the evidence for one product over the other becomes large enough, you'll make your decision and take the selected product off the shelf and place it in your basket.

There's still much more to be learned about this process. We don't yet know whether the basic mechanisms that help explain fast, two-item choices are also used for much slower and more complex choices. And, it's not yet possible to explain all of the biases I discussed in today's lecture.

But, this very simple sort of model holds promise. It's consistent with how our neurons work. It's consistent with basic psychological experiments. And, it's consistent with simple economic choices. So, there's good reason to believe that more complex decisions work in much the same way.

I began this lecture with the tragic story of Percival Lowell, an ambitious and talented astronomer who believed something in spite of all evidence to the contrary. He believed that on the planet Venus were cities and canals, an entire alien civilization. He drew pictures of that civilization. And, he took his belief to his grave.

Why did he make this mistake? The natural answer has always been confirmation bias: He wanted to believe in something and ignored or reinterpreted evidence to the contrary. He believed what he wanted to believe.

But, there was always something mysterious about the fact that Lowell's drawings of Venus were so detailed. He was an exceptional observer using one of the best telescopes in the world, and day after day he drew the same pattern of hubs and spokes, none of which others saw. Almost 90 years after his death, Lowell's drawings were published in a magazine for amateur astronomers, and several of those amateurs sent letters, each solving the mystery.

You see, Lowell had indeed worked on the largest telescope in the world: a refractor with a light-gathering lens 24 inches across. Through that telescope, Venus was blindingly bright, so bright that one cannot look at it directly. So Lowell did what astronomers often do when observing very bright objects: He covered up all but three inches of its lens. That dimmed the image of Venus enough to be viewable, but it also made that image very small, like light coming through a pinhole.

You've probably experienced what Lowell saw, yourself. When you have your eyes checked, the eye doctor will wave a very small light in front of your eyes, and you'll see both the light, and the shadows it casts of the blood vessels in your eye. You'll see a central dark spot and then a set of lines radiating from that spot—those are blood vessels. You'll see the same thing that Percival Lowell saw. He wasn't looking at canals on Venus; he was looking at blood vessels in his own eye.

We want to find evidence that supports our beliefs, that helps us make dramatic discoveries or win arguments. We're very good at seeking out that supporting evidence, and we're very good at developing counterarguments against evidence in which we don't believe. But we need to be skeptical, not just about others, but about ourselves. Sometimes, we just shouldn't believe our own eyes.

In the next lecture, we'll move from evidence to experience. We'll consider how we should make decisions about our own experiences. When we're deciding how to spend our money, how can we compare intangible experiences like vacations or concert tickets to physical goods like electronics or cars? How much of a price should we put on our memories? We'll learn about value of our experiences.

# The Value of Experience
## Lecture 15

This lecture will consider how we should make decisions about our own experiences. When we're deciding how to spend our money, how can we compare intangible experiences like vacations and concerts to physical goods like electronics and cars? What price should we put on our memories? In this lecture, you will learn about value of our experiences. This lecture will argue something that may seem irrational: Experiences are undervalued. They aren't as fleeting as they seem, and we're often better off spending money on experiences than we are on material goods.

**What Is an Experience?**
- Material goods are computers, furniture, clothes, cars, books, and houses. They are things that exist in our physical world. We can trade them to others. We can save them for later—in some cases indefinitely.

- Experiences are a little more difficult to define than material goods. For this lecture, experiences are the perceptions, emotions, and memories evoked by some event. Experiences are internal to each of us, and thus, we can't trade them to others; we can't save them for later.

- We are acting under the assumption that material goods and experiences are two distinct categories, but they aren't completely distinct. Think about material goods and experiences as two extremes on a continuum. And if it's helpful to think of one feature that distinguishes them, then think about time. Material goods last; experiences are fleeting.

**Undervaluing Experiences**
- In the early 2000s, psychologist Tom Gilovich and his colleagues began to explore what generated the most happiness: experiences or material goods. In their first laboratory study, they instructed half of

their participants to describe the most recent material purchase that had cost them at least 100 dollars. The remaining participants were instructed to describe their most recent experiential purchase of at least 100 dollars.

- Then, the participants answered a series of questions about that specific purchase, including how happy it made them feel and whether the money seemed well spent. The results were simple and striking: Experiential purchases led to more happiness, both when thinking back to the purchase and more generally in one's life. Experiential purchases were more likely to be seen as money well spent. In addition, experiential purchases generated less regret.

- A follow-up study was conducted in a large, nationwide, random sample. Each person was asked to think about two recent purchases—one material and the other experiential—that had been purchased in order to increase his or her personal happiness. Then, each person was asked which of those two actually makes him or her happier. Experiential purchases made people happier, and that advantage held for every demographic group tested.

- There was only one factor that made the advantage of experiential purchases go away: income. People with incomes less than about 25,000 dollars reported that material goods and experiences evoke the same relative happiness. But as income increased above that level, there was a greater and greater bias toward experiential purchases. Of people with incomes about 150,000 dollars per year, the highest category used, about 70 percent reported that their recent experiential purchase made them happier.

- Experiences make people happier than material goods. This result has been replicated in multiple studies by many other psychologists and marketing scientists. Furthermore, when researchers ask people to evaluate others' purchases of experiences and goods, the effects become even stronger.

**Memory**

- For experiential purchases, people don't show the normal biases of comparison. They don't do as much comparison before they purchase, they don't need to justify their purchase afterward, they aren't bothered if they could have gotten a better deal, and they aren't jealous if someone else gets a better deal.

- As a general rule, experiences don't lend themselves to comparison in the same way as material goods. That's partially due to the fact that experiences are subjective and internal; it's harder to compare vacations or concerts or cooking classes than it is to compare electronics or cars. But there's an even deeper reason— one that explains why experiences have such a lasting effect on our happiness: Experiences are fleeting, but memories last.

- The first and most important fact about memories is that they aren't accurate—at least, they aren't anything like a literal recording of an experience. Scientists who study memory now think that memories about our past consist of a set of sensations and emotions that are linked together when necessary, such as when a memory is formed and when that memory is brought to mind.

- Your memory of going to Disney World as a young child might include the visual image of staring up at Cinderella's castle, the tactile sensation of holding your father's hand, the noise of the street performers behind you, and the intertwined emotions of awe and excitement.

- Those different sensations and emotions are actually stored independently in your brain. Visual features of a memory are stored in brain regions that support vision, tactile features are stored in brain regions that support touch, and so on. But when a memory is retrieved, your brain has to access all of those different components of a memory and to bind them together again into one coherent experience.

**When retrieving memories from past experiences—for example, when looking through old pictures—we feel like the same way that we feel when we are being rewarded with something tangible.**

- The act of successfully retrieving a memory turns out to be extraordinarily rewarding. We like it when we're prompted to remember an event from our past. Think of how hypnotizing it can be to watch old photos rotate through a slideshow on a computer or television. When we retrieve memories of our past, our brain's reward system becomes active—in much the same way as when we win money or sip a glass of wine.

- Memories aren't literal recordings of our experiences. They change over time; they tend to become more positive. Think back to some vacation or other trip in which you went camping, hiking, canoeing, or something else outdoors. Most outdoor vacations combine both good and bad elements: Roasting marshmallows is followed by freezing in a cold tent.

- However, our memories of those vacations do something amazing over time. They change. The bad parts of the memories—the frustration, delays, cold—are likely to fade away. Or, they become more positive, as we reinterpret an unpleasant experience into something that gives us a good story. And the positive parts of the trips remain and get stronger as we remember them.

- In some ways, our memories become better over time. It's not that they become more accurate, but they become more positive. They become better stories; they become more valuable.

- This idea—that memories have substantial and increasing value—helps explain why experiential purchases generate such long-term happiness. Experiences generate memories. We enjoy retrieving those memories and reexperiencing the events from our past. And those memories actually become more and more valued over time.

- But there's an important caveat to raise. Bad experiences are no better than bad material goods, and a very bad experience can last longer in memory than a bad material purchase. Many bad material purchases are simply worthless; their negative features end when they are discarded. So, it's worth thinking about memory as something that extends our experiences in time: Good experiences become better as they last, but bad experiences disappear or change, albeit slowly.

**Memory as Identity**
- Do memories explain our satisfaction with spending money on experiences? In one study by the psychologists Tom Gilovich and Travis Carter, research participants were first asked to remember a significant experiential or material purchase they had made and to describe their satisfaction with that purchase. After the participant described that purchase—maybe a beach trip or perhaps a new car—he or she was given the following instructions.
    o Imagine that you could go back in time for just an instant and make a different decision, choosing one of the alternatives instead, and then come back to the present. All of your current memories of that purchase would be replaced with new memories that were formed as a result of the different choice,

but ultimately you have arrived back at the same place and time, right where you are now.

- Would you go back in time and switch all of your memories of your beach trip with new memories—for example, of a trip you *didn't* take to the mountains? The participants were asked to rate how willing they would be to trade in their memories of their experience or of their material good.

- The participants were more satisfied with experiential purchases than material purchases. However, that effect was driven by memory. The most satisfying purchases were those that generated memories that people wouldn't give up. Most experiences are better than most material goods at generating memories, so people tended to find experiential purchases more satisfying.

- Although it might seem a little counterintuitive, experiences generate more happiness and less regret than material goods, but it's not because of the pleasure of the experience at that time—it's because of the later memories the experience creates. And, over time, our memories help define our identity.

- Most people prefer to know about other people's experiences than about their material goods; they see people's experiences as more revealing of their true selves. We judge people by the experiences that they seek out. This preference is weaker in people who are more materialistic, but it doesn't go away. Our experiences become part of us; they define who we are. And we can use knowledge of others' experiences to judge them.

## Being Satisfied with Your Decisions
- Prioritizing experiences over material goods is often a very good idea. In general, once basic needs are met, purchases of experiences lead to more immediate happiness, more satisfaction with those purchases, and better memories. There's a really obvious recommendation here: Spend more money on experiences. However, that's not always possible. You can't spend all of your

money on experiences, and you shouldn't try to. Material goods can certainly generate happiness, under the right circumstances.

- There are a few tools that can help you become more satisfied with your decisions—of all sorts. The first is to think about your purchases, whether experiential or material, in terms of the experiences they provide. That's easy for a vacation or concert; it's harder for material goods like cars or computers. But it's still possible.

- The second recommendation is to think in terms of time, not money. Thinking about time forces us to consider our experiences—how we'll feel, what we'll get to do. We start prioritizing different things—with whom we'll connect, how we'll feel, what we'll remember.

## Important Terms

Carter and Gilovich, "The Relative Relativity of Material and Experiential Purchases."

Mogilner and Aaker, "The Time vs. Money Effect."

## Questions to Consider

1. Under what circumstances can experiences be better purchases than physical goods?

2. What makes experiences so valuable?

# The Value of Experience
## Lecture 15—Transcript

When you think about economic transactions, the image that probably comes to mind is a consumer purchase, perhaps buying a new car, some running shoes, or a new television. In all of those cases, the economic transaction involves giving up some of your money for a physical consumer good.

But not all economic transactions involve physical goods. When you go out to dinner at a nice restaurant, what are you paying for? It's not the calories in the food, you can obtain food of similar or greater nutritional value for much, much cheaper. You're paying for the experience—the ambience of the dining room, the attentive service, the opportunity to have a good conversation with someone close to you, and yes, the taste of the food.

When you think about it, paying for experiences seems a little odd. Experiences exist for a fleeting moment, and then they are gone. But people are willing to pay enormous amounts of money for seeming simple experiences.

If you've ever stayed at a beachfront hotel, you know that rooms with a view of the ocean cost much more than non-ocean-view rooms. How much more depends on the hotel and the view. In many cases, though, a true oceanfront room, one with the best view, will cost between 10 percent and 25 percent more than an identical room that doesn't face the ocean.

Is that worth it? Let's do some math. Let's suppose that the difference in price between ocean-view and non-ocean-view rooms is $50 a night. For some hotels it'll be less and for others it will be much more. And, let's further suppose that you spend 30 minutes each day, just sitting in your hotel room and admiring the view (that's probably an overestimate for most people). Together, those numbers imply that looking out at the ocean from your hotel room is an activity worth approximately $100 per hour. That's a pretty high rate to pay for a simple experience, probably much more than for any other activity on your vacation.

This ocean-view premium extends to housing purchases as well. Again, the exact numbers will vary somewhat depending on the location, but in general ocean-view properties carry a premium of something like 30–40 percent, on average, compared to nearby similar properties. For many beachfront locations, that means that the house on the ocean side of the street would cost hundreds of thousands of dollars more than its neighbor across the street, even if they had similar amenities and even similar beach access.

It seems simply irrational, in any sense of that word, to spend substantial amounts of money on a fleeting, insubstantial experience. You close your eyes and the ocean view disappears. Rather than staying a week in the ocean-view suite, you could have stayed in the garden view suite across the hallway, and saved enough money to buy that new computer or new television, or saved even more for your retirement.

But people are willing to spend impressive amounts of money on experiences. If anything, there is generally higher demand for ocean-view real estate than non-ocean view, even after accounting for the difference in price.

In today's lecture, I'll explore the idea of purchasing an experience. And, I'll argue for something that may seem irrational. I'll argue that experiences are undervalued. They aren't as fleeting as they seem, and we're often better off spending money on those experiences than we are on material goods.

So let's begin by defining material goods and experiences. Material goods are obvious; they are computers, furniture, clothes, cars, books, and houses. They are things that exist in our physical world. We can trade them to others. We can save them for later, in some cases indefinitely.

Experiences are a little harder to define. For today's lecture, I'll define experiences as the perceptions, emotions, and memories evoked by some event. An experience is what you feel when you look out an ocean-view window, or listen to a concert, or step into the cold water of a mountain stream. Experiences are internal to each of us, and thus we can't trade them to others, we can't save them for later.

I'll talk today as if these are two distinct categories (material goods on the one hand, and experiences on the other), but they aren't completely distinct. Many material goods can also convey experiences—cars, clothes, and houses all carry value both because of their physical nature and because of the experiences they enable. We don't just purchase a down winter coat because it protects us from the elements; we also value its comfort and the style it presents to others.

Food purchases have material elements and experiential elements. We purchase food to survive, but we usually choose one specific food over another because of the experiences it provides. And, our modern digital world can completely blur any lines between material goods and experiences. When we purchase a digital copy of a popular book, is that book material or experiential? There's no physical book, in any sense, but the book lasts for an extended period of time and can be moved around.

So think about material goods and experiences as two extremes on a continuum. And, if it's helpful to think of one feature that distinguishes them, then think about time. Material goods last. Experiences are fleeting.

It's been long recognized that experiences are valuable. In 1751 the Scottish philosopher David Hume ended his *Enquiry Concerning the Principles of Morals* with a meditation on this very issue. He valued experiences, what he called "the unbought satisfaction of conversation, society, study, even health and the common beauties of nature, but above all the peaceful reflection on one's own conduct." But he disparaged material goods, what he called "worthless toys and gewgaws … the feverish, empty amusements of luxury and expense."

Since the time of Hume, psychologists, economists, and even grandparents have recognized that happiness doesn't always come from material possessions. If you're like me, when you were young you got birthday cards from grandparents with a little bit of money inside, along with some instructions: "Do something fun. Get something you enjoy."

But, this advice was based on anecdotes and intuition, and there was surprisingly little empirical evidence one way or another. In the early 2000s, the psychologist Tom Gilovich and his colleagues began to explore what generated the most happiness, experiences or material goods. In their first laboratory study, they instructed half of their participants to describe the most recent material purchase that had cost them at least $100. The remaining participants were instructed to describe their most recent experiential purchase of at least $100. The young adults in this study described the sorts of purchases you might expect. Material purchases were things like clothing and jewelry; experiential purchases were things like concert tickets and trips to sporting events.

Then the participants answered a series of questions about that specific purchase, including how happy it made them feel and whether the money seemed well spent. The results were simple and striking. Experiential purchases led to more happiness, both when thinking back to the purchase and more generally in one's life. Experiential purchases were more likely to be seen as money well spent. And, experiential purchases generated less regret.

A follow-up study was conducted in a large nationwide random sample. Each person was asked to think about two recent purchases, one material and the other experiential, that had been purchased in order to increase their personal happiness. Then, each person was asked which of those two actually makes them happier. Experiential purchases made people happier, and that advantage held for every demographic group tested: young/old, employed/retired, male/female, Republican/Democrat, and so forth.

There was only one factor that made the advantage of experiential purchases go away: income. People with incomes less than about $25,000 reported that material goods and experiences evoke the same relative happiness. But as income increased above that level, there was a greater and greater bias toward experiential purchases. Of people with incomes about $150,000 per year, the highest category used, about 70 percent reported that their recent experiential purchase made them happier.

Experiences make people happier than material goods. This result has been replicated in multiple studies by many other psychologists and marketing scientists. What is more, when researchers ask people to evaluate others' purchases of experiences and goods, the effects get even stronger. That makes sense. Let me ask you this: Suppose that I tell you that I just spent

$1,000 on a beach vacation and another $1,000 on a new couch. Which one do you think made me happier?

So that's the basic phenomenon. The next step is to evaluate why experiences evoke more happiness. To think about why, we'll need to explore some other differences between experiential and material purchases. For now, let's contrast two prototypic purchases: the experiential purchase of a weekend stay at a mountain lodge and the material purchase of a new television set.

Let's first look at potential differences in the process of decision making. When people make experiential purchases they are more likely to search for an option that is good enough, rather than trying to find the best possible option. We try to find a good location for our vacation, but we try to find the best television. To use the term introduced in the lecture on bounded rationality, people are more likely to satisfice when they make experiential purchases.

Let's next consider what happens after the purchase is made. After material purchases, people still tend to be interested in other foregone options. Suppose that you purchased a television set and two weeks later you learned that there was a new and better model coming on the market. Or, you learned that the price on your set dropped by 20 percent. You'd probably be much less satisfied with your decision. You want to feel like you made the best purchase, and you didn't.

But after people have their experiences, people are less likely to think about what could have been. After you walk into your vacation hotel, you're probably not going to spend much time thinking about the other hotels in the area. And, you're not likely to be bothered if the price drops for other people. It's hard to know that in the first place, and you can explain away their discounted price as luck—they just got a good deal.

Finally, let's consider the effects of social comparison. Suppose that you set up your new television and invite a friend over. You proudly show off the great features of the new set, and your friend excitedly blurts out, "That's really great, I just got a new television, too." But your friend paid less for a television or got a better television or, worst of all, paid less and got a better television.

How would you feel? Most people find situations like this pretty frustrating. We're happy if our friends do well, but we don't want them to do better than us; that leads to jealousy.

But, replace "television" with "vacation." Your friend blurts out, "I just went on vacation, too." It's not as frustrating if a friend goes on a really great vacation or gets a better deal on a vacation. That doesn't evoke as much jealousy, as shown in laboratory studies. On the contrary, we share stories with friends who go to similar places.

There's something common about all of the effects that I just described. For experiential purchases, people don't show the normal biases of comparison. They don't do as much comparison before they purchase, they don't need to justify their purchase afterward, they aren't bothered if they could have gotten a better deal, and they aren't jealous if someone else gets a better deal.

As a general rule, experiences don't lend themselves to comparison in the same way as material goods. That's partially due to the fact that experiences are subjective and internal. It's harder to compare vacations or concerts or cooking classes than it is to compare electronics or cars. But there's an even deeper reason, one that explains why experiences have such a lasting effect on our happiness.

In 2011 the Disney Theme Parks announced that year's promotional campaign, called "Let the Memories Begin." The central concept of the new campaign was what they called a memory hub: an online site where visitors to Disneyland and Disney World could share their photographs and videos, along with stories about their vacations. In effect, people could share their memories.

Once shared, those electronic records of visitors' memories were used by Disney in several ways. They were featured on the website, used in Disney commercials, and even projected onto the facades of the park's central castles as part of a nighttime musical show.

At that time, every company was expanding rapidly into social media, trying to connect with its customers through non-traditional advertising channels. But what was striking about the Disney campaign was just how heavily it relied on memories. Strange as it might be to say, this media campaign wasn't emphasizing the pleasure you and your family will have during the visit—come to Disney World and you'll have fun while you're there. The campaign emphasized what you'll bring back after you come to Disney World, after you've ridden all the rides, met all of the characters, and are back at your home. You'll have memories. This campaign was very popular. It was extended into a second year before giving way to the next campaign, which actually also emphasized the transient nature of an experience (it was called "Limited Time Magic").

Experiences are fleeting, but memories last. It's important, however, to understand a bit about how memory works, so that we can see why memories are so motivating. As I introduced in a previous lecture, the first and most important fact about memories are that they aren't accurate, at least, they aren't anything like a literal recording of an experience. Scientists who study memory now think that memories about our past consist of a set of sensations and emotions that are linked together when necessary, such as when a memory is formed and when that memory is brought to mind.

So, your memory of going to Disney World as a young child might include the visual image of staring up at Cinderella's castle, the tactile sensation of holding your father's hand, the noise of the street performers behind you, and the intertwined emotions of awe and excitement. Those different sensations and emotions are actually stored independently in your brain. Visual features of a memory are stored in brain regions that support vision, tactile features are stored in brain regions that support touch, and so on. But when a memory is retrieved, your brain has to access all of those different components of a memory and to bind them together again into one coherent experience.

The act of successfully retrieving a memory turns out to be extraordinarily rewarding. We like it when we're prompted to remember an event from our past, as when we see an old vacation photo, and then momentarily relive the time we walked next to a Venice canal at sunset. Think of how hypnotizing it can be to watch old photos rotate through a slideshow on a computer or television. When we retrieve memories of our past, our brain's reward system becomes active, in much the same way as when we win money or sip a glass of wine.

Memories aren't literal recordings of our experiences. They change over time. They tend to become more positive. Think back to some vacation or other trip in which you went camping, hiking, canoeing, or you did something else outdoors. Most outdoor vacations combine both good and bad elements (roasting marshmallows is followed by freezing in a cold tent).

But, our memories of those vacations do something amazing over time. They change. The bad parts of the memories (the frustration, delays, cold) are likely to fade away. Or, they become more positive, as we reinterpret an unpleasant experience into something that gives us a good story. And, the positive parts of the trips? Those remain and get stronger as we remember them.

In some ways, our memories become better over time. By that I don't mean that they become more accurate. I mean that they become more positive, they become better stories, they become more valuable.

This idea—that memories have substantial and increasing value—helps explain why experiential purchases generate such long-term happiness. Experiences generate memories. We enjoy retrieving those memories and re-experiencing the events from our past. And, those memories actually become more and more valued over time.

But there's an important caveat to raise. Bad experiences are no better than bad material goods. And a very bad experience can last longer in memory than a bad material purchase. Many bad material purchases are simply worthless; their negative features end when they are discarded. So, it's worth thinking about memory as something that extends our experiences in time. Good experiences become better as they last, but bad experiences disappear or change, albeit slowly.

Now, let's connect memory back directly to our economic choices. Do memories explain our satisfaction which spending money on experiences?

In one study by the psychologists Tom Gilovich and Travis Carter, research participants were first asked to remember a significant experiential or material purchase they had made, and to describe their satisfaction with that purchase. After the participant described that purchase (maybe a beach trip or perhaps a new car) they were given the following instructions: "Imagine that you could go back in time for just an instant and make a different decision, choosing one of the alternatives instead, and then come back to the present. All of your current memories of that purchase would be replaced with new memories that were formed as a result of the different choice, but ultimately you have arrived back at the same place and time, right where you are now."

Would you go back in time and switch all of your memories of your beach trip with new memories, say, of a trip you didn't take to the mountains? Would you do that? The participants were asked to rate how willing they would be to trade in their memories of their experience or of their material good.

Consistent with everything I've described in this lecture, the participants were more satisfied with experiential purchases than material purchases. But, that effect was driven by memory. The most satisfying purchases were those that generated memories that people wouldn't give up. You wouldn't give up the memories from your last vacation or from the last play you attended. Most experiences are better than most material goods at generating memories, and so people tended to find experiential purchases more satisfying.

Let me emphasize this point, because it might be a little counterintuitive. Experiences generate more happiness and less regret, but it's not because of the pleasure of the experience at that time, it's because of the later memories the experience creates. And, over time, our memories help define our identity. Suppose that you were about to meet someone who would soon be entering your life, it could be a blind date or a new partner at work. What would you rather know about them, what kind of car they drive or where they last went on vacation?

Most people prefer to know about other people's experiences; they see those experiences as more revealing of someone's true self. We judge people by the experiences that they seek out. This preference is weaker in people who are more materialistic, but it doesn't go away. Our experiences become part of us. They define who we are. And we can use knowledge of others' experiences to judge them.

Prioritizing experiences over material goods is often a very good idea. In general, once basic needs are met, purchases of experiences lead to more immediate happiness, more satisfaction with those purchases, and better memories. There's a really obvious recommendation here. Spend more money on experiences! Go on that vacation. Splurge on that Broadway show.

But, that's not always possible. You can't spend all of your money on experiences, and you shouldn't try to. Material goods can certainly generate happiness, under the right circumstances. So, I want to end by giving you a couple of tools that can help you become more satisfied with your decisions of all sorts.

The first recommendation is to think about your purchases, whether experiential or material, in terms of the experiences they provide. That's easy for a vacation or concert. It's harder for material goods like cars or computers, but it's still possible.

Suppose that you purchased a new computer last year. I can promise you that since that time, someone else paid less for a much better computer. That always happens. It's easy to regret technological purchases when you think in terms of price and features. Since the beginning of the electronic age, prices have always gone down and features have always improved.

But, think about the experiences that computer has provided: watching digital photos, communicating with distant relatives, or even playing games. Research shows that thinking about material goods in terms of the experiences they provide leads to more satisfaction with that purchase. That's a good thing. It's not healthful to regret our purchases, especially when that regret comes from factors outside our control, like the fact that there's now a better deal.

And, a moment's reflection will reveal that nearly all material purchases can be framed in terms of experiences—toys, clothes, food, artwork. These all hold value in part because of the experiences they provide. Thinking about those experiences and the resulting memories makes it easier to see the value of those material goods. When you think about your experiences, you'll have a better sense of what's really important.

The second recommendation is to think in terms of time, not money.

Two researchers in a business school ran a wonderful experiment. They set up a lemonade stand in a San Francisco park with real six-year-olds as the salespeople. On a large easel to the left of the stand, they placed several signs to attract customers. One of the signs read "Spend a little money, and enjoy C&D's lemonade." Another read "Spend a little time, and enjoy C&D's lemonade." And the third didn't mention either money or time. The researchers changed to a different sign every 10 minutes, and measured how many people purchased lemonade while each sign was being displayed.

They found that people were twice as likely to stop and buy lemonade when the sign read "Spend a little time" compared to when it read "Spend a little money." Customers were also allowed to pay what they wanted for the lemonade, as little as one dollar or as much as three dollars. The "Spend a little time"-customers paid near the maximum, almost twice as much as the cheapskate "Spend a little money"-customers.

A simple sign prompted people to think about time, and suddenly they became more likely to purchase a product and they paid more for it. The likely reason was that people started thinking about purchasing lemonade as an experience. They would stop, talk to the cute kids, support a worthy cause, and then enjoy a nice glass of lemonade on a Saturday afternoon. Those experiences are worth much more than three dollars. The sign reminded people why they were in the park in the first place: to have a positive experience.

A sign emphasizing money, in contrast, makes people think of the lemonade as a material good. Most potential customers weren't in the park seeking out something to drink. And, besides, the stand is being manned by six-year olds; they probably don't make particularly good lemonade. If you just want a material good, some drink to quench a thirst, your money might get you more at the professional vendor or the vending machine instead.

Thinking about time forces us to consider our experiences, how we'll feel, what we'll get to do. We start prioritizing different things, with whom we'll connect, how we'll feel, what we'll remember. We'll see the smiling kids standing behind the stand, not just their watered-down lemonade.

Happiness comes from our experiences. That's an old idea. It predates behavioral economics and even scientific psychology. But even old ideas can be clarified and given structure by new science. David Hume knew the importance of this idea. He ended his masterwork on moral philosophy with these simple words: "Natural pleasures, indeed, are really without price; both because they are below all price in their attainment, and above it in their enjoyment."

In our next lecture, we'll explore decisions about a different sort of non-material experience: our health. Medical decisions involve uncertainty, complex science, temporal discounting, large consequences for ourselves and often others, and, yes, they affect what we'll experience on a daily basis. It's no wonder that decisions about our health are some of the most important and most challenging that we face in our lives.

# Medical Decision Making
## Lecture 16

In this lecture, you will learn about three factors that influence how we make medical decisions: how we deal with uncertainty, how we evaluate good and bad outcomes, and how we're guided by others' opinions. In one sense, there's nothing special about medical decisions: All of these factors influence nonmedical decisions, and we don't have any sort of brain module specific for medical decisions. However, in another sense, medical decisions are special. They involve our bodies, our capacities, our sense of self—even life and death. Medical decision making has the same biases as other forms of decision making, but there are also some key differences.

**Uncertainty**
- The first factor that shapes medical decisions is how we deal with medical uncertainty. Researchers have examined how real patients use probabilities when evaluating treatment options. When patients are told that a medicine has a 40-percent chance of controlling your disease, some people know what this means: The medicine works for 40 people out of every 100. But many people don't know what this means. They think of that 40 percent more abstractly, as if the physician was relating the chance of rain—it could reflect the physician's confidence or how much the symptoms would be reduced.

- Sometimes physicians describe probabilities in verbal labels: A side effect is "common" or "rare," and the success of the surgery is "likely" or complications are "unlikely." These labels are simpler for people to understand than probabilities, but different people treat the same label very differently, and what you think a probability label means could have dramatic effects on the treatment you choose.

- People also care not just about their own risk, but also about relative risk—how their probability compares to other people's probability.

If a diabetes medication reduces the probability of cardiovascular disease from 40 percent to 30 percent, it's not clear how good that is. What's the reference point?

- For medical decisions, people often care about whether their chances are higher or lower than their peers. This can cause problems. If we see ourselves as doing better than our peers, then we're less likely to take preventative actions. Other people's risk shouldn't affect our decisions, but it does.

- Even more challenging to process is information about changes in risk, such as the following statement: "Taking a statin medication reduces your long-term risk of cardiovascular disease by 50 percent." Emphasizing changes in probability can be very misleading. Statements like "Your chance of heart disease doubles if you don't take the medication" typically cause people to overestimate risks.

- What seems to work best is giving people absolute probabilities and presenting those probabilities in terms of frequency: Without taking this medication, four out of 10 people with diabetes like yours will develop heart disease, but with the medication, it drops to only three in 10. That is, about one in 10 people can prevent heart disease just by taking this medication.

- Using absolute probabilities makes the consequences of different decisions much more concrete. But it's not perfect. The common bias in how people use probabilities is they overestimate the probability of rare events, underestimate very common events, and are largely indifferent for events of intermediate probability.

- These biases not only hold when people make decisions about medical outcomes, but they're even exaggerated. The difference between certainty and a little bit of uncertainty looms very large. We want cures, not changes in probability.

- Many medical outcomes are rather rare. Read the safety sheet for any drug and you'll find a very long list of potential side effects, most of which are of very low probability. These rare outcomes can be vividly brought to mind, and we want to avoid them entirely, not have a small chance looming over us.

**Reward/Cost**
- The second factor that shapes medical decisions is the vividness of good and bad outcomes. As a general rule, outcomes that are more vivid, more tangible, and have better defined consequences exert greater influence on our decisions.

- People recognize that mental health can be more burdensome than physical health, but chronic depression is less tangible than chronic diabetes, for example, so research has shown that people are willing to pay more money to avoid diabetes than depression.

- Historically, there's been much more money spent on research and treatment of physical illness than mental illness, even though people understand just how debilitating mental disorders can be. Similar discrepancies can be seen when you ask people how much of their life span they'd be willing to give up to avoid different diseases; their answers don't necessarily match their sense of disease burden.

**Depression is a serious mental illness, but it isn't viewed as being as serious as a physical illness.**

- Vividness influences our medical decisions in other ways, too. People sometimes avoid taking action because they fear the regret associated with making a choice that leads to harm. This is sometimes called the omission bias—harms of omission aren't our fault. This bias works against us when we face rare or unknown risks.

- Many children have become sick or died because they didn't receive a freely available vaccine. When parents are surveyed, the primary factors that predict that their children won't be vaccinated are the perceptions that vaccines are dangerous and ineffective—and the omission bias. Parents who don't vaccinate their children are more fearful of taking an action that they perceive could harm their child, as compared to parents who vaccinate.

- Our decision biases matter. Many public health problems arise because of behaviors whose potential negative consequences are long term and uncertain. Just because you have dessert every evening doesn't guarantee that you're doomed to cardiovascular disease, diabetes, and an early death.

- Behavioral economist George Loewenstein points out that, in many medical decisions, the option that's best for us and best for society involves tangible costs but intangible benefits. It's no wonder that people aren't willing to pay a cost—for example, by exercising regularly or giving up fatty foods—in order to receive some uncertain, distant benefit.

**Others' Opinions**
- The third and final factor that shapes our medical decisions is others' opinions. We often consider what other people think when making our own medical decisions, for at least two reasons.

- One reason is that our medical decisions have consequences for others. We think about how our own medical choices will affect our partners, parents, children, and friends.

- A second reason is how we use others' opinions to make medical decisions. The health-care system in the United States—and in many other countries—relies on interactions between patients, their physicians, and other health-care workers.

- When recommending something to another person, especially someone unconnected to us, we try to think about his or her needs. We distance ourselves from the decision; it doesn't generate strong emotions.

- Often, our decisions focus on specific trade-offs that can be readily justified to others. For example, you can justify a complicated surgery by thinking that there might be a few potential complications, but they are very rare, and they're still much better than death.

- The idea that advisors seek to make decisions that can be justified to others connects back to the concept of regret aversion. Physicians want to avoid regret, too—and that can change what they recommend. Keep in mind that physicians exhibit the same biases as the rest of us.

- Medical decisions often rely on advice from others, particularly physicians and other health-care workers. Getting recommendations from others can often improve our decisions, because those recommendations aren't as influenced by emotional reactions to rare events and other biasing factors. However, we should be aware that advisors aren't bias-free. Like us, they want to avoid regret, and that can push them toward safe, default choices that can be easily defended, rather than a risky choice that might be best for us.

## Making Better Medical Decisions

- Even more than financial decisions, medical decisions are intensely personal, and there's no simple rule that can guarantee good outcomes or even good decisions. Everyone's medical situation is unique. The following recommendations, accordingly, are intended to help apply general principles of behavioral economics so that the process of decision making improves.

- The primary recommendation is that you should make decisions about yourself, but with others. Decisions will be better, overall, if you consider your potential benefits, costs, and risks independently from others' outcomes. Think in absolute terms, not relative terms; don't compare yourself to others.

- This is particularly important for decisions about prevention. You should evaluate your own risk. You might only have a 40-percent chance of cardiovascular disease, compared to more than a 50-percent chance in the general population—but that's still a 40-percent chance. You may still be able to take steps that reduce your own chance dramatically, improving your expected quality of life.

- Absolute probabilities are often most easily processed by thinking in terms of frequency. Most people do better when thinking about frequencies, especially in the middle range where events might occur or might not—for example, 60 out of every 100 people like you will develop this disease in the next 10 years. Thinking in terms of frequency helps make probabilities more concrete, especially when dealing with changes in probability.

- We rightly focus on cures and vaccines because of their power for eliminating disease, but we tend to overvalue changes in very high or very low probabilities. Steps that reduce the risk of common conditions can be much more important, even if they can't eliminate all risk.

- You should also recognize that you're not a perfect decision maker. None of us is. When you're facing a complex medical decision, you're not even at your best. You might be feeling extreme emotions, you might be stressed, and you might have ongoing depression or racing thoughts. Some disorders even affect the very systems in your brain that support decision making.

- Therefore, advice from others can be critical for making good decisions. The key is to use that advice in the right way. Avoid relying on anecdotes and stories about what has worked in the past. Stories are vivid and easy to remember, but they can also bias us. Seek out evidence, and get others' opinions on how to use that evidence, so that you aren't facing a complex decision alone.

- Finally, be optimistic. Suppose you learn that a surgery has a 10-percent chance of failure. That focuses your mind on the negative outcome, causing it to influence your decisions. However, the same surgery has a 90-percent chance of success. When people think in terms of success, they're less likely to avoid risks unnecessarily, often making much better decisions. And that positive mindset has many other benefits for your health.

## Suggested Reading

Loewenstein, Brennan, and Volpp, "Asymmetric Paternalism to Improve Health Behaviors."

Ubel, *Critical Decisions*.

## Questions to Consider

1. In what ways are decisions about our health different from decisions about our finances?

2. Why might thinking about medical outcomes in terms of frequency instead of probability lead to better decisions?

# Medical Decision Making
## Lecture 16—Transcript

Medical decisions can be extraordinarily difficult. They involve our most valuable asset: our health. They almost always involve some uncertainty. Because of the complexity of the human body, we can't know outcomes in advance. They can generate strong emotions, elicit our deepest fears, and fill us with regret. They are difficult, but important. We want to make the right decisions about our health.

You might think that because medical decisions have such large stakes, they wouldn't be influenced by the biases I've introduced in previous lectures. But they are.

Let me tell describe a very simple experiment run by Peter Ubel, who's both a behavioral economist and a physician. Here's the dilemma (fortunately, it was hypothetical) that he gave to his participants. Suppose that you are diagnosed with a form of treatable cancer. For now, let's assume that it is colon cancer. Your physician comes to you with two courses of treatment, what she calls the complicated and uncomplicated surgeries.

The uncomplicated surgery has only two potential outcomes, both with well-defined probabilities. There's an 80-percent chance that the surgery goes as expected and you recover completely, with no ill effects, no other health issues, and no chance of cancer recurrence. But there's a 20-percent chance you'll die during the surgery.

The complicated surgery is pretty similar, but it has slightly different outcomes. There's an 80-percent chance that you'll recover completely with no chance of recurrence and no ill effects, as before. And, now there's only a 16-percent chance you'll die during the surgery. But there are four unpleasant potential complications, each occurring in one percent of the patients who survive the surgery cancer free. There could be severe scarring, uncontrollable abdominal pain, recurring diarrhea, or a colostomy. The only difference between the uncomplicated and the complicated surgeries is that a four-percent chance of dying in the uncomplicated surgery is replaced by a four-percent chance of various unpleasant surgical complications.

Ubel first asked participants about their preferences for the surgical complications. When participants were asked which is better, severe scarring or death, they'll say severe scarring. The same answer holds for all of the different complications. People go through surgeries all the time that save their lives, but reduce their quality of life in some way. People prefer the complications to death.

But, when Ubel asked participants about their preferences for the surgeries, there was a surprising result. A majority of people in his experiment picked the uncomplicated surgery, the one with a higher chance of death. That choice just doesn't make sense, at least if one assumes that patients make decisions by comparing the sets of outcomes associated with each potential treatment. The same people prefer the outcomes of the complicated surgery, individually, but when faced with the surgeries as a whole, they pick the uncomplicated surgery.

This result is emblematic of the puzzle of medical decisions. They are high-stakes, important decisions. There's lots of information available. There's usually a physician or other expert to help. And, yet people make what seem like objectively bad decisions.

In today's lecture, I'll discuss three factors that influence how we make medical decisions: how we deal with uncertainty, how we evaluate good and bad outcomes, and how we're guided by others' opinions. In one sense, there's nothing special about medical decisions. All of these factors influence non-medical decisions, and we don't have any sort of brain module specific for medical decisions.

But, in another sense, medical decisions are special. They involve our bodies, our capacities, our sense of self, even life and death. So, I'll balance describing how medical decision making elicits the same biases as other forms of decision making, while also giving some insight into some key differences.

Before I discuss each of those three factors in more depth, let's see how they can jointly explain the decisions in Peter Ubel's experiment. First, let's think about uncertainty. Remember from the lecture on probability that a core finding of behavioral economics is that people give too much weight to very rare events—an event that objectively has only a one-percent chance of occurring might seem subjectively as if it had a five-percent chance of occurring. So, the surgical complications may only each have a one-percent chance of occurring, but they influence the decision much more.

Second, let's consider the vividness of good and bad outcomes. These surgical complications were specifically chosen because they seemed rare and scary. It's frightening to consider life with constant abdominal pain or recurring diarrhea. Vivid outcomes carry more weight in our decisions.

Third, let's evaluate the role of others' opinions on our decisions. These outcomes are not just personally unpleasant; they evoke disgust in others. We don't want to face the possibility that a surgical complication might alienate our friends or family, or might diminish our self-pride.

Together, these three factors lead to paradoxical medical decisions. People would rather have the surgical complication to death, if either was certain. But they'd rather have a surgery with an increased risk of death than one with a lesser risk of death along with those complications.

Let's begin by exploring how we deal with medical uncertainty. Suppose that you are a physician trying to communicate with a diabetes patient about different treatment options. (In this example, and in all the others in the lecture, I'll use hypothetical treatments and outcomes just to avoid any specific medical recommendations.) You know that clinical research trials have shown that a new medication reduces similar patients' chances of severe cardiovascular disease from 40 percent to 30 percent, over the next 10 years. How do you give her that information?

One obvious way to do that is just to relate the scientific study, very factually and slowly: "In randomized clinical trials of patients with similar symptoms, life history, and demographics, taking this medication reduced the overall incidence of cardiovascular disease from 40 percent in the control group to only 30 percent in the treated group, for a period of 10 years following the onset of treatment." I purposefully simplified that. It was much less complicated than how the same would be written in an academic journal or on a medical label. But it was still complicated.

You can imagine what the patient might be thinking: Doctor, I understand that this medicine can help some people, but what will it do for me?

Researchers have examined how real patients use probabilities when evaluating treatment options. When patients are told that a medicine has a 40-percent chance of controlling your disease, some people know what this means: the medicine works for 40 people out of every 100. But many people don't. They think of that 40 percent more abstractly, as if the physician was relating the chance of rain; it could reflect the physician's confidence or how much the symptoms would be reduced.

Sometimes physicians describe probabilities in verbal labels: a side effect is common or rare. Success of the surgery is likely, complications are unlikely. These labels are simpler for people to understand than probabilities, but different people treat the same label very differently. When people in one study were told that a side effect is very likely and then asked what that means in terms of numerical probability, their interpretations ranged from 30 percent to 90 percent. What you think a probability label means could have dramatic effects on the treatment you choose.

People also care not just about their own risk, but also about relative risk, how their probability compares to other people's probability. If a diabetes medication reduces the probability of cardiovascular disease from 40 percent to 30 percent, it's not clear how good that is. What's the reference point?

For medical decisions, people often care about whether their chances are higher or lower than their peers. This can cause problems. Someone who is at high absolute risk for cardiovascular disease might compare themselves to peers who are similarly overweight, also smoke, and also lead a sedentary lifestyle. If we see ourselves as doing better than our peers, then we're less likely to take preventative actions. Other people's risk shouldn't affect our decisions, but it does.

Even more challenging to process is information about changes in risk. Listen to the following hypothetical statement: Taking a statin medication reduces your long-term risk of cardiovascular disease by 50 percent. How should you use that information? Fifty percent seems like a big effect. Does that statement imply that you'll go from likely to get heart disease to unlikely to get heart disease after you start taking the medication? Probably not. It might mean something much less dramatic. Perhaps you have a four-percent chance of heart disease without the medication, and a two-percent chance with the medication.

Emphasizing changes in probability can be very misleading. And, this problem goes in the other direction, too. Statements like "Your chance of heart disease doubles if you don't take the medication" typically cause people to overestimate risks.

What seems to work best is giving people absolute probabilities, and presenting those probabilities in terms of frequency—Without taking this medication 4 out of 10 people with diabetes like yours will develop heart disease, but with the medication it drops to only 3 in 10. That is, about 1 in 10 people can prevent heart disease just by taking this medication.

Using absolute probabilities makes the consequences of different decisions much more concrete. But it's not perfect. Remember the common bias in how people use probabilities: They overestimate the probability of rare events, underestimate very common events, and are largely indifferent for events of intermediate probability.

These biases not only hold when people make decisions about medical outcomes, like changes in life expectancy; they're even exaggerated. The difference between certainty and a little bit of uncertainty looms very large. In laboratory experiments, a treatment that reduces the probability of a disease from 10 percent to 0 percent was actually seen as more valuable than another treatment that changes that disease's probability from 90 percent to 50 percent. We want cures, not changes in probability.

Let me emphasize that many medical outcomes are rather rare. Even routine anesthesia in healthy adults carries some risk of death, but the actual probability is extremely small, on the order of one in several hundred thousand. For a healthy adult, that's about the same as the chance of dying in an automobile accident next month.

Not all outcomes are that rare, but many are still very, very unlikely. Read the safety sheet for any drug. You'll find a very long list of potential side effects, most of which are of very low probability. These rare outcomes can be vividly brought to mind, and we want to avoid them entirely, not have a small chance looming over us.

This provides a natural transition to the second factor that shapes medical decisions: the vividness of good and bad outcomes. As a general rule, outcomes that are more vivid, more tangible, and have better defined consequences exert greater influence on our decisions. We can see this in medical decision making by comparing disorders that differ in how vivid they are, how tangible they are.

Let's take two disorders, chronic diabetes and chronic depression. Both are frankly debilitating and both can greatly reduce one's quality of life. When surveyed, people report that depression leads to greater reductions in quality of life, compared to diabetes. Mental illnesses are seen as particularly burdensome; they affect one's quality of life more than physical illnesses. But the same people were asked how much they'd be willing to pay to avoid each condition, and they were willing to pay more money to avoid diabetes than they were to avoid depression.

People recognize that mental health is more burdensome (but it's less tangible than something like diabetes), and so people are less willing to sacrifice large amounts of money to avoid it. Now this question was hypothetical; you can't just make diabetes or depression disappear with a monthly co-payment. But, the general principle can be seen in our society's priorities. Historically, there's been much more spent on research and treatment of physical illness than mental illness, even though people understand just how debilitating mental disorders can be.

This doesn't just hold for money. Similar discrepancies can be seen when you ask people how much of their lifespan they'd be willing to give up to avoid different diseases. Their answers don't necessarily match their sense of disease burden.

Vividness influences our medical decisions in other ways, too. Suppose that you are an older adult in a high-risk demographic group for prostate cancer. A series of tests indicates a likely prostate tumor, with unknown prognosis. You have the choice of taking action, perhaps by a combination of radiation therapy and surgery, or taking no action now and instead monitoring the possible progression of the tumor. Again, this is a hypothetical example, but I've chosen prostate cancer because it often involves a slow-growing tumor that doesn't necessarily require treatment.

What do you do, take action or wait? When faced with decisions with this general flavor, there's often a bias toward action. We want to take action for known and vivid risks, because we don't want the regret of failing to act.

Let's switch to a different hypothetical scenario. You are in a high-risk group for, say, Parkinson's disease. It's estimated that you'll have about a five-percent chance of suffering from that disease over the next decade. There's an experimental drug that has been shown to reduce the risk of people in your high-risk group to about two percent, but it also has a small chance, say one percent, of damaging the dopamine neurons in your brain directly, leading to symptoms that are similar to Parkinson's disease anyway.

As I've described this scenario, the choice seems clear: You have a five-percent chance of contracting the disease without the drug, and only a three-percent total chance of having the disease or similar symptoms with the drug. So, you should take the drug.

But, when faced with scenarios of this sort, people often avoid taking action. Why? Because they fear the regret associated with making a choice that leads to harm. This is sometimes called the omission bias; harms of omission aren't our fault.

This bias works against us when we face rare or unknown risks. Many children have become sick or died because they didn't receive a freely available vaccine. When parents are surveyed, the primary factors that predict that their children won't be vaccinated are the perceptions that vaccines are dangerous and ineffective, and the omission bias. Parents who don't vaccinate their children are more fearful of taking an action that they perceive could harm their child, compared to parents who do vaccinate.

Our decision biases matter. Many public health problems arise because of behaviors whose potential negative consequences are long-term and uncertain. Just because you have dessert this evening, or every evening for that matter, doesn't guarantee that you're doomed to cardiovascular disease, diabetes, and an early death.

The behavioral economist George Loewenstein points out that, in many medical decisions the option that's best for us and best for society involves tangible costs but intangible benefits. It's no wonder that people aren't willing to pay a cost—say, by exercising regularly or giving up fatty foods—in order to receive some uncertain, distant benefit.

I'll move now to the third and final factor that shapes our medical decisions: others' opinions. We often consider what other people think when making our own medical decisions, for at least two reasons. One is that our medical decisions have consequences for others. We think about how our own medical choices will affect our partners, parents, children, and friends. If a parent is temporarily incapacitated following surgery, they'll need to rely on others for their children's care. I won't spend more time right now discussing how consequences for others affect our decisions. That's a topic called other-regarding preferences, and it's a key part of the upcoming lectures on altruism and social cooperation. Instead, I want to explore a second reason: how we use others' opinions to make medical decisions.

The health-care system in the United States, and in many other countries, relies on interactions between patients, their physicians, and other healthcare workers. I'll focus on how physicians influence patients' decision making because that's what's attracted the most research, but similar conclusions could be drawn for interactions with nurses, pharmacists, and other caregivers.

Let's think back to the colon cancer scenario from the beginning of the lecture. Remember, there were two surgeries: an uncomplicated surgery that had a higher chance of death and a complicated surgery that had a lower chance of death but several vivid adverse effects. And I told you that most people prefer the uncomplicated surgery, even though they otherwise judge that its complications aren't as bad as death.

The researchers gave the same scenario to primary care physicians, selected randomly from a large database. These are our physicians, the ones who take care of you and me. They are trained in objectively evaluating outcomes and understanding probabilities. On average, they had almost 20 years' experience making medical decisions.

When the physicians were asked which treatment they would choose for themselves, a little less than 40 percent chose the uncomplicated surgery. That's less bias, overall, than non-physicians, who chose the uncomplicated surgery a bit more than 50 percent of the time. It still means, however, that almost half of these physicians chose the objectively worse outcome, despite their medical training and experience.

But the physicians were also asked which treatment they would recommend for their patients. That changed many of those physicians' decisions. They became significantly less likely to recommend the uncomplicated surgery, doing so only 25 percent of the time, and more likely to pick the objectively better but complicated surgery. Let me emphasize this important point: In this study, physicians made objectively better decisions for their patients than for themselves.

When recommending something to another person, especially someone unconnected to us, we try to think about their needs. We distance ourselves from the decision; it doesn't generate strong emotions. Often, our decisions focus on specific trade-offs that can be readily justified to others. In this scenario, you can justify the complicated surgery—yes, there are a few potential complications, but they are very rare and they're still much better than death. This idea—that advisors seek to make decisions that can be justified to others—connects back to the concept of regret-aversion introduced earlier. Physicians want to avoid regret, too, and that can change what they recommend.

One set of family practitioners were given the following sort of scenario. A patient comes into your office with chronic hip pain. They've tried a number of medications to help with their pain and none have worked. You refer them to an orthopedic consultant so that they can be evaluated for surgery. At the end of the visit, you notice that there's one medication they haven't yet tried. Do you start them on that medication? About half of the physicians said, yes, they'd prescribe that pain-relief medication, and about half said no, they wouldn't start any new medication. That seems reasonable, either answer can be justified.

A different group of family practitioners were given a modified version of the scenario. Everything was the same, but at the very end they were told that there were two medications that the patient hadn't tried. The two medications were pretty similar; both were well known and widely used for pain management. And one of them was the same medicine listed in the first scenario. So, basically, this group of physicians had the same decision as the first group, but with one additional option. But now, only a quarter of the physicians said that they'd prescribe either pain-relief medication, and the rest took the default option: referral with no new medications.

Physicians exhibit the same biases as the rest of us. Here, the challenge is that the two medications are very similar, so it's hard to choose between them. There's more potential to make a decision that you'd later regret, like starting the patient on the wrong medication. That pushes their decisions toward not starting any medicine at all.

In summary, medical decisions often rely on advice from others, particularly physicians and other health-care workers. Getting recommendations from others can often improve our decisions, because those recommendations aren't as influenced by emotional reactions to rare events and other biasing factors. But, we should be aware that advisors aren't bias free. Like us, they want to avoid regret, and that can push them toward safe, default choices that can be easily defended rather than a risky choice that might be best for us.

Now I want to end with a few recommendations for how to make better medical decisions. Even more than financial decisions, medical decisions are intensely personal, and there's no simple rule that you have good outcomes or even make a good decision. Everyone's medical situation is unique. These recommendations, accordingly, are intended to help apply general principles of behavioral economics so that the process of decision making improves.

My primary recommendation is that you should make decisions about yourself, but with others. What I mean by about yourself is that decisions will be better, overall, if you consider your potential benefits, costs, and risks independently from others' outcomes. Think in absolute terms, not relative terms. Don't compare yourself to others.

This is particularly important for decisions about prevention. You might be in pretty good shape for your age—you exercise a couple of times a week, don't smoke, and usually eat healthful foods. If so, your risk of cardiovascular disease is probably less than your peers. Does that mean that you shouldn't take preventative medications or adopt lifestyle changes to cut your risk further? No. You should evaluate your own risk. You might only have a 40-percent chance of cardiovascular disease, compared to more than 50 percent in the general population. But that's still a 40-percent chance. You may still be able to take steps that reduce your own chance dramatically, improving your expected quality of life.

Absolute probabilities are often most easily processed by thinking in terms of frequency. Remember that most people do better when thinking about frequencies, especially in that middle range where events might occur or they might not. Sixty out of every 100 people like you will develop this disease in the next 10 years. Thinking in terms of frequency helps make probabilities more concrete, especially when dealing with changes in probability. For a rare disease, a vaccine or behavior modification might reduce your chances from 1 out of 100 to 0 out of 100. That means for every 100 people who try to prevent the disease, 1 will be helped.

But for a common problem, like heart disease, preventative steps might reduce your chances from 60 out of a 100 to 30 out of 100. That means for every 100 people who try to prevent the disease, 30 will be helped. We rightly focus on cures and vaccines because of their power for eliminating disease, but remember that we tend to overvalue changes in very high or very low probabilities. Steps that reduce the risk of common conditions can be much more important, even if they can't eliminate all risk.

You should also recognize that you're not a perfect decision maker. None of us is. When you're facing a complex medical decision you're not even at your best. You might be feeling extreme emotions, you might be stressed, and you might have ongoing depression or racing thoughts. Some disorders even affect the very systems in your brain that support decision making.

So, advice from others can be critical for making good decisions. The key is to use that advice in the right way. Avoid relying on anecdotes and stories about what's worked in the past. Stories are vivid and easy to remember, but they can also bias us. Seek out evidence and get others' opinions on how to use that evidence, so that you aren't facing a complex decision alone.

Finally, be optimistic. Suppose you learn that a surgery has a 10-percent chance of failure. That focuses your mind on the negative outcome, causing it to influence your decisions. But, the same surgery has a 90-percent chance of success. When people think in terms of success, they're less likely to avoid risks unnecessarily, often making much better decisions. And, that positive mindset has many other benefits for your health.

Medical decisions can be difficult and scary; we naturally think about them as involving risks to our health. But there's another way to think about them: They are opportunities for us to preserve our health and to take control of our future.

In the next lecture we'll move to the domain of social decisions: how we combine our own judgments and others' judgments to reach a final decision. Understanding how social information contributes to decision making can help improve a wide range of our decisions, by helping us better use advice and by evaluating the judgments of others.

# Social Decisions—Competition and Coordination
## Lecture 17

This lecture transitions from a focus on decisions made by individuals in isolation to decisions made by individuals in social settings, specifically settings in which two people or a small group of people interact. Regulations are often criticized because they limit our freedom of choice, and there are surely situations in which those criticisms hit their mark. But the idea that we are free to choose is based on the idea of the single decision maker, acting in isolation. As game theory shows, sometimes we're better off by restricting our own choices—as counterintuitive as that may seem.

### Core Principles of Game Theory

- Economists and other social scientists have used a branch of mathematics called game theory to model interactions during strategic decision making. A "game" in this sense is basically an abstracted version of the decision situation—something that specifies the decision makers, or players, their potential choices, and the outcomes of their choices.

- During the early days of the National Hockey League, and up until the 1970s, players never wore helmets, simply because other players weren't wearing them. If one player wore a helmet, he'd be safer, but he wouldn't see or hear as well as the other players, so he'd be playing at a disadvantage. A player who wore a helmet might lose his spot on the team to someone else who didn't wear a helmet.

- Suppose that there are two similarly talented players competing for a spot on the same hockey team. They each have two potential choices: to wear a helmet or to not wear a helmet. And the outcomes each receives depend not just on their own choice, but also on the choice of the other player.

- Game theorists use numbers to represent the desirability of each outcome. In game theory, this is called the relative utility of the outcome. For this example, let's use arbitrary numbers from 0 to 10, with larger numbers indicating better outcomes—that is, outcomes with higher relative utility.

- Suppose that both players show up for training camp wearing helmets. They each have equal chances of making the team, and they are better protected from injury. So, that outcome seems pretty good for both of them—let's call it a 7.

- Suppose that one of those players now decides to play without his helmet; his odds of making the team now go up considerably, even though he's risking head injury. He thinks that's a trade-off worth making, so let's call that outcome a 9.

- But the other player is still wearing his helmet, so he's very unlikely to make the team. That's the worst outcome, even though his head is protected. So, let's call that outcome a 1.

- The following day, both players show up without helmets. They're back to a fair competition, although neither player's head is protected, and both are risking injury. So, let's call that outcome a 3.

- Clearly, the players are better off when both wear helmets than when neither wears a helmet. In both cases, the competition is fair, but the injury risk is much higher when not wearing a helmet. But they end up without helmets, in the worst collective outcome.

- This simple situation turns out to be equivalent to the most famous scenario in all of game theory: the prisoner's dilemma, an early version of the game that involved two prisoners jailed for jointly committing a crime. Each of them had to decide whether to remain quiet or inform on his partner.

- In the hockey scenario, the players will inevitably end up not wearing helmets. That pair of choices is known as an equilibrium point, because neither player has incentive to change their choice unilaterally.

- You shouldn't think about an equilibrium point as something that represents the optimal set of choices. The players would be better off if they both wore helmets, in this case. You should instead think about an equilibrium point as a stable set of choices. It's the set of choices from which no one has any incentive to deviate on their own. For hockey players, if your competitors aren't wearing helmets, then you're only going to make yourself worse off by starting to wear one.

## Coordination Games

- Not all social interactions involve direct competition. In many cases, small groups of people do best when they coordinate their behavior, especially when their interests are aligned.

- Coordination introduces its own set of challenges for decision making. Consider the following example. A group of hunters are working together to trap a stag in a forest. They each enter the forest from different directions and walk toward the center, forming a shrinking circle around the stag. As long as they all work together, the stag can't escape, and they'll each get a big reward.

- However, there's another game in the forest—small hares are plentiful and easy to catch. If one of the hunters decides to go after a hare instead, that hunter will be sure to get a small reward, but the stag will be able to escape the trap.

- In games like these, if every player cooperates, they'll all get a large reward. But if at least one person doesn't cooperate and takes the sure small reward, then all the rest will get nothing. So, cooperation depends on mutual trust; if everyone trusts the others, then the system works well. But once trust breaks down, the system breaks down.

- Many of our economic institutions rely on shared trust, and when that trust falters, there are runs on banks, collapses of industries, and other tears in our economic fabric.

**Backward Induction**
- Game theory is very powerful because it can take complex real-world problems and reduce them to simple models that can be solved mathematically. However, like the other models in this course, game theoretic models require assumptions about how people should behave.

- Players should be rational; they are motivated by their own outcomes. Players should think that other players are rational, too. Players can't communicate during the game and can't collude to split their payoffs after the game. In addition, there aren't any sort of hidden external influences that aren't represented in the game's explicit outcomes. These are the basic assumptions.

- By assuming that players are rational—that they consistently follow their self-interest—game theorists can find solutions to games that explain complex real-world problems. But people's behavior doesn't always follow the predictions of game theory. In particular, people can't always think through all the steps of how their choices should influence other people's choices, which should influence their own choices, and so on. That problem is known as backward induction.

- In principle, a rational player should be able to perform as many steps of backward induction as possible to reach an optimal decision—but we can't.

- Optimal choices in real-world games depend on your assessments of the rationality of the other players. And you can use your own limitations as a good guide to the limitations of the others. Your own doubt might be a good guide to others' doubt—and to the likelihood that at least one person won't cooperate. So, you switch your choice to the safe option, just like many of the others.

## Focal Points

- We don't have the computational abilities to reason through all the steps of a complex decision problem. We have bounded rationality, which means that our decision processes have limitations; we don't approach these games in a mathematically optimal way. Instead, we approach problems in a way that's suited to our own computational limitations and that tries to take advantage of the structure in the world around us.

- One very powerful tool for using the structure in our world is to look for a focal point, an idea coined by economist and Nobel Laureate Thomas Schelling. Focal points have special properties that distinguish them from other choices, and thus, they facilitate coordination even when people can't communicate directly.

- For example, suppose that you and your friend have to coordinate your behavior by each selecting one coin from a bag of 100 coins, independently. If all 100 coins are pennies, you are really unlikely to select the same one. But if 99 of the coins are pennies and one is a nickel, you'll be able to coordinate. That one meaningful outlier is a focal point.

- Focal points turn out to be extraordinarily important for real-world markets. They can change competitive markets into cooperative ones, which can be very bad for consumers.

## Emotion and Recommendations

- Our emotions also provide a powerful tool for our interpersonal decisions. Emotional reactions are assumed to be part of the outcomes of games—something wrapped into the utility values assigned to those outcomes. Emotion isn't seen as something that should shape the strategies players take in games; however, emotion does matter.

- The first recommendation for this lecture is that limiting your ability to make choices can give you power. Suppose that you and your friend want to meet at a restaurant. You'd rather have her come to your side of town; she'd rather have you come to her side of town. She gets her way by calling you, telling you where she's going, and then turning off her phone.

- She has purposefully limited herself to a single choice: She can only go to one restaurant, and she can't communicate with you anymore. However, by limiting her own options, she shapes what *you* will do—she knows that you'll come meet her.

- You can't just turn off your emotions, even if you wanted to. Emotion limits our choices, but it can also give us power over others.

- The second recommendation is that cooperation doesn't always require communication. You can coordinate your choices with someone by exploiting the structure of the world, by looking for focal points.

- Focal points—like cooperation itself—aren't necessarily good or bad. Focal points can help us reach consensus in group discussions and help us negotiate to a mutually beneficial outcome. However, they can also lead to unwanted collusion. Focal points provide a potential tool for increasing the efficiency with which we collaborate, for better or worse.

- The final recommendation is that institutional actions are often needed to disrupt unwanted equilibria. In many competitive markets—for example, consumer electronics—businesses would often prefer to upgrade their products to take advantage of some new technology, such as a better plug that connects devices to computers. But they only can change their own production if everyone else also changes their production. That's exactly the sort of situation where institutional actions are most valuable. Industry groups can collectively come up with a new standard that then becomes adopted more widely.

## Suggested Reading

Camerer, *Behavioral Game Theory*.

Schelling, *The Strategy of Conflict*.

## Questions to Consider

1. Why don't people's decisions in interactive games match what's predicted by rational choice models?

2. What are focal points, and how do they facilitate cooperation?

# Social Decisions—Competition and Coordination
## Lecture 17—Transcript

So far in this course, I've talked primarily about individuals who make decisions in isolation: a consumer deciding between cars to purchase, a gambler deciding whether to make one more bet, a near-retiree deciding whether to move their investments from stocks to bonds. But many real-world decisions aren't made in isolation. They involve consideration of the goals and plans of other people, and those goals and plans aren't necessarily aligned with our own.

In today's lecture I'll talk about how the decision process changes when there's another person involved, when we coordinate our decisions with someone else for mutual benefit, or when we compete with someone else over a limited resource. Such social decisions can involve a rather counterintuitive process of decision making. Let me give you an example, one you may have experienced before.

Suppose that you are arranging dinner plans with a friend who lives on the other side of town. The highest priority is to meet at a restaurant that you'd both like, and both you and your friend share that goal. But, you'd prefer a particular restaurant on your own side of town to minimize your travel time, and your friend prefers a restaurant on her side of town for the same reason. Each of you has a different, competing goal for the location of dinner. How could you resolve that competition?

Your first thought, naturally, is to call your friend and discuss the location of dinner. Maybe you can talk her into coming to your side of town. So, you call her and there's no answer. You soon get a short e-mail message from her. "Hi. My phone's out of charge and I'm going offline. I'll meet you at the restaurant down the street from my house at 7 o'clock. Bye!" With that simple message, she ensures that you go where she wants.

This seems like a trivial example; It just involves two friends deciding on the location for dinner. But, think about how it was solved: In a sense, your friend won the negotiation by purposefully limiting her ability to make decisions. As we'll discuss later in this lecture, that simple idea turns out to have extraordinary implications for how people, institutions, and governments interact.

Today I'll transition from a focus on decisions made by individuals in isolation to decisions made by individuals in social settings, specifically settings in which two people or a small group of people interact. We'll consider larger groups, how people interact in societies, and the influences of social norms on decision making in the next few lectures.

Economists and other social scientists have used a branch of mathematics called game theory to model interactions during strategic decision making. But what do they mean by a game? It's basically an abstracted version of the decision situation, something that specifies the decision makers or players, their potential choices, and the outcomes of their choices. So, let's take a real-world situation and reduce it to a game, specifically, a game in which people's goals are competing.

During the early days of the National Hockey League, and up until the 1970s, players never wore helmets. That wasn't because the players thought helmets were useless; on the contrary, many of them had experienced concussions from hard hits or had lost teeth to flying pucks. And, they all knew of other players who had suffered injuries from hockey sticks to the head.

So, why didn't they wear helmets? The simple answer was because other players weren't wearing them. If one player wore a helmet he'd be safer, but he wouldn't see or hear as well as the other players, so he'd be playing at a disadvantage. A player who wore a helmet might lose his spot on the team to someone else who didn't wear a helmet.

Let's simplify this situation to something we can model using game theory. There are two similarly talented players competing for a spot on the same hockey team. They each have two potential choices, wear a helmet or don't wear a helmet. And, their outcomes depend not just on their own choice, but also on the choice of the other player.

Game theorists use numbers to represent the desirability of each outcome. In game theory, this is called the relative utility of the outcome. So, for this example, I'll just use arbitrary numbers from 0 to 10, with larger numbers indicating better outcomes, that is, outcomes with higher relative utility.

Suppose that both players show up for training camp wearing helmets. They each have equal chances of making the team, and they are better protected from injury. So, that outcome seems pretty good for both of them, let's call it a 7.

Suppose that one of those players now decides to play without his helmet. His odds of making the team now go up considerably, even though he's risking head injury. He thinks that's a tradeoff worth making, so let's call that outcome a 9. But the other player is still wearing his helmet, so he's very unlikely to make the team. That's the worst outcome, even though his head is protected. So, let's call that outcome a 1.

What might happen next? The following day both players show up without helmets. They're back to a fair competition, although neither's head is protected and both are risking injury. So, let's call that outcome a 3.

Let's think about this situation. Clearly, the players are better off when both wear helmets than when neither wears a helmet. In both cases, the competition is fair, but the injury risk is much higher when not wearing a helmet. But they end up without helmets, in the worst collective outcome.

This simple situation turns out to be equivalent to the most famous scenario in all of game theory: the Prisoner's dilemma. The name Prisoner's dilemma comes from an early version of the game that involved two prisoners jailed for jointly committing a crime. Each of them had to decide whether to remain quiet or inform on his partner. I've always found that story a bit confusing and contrived. So, let's just stick with the real-world example.

In the hockey example, the players will inevitably end up not wearing helmets. That pair of choices is known as an equilibrium point, since neither player has incentive to change their choice unilaterally. You shouldn't think about an equilibrium point as something that represents the optimal set of choices. The players would be better off if they both wore helmets, in this case. You should instead think about an equilibrium point as a stable set of choices. It's the set of choices from which no one has any incentive to deviate on their own. For hockey players, if your competitors aren't wearing helmets, then you're only going to make yourself worse off by starting to wear one.

Not all social interactions involve direct competition. In many cases, small groups of people do best when they coordinate their behavior, especially when their interests are aligned. Think about your own social interactions. Often, you and your social partners both want the same outcome, and when one person does well the other person also does well. When you and your friends meet at a movie theater with 20 screens you each could choose any of those 20 movies, but you'd rather go to the movie together than to go to separate movies. So, you discuss your preferences and end up seeing a movie you'll both enjoy.

Coordination introduces its own set of challenges for decision making. Consider the following example. A group of hunters are working together to trap a stag in a forest. They each enter the forest from different directions and walk toward the center, forming a shrinking circle around the stag. As long as they all work together, the stag can't escape, and they'll each share in a big reward. But, there's other game in the forest; small hares are plentiful and easy to catch. If one of the hunters decides to go after a hare instead, that hunter will be sure to get a small reward, but the stag will be able to escape the trap.

In a game like this, if every player cooperates, they'll all get a large reward. But if at least one person doesn't cooperate and takes the sure small reward, then all the rest will get nothing. So, cooperation depends on mutual trust. If everyone trusts the others, then the system works well. But once trust breaks down, the system breaks down. This probably seems familiar to you. Many of our economic institutions rely on shared trust, and when that trust falters, there are runs on banks, collapses of industries, and other tears in our economic fabric.

Game theory is very powerful because it can take complex real-world problems (like helmet wearing in hockey or trust in economic institutions) and reduce those problems to simple models that can be solved mathematically. But, like the other models we've considered throughout this course, game theoretic models require assumptions about how people should behave. Some of the basic assumptions are consistent with the rules for behavioral economics experiments that I introduced in an early lecture.

Players should be rational; they are motivated by their own outcomes. Players should think that other players are rational, too. Players can't communicate during the game and can't collude to split their payoffs after the game. And, there aren't any sort of hidden external influences that aren't represented in the game's explicit outcomes.

These are the basic assumptions, and modern game theory relaxes those assumptions in many ways that are well beyond the scope of today's lecture. But by assuming that players are rational, that they consistently follow their self-interest, game theorists can find solutions to games that explain complex real-world problems.

But people's behavior doesn't always follow the predictions of game theory. In particular, people can't always think through all the steps of how their choices should influence other people's choices, which should influence their own choices, and so on. That problem (I know that you know that I know, and so on) is known as backward induction. In principle, a rational player should be able to perform as many steps of backward induction as possible to reach an optimal decision. But, we can't. Let's see why by considering decisions in markets where value depends on what other people are thinking, like in the stock market.

In 1936 the economist John Maynard Keynes described the business of picking stocks in unflattering terms, saying that: "Professional investment may be likened to those newspaper competitions in which the competitors have to pick out the six prettiest faces from a hundred photographs, the prize being awarded to the competitor whose choice most nearly corresponds to the average preferences of the competitors as a whole."

In this conception, the most successful investors are those who can accurately assess the general sentiment of other investors and then stay one step ahead of the rest. Economists have taken a cue from Keynes and modeled this sort of problem in what's often called a beauty contest game.

Suppose that I give you the following game. You and nine other players each must choose a number between 1 and 100. The winner of the game is the one whose number is closest to two-thirds the group's average. So, if the average of the group were 60, then someone whose choice was near 40 would be the winner. Now, let's use backwards induction to try to solve this game. You might expect that the average of 10 random numbers would be around 50. So, you should choose 33, which would be two-thirds of that average.

But wait, the other players are rational, just like you. They know that they should pick 33, so to outsmart them, you'll need to pick two-thirds of that, or 22. But wait again, the others know that, too. They'll pick 22, so you need to pick two-thirds of that, and so on. If you follow this logic to its conclusion, then everyone should pick the smallest number possible: one. That's the solution to this game. And it never happens.

Whenever groups of people have played this sort of beauty pageant game in the laboratory, they never all agree on the same number. They give a range of numbers, the average of which is usually in the 20s or 30s. This means that people on average only follow one or two steps of backwards induction. They think, "I know that they know that I know," but not much more than that.

And, who wins the game? The best strategy isn't the rational solution to the game. It's one more step than the rest of the group—if the group's average were 33, then you win by choosing 22. But if the group's average were 20, you'd only win if your answer were around 14.

The key idea here is that optimal choices in real-world games depend on your assessments of the rationality of the other players. And, you can use your own limitations as a good guide to the limitations of the others. Think back to the stag hunt game I introduced a few minutes ago. Suppose that there are 10 hunters in your group; if everyone cooperates, you'll each get a big reward.

Imagine yourself walking toward the center of the forest. What might you be thinking? You know that the others might be tempted by the sure-thing smaller reward. And you know that each of them is thinking the same thing. Everyone recognizes that there's some risk that someone will fail to cooperate, either because of temptation or just a mistake. In this case, your own doubt might be a good guide to others' doubt and to the likelihood that at least one person won't cooperate. So, you switch your choice to the safe option just like many of the others.

We don't have the computational abilities to reason through all the steps of a complex decision problem. To return to an idea from an earlier lecture, we have bounded rationality. Bounded rationality means that our decision processes have limitations—we don't approach these games in a mathematically optimal way. Instead we approach problems in a way that's suited to our own computational limitations, and that tries to take advantage of the structure in the world around us.

One very powerful tool for using the structure in our world is to look for a focal point.

Before I define a focal point, let's play a game, one I've adapted from similar games proposed by the economist and Nobel laureate Thomas Schelling. You have been selected to be one of two participants in an American game show. You will win $10 million if you can shake hands with your fellow participant at a particular place, date, and time, somewhere in the United States during the next calendar year. You will have to write down your place, date, and time right now, and your partner is a random American adult who has the identical instructions and is doing the same thing. If your locations do not match, then neither of you wins anything. Good luck.

I want you to think for a moment. What place would you pick? What date and time? Hold on to your answer for a moment. Let's think about how many places there are in the United States. The number is so large that coordination by random chance is essentially impossible, even before you add the additional challenge of agreeing on the right day and at the right time. So, we should expect that you and your fellow contestant would never win the game show. You'd be much more likely to each draw a lottery ticket and have the same set of numbers.

But, when I run this game in my classes (without the promise of a jackpot) I usually get the same answers. Students say Times Square, New York City, January 1st, midnight. Or, the Statue of Liberty, July 4th, noon. Or, the White House or U.S. Capitol, usually on July 4th at noon.

Any answer is possible. But a few answers are much, much more probable than the rest. Schelling called those answers focal points. Focal points have special properties that distinguish them from other choices, and thus they facilitate coordination even when people can't communicate directly.

Let's consider another example, one you could test yourself. Suppose that you and a friend have to coordinate your behavior by each selecting one coin from a bag of 100 coins, independently. If all 100 coins are pennies, you are really unlikely to select the same one. But, if 99 of the coins are pennies and one is a nickel, I'm completely sure that you'll be able to coordinate. That one meaningful outlier is a focal point.

Focal points turn out to be extraordinarily important for real-world markets. They can change competitive markets into cooperative ones, which can be very bad for consumers.

In 2000 the state of Colorado passed legislation that set a maximum loan rate that payday lenders could charge. The assumption was that setting that maximum rate would lower rates overall. But exactly the opposite happened, rates went up. Before the legislation passed, the market in these loans was competitive. Different lenders would undercut each other; they'd rather everyone charge high loan rates, but they wouldn't just raise their own rates unilaterally. Then, when the law passed, the new maximum loan rate established a focal point, and lenders could collude by all charging that same maximum rate. This collusion was most pronounced in the larger markets. Before they had been the most competitive, but now the lenders could coordinate on their pricing.

Our emotions also provide a powerful tool for our interpersonal decisions. I didn't mention emotion when I introduced the basic principles of game theory, nor when I talked about how game theorists find solutions to game. That's because emotion isn't part of game theory. Emotional reactions are assumed to be part of the outcomes of games, something wrapped into the utility values assigned to those outcomes. But emotion isn't seen as something that should shape the strategies players take in games.

But emotion does matter. Let me give one striking example: the ultimatum game. Suppose that you come to the laboratory. You are told that you are going to play a two-person game. Your partner in the game is anonymous—it's someone in another room. You can't communicate with them, don't know them, and won't find out anything about them.

That player, let's call them the proposer, begins the game with $20. They then have to propose a division of that $20 —they'll give you some and keep the rest—and then you can respond to their offer. If you don't accept their offer, then no one gets any money. It's called the ultimatum game because it's a take-it-or-leave-it offer. There's one shot, no negotiation. So, you sit in the laboratory room and wait for their proposal. They propose to keep $19 and give you only 1 dollar. What do you do? Do you accept the dollar? Or, do you reject their offer and then walk away with nothing?

In cases like this, responders almost always reject the offer. They often get angry, turn down the money, and walk away with nothing. Now you might think that's because one dollar is essentially worthless. But, in the game I just described, people still commonly reject offers of $2, $3, $4, even $5. Only when the split seems closer to fair, say, when the proposer offers $8 out of $20, do responders accept the ultimatum nearly all of the time. You may still be thinking, that's not that much money. Even poor college students might act in irrational ways when faced with small stakes. So, let me tell you about some variations of this experiment.

In one case, the experimenters tested U.S. college students using payouts of $400 dollars. The proposers could offer any amount to the responders, and if that offer was accepted, they'd get to keep the rest for themselves. So, some proposers offered about $30. You know, to a college student, that's a meaningful amount of money for a five-minute experiment. The responders rejected those offers more than half of the time. Some proposers offered about $60. The responders rejected those offers more than a quarter of the time.

So, college students will turn down $30 or even $60, if the offer seems unfair. If that doesn't seem that meaningful to you, consider this example. Economists have run variants of the ultimatum game in a number of different countries, including some where the standard of living is much lower than in the United States, which allows them to run the same experiments with very large stakes. There's considerable variability across individuals and cultures, but people still sometimes turn down offers equivalent to several day's wages, or more, if those offers seem unfair.

Behavior in the ultimatum game just doesn't make sense. Why would people reject large sums of money that are given to them by an anonymous other person just because the offer seems unfair? It isn't because people don't want the money.

There's a related game called the dictator game. It has the same basic format with one key difference: the offer can't be rejected. So, if the dictator player is handed $20 at the start of the game, they can decide how much they want to keep for themselves and how much they want to give to the other person. Suppose that you are in one of these experiments, and the anonymous dictator player keeps $18 and gives $2 to you. The experimenter places $2 on the table in front of you. Would you just storm out of the room? Probably not. People receiving money in dictator games don't turn down the money they've just been given.

So what's different about these two games: the ultimatum game, where people sometimes turn down even large amounts of money, and the dictator game, where they don't? The key difference is that the responder in the ultimatum game has the power to influence the proposer but only if they behave irrationally.

Suppose that a responder in the ultimatum game is completely rational. They prefer more money to less. So, they accept whatever they're offered. A proposer can take advantage of them and offer the smallest amount possible knowing that they'll accept. That's the rational, equilibrium point for the ultimatum game.

But if the responder might not be rational, if they might turn down money, then the proposer can't just assume that they'll accept any amount offered. The proposer needs to offer something that seems more fair. So, the threat of irrational behavior, of acting against one's self interest, pushes the proposer to offer more money.

But how can the threat of rejection be credible? There's no contract in this game. In many experiments, the proposer and responder interact via computers, so they never even see each other. So, there's no way that an individual responder can send a signal of threat.

There is a solution, and it's related to the first of my recommendations for today's lecture: Limiting your ability to make choices can give you power. Remember the example from the beginning of the lecture. You and your friend want to meet at a restaurant. You'd rather have her come to your side of town; she'd rather have you come to her side of town. She gets her way by calling you, telling you where she's going, and then turning off her phone.

She's purposefully limited herself to a single choice. She can only go to one restaurant, and she can't communicate with you anymore. But, by limiting her own options, she shapes what you will do; she knows that you'll come meet her. Thomas Schelling won the Nobel prize in economics for this basic idea: that limiting your own ability to make choices can give you power.

So, let's apply this idea to the ultimatum game. When responders are given an unfair offer, say $2 out of $20, they get angry. They want to retaliate against the proposer. They are willing to sacrifice their own earnings if it teaches the proposer a lesson. And, they can't just turn off the emotion, even if they wanted to. That willingness to sacrifice one's own potential earnings, to behave irrationally and against our own self-interest, provides the credible threat we need to discourage unfair offers. Emotion limits our choices, but it can also give us power over others. I'll revisit this idea at the very end of the course, when we talk about precommitment.

My second recommendation is that cooperation doesn't always require communication. You can coordinate your choices with someone by exploiting the structure of the world, by looking for focal points. I want to emphasize that focal points, like cooperation itself, aren't necessarily good or bad. Focal points can help us reach consensus in group discussions and help us negotiate to a mutually beneficial outcome. But, they can also lead to unwanted collusion, as in the case of payday lenders. Focal points provide a potential tool for increasing the efficiency with which we collaborate, for better or worse.

My final recommendation is that institutional actions are often needed to disrupt unwanted equilibria. In many competitive markets, say consumer electronics, businesses would often prefer to upgrade their products to take advantage of some new technology, like a better plug that connects devices to computers. But they only can change their own production if everyone else also changes their production.

That's exactly the sort of situation where institutional actions are most valuable. Industry groups can collectively come up with a new standard that then becomes adopted more widely. Similarly, as soon as the National Hockey League adopted a regulation enforcing helmet usage, the undesirable equilibrium was disrupted, and players moved collectively to a more desirable equilibrium, with everyone wearing helmets.

Regulations are often criticized because they limit our freedom of choice. And, there are surely situations in which those criticisms hit their mark. But the idea that we are free to choose is based on the idea of the single decision maker, acting in isolation. As game theory shows, sometimes we're better off by restricting our own choices, counterintuitive as that may seem.

# Group Decision Making—The Vox Populi
## Lecture 18

The idea of the wisdom of crowds has become so well known that it's hardly questioned anymore. Many people—from politicians to venture capitalists—now assume that crowds simply do better than individuals when forming judgments and making decisions. However, in this lecture, you will discover that the true nature of this phenomenon is a bit more complex than the popular story. Sometimes the crowd does very well indeed, but other times the crowd goes systematically astray—for systematic, predictable reasons.

**The Wisdom of Crowds**

- The wisdom of crowds is an old idea, dating back more than a century, that's continually being shaped by new research. The spark of the idea came from a short paper published in 1907 by the English social scientist and statistician Francis Galton.

- His essay, published in the scientific journal *Nature*, described data he collected from judgments of the dressed weight of an ox, as made by visitors to the Plymouth livestock show. Almost 800 people had made judgments; some of those people were ranchers or other experts, while others were just random visitors of the exhibition. Each, though, had purchased a ticket and written down their guess, in hope of a large prize.

- Galton's scientific report was prompted by an unusual feature of those guesses. Even though people's individual guesses varied considerably, the median value of the guess was very close to the true weight. In statistics, the median is just the middle of some set of numbers. In this competition, it's the guess that was exactly in the middle of the range of guesses, with half of the people guessing more and half guessing less. That median was 1,207 pounds. The actual dressed weight of the ox was 1,198 pounds, only nine pounds from the median guess.

- Suppose that you were at that same fair more than 100 years ago. You know nothing about oxen, but unlike the other fairgoers at that livestock show, you look at many of the other people's guesses. You take the middle of all those guess and write that down as your guess. You'd do much better than the typical butcher, rancher, or other expert.

- Galton described this effect as the vox populi—the voice of the people. In modern times, it's called the wisdom of crowds. It's not magic; it arises because there's always error in people's guesses. In many situations, some people will guess too high, and others will guess too low, and those different guesses will bracket the true value. If that happens, taking the middle guess from a crowd is more likely to be close to the true value than just taking a guess from a single person.

- There's a frequent misconception that the best way to aggregate data from a crowd is to take the average. The average value can be fine for some sorts of judgment, primarily when people's judgments are all on the same scale, but when people's judgments are on vastly different scales, then the average can be misleading.

- For many real-world judgments, people might not even guess the right order of magnitude—they could be off by factors of 10 or more. So, the median, or middle, guess usually provides a better estimate of the true value being judged.

- Another misconception is that it's vital to have a crowd of experts. Expertise isn't as important as two other factors. The first is pretty simple: The size of the crowd matters, to a point. As the group size increases from just a few people to a few dozen people to hundreds of people, the accuracy of the crowd's judgment usually increases. It's often better to have a large crowd of nonexperts than only a few experts. However, once the crowd becomes sufficiently large, there are diminishing returns.

## Diversity

- The second factor is the primary reason for the wisdom of crowds: diversity. Diversity has become a loaded term, one that carries social and political baggage. In this lecture, diversity means something very simple: the degree to which different people approach a decision in different ways.

- Diversity isn't something absolute; it is defined with regard to something. For many sorts of judgments and decisions, we care about intellectual diversity, where people bring different information and different approaches to the same problem.

- There are many factors that influence group decision making: what knowledge each person brings to the decision, whether people share similar or different personalities, whether and how they communicate, and so forth.

**Diversity in thought is advantageous to any problem that a group of people is trying to solve.**

- Researchers have shown that a group made up entirely of high-performing individuals can often do worse than more diverse groups, those that contain some high performers and some low performers. That's because individuals in the diverse groups are more likely to approach the decision in different ways, so the group becomes more effective as it gets larger.

- In addition, groups whose members differ in personality will make better decisions, on average, than groups whose members have more similar personalities. Part of the explanation comes from group dynamics; groups with diverse personalities are more likely to challenge each other in discussions. Our personality can predict, albeit imperfectly, some aspect of how we approach decision problems. Thus, diverse personalities make groups or crowds more effective decision makers.

- In some ways, communication at the wrong time is the enemy of good decision making. Social influence through communication before making decisions can disrupt the wisdom of crowds. Communication from a few prominent individuals in advance of decisions can reduce the diversity of the crowd and potentially introduce bias.

- In real-world judgments, the wisdom of the crowd can be systematically biased by media reports, by very salient news events, and by the opinions of a few influence makers. What's particularly striking is that people often become more confident when they are exposed to less diverse information.

- There's a surprising potential solution, though. Researchers have shown that uninformed people can actually help stem the tide of biased communication.

## Limitations
- It's easy to get caught up in the power of crowd decisions and to lose sight of when crowds fail. Crowds fail when they have a shared error in judgment. And when that's the case, there's a deeper

problem: The people who are most confident about their judgments are often the most wrong.

- When the crowd tends to get a judgment right, the people who are more accurate tend to be more confident. But when the crowd tends to get a judgment wrong, then confidence is higher in people who are more inaccurate.

- We think that confident people are more likely to be right, and we place our trust in them. But just because someone is confident about their judgment doesn't make them accurate—they're just more likely to be like the rest of the crowd.

- We can be overconfident in our own judgments as well, and that can also cause the wisdom of crowds to fail. When betting on football games, casual gamblers generally prefer to bet on the favored team, even though the advantage of the favorite is essentially negated by the point spread, or betting line. Systematic biases like this one can reduce or eliminate any advantage of crowds.

- In addition, crowds fail when people ignore them. In many of our decisions, we have the opportunity to collect information from other people, but we tend to undervalue that information.

- When people receive advice from someone else about a judgment, they tend to adjust their judgment by only about 25 percent toward whatever the advisor recommended. This number is itself an aggregate across three types of people: Most people ignore advice and keep their original judgment, some split the difference between their original judgment and the advisor's, and a small minority actually adopt the advisor's position.

- This pattern of results means that people treat their own judgments as much more accurate than someone else's. They don't use information from other people as much as they should, even when those other people should be just as good at the judgment or decision.

- And people don't recognize the importance of sample size. When given the choice of following the advice given by one confident person or the aggregate of several less confident people, a majority of people will choose to follow the confident person. Remember, people tend to overestimate the quality of their evidence and underestimate the importance of the quantity of evidence.

- However, confidence isn't necessarily predictive of accuracy. In fact, situations where one confident person disagrees with a group of less confident people are precisely those in which the confident person is most likely to be wrong.

**Using the Wisdom of Crowds**
- Using the wisdom of crowds can lead to good decisions in some circumstances and poor decisions in other circumstances. The main challenges lie in knowing when to use the wisdom of crowds and in how to improve the process of decision making so that crowd-sourced decision making can be more effective. The following are three recommendations, each of which applies to a wide range of decisions.

- The first one is the simplest: Diversity matters. Take it seriously. Groups tend to be more effective than individuals when they consist of a diverse set of individuals who bring different perspectives to a decision. However, groups are actually less effective than individuals when they aren't diverse—when different people bring the same biases to the decision.

- Second, encourage people to make independent contributions to a decision. You can have a large group filled with people who bring different perspectives, but if that group communicates before people think independently about that decision, then the advantage of their diversity may be lost.

- Communication isn't always a good thing. In the extreme case, where group members prioritize social cohesion over independent thought, communication can actually lead to closed-mindedness, where people think much more alike than they really should and become overconfident in the accuracy of their beliefs. This phenomenon is known as groupthink, and it's most evident when a small group of similar people works together on a high-pressure decision.

- Finally, you can use the wisdom of crowds to make better judgments and better decisions by simulating a crowd of two—in your own guessing. When people make two guesses after thinking about different information, or after just waiting a while, the average of their guesses turns out to be a better estimate than one guess in isolation. So, don't get fixated on a first guess. Force yourself to think again, consider what else is important, and make a new estimate.

## Suggested Reading

Koriat, "When Are Two Heads Better Than One and Why?"

Surowiecki, *The Wisdom of Crowds*.

Vul and Pashler, "Measuring the Crowd Within."

## Questions to Consider

1. What factors drive the wisdom-of-crowds effect?

2. What circumstances lead crowds to make the wrong decisions?

# Group Decision Making—The Vox Populi
## Lecture 18—Transcript

*Who Wants to Be a Millionaire?* is one of the most popular game shows in history. Its basic premise, which has now been replicated in dozens of countries, is that a single contestant answers a series of multiple-choice trivia questions for ever-increasing amounts of money. The questions are drawn from any area of knowledge—sports, geography, literature, anything at all.

The contestant has several lifelines to help with difficult questions; for example, he or she can poll the audience members to get their collective answer. And, if the contestant makes it all the way to the end of the game without missing a question, they win the titular prize of a million dollars (or pounds, etc.). The first few questions are generally very easily answered. They're simple general-knowledge questions that allow the television audience to get to know the contestant and that allow the contestant to answer a few questions with confidence before getting to harder trivia.

On one episode of the French version of *Who Wants to be a Millionaire?* the contestant faced a typical early question: "Which of these revolves around the Earth?" The potential answers were the moon, the sun, Mars, and Venus. As these answers were revealed, the contestant visibly sighs and swallows. He repeats the question. Which of these revolves around the earth? His eyes scan the different options. Then, he says, "I'm going to ask the audience."

The host instructs the studio audience to pick up their electronic controllers and place their vote. Then, after a few seconds of upbeat music, the audience poll is revealed. Fifty-six percent answer that the sun rotates around the earth, 42 percent say that the moon rotates around the earth, and negligible fractions answer Mars or Venus. The contestant nods his head, and then starts talking his way through his answer. Mars, definitely not. Venus, no. After a pause, he says, "Response B," the sun.

He goes with the crowd's response, and he loses. The moon, of course, rotates around the earth, but he was led astray by his own ignorance, or perhaps nervousness, and by the majority opinion of the studio audience. Why did the audience's majority judgment lead him astray? It's probably not because the audience didn't know that the moon rotates around the earth. Instead, the audience was split. Slightly less than half told him the correct answer, to help him. But slightly more than half told him the incorrect answer—probably on purpose, as a punishment for soliciting their help on such an easy question.

In many cases, groups of individuals make more accurate judgments and better decisions than single individuals. This phenomenon, which has come to be known as the wisdom of crowds, explains why the studio audience in *Who Wants to Be a Millionaire?* usually provides the correct answer. It has also been applied to many real-world problems: estimating numbers, developing consumer products, betting on sports and political events, and brainstorming for creative solutions.

The idea of the wisdom of crowds has become so well known that it's hardly questioned any more. Many people, from politicians to venture capitalists, now assume that crowds simply do better than individuals when forming judgments and making decisions. But, in today's lecture, I'll present a more nuanced view. As is often the case, the true nature of this phenomenon is a bit more complex than the popular story. Sometimes the crowd does very well indeed. But other times the crowd goes systematically astray, for systematic, predictable reasons.

Wisdom of crowds is an old idea, dating back more than a century, that's continually being shaped by new research. The spark of the idea came from a short paper published in 1907 by the English social scientist and statistician Francis Galton. Throughout his long life, Galton had been interested in averages. As a statistician, he invented the measure that's used to explain variation around averages, called the standard deviation. He showed how extreme values of data tended to move back toward an average as more data are collected—that's regression to the mean. And, he measured countless people's faces and body parts, trying to identify average characteristics of the groups from which they came.

His essay, published in the scientific journal *Nature*, described data he collected from judgments of the dressed weight of an ox, as made by visitors to the Plymouth livestock show. Almost 800 people had made judgments. Some of those people were ranchers or other experts, while others were just random visitors of the exhibition. Each, though, had purchased a ticket and written down their guess, in hope of a large prize.

Galton's scientific report was prompted by an unusual feature of those guesses. Even though people's individual guesses varied considerably, the median value of the guess was very close to the true weight. In statistics the median is just the middle of some set of numbers. In this competition, it's the guess that was exactly in the middle of the range of guesses, with half of the people guessing more and half guessing less. That median was 1,207 pounds. The actual dressed weight of the ox was 1,198 pounds, only 9 pounds from the median guess.

Let me describe this result a different way. Suppose that you were at that same fair more than 100 years ago. You know nothing about oxen. You're no expert butcher, no rancher; perhaps you've never even seen an ox before. But, unlike the other fairgoers at that livestock show, you look at many other people's guesses. You take the middle of all those guess, and write that down as your guess. You'd do much better than the typical butcher, rancher, or other expert.

Galton described this effect as the vox populi—the voice of the people. Now, it's called the wisdom of crowds. It's not magic. It arises because there's always error in people's guesses. In many situations, some people will guess too high and others too low; those different guesses will bracket the true value. If that happens, taking the middle guess from a crowd is more likely to be close to the true value than just taking a guess from a single person.

There's a frequent misconception that the best way to aggregate data from a crowd is to take the average. The average value can be fine for some sorts of judgment, primarily when people's judgments are all on the same scale. But, when people's judgments are on vastly different scales, then the average can be misleading. Suppose that I ask three people the question: How many miles of road are there in the United States? The first answers 500,000; the second answers 5 million; and the third answers 50 million.

The average of those three guesses is more than 18 million (the average is most influenced by the very large guess). But the median, or middle, guess is only 5 million—that's much closer to the true answer, which is about 4 million miles of road. For many real-world judgments, people might not even guess the right order of magnitude. They could be off by factors of 10 or more. So, the median or middle guess usually provides a better estimate of the true value being judged.

Another misconception is that it's good to have a crowd of experts. If you look back at Galton's ox-judging contest, those fairgoers were indeed pretty expert. About 60 percent of their guesses came within 50 pounds of the correct weight. I suspect that if you took 21$^{st}$-century Americans, most of them wouldn't do anywhere near as well. But expertise isn't as important as two other factors.

The first is pretty simple: the size of the crowd matters, to a point. As the group size increases from just a few people to a few dozen people to hundreds of people, the accuracy of the crowd's judgment usually increases. It's often better to have a large crowd of non-experts than only a few experts. But, once the crowd gets sufficiently large, there are diminishing returns, just as in our discussion of sample size in opinion polls from a previous lecture.

But, there's a second factor, and it's the primary reason for the wisdom of crowds: diversity. Diversity has become a loaded term, one that carries social and political baggage. I'll use diversity in this lecture to mean something very simple: the degree to which different people approach a decision in different ways.

Diversity isn't something absolute, it is defined with regard to something. For many sorts of judgments and decisions, we care about intellectual diversity, where people bring different information and different approaches to the same problem. Let me explain this two ways, first with a simple example and then with something more complex.

Suppose that you're an economist trying to predict how much the U.S. economy will grow over the next six months. In its semi-annual survey of economic forecasts, the *Wall Street Journal* collects and aggregates such predictions from about 50 leading economists, and then it tracks those predictions over time, to see who does best.

Suppose that the *Wall Street Journal* surveyed only economists who studied consumer confidence. The predictions of those economists would tend to be correlated; that is, they might all prioritize the same information in making their predictions. They might all overestimate economic growth when consumer confidence is high, and underestimate growth when confidence is low. Without diversity of thought, people's judgments tend to be correlated, and the value of the crowd is lost.

The aggregate prediction is much more likely to be accurate if the individual predictions are uncorrelated, if the economists use different information and different models when making their predictions. For any given prediction, some economists might be too high and some might be too low, but the middle prediction would be more likely to be accurate.

Of course, this example is purposefully simplified. It would be very unlikely for all of the economists in the *Wall Street Journal* survey to use the same information. But, I picked this example for a particular reason: The future of the economy is difficult to predict, and it's not the case that the best prediction is made by the best predictor.

A wonderful feature of that *Wall Street Journal* survey is that all of the predictions are shown publicly, so anyone can track who was accurate one year, and whether they remained accurate the next year. One year, a forecaster correctly predicted that interest rates would be unusually high, when the rest of the crowd thought that they would be low. He was the most accurate predictor that year. Was he using different information than the rest? Yes. According to the *Wall Street Journal*, he had visited a jeans factory and seen the demand for $250 jeans. He based his inflation forecast on this visit, reasoning that consumers must have discretionary money if they were buying such expensive jeans.

It's probably not a good idea to base one's predictions about the entire U.S. economy on such an idiosyncratic observation. But this example might not be that atypical. It turns out that when an individual economist was correct, and the crowd wasn't, then that individual's predictions tended to be much worse than average on other occasions. That is, being right when the crowd is wrong might often be a sign of poor judgment, not good judgment.

Let's move to a much more complex example. Suppose that you bring a group of 12 people into a room, and they have to communicate with each other and reach an aggregate decision. For the moment, the specific decision doesn't matter, but you could think about this example as a group of jurors debating guilt or innocence, a set of marketing executives arguing about an advertising campaign, or whatever fits your interests.

I labeled this as a more complex example because there are so many factors that influence group decision making: what knowledge each person brings to the decision, whether people share similar or different personalities, whether and how they communicate, and so forth. What factors would predict whether this group makes a good or bad decision?

Let's first think about knowledge. It seems obvious that knowledge is a good thing. Our ideal group should be composed of knowledgeable, high-performing people. That is, we should form our group from a set of people who would be pretty good at the task, individually. But, that's not necessarily a good idea. Researchers have shown that a group made up entirely of high-performing individuals can often do worse than more diverse groups, those that contain some high-performers and some low-performers. That's because individuals in the diverse groups are more likely to approach the decision in different ways, so the group becomes more effective as it gets larger.

Let's next think about personality. It might also seem obvious that we want a group of people who are generally similar in personality, but that's not a good idea either. Groups whose members differ in personality will make better decisions, on average, than groups whose members have more similar personalities. Part of the explanation comes from group dynamics. Groups with diverse personalities are more likely to challenge each other in discussions.

But, personality is helpful even when people can't interact. Researchers took several hundred people, gave them the most common personality survey, and then asked them to estimate the probabilities that specific teams would win games in the upcoming World Cup soccer tournament.

After they had collected data from everyone, they then constructed virtual two-person groups by taking each person and pairing them with the person whose personality was most dissimilar. The average estimates from pairs of dissimilar people were much more accurate than estimates from pairs of people with similar personalities, more accurate than random pairs of people, and more accurate than estimates given by individuals. Our personality can predict, albeit imperfectly, some aspect of how we approach decision problems. Thus, diverse personalities make groups or crowds more effective decision makers.

Let's also think about communication. You might think that crowds make the best decisions when people can talk to each other, when people who know a lot can influence those who don't. But that's wrong. In some ways, communication at the wrong time is the enemy of good decision making.

Social influence through communication before making decisions can disrupt the wisdom of crowds. To provide an intuition, imagine that you are sitting in the middle of a large theater filled with people. Visible on the stage in front of you are a large barrel filled with marbles and a microphone on a stand. A host walks to that microphone, and asks the members of the crowd to each guess how many marbles are in the barrel.

Based on the examples so far, you should expect that different people would make very different guesses, but that the median guess of the crowd would tend to be better than that of any random individual. We'd get the standard wisdom-of-crowds effect if everyone answered independently. But suppose that the host invited one audience member up to the stage and that audience member looked at the barrel, stepped to the microphone, and said, "There are 10,000 marbles in the barrel," and then she proceeded to explain her reasoning.

What would happen to the crowd's guesses? They'd become more correlated. That first public guess of 10,000 marbles would serve as an anchor—remember that heuristic?—and people would adjust their own guesses up or down from that anchor. So, communication from a few prominent individuals in advance of decisions can reduce the diversity of the crowd and potentially introduce bias.

In real-world judgments, the wisdom of the crowd can be systematically biased in a similar manner by media reports, by very salient news events, by the opinions of a few influence-makers. What's particularly striking is that people often become more confident when they are exposed to less diverse information.

There's a surprising potential solution, though. Researchers have shown that uninformed people can actually help stem the tide of biased communication. To return to the theater example, imagine that half of the audience was outside in the lobby for that first public guess of 10,000 marbles. When those people return to their seats they chat with those around them. They didn't hear the initial guess, so their reasoning hasn't been influenced, and it helps those around them think more clearly about the problem.

So the key contributor to the wisdom of crowds is diversity, and any factors that undermine diversity can also undermine the wisdom of crowds.

I want to move to some very specific limitations. It's easy to get caught up in the power of crowd decisions, and to lose sight of when crowds fail.

Let's think back to the beginning of the lecture, to the French studio audience of *Who Wants to Be a Millionaire?* That audience led the contestant astray by telling him that the sun rotates around the earth. In this case, the crowd failed (from the contestant's perspective) because a good fraction of the studio audience had a shared and unexpected bias: They wanted him to lose.

Crowds fail when they have a shared error in judgment. And, when that's the case, there's a deeper problem. The people who are most confident about their judgments are often the most wrong.

In a clever study, people were asked to make judgments about simple drawings; for example, which of two line drawings was created from a longer line. The researchers chose the questions so that there would be some that most people would get correct, and so that there were others that most people would get incorrect. These mistakes occurred because of systematic perceptual biases that we all share. For example, people tend to overestimate the length of shapes composed of curved lines compared to shapes composed of straight lines and angles, and they tend to see vertical lines as longer as horizontal lines.

When the crowd tends to get a judgment right, the people who are more accurate tend to be more confident. But, when the crowd tends to get a judgment wrong then confidence is higher in people who are more inaccurate. We think that confident people are more likely to be right, and we place our trust in them. But just because someone is confident about their judgment doesn't make them accurate, they're just more likely to be like the rest of the crowd.

We can be overconfident in our own judgments, as well, and that can also cause the wisdom of crowds to fail. When betting on football games, casual gamblers generally prefer to bet on the favored team even though the advantage of the favorite is essentially negated by the point spread, or betting line.

In one experiment, those point spreads were manipulated to help the underdog team—for example, changing the bet from a 50/50 gamble to something where the underdog might have a 60-percent chance of winning the bet. Casual gamblers still picked the favorites. And, they picked the favorites even when they were warned about that bias.

Gamblers just like picking favorites, probably because of a combination of two effects we've discussed in this course: a preference for betting on things that are more familiar, and the ease with which they can envision the favorite winning, compared to the underdog. Systematic biases like this one can reduce or eliminate any advantage of crowds.

And crowds fail when people ignore them. In many of our decisions, we have the opportunity to collect information from other people – but we tend to undervalue that information.

When people receive advice from someone else about a judgment—whether guesses about the number of M&Ms in a jar or predictions about investment—they tend to adjust their judgment by only about 25 percent toward whatever the advisor recommended. This number, 25 percent, is itself an aggregate across three types of people. Most people ignore advice and keep their original judgment. Some split the difference between their original judgment and the advisor's. And, a small minority actually adopt the advisor's position.

This pattern of results means that people treat their own judgments as much more accurate than someone else's. They don't use information from other people as much as they should, even when those other people should be just as good at the judgment or decision.

And people don't recognize the importance of sample size, as I introduced in the lecture on evidence. When given the choice of following the advice given by one confident person or the aggregate of several less confident people, a majority of people will choose to follow the confident person. Remember, people tend to overestimate the quality of their evidence and underestimate the importance of the quantity of evidence.

But, as I've emphasized in today's lecture, confidence isn't necessarily predictive of accuracy. In fact, situations where one confident person disagrees with a group of less confident people are precisely those in which the confident person is most likely to be wrong.

Throughout today's lecture, I've emphasized that using the wisdom of crowds can lead to good decisions in some circumstances and poor decisions in other circumstances. The main challenges lie in knowing when to use the wisdom of crowds and in how to improve the process of decision making, so that crowd-sourced decision making can be more effective.

Let me end with three recommendations, each applies to a wide range of decisions. The first one is the simplest: Diversity matters. Take it seriously. Groups tend to be more effective than individuals when they consist of a diverse set of individuals who bring different perspectives to a decision. But, groups are actually less effective than individuals when they aren't diverse, when different people bring the same biases to a decision. I've emphasized this over and over again in today's lecture. It's the single most critical factor for helping groups make good decisions.

Second, encourage people to make independent contributions to a decision. You can have a large group filled with people who bring different perspectives, but if that group communicates before people think independently about that decision, then the advantage of their diversity may be lost. This may seem very counterintuitive, so I'll repeat it: Communication isn't always a good thing.

In the extreme case, where group members prioritize social cohesion over independent thought, communication can actually lead to closed-mindedness, where people think much more alike than they really should, and they become overconfident in the accuracy of their beliefs. This phenomenon has been labeled groupthink, and it's most evident when a small group of similar people works together on a high-pressure decision.

One technique for increasing independent thought is selective communication. If there's a complex decision to be made by a group of, say, 20 people, it's a good approach to have them each write down their initial thoughts about that decisions before any intragroup communication takes place. This works for brainstorming, too. Good brainstorming often requires individuals working independently to generate many ideas, and then a group working collectively to evaluation those ideas. It's often effective to go back and forth between individual brainstorming and collective evaluation, alternating these two approaches over and over.

Finally, I want to end with a way you can use the wisdom of crowds to make better judgments and better decisions. Let's consider another trivia question. What's the distance—in a straight line, as the airliner flies—between Rome and London? Think for a moment, and then state your estimate out loud. Ok, now, assume that your first guess was wrong. Think for a moment about why it might have been wrong. What didn't you consider when making your estimate? Now, based on what you are thinking about now, make a new, alternative estimate.

What did you just do? You just simulated a crowd of two, in your own guessing. When people do this, when they make two guesses after thinking about different information (or after just waiting a while) the average of their guesses turns out to be a better estimate than one guess in isolation.

Someone who answered the Rome to London question by saying 1,500 miles would be likely to reduce their estimate the next time, thinking about European geography a different way. Perhaps they'd now say only 700 miles. The average, here 1,100 miles, is much more likely to approximate the true value of about 900 miles.

This is a really easy trick for improving your judgments and even some complex decisions. Don't get fixated on a first guess. Force yourself to think again, consider what else is important, and make a new estimate. It even works well for consumer decisions. If you ask yourself how much something is worth—say, a used car on which you might make an offer—don't stop after your first estimate. Try again, and see how your estimate changes.

Even if you can't collect data from a diverse and independent crowd, even if you can't rely on a trusted friend, you still can improve your own judgments just by asking yourself to think again.

In the next lecture, we'll move from gaining information from others to making decisions about others. We'll explore pro-social decisions like helping others and giving to charity, and we'll see how decisions about others can be very different from decisions about ourselves.

# Giving and Helping—Why Altruism?
## Lecture 19

This lecture moves from gaining information from others to making decisions about others. In this lecture, you will explore prosocial decisions like helping others and giving to charity, and you will see how decisions about others can be very different from decisions about ourselves. This lecture explores why we often act in ways that help or hurt others, even when those actions might not be in our own interest. We can't guarantee that our actions—well intended as they may be—will lead to success. But by helping others, we may end up helping ourselves.

**Why Do We Give?**

- There's a strand of research in economics that considers motivations beyond one's own interest—what are known as other-regarding preferences. Preferences about one's own outcomes are self-regarding preferences; preferences about others' outcomes are other-regarding preferences.

- Other-regarding preferences can be much more difficult to explain than self-regarding preferences; we often don't know why someone sacrifices of themselves on behalf of another. But there's a general theme that separates self-regarding and other-regarding preferences. Other-regarding preferences are often connected to our sense of identity. How we see ourselves, and how we see others, shape whether and how we give to others. And, in many cases, our sense of self leads us to value some public good or a social norm over our own interests.

- Why do we give of ourselves to help others? Are we really altruistic? The term "altruism" has been defined—and criticized—in many ways; the following is a simple definition: Altruistic actions reduce one's own well-being to fulfill an other-regarding preference.

- Altruism isn't supporting your kids or helping your other relatives. Doing so provides clear personal benefits to you—or at least to your genetic fitness. It isn't showing reciprocity to your friends or entering into alliances of convenience with your enemies. Acts aren't altruistic if they are done strategically, in anticipation of some reciprocity later—that's closer to cooperation than altruism.

- Not all good works are altruistic. When a major corporation starts supporting the Red Cross or a local school system, that support might be driven by the desire to change a brand image instead of helping those less fortunate. And altruism doesn't require that someone obtain no benefit from one's action, just that the benefit doesn't outweigh the cost.

- Economists think about altruism in the context of public goods—things like national parks, highway systems, a clean environment, or public radio or television channels. A public good is something that benefits many people, all of whom want the public good to continue to exist. However, because most public goods can be accessed without charge, there's little incentive for any one person to contribute to their upkeep. People can become free riders, using the public goods without paying for them.

- This problem is solved in different ways for different public goods. Some public goods, like national parks and highway systems, are supported primarily by forced contributions through taxes. But others, like public radio and television, need substantial support from charitable giving.

- To explain why people donate to such public goods, economists have assumed that people are altruistic; they want the public good to exist, and they give of themselves—independently of any other motive. Economic models of public goods have made some strong predictions about how people should behave, if they are motivated by this sort of altruism.

- One strong prediction is that government support through taxation should substitute for, or crowd out, personal giving. This is because both taxation and private gifts have the same effect on the public good. Another prediction is that charitable giving should show strong income effects. If the public good is equally valued by everyone, only the wealthy would give, because only to them is the donated money insignificant enough to be outweighed by the public good. But we know that these predictions aren't true.

**Charity: Social Benefits**
- Charitable giving can't be explained by pure altruism. There are a few alternative explanations: one involving external benefits and the other involving internal benefits.

- Charitable giving carries noneconomic benefits, particularly in terms of social status. It provides entry into particular social networks, those in which other givers circulate. Giving can provide status, and charitable giving can be a socially acceptable signal of wealth.

- Evidence that people are motivated by the noneconomic benefits of giving has been found in a surprising place—the annual reports from charities that have tiers of giving. Some charities list their donors by tier in their annual reports.

- If the charity lists the total amount donated by each tier, as well, you'll probably find that the total is pretty similar to what would be expected if most people gave the minimum amount necessary for a given tier. That's consistent with the idea that people don't decide on a gift and then see which tier they fall into. Instead, they use information about tiers to calibrate what they want to give, based on the status they want to signal.

**Charity: Warm Glow**
- Noneconomic benefits surely motivate many people to give. If anything, some people will be motivated by the desire to avoid scorn; they don't want to be seen as a deadbeat or free rider by their

peers. But we need more to explain why people give even when social status is minimal.

- Research in economics, psychology, and neuroscience now all converges on an alternative explanation: that people are motivated by internal benefits. The very act of giving leads to a good feeling about oneself—what's sometimes called a warm glow feeling—that provides utility to those who give.

- The economist James Andreoni has incorporated the idea of a warm glow feeling into a model of what he calls impure altruism. This model can explain real-world charitable giving better than models based on pure altruism. If people give, in part, because giving feels good, then government subsidies shouldn't completely offset private giving. Tax dollars that support public radio don't substitute for one's own gift, because the tax dollars don't lead to a warm glow.

- In addition, impure altruism can explain why people give to public goods that have a very large reach, such as the Red Cross or a national park. When many people could give, the incentive for any one person to give is very small; one person's gift isn't likely to make much difference in the existence of the public good. However, if people are motivated by the feeling they get by acting altruistically, then they'll still give even when they know others are likely to give, too. Impure altruism is a powerful idea, and it can explain some anomalies in charitable giving.

**Even though charity involves donating money, time, or resources, it carries noneconomic benefits to the provider.**

**Social Cognition Explanations**

- The warm glow we feel when giving to a deserving charity explains why we choose to give our own money to support a charity, rather than depend on the generosity of others, but it doesn't explain why we give to some causes and not others. Of course, we each have our own reasons for giving and our own personal set of causes to support. But there's one factor that seems to be critical for encouraging people to act on their other-regarding preferences: seeing others in need.

- People are more willing to give when they know that a specific, identifiable other person will benefit from their actions. This isn't necessarily a good approach to charitable giving. When a child's suffering makes the national news, spontaneous donations to that one child might total hundreds of thousands of dollars. Such giving is very generous, but it helps only one person or one family—at the expense of many others who might have similar needs.

- In addition, people are often less willing to give when many thousands or millions of people need help, as when famine afflicts an entire region or when war or genocide tears a country apart. In a general sense, the larger the problem, the less likely it is to elicit charitable giving. What could explain this paradox: We give to the few, but not to the many?

- When one person suffers, we can empathize with them or their family. We can imagine what it must be like to experience some tragedy. We engage in what psychologists call social cognition mechanisms—processes that help us understand someone else's thoughts, goals, or feelings. And we can envision how our donation could make that person's life a little better.

- But when a tragedy affects many people, we think about the harm to the community—the number of people homeless, the size of the area affected by famine. We can't empathize as easily with one person; there might not even be any identifiable people whose stories are being told. And we can't imagine how our minor contribution could possibly make a difference in such a terrible situation. So we shake our heads, mutter at the unfairness of life, and move on.

- As a general rule, people are more likely to give when they can identify and empathize with specific people who will benefit from their generosity. This rule doesn't mean that the only thing that matters is having a single identifiable target; instead, think of it as saying that the more identifiable the target, the more likely the giving.

- A consequence of this rule—giving is greater to an identifiable target—is that giving should also be reduced when people can't or don't empathize with those in need. We don't empathize with the person who seems like an outsider, a member of a different group, or someone not like us. Those people are dehumanized, to use a term from social psychology. And, sadly enough, when people are so affected by ongoing tragedy that they don't seem like us anymore, then they don't engage our processes of social cognition. They don't elicit our empathy, or our charitable gifts.

## Encouraging Charitable Giving

- We can't just tell people that their decisions are biased and expect change. It's more effective to identify ways in which people can use their biases as tools to make better decisions. To encourage charitable giving, there are two primary tools.

- First, giving comes in part from an internal sense of motivation—the warm glow we feel when helping others. If you are running a charity, you should make that motivation as tangible as possible. Build a community of givers. Tell donors that they are part of your community, that they are one of you. Provide testimonials not only from the people who benefit, but also from the people who give. Emphasize the success of past fundraisers, not the challenge of reaching the goals. Potential donors want to feel like winners, like they are part of something great. Don't scare donors; celebrate them.

- Second, people are more likely to give to identifiable other people in need, not to masses affected by a tragedy. A good approach is to make the tragedy personal. Tell stories about specific people in need. Humanize them. Focus on the mundane, the normality of life before the disaster. Describe what specific people were doing beforehand—how they were thinking about what to eat for dinner or how to save for their kids' future. Don't present generic disaster victims but people whose full lives have been disrupted by tragedy.

### Suggested Reading

Fehr and Fischbacher, "The Nature of Human Altruism."

Harbaugh, Mayr, and Burghart, "Neural Responses to Taxation and Voluntary Giving Reveal Motives for Charitable Donations."

### Questions to Consider

1. What is impure altruism, and how does it help explain the prevalence of charitable giving?

2. Why might people be less likely to give following large disasters than small tragedies?

# Giving and Helping—Why Altruism?
## Lecture 19—Transcript

Welcome back. Today we'll explore some of the deepest facets of our humanity: why we sacrifice of ourselves to help other people, even when we don't benefit.

On January 7, 2007, Wesley Autrey was walking through a New York City subway station, awaiting the train that would take him and his two daughters home. While he walked through the turnstile toward the subway platform, he saw a young man lying on the platform having an epileptic seizure, and he ran to help. After Mr. Autrey and others helped the young man to his feet, the young man then stumbled off the platform, onto the subway tracks, and into the path of an oncoming train.

Mr. Autrey saw the man fall and then made a remarkable decision. He looked back at his daughters standing behind him and he leapt down onto the tracks. Mr. Autrey grabbed the man and wasn't able to pull him back toward the platform, there was no time, so he pinned the man down into the space between the rails, lying on top of him, as the train passed over both of them. As the train stopped amidst the clamor of brakes and screams, Mr. Autrey shouted, "We're OK down here, but I've got two daughters up there. Let them know their father's OK."

What an amazing story. Every time I hear it or tell it I get goosebumps. This man saw a stranger helpless and about to die, and he decided to jump in front of and under a train himself to save that stranger's life. So, why did he do it? Why did he risk his life to potentially save a stranger?

It wasn't because the potential benefits outweighed the potential costs. Yes, after this act of unadulterated heroism, Wesley Autrey was celebrated throughout New York and beyond. He received thousands of dollars in gifts, a family trip to Disney World, and a medal for his bravery. He became famous; he made appearances on major talk shows and was even honored at a U.S. State of the Union address.

But, the potential costs are obvious. There was no way for him to know the relative chances of success or death. None of us would have blamed him if he hadn't risked his life, if he had instead stayed there on the platform with his daughters. There are other, less-life-threatening ways to become famous besides diving under a train.

We'll probably never know why, even he probably doesn't remember exactly why, he decided to jump down to the track. But, we can get some hints from his own words, as quoted in the *New York Times* the day afterward: "I don't feel like I did something spectacular. I just saw someone who needed help. I did what I felt was right."

In today's lecture we'll explore why we often act in ways that help or hurt others even when those actions might not be in our own interest. There's a strand of research in economics that considers motivations beyond one's own interest, what are known as other-regarding preferences. Let me define that bit of jargon.

So far I've emphasized preferences about personal outcomes—someone might prefer receiving $100 today compared to $120 in a year, or might prefer to own a new jacket compared to the $200 it costs. Preferences about one's own outcomes are self-regarding preferences. A preference about someone else's outcomes is an other-regarding preference. If you want the Red Cross to have more money, compared to less money, that's an other-regarding preference. If your decisions are affected by notions of fairness or equity, then you have other-regarding preferences.

Other-regarding preferences aren't necessarily positive. Consider the Grinch, the mean-spirited titular character of the classic children's story *How the Grinch Stole Christmas*. The Grinch hated merriment. He hated singing, celebration, and holiday cheer. He preferred others to be sad, not merry. Those are all other-regarding preferences. Other-regarding preferences can be much more difficult to explain than self-regarding preferences. We often don't know why someone sacrifices of themselves on behalf of another.

But there's a general theme that separates self-regarding and other-regarding preferences. Other-regarding preferences are often connected to our sense of identity. How we see ourselves and how we see others shape whether and how we give to others. And, in many cases, our sense of self leads us to value some public good or a social norm over our own interests.

Let's think about charitable giving. Why do we give of ourselves to help others? Are we really altruistic? Because the term "altruism" has been defined and criticized in so many ways, I want to offer a simple definition. Altruistic actions reduce one's own well-being to fulfill an other-regarding preference.

So, what's not altruistic? Altruism isn't supporting your kids or helping your other relatives. Doing so provides clear personal benefits to you, or at least to your genetic fitness. It isn't showing reciprocity to your friends, or entering into alliances of convenience with your enemies. Again, acts aren't altruistic if they are done strategically, in anticipation of some reciprocity later; that's closer to cooperation than altruism.

And, not all good works are altruistic. When a major corporation starts supporting the Red Cross or a local school system, that support might be driven by the desire to change a brand image instead of helping those less fortunate. And altruism doesn't require that someone obtain no benefit from one's action, just that the benefit doesn't outweigh the cost.

Economists think about altruism in the context of public goods, things like national parks, highway systems, a clean environment, or public radio or television channels. A public good is something that benefits many people, all of whom want the public good to continue to exist. However, because most public goods can be accessed without charge, there's little incentive for any one person to contribute to their upkeep. People can become free riders; they use the public goods without paying for them.

This problem is solved in different ways for different public goods. Some public goods, like national parks and highway systems, are supported primarily by forced contributions through taxes. But others, like public radio and television, need substantial support from charitable giving.

To explain why people donate to such public goods, economists have assumed that people are altruistic—they want the public good to exist, and they give of themselves—independently of any other motive. Economic models of public goods have made some strong predictions about how people should behave, if they are motivated by this sort of altruism.

One strong prediction is that government support through taxation should substitute for, or crowd out, personal giving. This is because both taxation and private gifts have the same effect on the public good. According to these models, government subsidies won't help. Every additional tax dollar that supports, say, Yosemite National Park, should be counteracted by one fewer dollar from private giving. Another prediction is that charitable giving should show strong income effects. If the public good is equally valued by everyone, only the wealthy would give, since only to them is the donated money insignificant enough to be outweighed by the public good.

But we know that these predictions aren't true. Government subsidies to our national parks don't completely crowd out private support. And, it isn't the case that only the wealthy give. Many charities receive substantial support from average, middle-income citizens. If anything, charitable giving tends to be greater at lower income levels, at least as a proportion of household income.

So, if charitable giving can't be explained by pure altruism, what are the alternatives? Let's consider two alternative explanations: one involving external benefits, and the other involving internal benefits.

Suppose that you donated a very large sum of money to your college alma mater. If you donated anonymously, you'd probably receive a phone call from the college's president, perhaps a letter of gratitude from the relevant dean. You'd be thanked privately for your generosity.

But, if you donated publicly, much more would happen. You'd be featured in the alumni magazine. You'd be invited to fundraising dinners to socialize with students, faculty, and other donors. You could be asked to serve on the college's board of trustees. You might even have a campus building named after you.

Charitable giving carries non-economic benefits, particularly in terms of social status. It provides entry into particular social networks, those in which other givers circulate. Giving can provide status; many charities have special labels like "President's Club" for their most generous donors.

And, charitable giving can be a socially acceptable signal of wealth. It may seem paradoxical but charitable giving is a form of conspicuous consumption—you're spending money on something that you don't need. And that social signal of wealth is evident to people even if they don't see your second home, luxury car, or vacation photos. Having your name on a college building might be the single most socially acceptable way to display your wealth.

Evidence that people are motivated by the non-economic benefits of giving has been found in a surprising place: the annual reports from charities that have tiers of giving. You might be able to perform this very experiment by looking at the annual report of a charity you support. Some charities list their donors by tier in their annual reports: One list includes everyone who gave between $100 and $249, another list includes those who gave between $250 and $499, and so on.

If the charity lists the total amount donated by each tier, as well, you'll probably find that the total is pretty similar to what would be expected if most people gave the minimum amount necessary for a given tier. That's consistent with the idea that people don't decide on a gift and then see what tier they fall into. Instead, they use information about tiers to calibrate what they want to give, based on the status they want to signal.

Non-economic benefits surely motivate many people to give. If anything, some people will be motivated by the desire to avoid scorn—they don't want to be seen as a deadbeat or free-rider by their peers. But, we need more to explain why people give even when social status is minimal. Why do people donate $10 a month to their public radio station, even though they could listen for free?

Research in economics, psychology, and now neuroscience all converges on an alternative explanation: that people are motivated by internal benefits. The very act of giving leads to a good feeling about oneself—what's sometimes called a warm glow feeling—and that provides utility to those who give.

The economist James Andreoni has incorporated the idea of a warm glow feeling into a model of what he calls impure altruism. This model can explain real-world charitable giving better than models based on pure altruism. If people give, in part, because giving feels good, then government subsidies shouldn't completely offset private giving. Tax dollars that support public radio don't substitute for one's own gift, since the tax dollars don't lead to a warm glow.

And, impure altruism can explain why people give to public goods that have a very large reach, such as the Red Cross or a national park. When many people could give, the incentive for any one person to give is very small. One person's gift isn't likely to make much difference in the existence of the public good. But, if people are motivated by the feeling they get by acting altruistic, then they'll still give even when they know others are likely to give, too. Impure altruism is a powerful idea, and it can explain some anomalies in charitable giving.

Over the past few decades, major universities have begun capital campaigns to raise hundreds of millions or even billions of dollars. When one of these capital campaigns starts, there's usually some glitzy ceremony where the university president announces a goal of, say, $3 billion. Why announce a goal? Wouldn't the university benefit from every dollar that's donated?

And, what makes it even stranger is that the starting point of a major capital campaign isn't zero. Usually, the campaign isn't officially started, and the donations aren't publicly announced, until after some significant fraction of the goal has been raised in what's called a silent phase of the campaign. That is, something like a third of the goal might already be pledged as seed money before publicly asking for donations.

Universities and other charities do this because donors are motivated by impure altruism. Donors want to feel part of a large collective enterprise; they want to feel that their donation was part of something much larger.

A well-defined goal and seed money toward that goal increase people's confidence that they'll feel that sense of accomplishment.

Empirical data support this explanation. Suppose that two similar and similarly deserving charities each want to raise $10 million, say for a new building. The first charity announces that they need $10 million. The second charity announces that they already have $5 million in seed money, and thus they only need $5 million more to construct the building. Who will receive more money from these announcements?

If anything, the first charity seems more deserving—they are in the most need. But, research shows that the second charity is likely to receive more money in new donations. People give more money when they feel confident that their gift will matter.

So, far, I've talked about a feeling, a warm glow that motivates our behavior. Now a skeptic might suspect that this feeling isn't anything tangible or measurable, it's just a variable that economists put in their models to improve explanations of real-world behavior. But, there's actually some pretty amazing evidence that translates the warm glow feeling into something tangible. The economist Bill Harbaugh and his colleagues were interested in distinguishing between pure and warm-glow explanations for altruism, so they used neuroimaging techniques to measure how the brain responded to charitable donations. Participants in their study were given an initial monetary endowment and then made decisions about money for themselves and for a local food bank.

Sometimes the participants were forced to donate money to the food bank. That's like taxation. Other times they could freely choose whether to donate; for example, they could decide to sacrifice $15 of their own money so that the charity would receive $30. The charity was real, the donations were real, and the experimenters went to great lengths to anonymize donations and to eliminate any effects of social status, meaning that there was no social pressure to please the experimenter by donating more money.

Harbaugh and his colleagues found that a brain structure called the nucleus accumbens, that key target for dopamine neurons, showed increased activity when subjects were taxed, when they were forced to give money to a worthy charity. By itself, that result would support the idea of altruistic giving, that people give because they want the public good to exist.

But they also found that there was more activation in that same region when people could give freely. And, those people who had the most activation in this brain region when the charity received money, compared to when they themselves received money, were the ones who were most likely to give. That's consistent with impure altruism—the public good matters, but our internal motivations matter, too.

These results represent a remarkable confluence of economic theory and neuroscience. The economic theory helps neuroscience identify a warm glow effect within the brain's dopamine system. And, neuroscience in turn helps refine economic theory. As I described in an early lecture, the dopamine system isn't associated with feelings of pleasure, themselves, but with motivation; its activity reinforces our actions so that we do them again. The warm glow we feel when giving to a deserving charity isn't just a feeling, it's a source of motivation, pushing us to give again.

This explains why we choose to give our own money to support a charity rather than to depend upon the generosity of others. But it doesn't explain why we give to some causes, and not others. Of course, we each have our own reasons for giving and our own personal set of causes to support. But there's one factor that seems to be most critical for encouraging people to act on their other-regarding preferences: seeing others in need.

Think back to Wesley Autrey's quote, "I just saw someone who needed help." People are more willing to give when they know that a specific, identifiable other person will benefit from their actions. This isn't necessarily a good approach to charitable giving. When a child's suffering makes the national news, spontaneous donations to that one child might total hundreds of thousands of dollars. Such giving is very generous, but it helps only one person or one family at the expense of many others who might have similar needs.

And, people are often less willing to give when many thousands or millions of people need help, as when famine afflicts an entire region or when war or genocide tears a country apart. In a general sense, the larger the problem, the less likely it is to elicit charitable giving. What could explain this paradox: we give to the few, but not to the many?

When one person suffers, we can empathize with them or their family. We can imagine what it must be like to experience some tragedy. We engage in what psychologists call social cognition mechanisms: processes that help us understand someone else's thoughts, goals, or feelings. And, we can envision how our donation could make that person's life a little better.

But when a tragedy affects many people, we think about the harm to the community, the number of people homeless, the size of the area affected by famine. We can't empathize as easily with one person; there might not even be any identifiable people whose stories are being told. And, we can't imagine how our minor contribution could possibly make a difference in such a terrible situation. So we shake our heads, mutter at the unfairness of life, and move on.

As a general rule, people are more likely to give when they can identify and empathize with specific people who will benefit from their generosity. This rule doesn't mean that the only thing that matters is having a single identifiable target; instead, think of it as saying that the more identifiable the target, the more likely the giving.

For example, the charity Habitat for Humanity provides homes for needy families through donations of money and time from volunteers. In one study, people in the community were asked to give money to Habitat for Humanity. They were either told that the needy family "has been selected" or that the family "will be selected." More money was donated by people who were told the family has been selected, even though the family was never named. People were motivated simply by knowing that there was a specific family they were helping.

A consequence of this rule—giving is greater to an identifiable target—is that giving should also be reduced when people can't or don't empathize with those in need. We don't empathize with the person who seems like an outsider, a member of a different group, or someone not like us. Those people are dehumanized, to use a term from social psychology. And, sadly enough, when people are so affected by ongoing tragedy that they don't seem like us anymore, then they don't engage our processes of social cognition. They don't elicit our empathy or our charitable gifts.

Now, I've told you that we're likely to give to identifiable targets, perhaps even more likely than we should. And, we're not likely to give when tragedies or continuing problems lead to mass suffering. So, could we just teach people about this bias, so that they'll become more generous to victims of large tragedies?

A group of behavioral economists tried to do exactly that. They had research participants fill out a short survey about some unrelated topic, and they paid them in cash for participating. They then gave them a form and an envelope. The form told them that they could donate any part of their earnings to a charity. And half of the participants were just given the name of a well-known charity and statistics about the problem it addressed, while the other half were given the name of the same charity along with a picture of a young girl and a description of her needs.

If they had stopped there, this would have just been the standard identifiable target effect: People should give more when the young girl's face and description were shown. And, in one condition of the experiment that's exactly what they found. People gave about half of their earnings when the young girl was shown, but only a quarter of their earnings when statistics were provided.

But in another condition of the experiment, they also told people about the scientific principle, much as I'm telling you now. They said that "research shows that people typically react more strongly to specific people who have problems themselves than to statistics about people with problems," and they went on to give specific examples.

The natural prediction for this second condition would be that teaching people about their own bias should help them—they should give more money when victims are described through statistics. But that's not what they found. Giving actually went down. In both conditions people only gave about a quarter of their earnings. Teaching people about their bias actually made things worse. People weren't any more likely to give to statistical victims, and the deliberative thinking evoked by the instructions actually reduced people's connection to the identifiable victims.

I want to emphasize this point: We can't just tell people that their decisions are biased and expect change. It's more effective to identify ways in which people can use their biases as tools make better decisions. To encourage charitable giving, there are two primary tools.

First, I've emphasized that giving comes in part from an internal sense of motivation, the warm glow we feel when helping others. If you are running a charity, you should make that motivation as tangible as possible. Build a community of givers. Tell donors: "You are part of our community; you are one of us." Provide testimonials not only from the people who benefit, but from the people who give. Emphasize the success of past fundraisers not the challenge of reaching the goals. Potential donors want to feel like winners. They want to be part of something great. Don't scare donors, celebrate them.

Second, I've also emphasized that people are more likely to give to identifiable other people in need, not to masses affected by a tragedy. After a natural disaster, news coverage often focuses on its scope: the number of people affected, the breadth of the devastation. Interviews with victims describe how people are left homeless and in dire need of food and shelter. But to your average American, sitting in a living room chair, safe within a sturdy home, the images of devastation are distancing. It's difficult to comprehend a major natural disaster, much less to identify with the victims.

A better approach is to make the tragedy personal. Tell stories about specific people in need. Humanize them. Focus on the mundane, the normality of life before the disaster. Describe what specific people were doing beforehand, how they were thinking about what to eat for dinner, or how to save for their kids future. Don't present generic disaster victims, but people whose full lives have been disrupted by tragedy.

Convincing people to sacrifice of themselves to help others can be an extraordinarily difficult task, as any charitable fundraiser knows. But, people can be extraordinarily generous and self-sacrificing when they see someone in need. Wesley Autrey was an extreme example. Few of us will face such a terrible choice, and even fewer will have the courage to risk their own life to save someone they don't know.

But there's nothing really magical about wanting to help others. Other-regarding preferences are part of the human condition. Generosity and heroism come from people just like you and me.

I want to end with a second story about Wesley Autrey, one that humanizes him. About four months after his heroic act, he again faced pressure, this time as a contestant on the game show *Deal or No Deal*. He remained in the game until the very end, turning down very large amounts of money on the chance that his briefcase contained one million dollars. And, in the end he walked away with $25. He tied with Frank, the contestant discussed in the very first lecture, as the worst *Deal or No Deal* contestant of all time. But, there's a small silver lining here. For his past heroism, the television network rewarded him with a new car. We can't guarantee that our actions, well intended as they may be, will lead to success. But by helping others, we may end up helping ourselves.

In the next lecture, we'll see how other-regarding preferences provide a foundation for one of the most important social decisions: cooperation.

# Cooperation by Individuals and in Societies
## Lecture 20

Cooperation is a fundamental feature of social life. But encouraging cooperation, and enforcing it, can be surprisingly difficult. In this lecture, you will learn about cooperation—why we work together for mutual gain. Cooperation seems like a prototypic phenomenon within behavioral economics, but it has importance that goes well beyond behavioral economics, and we shouldn't underestimate how cooperation is shaped by traditional economic, political, and cultural institutions. It's present in all human societies, but it can take very different forms.

**Cooperation**

- The trust game is a simple game that allows us to measure cooperation in the laboratory. This game is played by two people at a time: an investor and a trustee. For now, imagine that these people are sitting at computers in two different rooms; they don't know each other's identity, won't meet each other during the game, and can only communicate through their decisions in the game.

- When the game begins, the investor is allocated a starting endowment of 20 dollars, for example. Then, the investor must decide how much of the money to invest with the trustee. Any money invested is multiplied by some factor—let's say that the money is tripled. So, if 10 dollars were invested, then the trustee would have 30 dollars. The trustee then decides how much money to give back to the investor and how much to keep.

- This is a powerful game because it distills trust down to its essence—the belief that another person will reciprocate a prosocial action, even against their self-interest. What would rational, self-interested players do if they played this game once? What should you do, if you are playing?

- Suppose you're the trustee. A random, anonymous person has just given you 30 dollars, and there's nothing forcing you to send any money back. So, if you are purely self-interested, you should keep the money. A self-interested trustee should keep any money given to them. Knowing that, a self-interested investor shouldn't invest anything; there should be no trust in the trust game.

- But that equilibrium solution—no investment, no repayment—only rarely happens. Most people invest at least some money. Across many different studies, the investors typically send about 50 percent of their initial endowment to the trustee. And most trustees return a significant amount of money, but a substantial minority do not. On average, trustees return slightly less than what the investor sent.

- There's considerable variation in this game. Some of the time, investors benefit from being trusting, but often they don't. And there's also evidence for cultural variation. This game has been used in experiments in many different countries, and the varying outcomes point to the potential for quantitative measurement of something that seems so subjective—trust.

- However, real-world cooperation often involves interactions among people in groups. When the trust game is expanded so that people aren't interacting with a single partner, but with someone randomly chosen from a group, there's a notable change in people's behavior.

- In one experiment, there was a group of investors and another group of trustees. When a given trustee received an investment, their repayment could go to any of the investors, not necessarily the one who initially invested.

- In this situation, the rate of reciprocation drops dramatically. People no longer expect others to behave fairly, because there's no ability to track others' actions, and thus, people can't build up a trustworthy reputation. If interactions are just random and anonymous, people can't send signals that they are trustworthy nor send signals that disapprove of others' behavior.

## Signaling

- What leads to cooperative behavior in the real world? There are three types of explanations: signals, norms, and enforcement.

- When people interact in social settings, their actions send signals about their intentions. We can send signals in many ways—through our body language, through our tone of voice, how we move toward or away from someone.

- When people interact in laboratory games, though, the researchers don't necessarily want to allow all of those realistic signal; they're just too complex to easily characterize. Instead, people need to send signals through their actions in the game, whether their decisions signal an intent to cooperate or to compete.

- In a clever study, a team of economists and neuroscientists brought two people to the laboratory to play the trust game against each other. However, in a twist, the two players each went into their own MRI scanner, and the two scanners were synchronized so that images of both players' brains were collected simultaneously while the players played the game 10 times in a row with each other.

- They found that when players interacted in a benevolent way, such as when a player increased the amount they sent to their opponent from one game to the next, there was increased activation in a brain region called the nucleus accumbens, one of the major targets for the dopamine neurons that guide how we learn about reward.

- What's even more interesting was how this brain activation changes as the two players develop trust. In the first few games, the brain activation occurs relatively late in each game, after the investor makes an investment that shows trust. However, as the two players start to trust each other more and more, the activation in this brain region moves earlier in the game. It now anticipates the investor's signal that he or she is willing to trust.

- Cooperation is rewarding, and as we develop trust, that sense of reward is not only present following cooperative acts, but also when we first receive a signal of cooperation.

## Social Norms

- Signaling is clearly important for cooperation, but it can't explain the variety of real-world cooperation that people show. We often cooperate with people we've never met, even before we've received any signals from them. And we do that because of what are called social norms, which are generally accepted rules about how we should behave.

- Economists and psychologists generally advance three explanations for the social norm of cooperation. The first explanation is simple: We cooperate because of a sense of altruism. We want to help our social partners. However, pure altruism only works in very limited circumstances that don't really apply to social cooperation.

- Impure altruism assumes that we have an internal feeling—a warm glow—that motivates us to help others. That's consistent with the sense of reward that we get from interacting with a specific partner, but it doesn't explain why we have social norms that encourage cooperation.

- A second explanation is that of inequality aversion. People dislike it when what they receive differs from what someone else receives. The behavioral economist Ernst Fehr and his colleagues have shown that incorporating inequality aversion into their models allows them to predict whether people will cooperate or be selfish in economic situations. Their inequity aversion model implies that in some situations, people will be willing to sacrifice some of their own money in order to reach a more equitable outcome. Inequity aversion can explain some biases in people's choices, but by itself, it can't explain the prevalence of cooperation.

- The third explanation is that of reciprocity. In terms of intentions, reciprocity can be defined as follows: When we interact with others, we make judgments about their motives, and then we act in the same way. We reciprocate good intentions, leading to cooperation. Reciprocation, like inequity aversion, provides a potentially necessary condition for cooperation. But it isn't sufficient. We still need some enforcement mechanism.

**Altruistic Punishment**
- Suppose that you are watching two other people play a trust game. The investor offers everything to the trustee, but the trustee keeps everything. The trustee breaks the social norm of cooperation. Now also suppose that you have the opportunity to spend five dollars of your own money to punish the uncooperative trustee; if you spend five dollars, the trustee will lose 20 dollars from their ill-gotten gains.

- People are willing to engage in such altruistic punishments—in both laboratory and real-world situations—in order to enforce social norms. They get angry at the cheaters, and that emotion pushes people to take actions against their own self-interest.

- When people engage in altruistic punishment, there are two primary effects. First, it corrects deviant behavior when a partner fails to cooperate; the punished cheater cooperates in the next game. Second, altruistic punishment increases one's confidence that an unknown partner will cooperate in the future.

- If people can't be punished for failing to cooperate, then social cooperation unravels with even a few bad apples. People see antisocial behavior that goes unpunished, and they lose confidence in others. That leads to a cycle of diminishing cooperation over time. But if altruistic punishment is possible, a few good apples can enforce cooperation even in very large groups.

- Altruistic punishment is powerful but expensive. It requires time and energy to confront someone who is disturbing their social group or shirking their duties in the workspace. Even if you have good intentions, you might not find altruistic punishment worth the effort.

- However, when someone misbehaves in your social group or workplace, often multiple people will be affected by their misbehavior. Therefore, corrective actions don't have to come from one person in isolation, but can come from a group in coordination.

- Conditional cooperation involves cooperating when cooperating is deserved but punishing when that's necessary. Real-world groups that include a substantial portion of conditional cooperators are better able to manage their shared resources.

**Altruistic Reward**

- As opposed to altruistic punishment as a method for enforcing norms of social cooperation, there's another possibility: altruistically rewarding people who cooperate with you. The key advantage of reward, compared to punishment, is that it promotes social ties. Rewarding someone builds a social relationship with him or her. Punishments, on the other hand, break down social ties. Altruistic punishments can be used as weapons or threats.

- There's much less known about altruistic reward, compared to altruistic punishment, but the best evidence suggests that reward might work at least as well as punishment in encouraging cooperation.

- If altruistic punishment and altruistic reward are both effective and encourage cooperation, why might we prefer only altruistic reward? Altruistic punishment takes away resources, either because of literal costs or lost time or energy. Altruistic punishment makes the group worse off, overall. But rewarding someone doesn't make the group worse off; it just transfers money from one person to another. Altruistic rewards serve as signals of trust that don't reduce the overall resources of the group.

- We know much more about how altruistic punishment can enforce cooperation than about how altruistic reward can encourage cooperation, but there's something reassuring about the idea that cooperation doesn't necessarily need enforcement through punishment, if the right incentives can be provided at the right time.

## Suggested Reading

Bshary and Grutter, "Image Scoring and Cooperation in a Cleaner Fish Mutualism."

Henrich, et al, "Markets, Religion, Community Size, and the Evolution of Fairness and Punishment."

## Questions to Consider

1. Why is conditional cooperation so important for group dynamics?

2. How does altruistic punishment facilitate cooperation?

# Cooperation by Individuals and in Societies
## Lecture 20—Transcript

Cooperation is a fundamental feature of social life. But encouraging cooperation and enforcing cooperation can be surprisingly difficult. Let me illustrate this with a story. It's a story about pairs of workers who collaborate on cleaning jobs.

Several times a day, each pair will perform a cleaning job, each time for a different client. When they are at their job, each of the two workers can choose do their job well, cleaning like they are supposed to. Or, each worker can choose to shortchange the client, not doing the job that the client expects.

Let's represent each cleaning job as a simple game. When each worker does the job they are supposed to, their payoff in the game is the difference between what they receive for the job and the effort they expend. If they shortchange the client, then their net payoff actually increases, since they receive the same amount but they are not expending as much effort. And since each worker's payoff doesn't depend on what the other worker does, each not only has significant incentive to cheat, but also has no incentive to monitor their partner's cheating.

In a game like this one, you might expect that the workers would systematically shortchange their clients; they're better off individually for doing so. But that's not what happens. Let me tell you a little more about these workers, because they aren't who you might expect.

The workers are actually small fish called cleaner wrasse. Their clients visit them on cleaning stations in coral reefs, where pairs of cleaner fish work together to remove dead skin and external parasites, sometimes even by swimming into the mouths of their client. When the pair of fish work together to clean the client, they each get a little bit of nutrition from the dead skin and parasites, and the client fish come back to the cleaning station over and over.

But, some of the time, one of the cleaner fish doesn't do its job. Instead of removing parasites, it might take a small bite out of the client, trying to get a little extra food. That could cause the client to swim away, if it notices. So, here's the amazing thing: When one of the cleaner fish cheats the client, the other cleaner fish chases the cheating cleaner fish away. That fish stops eating, expends energy unnecessarily, and potentially risks a dangerous swim through open water just so that it can punish its partner.

And, what happens next? The cheating fish cooperates the next time. It works together with its partner to do its job, and they both feed equally. Cooperation was enforced by punishment.

In today's lecture, I'll talk about cooperation: why we (and other animals) work together for mutual gain. Let's begin by walking through a simple game that allows us to measure cooperation in the laboratory, this time among humans instead of fish. It's called the trust game, and it's played by two people at a time: an investor and a trustee. For now, imagine that these people are sitting at computers in two different rooms. They don't know each other's identity, won't meet each other during the game, and can only communicate through their decisions in the game.

When the game begins the investor is allocated a starting endowment, say $20. Then, the investor must decide how much of the money to invest with the trustee. Any money invested is multiplied by some factor, for now let's say that the money is tripled. So, if $10 were invested, then the trustee would have $30. The trustee then decides how much money to give back to the investor, and how much to keep. This is a powerful game because it distills trust down to its essence: the belief that another person will reciprocate a pro-social action, even against their self-interest.

Let's think about the equilibrium solution to this game. What would rational, self-interested players do, if they played this game once? What should you do, if you are playing?

Suppose you're the trustee. A random, anonymous person has just given you $30 dollars, and there's nothing forcing you to send any money back. So, if you are purely self-interested, you should keep the money. A self-interested trustee should keep any money given to them. Knowing that, a self-interested investor shouldn't invest anything—there should be no trust in the trust game.

But that equilibrium solution—no investment, no repayment—only rarely happens. Most people invest at least some money. Across many different studies, the investors typically send about 50 percent of their initial endowment to the trustee. And, most trustees return a significant amount of money, but a substantial minority do not. On average, trustees return slightly less than what the investor sent.

I want to emphasize that there's considerable variation here. For example, if the investor sent $10 and that was multiplied to a total of $30 some trustees would return $15. That seems like a fair split, but some would only return a few dollars or nothing at all. So some of the time investors benefit from being trusting, but often they don't.

And there's also evidence for cultural variation. This game has been used in experiments in many different countries. In some countries, like Germany, trustees returned relatively little of what was invested, while in other countries, like Bulgaria, trustees returned much more. That doesn't necessarily mean Bulgarians are more trustworthy or cooperative than Germans, since many other factors can contribute to differences in experiments. But it does point to the potential for quantitative measurement of something that seems so subjective: trust.

So far, I've talked about cooperation between two people who interact once. But, real-world cooperation often involves interactions among people in groups. When the trust game is expanded so that people aren't interacting with a single partner but with someone randomly chosen from a group, there's a notable change in people's behavior.

In one experiment, there was a group of investors and another group of trustees. When a given trustee received an investment, their repayment could go to any of the investors, not necessarily the one who initially invested. In this situation, the rate of reciprocation drops dramatically. People no longer expect others to behave fairly since there's no ability to track others' actions, and thus people can't build up a trustworthy reputation. If interactions are just random and anonymous, people can't send signals that they are trustworthy nor send signals that disapprove of others' behavior.

So, if trust so easily breaks down when groups interact in the laboratory, what leads to cooperative behavior in the real world? Over the remainder of this lecture, I'll consider three types of explanations: signals, norms, and enforcement.

When people interact in social settings, their actions send signals about their intentions. We can send signals in many ways: through our body language, our tone of voice, how we move toward or away from someone. We've all been reassured by someone's smile or put off by someone's crossed arms and harsh tone of voice. When people interact in laboratory games, though, the researchers don't necessarily want to allow all of those realistic signals, they're just too complex to easily characterize. Instead, people need to send signals through their actions in the game whether their decisions signal an intent to cooperate or to compete.

In a clever study, a team of economists and neuroscientists brought two people to the laboratory to play the trust game against each other. But, in a twist, the two players each went into their own MRI scanner, and the two scanners were synchronized so that images of both players' brains were collected simultaneously, while the players played the game 10 times in a row with each other.

They found that when players interacted in a benevolent way, such as when a player increased the amount they sent to their opponent from one game to the next, there was increased activation in a brain region called the nucleus accumbens. That's the same region we've heard about several times before. It's one of the major targets for the dopamine neurons that guide how we learn about reward.

What's even more interesting was how this brain activation changes as the two players develop trust. In the first few games, the brain activation occurs relatively late in each game, after the investor makes an investment that shows trust. But, as the two players start to trust each other more and more, the activation in this brain region moves earlier in the game. It now anticipates the investor's signal that they're willing to trust. Cooperation is rewarding. And, as we develop trust, that sense of reward is not only present following cooperative acts but also when we first receive a signal of cooperation.

Signaling is clearly important for cooperation. But it can't explain the variety of real-world cooperation that people show. We often cooperate with people we've never met, even before we've received any signals from them. And we do that because of what are called social norms, generally accepted rules about how we should behave.

It's notoriously difficult to identify why particular social norms exist. For any social norm (say, wearing formal clothes to a job interview) explanations can come from psychology, sociology, economics, anthropology, or even evolutionary biology. Economists and psychologists generally advance three explanations for the social norm of cooperation.

The first explanation is simple: We cooperate because of a sense of altruism. We want to help our social partners. But, altruism doesn't get us very far. As I discussed in the previous lecture, pure altruism only works in very limited circumstances: when we value a public good, when our sacrifice is relatively insignificant, and when there aren't competing sources for support. Those conditions don't really apply to social cooperation.

Impure altruism assumes that we have an internal feeling, a warm glow, that motivates us to help others. That's consistent with the sense of reward that we get from interacting with a specific partner, but it doesn't explain why we have social norms that encourage cooperation. So, we'll put altruism aside as a potential explanation.

A second explanation is that of inequality aversion. People dislike it when what they receive differs from what someone else receives. The behavioral economist Ernst Fehr and his colleagues have shown that incorporating inequality aversion into their models allows them to predict whether people will cooperate or be selfish in economic situations.

They define two distinct forms of inequality aversion: envy and guilt. People strongly dislike having less than what others have. That's envy. And, they less strongly dislike having more than what others have. That's guilt. Both of these are examples of reference dependence, such that people care not just about absolute outcomes, but outcomes relative to some reference point.

Their inequity aversion model implies that in some situations people will be willing to sacrifice some of their own money in order to reach a more equitable outcome. Inequity aversion can explain some biases in people's choices, like rejection of unfair offers in the ultimatum game, as described in a previous lecture.

But, inequity aversion by itself can't explain the prevalence of cooperation. To get an intuition about why, imagine that there are a group of people interacting in a market, some are very inequity averse, but some aren't, they're just selfish. The inequity-averse people will be at a competitive disadvantage compared to the selfish people (those who act to maximize their own interest, without regard to cooperation).

The selfish people are willing to accept unfair divisions of resources as long as the unfairness works to their benefit. So, a selfish person would do better than an inequity-averse person when the deck's stacked in their favor. Without some mechanism for enforcement, inequity aversion can't explain the persistence of cooperation in the equilibrium states of markets.

The third explanation is that of reciprocity. I'll define reciprocation here in terms of intentions: When we interact with others, we make judgments about their motives, and then we act in the same way. We reciprocate good intentions, leading to cooperation.

In one such model of reciprocity in economic games, different choices are characterized as either involving nice or mean intentions. Players gain utility not just from their own outcomes, but from the product of their own intentions and the other player's intentions. If the other player is nice, then it's good to be nice. If the other player is mean, then it's good to be mean. This sort of model implies that our behavior in a social interaction depends on our inferences about someone else's character. We want to be nice to other nice people. Niceness can be mutually reinforcing, leading to cooperation.

But meanness can also be mutually reinforcing. As such, reciprocation, like inequity aversion, provides a potentially necessary condition for cooperation. But it isn't sufficient. We still need some enforcement mechanism. So, how can cooperation be enforced?

Let's think back to the cleaner fish from the introductory example. When one of the fish failed to cooperate, one of the fish sacrificed its own food and energy to chase the other. It sacrificed its own time and energy to punish another so that it could enforce a social norm. That's an example of what is called altruistic punishment.

In humans altruistic punishment takes a different form. Let's suppose that you are watching two other people play a trust game. The investor offers everything to the trustee, but the trustee keeps everything. The trustee breaks the social norm of cooperation. Now let's also suppose that you have the opportunity to spend $5 of your own money to punish the uncooperative trustee. If you spend $5, the trustee will lose $20 from their ill-gotten gains.

People are willing to engage in such altruistic punishments, in both laboratory and real-world situations, in order to enforce social norms. They get angry at the cheaters, and that emotion pushes people to take actions against their own self-interest.

When people engage in altruistic punishment there are two primary effects. The first is straightforward: It corrects deviant behavior when a partner fails to cooperate (the punished fish starts cleaning correctly, the punished human cheater cooperates in the next game). The second is more subtle: Altruistic punishment increases one's confidence that an unknown partner will cooperate in the future.

If people can't be punished for failing to cooperate, then social cooperation unravels with even a few bad apples. People see antisocial behavior that goes unpunished, and they lose confidence in others. That leads to a cycle of diminishing cooperation over time. But if altruistic punishment is possible, a few good apples can enforce cooperation even in very large groups.

Altruistic punishment is powerful but expensive. It requires time and energy to confront someone who is disturbing their social group or shirking their duties in the workspace. Even if you have good intentions, you might not find altruistic punishment worth the effort. But, think about what happens when someone misbehaves in your social group or in your workplace. Often, multiple people will be affected by their misbehavior. Therefore, corrective actions don't have to come from one person in isolation, but can come from a group in coordination.

Let me give you a real-world example. Within the forests of Ethiopia, local groups manage their forests as a common good. For example, they set their own rules about how individual members of their groups can harvest wood for fuel. This creates a classic problem of cooperation. Each member of the local group might benefit from collecting extra wood for themselves, but if everyone harvested wood indiscriminately, the common resource would disappear.

So, these groups set up patrols. They go through the forest, and they look for people who are taking more wood than they should. But that's quite a lot of work. Spending time wandering through the forest and looking for those cutting down too much wood reduces the time available for meeting the needs of one's own family.

Researchers ran simple two-player laboratory games with the members of 49 different local Ethiopian groups, and they used data from those games to characterize each person's attitude toward cooperation. About 50 percent of the people were what they called "conditional cooperators." If the other player cooperated, they'd cooperate right back. But if the other player doesn't cooperate, then they behave selfishly. About 10 percent were free riders: they tried to take advantage of the other player's generosity. The remaining people were either consistently altruistic or had a more variable set of attitudes.

Then, the researchers looked at each of those 49 groups and compared each group's real-world resource management to how its members played the games. They found that groups whose members were mostly conditional cooperators had the most trees remaining in their forests; they had managed their local forests most effectively for the common good. Why? Because the people who were conditional cooperators in the games tended to go out on patrol; they were the ones looking to enforce the social norm of cooperation. It's particularly striking that the people who most benefited their communities were the conditional cooperators in the game not the altruists, who always cooperated, and definitely not the free riders, who never cooperated.

Conditional cooperation involves cooperating when cooperating is deserved, but punishing when that's necessary. Real-world groups that include a substantial portion of conditional cooperators are better able to manage their shared resources. Let me summarize this key point: If people are allowed to coordinate their punishment of non-cooperators, then even a small group can be effective in shaping the long-term trajectory of their society, pushing it toward general cooperation, even if there's still a small minority of persistent misbehavers.

Communication is critical for that coordination. The Nobel Laureate Elinor Ostrom was a pioneer in the economic modeling of how common resources, like those shared forests in Ethiopia, can be managed successfully by local cooperation. She and her colleagues showed that altruistic punishment works best when people communicate freely.

Communication helps people coordinate their punishment, making conditional cooperation more effective. And, communication can be used as a low-cost social signal. Often, we don't want to punish violators of social norms immediately. That's too effortful and carries too much of a social cost. So, a threat provides an often-effective low-cost substitute.

Given how communication can make coordination more effective, one might expect that altruistic punishment works better in homogeneous groups than in diverse groups. But, that's not true. Field experiments have shown that altruistic punishment helps in diverse groups but has little effect in homogeneous groups, perhaps because the threat of punishment carries more weight in diverse groups, but less weight in groups held together by kinship and social ties.

So far, I've talked entirely about altruistic punishment as a method for enforcing norms of social cooperation. But there's another possibility: altruistically rewarding people who cooperate with you. The key advantage of reward, compared to punishment, is that it promotes social ties. Rewarding someone builds a social relationship with them. Think back to the examples of two-player trust games. Sending someone a signal that you trust them, that you approve of their behavior, can be a very powerful motivator for continued cooperation.

Punishments, on the other hand, break down social ties. Altruistic punishments can be used as weapons or threats. For example, free riders can use altruistic punishments against cooperators. Suppose that one merchant consistently provides lower-priced goods on an online marketplace. Unscrupulous competitors might post disparaging and false reviews of that merchant online, in order to reduce its reputation and drive its customers away.

There's much less known about altruistic reward, compared to altruistic punishment. But the best evidence suggests that reward might work at least as well as punishment in encouraging cooperation.

In one experiment, groups of people were brought into the laboratory to play a cooperative game, and different groups were allowed to engage in altruistic punishment, altruistic reward, both, or neither. As you might expect from everything I've said so far, cooperation completely broke down when neither punishment nor reward was possible. But when individuals could either reward good behavior or punish bad behavior, then the groups all tended to cooperate effectively. The overall rate of cooperation was about the same in either case, and wasn't any better or worse when both options were available.

So, if altruistic punishment and altruistic reward are both effective and encourage cooperation, why might we prefer only altruistic reward? Think about the consequences of punishment for the overall wellbeing of a group. Remember that altruistic punishment takes away resources, either because of literal costs or lost time or energy. Altruistic punishment makes the group worse off, overall. But rewarding someone doesn't make the group worse off; it just transfers money from one person to another. Altruistic rewards serve as signals of trust that don't reduce the overall resources of the group.

It's important to treat this claim with some caution. We know much more about how altruistic punishment can enforce cooperation than about how altruistic reward can encourage cooperation. But, there's something reassuring about the idea that cooperation doesn't necessarily need enforcement through punishment if the right incentives can be provided at the right time.

Cooperation seems like a prototypic phenomenon within behavioral economics. People's real-world behavior was difficult to explain using traditional economic models. Then economists created new models that incorporated psychological concepts like inequity aversion and desire for reciprocity. And, understanding how people can enforce social norms has helped economists and psychologists explain some unexpected real-world decisions.

But, cooperation has importance that goes well beyond behavioral economics, and we shouldn't underestimate how cooperation is shaped by traditional economic, political, and cultural institutions. It's present in all human societies, but it can take very different forms. Let's think about the diversity of human society, for a moment. Societies differ in many ways that might shape how the individuals therein cooperate. Group size is one key difference. Nomadic and hunting groups are smaller than farming groups, which are smaller than urban groups.

Some groups are interconnected through markets. In our modern urban societies, we are dependent on others when we purchase our food and everything else. But in some agrarian societies, families or other small groups are separately responsible for their own food. And, there are many other institutions that could promote cooperation, from religions to national pride to cultural practices.

For cooperation, these institutions matter. People who live in societies consisting of relatively small social groups tend to be more tolerant of antisocial behavior; they allow group members the most latitude before resorting to punishment. Those in societies consisting of larger social groups are less tolerant and punish more readily, which makes sense. Altruistic punishment is a key tool for enforcing cooperation in large groups. And, people in highly interdependent social groups—those societies where individuals don't produce or forage for their own food—tend to show the most fairness in their interactions with others. That also makes sense, given that social norms for fairness are likely to be strongest in highly interdependent groups.

Cooperation isn't necessarily a virtue in every setting. In some social groups, cooperation is much more important than in others. And, in almost every social group, it's better to be a conditional cooperator: someone who cooperates when others are cooperating, but who enforces social norms when others misbehave.

I want to end by returning to the little cleaner fish, swimming around reefs and waiting for their clients to arrive. I told you that some cleaner fish tend to cooperate and some don't, and that the cooperators will altruistically punish the non-cooperators. Well, there's even more to this story. Client fish surreptitiously watch the cleaner fish. They observe their behavior, how they treat their other clients. And they spend more time swimming near good cooperators than bad cooperators. It's as if the little cleaner fish develop a reputation for being a good or bad cooperator, and having a good reputation for cooperation helps them attract clients.

And, do the little cleaner fish learn from being observed? Yes. Over time, they actually learn to feed more cooperatively when observant clients are nearby. They act in a way to maximize their positive reputation. Cooperation begets more cooperation, leading to a stable, mutually beneficial social setting.

That's the key lesson here. Cooperation arises from the combination of self-interest, awareness to others' actions, and the gradual formation of social norms. These little fish could be more self-interested in any one interaction and get more food in the short term, but by cooperating over many interactions, they get much more food in the long run. We humans, with our ability to plan and our complex social networks, can only hope to do equally well.

In the next lecture, we'll move from how cooperation develops to how cooperation breaks down. We'll see how economic incentives can interfere with people's motivation to help others or to build social ties, as we explore the remarkable phenomenon of reward undermining.

# When Incentives Backfire
## Lecture 21

Money serves as an incentive for our behavior. We are more likely to seek out jobs that pay more money rather than less. When we shop, we prefer to spend less money rather than more. The fact that money serves as an incentive for behavior is central to our economy—and to almost every other facet of our lives. In this lecture, you will learn about one of the more striking findings from recent research in behavioral economics, psychology, and neuroscience: Economic incentives can backfire. They can actually discourage behavior rather than encourage it.

**Reward Undermining**

- The phenomenon where an incentive decreases motivation for a behavior has several names, one of which is reward undermining—when the external incentive undermines the sense of internal reward that normally motivates our behavior.

- Reward undermining is an extraordinarily powerful idea. Incentives can not only undermine small-scale interpersonal interactions, but also very large-scale social policies. Research has shown that economic incentives can decrease, or potentially even eliminate, people's actions to benefit an important social good, like blood donation.

- There are two different sorts of motivation: external and internal. External motivation and internal motivation aren't just two factors on the same scale of utility; they may represent different scales altogether.

- Economic theory has historically given pride of place to external sources of motivation. A monetary incentive, for example, should have much greater influence on behavior than any internal factors. In addition, external incentives should have more consistent effects, too. People should all be motivated by money in a generally similar way, even if their internal motivations are very different. However, reward undermining argues that internal sources of motivation can be more important, at least some of the time.

- What determines whether external incentives or internal motivations shape our decisions? One answer is that there are actually two different currencies for decision making. One currency is economic—our choices lead to physical gains and losses, good outcomes and bad. The other currency is social—our choices change how other people see us, or how we see ourselves.

- Different incentives change the currency in which we make our decisions, from social to economic, or vice versa. Monetary incentives change the context of a decision from a social relationship to an economic transaction, from social currency to economic currency.

- Money changes how we think about our social relationships. We resist lending money to friends and family—not because of the value of money, but because of the value of our social ties. We don't want to think about money whenever we think about our friends, and we don't want to risk our friendship over a loan.

- Incentives can work in the opposite way, too: Social relationships can change how we think about economic incentives. Salespeople in many industries know this. They want to build social relationships with their customers so that the customers choose their firm among many in a crowded marketplace. And we expect reciprocity in our social relationships. Gifts and favors are reciprocated—perhaps not consciously, but reciprocated nonetheless.

- These two currencies, economic and social, can compete with and even undermine each other, potentially leading to bad decisions.

## Psychological Explanations
- There are some different explanations for reward undermining. The first category of explanation comes from psychology, and it focuses

on the idea of motivation. A core concept in social psychology is that people don't simply know the reasons for their actions; instead, they have to infer their own reasons based on potential external and internal motivators.

- In one kind of reward undermining, initially called the overjustification effect, the external prize is enough to justify the behavior, so it prevents internal motivation from developing. This is an early undermining perspective, because it proposes that external incentives prevent internal motivation from forming in the first place.

- Alternatively, undermining might happen more gradually. Many studies have shown that external incentives don't necessarily extinguish internal motivation, especially if those incentives are infrequent and unexpected. For example, nearly all students in the United States are constantly exposed to external incentives, in the form of grades, and many of them remain curious and inquisitive learners.

- So, a late undermining perspective would propose, instead, that external incentives won't undermine internal motivation immediately, but will instead have effects later, as they are delivered repeatedly.

- It is very difficult to discriminate between these two perspectives, but the key message is that we now know that motivation is an important contributor to reward undermining, but it isn't the only contributor.

**Reward**
- Deep in the brain are neurons that use the chemical dopamine. Those neurons send signals to brain regions that help us learn so that we can learn to make choices that lead to good outcomes and avoid choices that lead to bad outcomes.

- Dopamine is not associated with pleasure, but instead with motivation. Rats whose reward system has been disrupted by brain damage show normal facial expressions of pleasure when food is placed in their mouths, but they aren't motivated enough to cross their cage to eat, even if they are hungry.

- So, if undermining is associated with disrupted motivation, as these psychological theories contend, then undermining should also disrupt the function of the brain's reward system.

- Recall that range effects occur because our sense of a meaningful difference in some quantity is inversely proportional to its range. It's reasonable to assume that the range in the activity of our reward system will be smaller when we're just playing a game for fun than when we're playing a game for money.

- There's good evidence that external rewards—particularly money— have greater effects on our reward system than internal rewards like satisfaction. There's a good reason for that: Those external rewards are very important for learning about the consequences of our decisions.

- From the perspective of our reward system, reward undermining is like a range effect. When an external incentive is provided, it increases the range of rewards to which our reward system responds, and internal rewards seem small by comparison. However, if all we experience are internal rewards, then those rewards seem much more important.

## Incentives as Social Signals

- Motivation isn't the whole story. Sometimes monetary incentives backfire in a way that can't easily be explained in terms of diminished motivation.

- Consider the following proposition: If there is a nuclear storage site in your community, then you will receive thousands of dollars yearly. When someone offers you money—particularly when they offer you a lot of money—you don't think that they are doing it out of the goodness of their heart.

- Incentives in economic transactions send signals about other people's motivations. If the government offers you money, they must want you to sacrifice something in return. And if a nuclear storage site is built in your community, you might be sacrificing your health, your children's health, and the local environment. When we bring those potential disadvantages to mind, the incentive backfires.

**Paying children to play video games might lead them to view it as "work," which might lead to a decline in play.**

- Incentives can also signal that someone doesn't trust us to make the right decision. Paying children to avoid a desirable behavior—for example, playing video games excessively—sends a very strong signal: Video games are really fun!

- There's a somewhat paradoxical prediction here. You shouldn't pay kids to avoid video games, in part because that sends the wrong social signal. What might work much better is paying kids to play video games. Make the game as work-like as possible so that their performance in the game earns them small amounts of money, and that money may undermine their internal motivation for the games.

- The presence of an incentive sends social signals. The opposite is true as well: When people take actions without incentives, it also sends social signals—to themselves and to others. When we act without external incentives, it says something about us. When we sacrifice of ourselves, when we take risks without any obvious external cause, then we signal that we're motivated by internal causes. We show others that we're not the sort of person who can be bought. We act because of our principles, our desire to help others, our honor.

## When Do Incentives Work?

- When and how do incentives work? This isn't just a question for economists and policymakers. We all use incentives. The following are four guidelines about when incentives work—when they don't backfire and don't undermine our behavior.

- First, incentives work when they establish social norms. Pro-conservation messages in hotel rooms that ask you to help save the environment by reusing your towels work best when they say something that suggests a social norm—for example, 80 percent of guests in this hotel were willing to reuse their towel.

- Other incentives, like small taxes on disposable plastic bags, have had mixed success, often because reduced consumption in one area is offset by increased consumption in another. However, they have been most successful when they establish a social norm: People now see the prosocial behavior as what good people do, rather than as the outcome of an economic transaction.

- Second, incentives work when they expose us to a good outcome. Suppose that you want to encourage your kids to eat more vegetables. An economic incentive could help. In one study, an incentive to eat vegetables broke down children's initial resistance to vegetables, and then they developed a taste for those vegetables over repeated exposures.

- Third, incentives work when internal motivation is absent or already crowded out. People are willing to pay money to ride their bikes, read novels, or work in their gardens. Many people find all of those tasks to be interesting. But people must be paid to work as a bicycle courier, to proofread magazine articles, or to clear other people's gardens. These tasks aren't interesting, or personally relevant, so incentives are critical.

- One solution for this problem is to provide minimal cost incentives—shaping behavior by providing positive feedback or by noting milestones, rather than by giving money. Many online sites have adopted this approach in what is known as gamification, which is the act of converting otherwise boring tasks into games.

- Fourth, incentives are better at encouraging good performance than at shaping our decisions. Incentives work very well in many situations. For example, people work harder and for longer periods of time when they can earn more money. That's a core principle of labor economics, and it's easily observed in workers' willingness to work overtime for a higher rate of pay.

- However, research indicates that incentives are less good at motivating people to engage in an action when they have free choice. What economic incentives can undermine is our motivation for specific choices—for better or for worse.

## Suggested Reading

Frey and Jegen, "Motivation Crowding Theory."

Gneezy and Rustichini, "A Fine Is a Price."

## Questions to Consider

1. Under what circumstances can economic incentives backfire, reducing the behavior they were intended to increase?

2. Why might small gifts—such as a pharmaceutical company sending a mug to a physician—have large effects on the recipient's behavior?

# When Incentives Backfire
## Lecture 21—Transcript

Are you motivated by money? You might answer, "Well, no, I'm motivated by helping others, by doing what's right. Money's not really that important to me." So, let me change the question: Are people motivated by money? Do they work hard to earn money? Do they give up their most precious resource—their time—to gain more money? Do they prefer more money to less money? If we are talking about people in general, the answers seem obvious: Yes, people are motivated by money.

To use a term from economics, money serves as an "incentive" for our behavior. We are more likely to seek out jobs that pay more money, rather than less. When we shop, we prefer to spend less money rather than more. That money serves as an incentive for behavior is central to our economy and to almost every other facet of our lives.

In today's lecture, I want to describe one of the more striking findings from recent research in behavioral economics, psychology, and neuroscience. Simply put: economic incentives can backfire. They can actually discourage behavior, rather than encourage it. I want to illustrate this concept by describing an elegant study conducted by the economists Uri Gneezy and Aldo Rustichini. They began their experiment by going to 10 daycare centers in Israel and just watching did parents pick up their kids on time, or were they late.

If you've ever had kids in daycare, or known someone who has, then you might know that parents are sometimes, despite their best efforts, late. Between work, errands, picking up other children, and all the demands of a busy family, parents are sometimes late. For four weeks, the economists counted how often parents were late in a given week.

On average, parents in a typical daycare were late about five percent of the time. That's not too bad, but it's still disruptive to the daycare center, since the caregivers can't go home until all the children have been picked up. Perhaps if there was some incentive to encourage timeliness, the number of late parents would go down.

So, after a month had passed, the economists worked with the daycare centers to institute a fine for being late. Each time a parent was late, their monthly bill would go up by the equivalent of a few dollars. This isn't a huge penalty, but it's enough to be a reasonable incentive for parents to pick their kids up on time.

What happened next was really remarkable. Over the next month, the number of late parents went steadily up. The parents were late twice as often as before. Instead of being late five percent of the time, they were now late 10 percent of the time even though they were now paying a fine for being late.

Let's think about this phenomenon for a moment. Before there was a fine, there was no economic incentive to show up on time. They didn't pay more money if they were late, and didn't save any money if they were early. But there was a social incentive to not be late. They didn't want to inconvenience the daycare workers, much less delay seeing their own kids.

When the fine was introduced, that same social incentive should be there: The daycare workers still want to go home as soon as possible. The fine provides an additional economic incentive: However motivated someone was before to show up on time, they should be even more motivated by the potential loss of money. The social incentive and the economic incentive should work together; they should add up to shape behavior even more strongly.

But that's not what happened. The fine did not add to parents' motivation to show up on time. If anything, it undermined their motivation. And, it gets worse. The economists measured how often parents were late for three months. Throughout that time, parents were consistently late about 10 percent of the time. Again, that's twice what it was before the fine.

Then, the daycare centers took the fine away. Did parents' behavior go back to what it was before the fine? No. The parents were still late about 10 percent of the time, and that high rate remained consistent until the end of the experiment a month later.

So, in this case, the introduction of an economic fine not only increased the very behavior it was intended to discourage, but the bad behavior lasted well after the fine went away. The incentive failed, spectacularly.

This phenomenon, where an incentive decreases motivation for a behavior, has several names. The one I'll use in today's lecture is reward undermining: The external incentive undermines the sense of internal reward that normally motivates our behavior. Reward undermining is an extraordinarily powerful idea. As we'll see in today's lecture, incentives can not only undermine small-scale interpersonal interactions (like in the daycare example) but also very large-scale social policies.

Take the example of blood donation from the very first lecture of this course. That's actually what sparked the idea of reward undermining. In 1970 the social scientist Richard Titmuss observed that people tended to donate more blood when they weren't being paid for their donations. For example, donation rates were higher in Great Britain, which did not pay donors, than they were in the United States, which did.

That's just a correlation, and other factors could contribute to higher donations in Great Britain. But more recently, economists have conducted randomized experiments that manipulate the incentives offered to different potential donors, and the basic result held. People who were offered payment for blood donation were less likely to donate, overall. So, economic incentives can decrease, or potentially even eliminate, people's actions to benefit an important social good, like blood donation. That's a big deal. Let's look at reward undermining in more detail, so that you can understand how different sorts of incentives can actually come into conflict.

I defined reward undermining by saying that an external incentive can undermine internal motivation. I want you to think about what that simple definition implies: There are two different sorts of motivation. External motivation and internal motivation aren't just two factors on the same scale of utility, they may represent different scales altogether.

Economic theory has historically given pride of place to external sources of motivation. A monetary incentive, for example, should have much greater influence on behavior than any internal factors. And, external incentives should have more consistent effects, too. People should all be motivated by money in a generally similar way, even if their internal motivations are very different. But, reward undermining argues that internal sources of motivation can be more important, at least some of the time.

So, what determines whether external incentives or internal motivations shape our decisions? One answer is that there are actually two different currencies for decision making. One currency is economic: Our choices lead to physical gains and losses, good outcomes and bad. The other currency is social: Our choices change how other people see us, or how we see ourselves. Different incentives change the currency in which we make our decisions, from social to economic, or vice versa.

When the economists who conducted the daycare study wrote the paper describing their surprising results, they summarized their study with a simple title: "A Fine is a Price."

A fine is a price. Before the fine was introduced, the parents were making decisions about social currency. They had to consider what the daycare workers would think about them, and what they would think about themselves. A parent who was regularly late might think of themselves as inconsiderate, irresponsible, someone who doesn't hold up their end of a social relationship.

But the fine set a price for being late. We don't have prices in our social interactions; we have prices in our economic transactions. Once the parents could think about being late as an economic transaction, they could then decide whether the additional time was worth the monetary cost.

Social relationships don't matter in our economic transactions. When we go shopping we don't worry about what the store thinks of us, and we don't think of ourselves as inconsiderate whenever we take advantage of a good deal at a store. Monetary incentives change the context of a decision from a social relationship to an economic transaction, from social currency to economic currency.

Money changes how we think about our social relationships. We resist lending money to friends and family, not because of the value of money, but because of the value of our social ties. We don't want to think about money whenever we think about our friends, and we don't want to risk our friendship over a loan.

And, incentives can work in the opposite way, too: Social relationships can change how we think about economic incentives. Salespeople in many industries know this. They try to build rapport with their customers getting to know them and their families. They host customers at dinners, at sporting events, on trips. They want to build social relationships with those customers, so that the customers choose their firm among many in a crowded marketplace.

Pharmaceutical and medical device companies have historically courted physicians by offering them small gifts: free meals, travel to conferences, or inexpensive goods like books or bags. Now, you might think that a $20 lunch isn't a large enough economic incentive to change what drug a physician prescribes or what device a physician implants. But, the primary effect of those small gifts isn't economic, it's social. Those gifts establish a social relationship between the company and the physician. And, what do we expect in our social relationships? Reciprocity. Gifts and favors are reciprocated, perhaps not consciously, but reciprocated nonetheless.

Research shows that even simple, small gifts like free meals can have powerful effects on physicians' practices; for example, they become more likely to prescribe drugs from those companies. And, this isn't good for patients. Reviews of real-world physician behavior show that small gifts lead to systematic and negative effects on clinical care.

So, these two currencies—economic and social—can compete with and even undermine each other, potentially leading to bad decisions.

I want to next describe some different explanations for reward undermining. The first category of explanation comes from psychology and it focuses on the idea of motivation.

A core concept in social psychology is that people don't simply know the reasons for their actions. Instead, they have to infer their own reasons based on potential external and internal motivators. Let's consider a real-world controversy related to reward undermining: giving students incentives, like money, for earning good grades. Proponents of this idea argue that incentives can motivate students to attend class, read course material, and pass end-of-year tests. But critics claim that paying students can eliminate students' internal motivation, robbing them of the love of learning and curiosity necessary for long-term success.

So, let's consider a simple experiment. A school introduces a new enrichment activity to two classrooms, say, a new drawing easel and markers. In one classroom, students are told that they can draw pictures on the easel for a chance to win a prize, say, a gold star. In another, students are simply drawing for drawing's sake; there's no prize or other external incentive. The key measure is how often students draw in the future, when they are given the opportunity to go back to the drawing easel in their free time.

In early studies of this sort, it was found that students who were rewarded for participating in a fun activity were much less likely to seek out that activity in the future. That is, if they were given an incentive the first time that they drew pictures, then they weren't motivated to draw pictures without that incentive. This sort of reward undermining was initially called the overjustification effect. The external prize was enough to justify the behavior, so it prevented internal motivation from developing. The drawing task becomes a means to an end, rather than an end in itself. This is an early undermining perspective, because it proposes that external incentives prevent internal motivation from forming in the first place.

Alternatively, undermining might happen more gradually. Many studies have shown that external incentives don't necessarily extinguish internal motivation, especially if those incentives are infrequent and unexpected. Besides, nearly all students in the United States are constantly exposed to external incentives, in the form of grades, and many of them remain curious and inquisitive learners. So, a late undermining perspective would propose, instead, that external incentives won't undermine internal motivation immediately, but will instead have effects later, as they are delivered repeatedly.

It is very difficult to discriminate between these two perspectives, but the key message is, we now know that motivation is an important contributor to reward undermining, but that it isn't the only contributor.

Think back to earlier in the course, when I described the brain's reward system. Deep in the brain are neurons that use the chemical dopamine. Those neurons send signals to brain regions that help us learn, so that we can learn to make choices that lead to good outcomes and avoid choices that lead to bad outcomes. I emphasized that dopamine was not associated with pleasure, but instead with motivation. Rats whose reward system has been disrupted by brain damage show normal facial expressions of pleasure when food is placed in their mouths, but they aren't motivated enough to cross their cage to eat, even if they are hungry. So, if undermining is associated with disrupted motivation, as these psychological theories contend, then undermining should also disrupt the function of the brain's reward system.

A group of neuroscientists ran a clever study to test this prediction. They allowed participants to play a simple stopwatch timing game. You may have played this sort of game yourself, if you've ever owned a digital watch. The participants just pressed a button once to start a timer, and again to stop that timer, and they tried to stop exactly on a target time, say, five seconds. Participants find this game surprisingly fun. It's difficult enough to be challenging, but it's also the sort of task that you get better at over time.

The researchers split their participants into two groups. The first group began by playing the game for money. The better they were at hitting the targets, the more money they earned. The second group began by playing the game just for fun. The researchers measured brain activation while the participants played this game, and found that both groups showed considerable activation within a brain region that receives input from dopamine neurons, which is a hallmark of motivation.

Then, they had both groups play the game for a second session without any monetary reward. In the group for which the economic incentive had been present, but was taken away, the activation in that brain region went back to baseline levels. It was as if the motivational signal in the brain disappeared.

But, in the group that wasn't paid the first time, the motivational signal in the brain was still there and just as large as before.

I want to remind you of something that I introduced in an early lecture: the idea of range effects. Range effects occur because our sense of a meaningful difference in some quantity is inversely proportional to its range. Let's apply this idea to motivation.

It's reasonable to assume that the range in the activity of our reward system will be smaller when we're just playing a game for fun than when we're playing a game for money. There's good evidence that external rewards, particularly money, have greater effects upon our reward system than internal rewards like satisfaction. There's a good reason for that: Those external rewards are very important for learning about the consequences of our decisions.

From the perspective of our reward system, reward undermining is like a range effect. When an external incentive is provided, it increases the range of rewards to which our reward system responds, and internal rewards seem small by comparison. But, if all we experience are internal rewards, then those rewards seem much more important. But motivation isn't the whole story. Sometimes monetary incentives backfire in a way that can't easily be explained in terms of diminished motivation.

In the early 1990s, the Swiss government was considering two small communities as potential storage sites for low-level waste from their nuclear power plants. At that time nuclear power was relatively popular in Switzerland; it was seen as a common good that benefited the country as a whole. The households in those two communities were surveyed about whether they would support or oppose a nuclear waste storage site in their community. I want to emphasize that this isn't a laboratory experiment conducted in college students. The researchers targeted the specific communities that were likely to be most affected by the storage site, and they interviewed more than two-thirds of all households in those communities.

Perhaps surprisingly, slightly more than 50 percent of the people interviewed actually supported building the storage site. They saw the storage site as something relatively safe, something that might have other benefits for their community, and something connected to the greater social good of nuclear power.

But, then the researchers added an economic incentive. People were asked whether they would support or oppose the storage site, if the Swiss parliament offered every resident in their community a yearly payment equivalent to several thousand U.S. dollars. When the incentive was added, only 25 percent of people supported the storage site. The incentive reduced people's willingness to support the public good rather dramatically.

It's hard to dismiss this result. This was a real issue in two real communities. Almost everyone in those communities was surveyed. And, the monetary incentive was substantial, equivalent to thousands of dollars. But the incentive backfired. About a quarter of the community switched from favoring the storage site to opposing the storage site, because of the incentive. Why did support drop so dramatically?

One explanation is that the incentive disrupted some internal motivation, say, a sense of charity, like in the stopwatch game I just discussed. But this situation is different. Here, undermining occurs while the external incentive is present. The external incentive seems to make the outcome less desirable, rather than more. We need an alternative explanation.

Think for a moment about the logic of this specific incentive. It's framed as an offer: If there is a nuclear storage site in your community, then you will receive thousands of dollars yearly. When someone offers you money—particularly when they offer you a lot of money—you don't think that they are doing it out of the goodness of their heart. Incentives in economic transactions send signals about other people's motivations. If the government offers you money, they must want you to sacrifice something in return. And, what might you be sacrificing if a nuclear storage site is built in your community? Your health. Your children's health. The local environment. When we bring those potential disadvantages to mind, the incentive backfires.

Incentives can also signal that someone doesn't trust us to make the right decision. Paying children to avoid a desirable behavior, say, playing videogames excessively, sends a very strong signal: Videogames are really fun. There's a somewhat paradoxical prediction here. You shouldn't pay kids to avoid videogames, in part because that sends the wrong social signal. What might work much better is paying kids to play videogames. Make the game as work-like as possible, so that their performance in the game earns them small amounts of money, and that money may undermine their internal motivation for the games.

So far, I've talked about how the presence of an incentive sends social signals. But, the opposite is true as well: When people take actions without incentives, it also sends social signals, to themselves and to others.

In 1914 the explorer Ernest Shackleton was assembling a crew for a voyage to Antarctica. His ambitious goal was the first crossing of that continent, which would be a hazardous task, to the say the least. Although no one has been able to confirm this story, legend has it that he placed the following advertisement in a newspaper: "Men wanted for hazardous journey. Small wages, bitter cold, long months of complete darkness, constant danger. Safe return doubtful. Honor and recognition in case of success." And, the story continues, he received some 5,000 applications for joining his crew.

When we act without external incentives, it says something about us. When we sacrifice of ourselves, when we take risks without any obvious external cause, then we signal that we're motivated by internal causes. We show others that we're not the sort of person who can be bought. We act because of our principles, our desire to help others, our honor.

If reward undermining is a real phenomenon, we're left with a puzzle: When and how do incentives work? This isn't just a question for economists and policymakers. We all use incentives. We use incentives when we reward our children for good behavior, when we help and support our friends, when we encourage employees or volunteers in our organizations, and even when we reward ourselves for our own accomplishments.

I'll end by describing four guidelines about when incentives work, when they don't backfire, and when don't undermine our behavior. First, incentives work when they establish social norms. We've all seen the pro-conservation messages in hotel rooms, things like "Help save the environment by reusing your towels." Those messages work best when they say something that suggests a social norm, something like "Eighty percent of guests in this hotel were willing to reuse their towel."

Other incentives, like small taxes on disposable plastic bags, have had mixed success, often because reduced consumption in one area is offset by increased consumption in another. But, they have been most successful when they establish a social norm. People now see the pro-social behavior as what good people do, rather than as the outcome of an economic transaction.

Second, incentives work when they expose us to a good outcome. Suppose that you want to encourage your kids to eat more vegetables. They hate broccoli, won't even try carrots, and they push away any plate with a green bean aboard. Could an incentive help? Absolutely.

Researchers created a randomized trial in which they varied whether or not kids were paid for eating their vegetables. The kids who were paid were more likely to try their vegetables, and they ate them whenever they were paid for eating them. And, guess what happened. The kids started liking the vegetables, and they ate more vegetables after the payments ended. The incentive broke down their initial resistance to the vegetables, and then they developed a taste for those vegetables over repeated exposures.

Third, incentives work when internal motivation is absent or already crowded out. People are willing to pay money to ride their bikes, to read novels, or to work in their gardens. Many people find those all interesting tasks. But people must be paid to work as a bicycle courier, to proofread magazine articles, or to clear other people's gardens. These tasks aren't interesting or personally relevant and so incentives are critical.

One solution for this problem is to provide minimal cost incentives, shaping behavior by providing positive feedback or by noting milestones, rather than by giving money. Many online sites have adopted this approach in what is known as gamification, converting otherwise boring tasks into games.

Fourth, incentives are better at encouraging good performance than at shaping our decisions. From the many examples I've provided, you might think that incentives always undermine internal motivation. That's not always true. Incentives work very well in many situations. For example, people work harder and for longer periods of time when they can earn more money. That's a core principle of labor economics and it's easily observed in workers' willingness to work overtime for a higher rate of pay.

But, research indicates that incentives are less good at motivating people to engage in an action when they have free choice. Think back to what's common to these examples: donating blood, children drawing on easels, playing a stopwatch game, and supporting a nuclear storage site. In all these cases, there's a free choice to take one action or another. What economic incentives can undermine is our motivation for specific choices, for better or for worse.

So, is reward undermining inevitable? No. Take the example that sparked research on this phenomenon: Blood donation. I've told you that paying people for donating blood actually decreases their willingness to do so. And, that's true; donation rates can go down. But that reward undermining can be counteracted by giving potential donors an additional option: If they wish, they can donate their payment to charity. When people are given that option, donation rates rise again. To be sure, a donation to charity is still an incentive. It's just the right incentive to encourage the right behavior.

In the next lecture, we'll begin to explore the key techniques for encouraging good decisions, beginning with one of the most powerful: a technique known as precommitment.

# Precommitment—Setting Rationality Aside
## Lecture 22

In this lecture, you will learn about one of the most powerful tools for making better decisions: precommitment. When you precommit to something, you are making a binding decision ahead of time, essentially locking in a choice option now rather than keeping flexibility for the future. It seems strange to want to precommit ourselves to a course of action. We usually value flexibility in our decision making; we want to keep our options open. However, as you will learn in this lecture, giving up that flexibility can often lead to better decisions.

**Precommitment Explained**

- Precommitment is a very powerful approach to improving decision making. It works, and it works well, especially under the right circumstances. A precommitment is a decision now to limit one's possible decisions in the future.

- Precommitment works, in large part, because we know that we don't always make good decisions. We think about ourselves in the future—perhaps facing some new temptation—and we don't trust that future self to make a good decision. So, we bind our future self's hands to prevent mistakes.

- If you're like most Americans, you've made New Year's resolutions before—whether to lose weight, volunteer more in your community, or take up a new and time-consuming hobby. And if you're like most Americans, you didn't keep all of your resolutions. Just resolving to do something doesn't help much. And it can actually backfire. Just making a resolution about your goal can make you less likely to take action to reach that goal.

- New Year's resolutions aren't binding. Therefore, resolving to do something can substitute for real action. We're comforted by our plans to get in shape. We become confident that our resolute future self will exercise regularly and eat well, which gives our present self permission to indulge.

- Resolutions aren't completely useless. They can highlight important goals and thus provide a roadmap toward some desired outcome. But they aren't binding, and thus, they can backfire on us.

**Costly Precommitment**
- Precommitment works best when it is credible—when people can't readily change the committed course of action because of the effort required, because of a financial cost, or because the decision is irrevocable.

- A common example is that of cutting up one's credit cards to prevent future spending. But precommitment doesn't have to be so extreme. If you know you tend to overspend when shopping for holiday presents, then just resolving to spend less is unlikely to be effective. A better step toward responsibility would be to leave credit cards at home when shopping; by only bringing cash, you set an upper limit on what can be spent during that shopping trip.

**An example of precommitment is cutting up your credit cards so that you cannot use them.**

- Credible precommitment has been used to help addicts and people at risk for addiction manage their behavior. Many casinos have self-exclusion programs that allow patrons to establish binding limits on their play. For example, you could voluntarily establish limits on how much you can bet, how much credit you can be extended, or even whether you can enter a particular casino.

- Credible precommitment works even for problem gamblers; they can't feed their addiction when they can't enter in the first place. However, when a commitment isn't credible—like when casinos or states remind people about the dangers of gambling but don't bar entry into the casinos—then it doesn't help problem gamblers and has only very limited benefits for everyone else.

- People engage in precommitment at great potential cost to themselves. They'll purposefully establish penalties for missing deadlines in order to motivate themselves to complete tasks. Research by the behavioral economist Dan Ariely and his colleagues showed that costly precommitment really helps, especially when people are sophisticated about how they set their deadlines.

## Emotions as Precommitment Devices

- Precommitment works when it binds us to a course of action—when we can't change from our original plan without penalty. This aspect of precommitment turns out to be critical for ensuring cooperation in social interactions.

- When we interact with others in economic settings, we need to convince them that we can be trusted—that our promises bind our future actions. In modern society, there are external tools for making binding promises, like legal contracts. Our reputations also suffer when we break our promises, and people will readily punish promise breakers in order to enforce social norms.

- However, what about very simple sorts of economic interactions, like two people haggling over a price, where there are no contracts and no reputations to consider? What can cause people to cooperate for mutual benefit? Promises aren't enough; most verbal promises are just cheap talk without any precommitment mechanism. So, we need some way to bind ourselves to a course of action so that we can't take a different action later.

- The economist Robert Frank argues that our emotions make our promises credible. Think about anger. You can tell if someone is really angry—you can see it in their face, in the tensing of their muscles, how they stomp around the room with undirected energy. And that anger does not dissipate instantaneously; instead, it takes time to dissipate, and all the while, you're fearful of what that angry person might do next.

- When we receive clear signals that someone else is committed to a course of action, even if it wouldn't be in their self-interest, it shapes our actions. We back down in negotiations, for example.

**Institutional Precommitment**

- Precommitment can be a powerful tool for making good decisions, and it's been recently applied by a range of institutions—both governmental and nongovernmental—in hopes of shaping real-world decisions.

- A striking example has come in the realm of organ donation. Making one's vital organs available to others, in the event of death, can save the lives or improve the quality of life of several other people. Organ donation has extraordinary social benefits, but in many countries, too few people register to be donors.

- In the United States, donor rates have risen steadily as people become more aware of organ donation and as signing up becomes increasingly convenient. But participation remains lower than it should; only recently has the proportion of eligible donors risen above 40 percent. In addition, many of our peer countries have similar or lower rates.

- But in some countries—such as France, Hungary, and Portugal—nearly 100 percent of all adults are registered organ donors. Is this because their citizens are more altruistic than Americans? No. It's because those systems use an opt-out approach to organ donation: Everyone is assumed to be a donor, unless they expressly indicate that they wish to opt out of the donation program. But almost no one does.

- A simple difference in policy—from opting in to opting out of donation—dramatically increases the number of eligible donors. This seems like a relatively noncontroversial use of precommitment and of behavioral economic methods, more generally. Thousands of additional lives are saved yearly in these countries; there's a clear benefit to their societies.

- Most people report approving of organ donation. In fact, within the United States, the number of people who support organ donation has historically been much larger than the number of eligible donors. So, the precommitment approach pushes them toward making a decision they'd prefer anyway. In addition, those people who don't wish to become organ donors can still decline participation, if they choose.

- However, even this case raises ethical issues. Think about someone who is really against organ donation—who doesn't wish to participate—but because he or she is susceptible to all the same biases as the rest of us, he or she doesn't take any action to change the default. People like this would end up being an organ donor—in a sense, against their wishes—because of their own inertia.

- There are obvious counterarguments. There's still an enormous societal benefit from increasing the pool of organ donors. And even this hypothetical person still could have opted out, if he or she had just mustered the energy. So, that's hardly the most compelling case against an opt-out plan.

- Even the nonbinding precommitment of an opt-out program involves ethical tradeoffs. Precommitment works. People stick with default options—perhaps because they really prefer that option, perhaps because of their own inertia, or perhaps because the default establishes a new social norm.

- So, changing the organ donation program from opt-in to opt-out program changes that program's mistakes. An opt-in program misses people who really prefer to participate but haven't enrolled, while an opt-out program includes people who would rather not participate but haven't withdrawn.

- For organ donation, this tradeoff seems justified; almost everyone benefits from the move to an opt-out program. But it isn't hard to imagine a circumstance in which a precommitment strategy might not be so benign—for example, a dubious investment vehicle—one where many people end up, by default, making decisions against their preferences.

**Precommitment Strategies**
- We can easily use precommitment strategies in our everyday lives, and they don't have to be as extreme as cutting up our credit cards. Most of the time we use precommitment to avoid temptation, for which it is very effective. Indeed, the best approach to managing temptation is to avoid it in the first place.

- Don't trust your future self to make good decisions. It'll be just as hard to skip dessert tomorrow as it is today. Help out your future self by precommitting. If you rarely have money at the end of each pay period to invest for the long term, force yourself to save money by an automatic payroll deduction, which is more likely to be successful than trusting in your future willpower.

- In addition, avoid empty commitments. Just making a resolution isn't enough, and small steps toward a large goal can backfire. Make small commitments that are readily managed, and make them credible; you're better off if there are specific outcomes that depend on meeting your goals.

### Suggested Reading

Frank, *Passions within Reason*.

Johnson and Goldstein, "Do Defaults Save Lives?"

## Questions to Consider

1. Why are opt-out approaches to retirement saving so effective?

2. How do our emotions facilitate precommitment?

# Precommitment—Setting Rationality Aside
## Lecture 22—Transcript

We all want to make better decisions, and throughout this course I've emphasized that just knowing about the mistakes we make isn't enough. We need to understand what we do well so that we can identify the tools we already have, and can use them in the right way at the right time. In today's lecture, I'll talk about one of the most powerful tools for making better decisions: precommitment.

When you precommit to something, you are making a binding decision ahead of time, essentially, locking in a choice option now, rather than keeping flexibility for the future. It seems strange to want to precommit ourselves to a course of action. We usually value flexibility in our decision making; we want to keep our options open. But, as I'll show you today, giving up that flexibility can often lead to better decisions.

Let's start by considering the largest and longest-term financial challenge faced by most Americans: saving for retirement. There are three primary contributors to retirement savings for workers in the United States. First, the government-managed Social Security system provides a defined benefit to each worker based on their tax-mandated contributions. But Social Security is rarely enough on its own to support a comfortable retirement. It typically replaces a little less than half of the pre-retirement income of the average taxpayer.

Second, some Americans have employer-sponsored, defined-benefits plans. Often, those are in the form of a pension. Those plans guarantee a specific income each year after retirement, simplifying planning. But, they are increasingly rare, in large part because of the financial uncertainty they introduce for employers.

Third, the remaining Americans depend on their own ability to save for retirement, often through defined-contributions savings plans offered through their employer. These are known by a variety of names including 401(k) and 403(b) plans. There are two important reasons for saving for retirement through one of these plans, rather than through other investment vehicles. There are typically significant tax advantages, and employers often contribute matching funds to the plans.

Defined-contributions plans can provide a very effective method for people to take control of their retirement savings. If there's an employer match on, say, up to 6 percent of annual income, then a worker can contribute 6 percent of their income annually, pre-tax, but actually save 12 percent annually. Current balances can be easily tracked over time, so that people know exactly how much has been saved and how much is still needed. And, the vesting period for benefits is usually much shorter than for traditional pension plans.

These plans can be very effective both for individuals and for society. There's just one problem. Many people don't bother to enroll.

Enrollment rates vary dramatically from company to company, for reasons you might expect. Financial circumstances affect whether someone has the capacity to save for the future, and workers with higher incomes and more education are more likely to enroll. And, it's not necessarily the case that everyone should enroll in a retirement plan. Someone who has overwhelming immediate financial needs, like the burden of a catastrophic illness, might reasonably prioritize those expenses over saving for retirement. But even taking financial and other factors into consideration, it's pretty clear that fewer people participate than should.

In one survey of three large companies, only about one in three employees signed up for the retirement plan within six months of beginning work. And, that rate only jumped to about two in three after three years working at the company. You might argue that, indeed, many of those non-participating workers couldn't contribute. They didn't have the discretionary income each month to devote to a distant retirement. To counter that argument, let me focus on a specific group of workers.

Some U.S. workers nearing retirement age can withdraw money, including the employer match, from their retirement accounts immediately and without any penalty. All they have to do is designate some part of their paycheck to their retirement fund, then they get the employer match in each paycheck, and then they can withdraw both their own contribution and the employer match right away. This is arbitrage: The employer match represents free money just for the taking. And it's not an inconsequential amount of money. For most employees the employer match would be thousands of dollars a year.

But, only about 40 percent of eligible workers surveyed in one study actually took advantage of this free money. The remainder are losing perhaps thousands of dollars each year, right in the pre-retirement period where every dollar is critical. And, this lack of participation isn't limited to the United States. Another study examined a class of retirement savings plans in the United Kingdom. These were fully employer-supported. They required no personal contribution. Let me emphasize that: All people had to do was sign up, and their employer would start contributing money to a retirement account. And still, only about half of eligible employees took action to enroll in the plans. The rest simply didn't sign up for the benefits coming to them.

Why don't people participate in retirement plans, even when they know that saving is important and they can do so very simply (often by mailing a single card or clicking on a single webpage)? There's a one-word explanation: inertia. When you aren't already enrolled in a plan, it can be hard to start. You have to sacrifice some of your monthly income right now. And, you have to make a decision about how to invest your money. That can be complicated and discouraging.

The proportion of people participating in a 401(k) or similar retirement plan actually decreases when the employer offers more investment options. For example, companies that only offer 2 mutual funds to choose from have higher participation than those that have 10 funds, and much higher than those that have 40 or more options. As I've emphasized throughout this course, people want to make decisions that they won't regret later, and complicated decisions that involve many potential funds for investment are more likely to generate regret.

What can be done about this? Some employers have moved to an opt-out approach to retirement savings. That is, employees are automatically enrolled in the retirement plan shortly after hiring, with some default contribution level, and they stay in the plan unless they expressly choose to withdraw. That's what's meant by opt-out. It's a precommitment strategy, in that workers are committed to a particular decision ahead of time, but it's not a binding precommitment. They can choose to leave the plan when they wish.

So, what happens when a company changes to an opt-out approach? The history at one large chemical company is typical. That company offered a very generous dollar-for-dollar match up to 6 percent of pay, but still only about 70 percent of employees signed up for the retirement plan. When that company began automatically enrolling new employees into the program, nearly everyone continued to participate. Almost no-one opted out.

And, let me tell you the most amazing effect. That same company automatically enrolled all of its current employees who weren't participating. Again, these are people who could have signed up, but just didn't. More than 95 percent of those people now stayed in the program and started building savings for retirement.

One simple change in how a retirement plan was presented to employees—moving from an opt-in to an opt-out approach—led to a dramatic increase in participation. This sort of story is pretty typical; it's been documented in a number of different companies, under a wide range of conditions.

And, employers don't have to go all the way to an opt-in approach. Just requiring employees make an active decision—they have to indicate whether they want to sign up or not—can lead to much better participation than when people must take action to join the plan.

As this example illustrates, precommitment is a very powerful approach to improving decision making. It works, and it works well, especially under the right circumstances. A precommitment is a decision now to limit one's possible decisions in the future. Precommitment works, in large part, because we know that we don't always make good decisions. We think about ourselves in the future, perhaps facing some new temptation, and we don't trust that future self to make a good decision. So, we bind our future self's hands to prevent mistakes.

The classic example of precommitment involves a literal binding. In Homer's *Odyssey*, the protagonist (Odysseus) had to sail his ship past the sirens (half-human, half-bird creatures who lured sailors to their deaths through a mesmerizing song). The sorceress Circe took Odysseus aside and advised him to stop up the ears of his crewmen with wax, and to bind himself with strong ropes to the ship's mast so that they couldn't hear the sirens' song, and so that he couldn't act when he heard it. Odysseus was tempted by the sirens' song, which promised him what he most desired, knowledge. But he couldn't give into that temptation. He was physically unable to leave his ship. His precommitment during a moment of cautious reflection saved him during a later moment of temptation.

Odysseus' precommitment worked because it was credible and costly. There was no way he could escape the bindings when he was later tempted. I emphasize this because precommitment often doesn't work when it's not credible, when it doesn't carry any cost.

If you're like most Americans, you've made New Year's resolutions before. You might have resolved to lose weight, volunteer more in your community, or take up a new and time-consuming hobby. And, if you're like most Americans, you didn't keep all of your resolutions.

Just resolving to do something doesn't help much. And, it can actually backfire. Just making a resolution about your goal can make you less likely to take action to reach that goal. Let me illustrate with an example from everyday life.

In one experiment, the marketing scientist Gavan Fitzsimons and his colleagues gave young adults a menu of several sandwich items and asked them which item they'd want for lunch. Some participants viewed a menu containing a fish sandwich, a chicken sandwich, and a bacon cheeseburger. On that menu, the bacon cheeseburger is clearly the least healthful. On average, participants made pretty good choices. They only chose the bacon cheeseburger about 20 percent of the time. And the participants who were resolved to control their eating chose it much less, only about 5 percent of the time. That seems pretty good. People rarely chose the least healthful option, and the people with clear goals made the best choices.

But, the researchers also gave a different menu to another group of participants. Those participants saw a menu with a bacon cheeseburger, a chicken sandwich, and a vegetarian burger. This menu differs from the first in that it replaces a somewhat neutral item with a clearly healthful item, the veggie burger.

And, people's choices got worse. This second group chose the bacon cheeseburger about 40 percent of the time, that's twice as much as before. What's even more remarkable is that the people who reported clear goals to control their eating now chose the bacon cheeseburger the most, more than half of the time. Just seeing a veggie burger on the menu made them much, much more likely to pick the least healthful option.

What happened here? Well, it seems that when people with a strong goal and high self-control viewed an option consistent with that goal (like the veggie burger) they didn't necessarily choose that option. Instead, just viewing it seemed to fulfill their goals. That's what the researchers called vicarious goal fulfillment. Those people then relax their self-control, and they ignore their plans.

New Year's resolutions can have the same effect. They aren't binding. They're what economists call "cheap talk." And so, resolving to do something can substitute for real action. We're comforted by our plans to get in shape. We become confident that our resolute future self will exercise regularly and eat well, and that gives our present self permission to indulge.

Resolutions aren't completely useless. They can highlight important goals and thus provide a roadmap toward some desired outcome. But, they aren't binding, and that means they can backfire on us.

Precommitment works best when it is credible, when people can't readily change the committed course of action because of the effort required, because of a financial cost, or because the decision is irrevocable. A common example is that of cutting up one's credit cards to prevent future spending. But precommitment doesn't have to be so extreme. If you know you tend to overspend when shopping for holiday presents, then just resolving to spend less is unlikely to be effective. A better step toward responsibility would be to leave credit cards at home when shopping. By only bringing cash, you set an upper limit on what can be spent in that shopping trip.

Credible precommitment has been used to help addicts and people at risk for addiction to manage their behavior. Many casinos have self-exclusion programs that allow patrons to establish binding limits on their play. For example, you could voluntarily establish limits on how much you can bet, how much credit you can be extended, or even whether you can enter a particular casino.

In the city-state of Singapore, there was great apprehension in advance of the opening of two mega-casinos in 2010. Lawmakers and the public alike were concerned that many people wouldn't be able to control their gambling. So, the government gave people the option to self-exclude, to prevent themselves from entering, and within two years about 100,000 people had enrolled in that program.

Think about this for a moment. The people who have no interest in gambling whatsoever, who don't derive enjoyment from gambling, wouldn't bother to self-exclude; they don't need to. People self-exclude precisely because they recognize that they do derive enjoyment from gambling, that they could be tempted, that their future self might not be able to make the right decisions, and so they eliminate any concern by pre-committing.

Credible precommitment works even for problem gamblers. They can't feed their addiction when they can't enter in the first place. But when a commitment isn't credible, as when casinos or states remind people about the dangers of gambling but don't bar entry into the casinos, then it doesn't help problem gamblers and has only very limited benefits for everyone else.

People engage in precommitment at great potential cost to themselves. They'll purposefully establish penalties for missing deadlines in order to motivate themselves to complete tasks. Research by the behavioral economist Dan Ariely and his colleagues showed that costly precommitment really helps, especially when people are sophisticated about how they set their deadlines.

For example, people in one study were given tasks that had to be completed in a three-week period, in order to maximize their earnings. They were allowed to pre-commit to particular deadlines with financial penalties for missing those deadlines. Think about this option for a moment—it's like voluntarily taking money away from your future self. Or they could just plan to complete all tasks by the end of the three-week period. Those people who pre-committed by self-imposing weekly deadlines did very well, overall, while those people who just planned to complete everything by the end of the experiment did very poorly.

Precommitment works when it binds us to a course of action, when we can't change from our original plan without penalty. This aspect of precommitment turns out to be critical for ensuring cooperation in social interactions. When we interact with others in economic settings, we need to convince them that we can be trusted, that our promises bind our future actions. In modern society, there are external tools for making binding promises, like legal contracts. Our reputations also suffer when we break our promises, and as I discussed in the lecture on cooperation, people will readily punish promise-breakers in order to enforce social norms.

But, what about very simple sorts of economic interactions (like two people haggling over a price) where there are no contracts and no reputations to consider? What can cause people to cooperate for mutual benefit? Promises aren't enough. Most verbal promises are just cheap talk without any precommitment mechanism. So, we need some way to bind ourselves to a course of action, so that we can't take a different action later.

Let's think back to the ultimatum game, which I introduced in an earlier lecture. As a reminder, the standard form of this game involves two players who don't know each other, have no other interactions besides the game itself, and who play the game once. The first player, the proposer, has access to a sum of money, say $100, and can propose a division of that money, say they get $90 and the second player gets $10. The second player, the responder, can choose to accept that division or reject it, in which case no one gets anything.

A rational responder would accept any proposed division—after all, some money is better than no money—which means that a rational proposer would offer a very small amount.

I told you that when people play this game for real money, responders will reject offers that seem unfair, even when the stakes are pretty large. And, because responders do reject unfair offers, against their self-interest, proposers' offers tend to be relatively fair.

What causes this? Emotion. When responders are given an unfair offer, they recognize it as unfair, and they get angry. Anger has two key effects on people's behavior. It pushes us toward action. Angry people want to strike out at the source of their anger. And, it reduces our self-concern. Angry people are willing to sacrifice their own well-being to harm others.

The economist Robert Frank argues that our emotions make our promises credible. Think about anger. Can you tell if someone is really angry? Yes. You can see it in their face, in the tensing of their muscles, how they stomp around the room with undirected energy. And, does that anger dissipate instantaneously, as if turning off a light switch? No, anger lasts. It takes time to dissipate, and all the while you're fearful of what that angry person might do next.

There's a great cartoon by the New Yorker artist Frank Modell called "The Extortionist." Two pedestrians approach a street vendor selling pencils. The vendor stares off in the distance with an angry look on his face. He holds the pencils in his left hand and a whip in his right hand, and he wears a sign that reads "Irrational."

When we receive clear signals that someone else is committed to a course of action, even if it wouldn't be in their self-interest, it shapes our actions. We back down in negotiations, we propose a more fair offer in the ultimatum game, and yes, we buy pencils that we don't want.

Precommitment can be a powerful tool for making good decisions. And, it's been recently applied by a range of institutions, both governmental and non-governmental, in hopes of shaping real-world decisions.

A striking example has come in the realm of organ donation. Making one's vital organs available to others in the event of death can save the lives or improve the quality of life of several other people. Organ donation has extraordinary social benefits, but in many countries too few people register to be donors.

In the United States donor rates have risen steadily as people become more aware of organ donation and as signing up becomes increasingly convenient. But participation still remains lower than it should. Only recently has the proportion of eligible donors risen above 40 percent. And many of our peer countries have similar or lower rates.

But in some countries, such as France, Hungary, and Portugal, nearly 100 percent of all adults are registered organ donors. Is this because their citizens are more altruistic than Americans? No. It's because those systems use an opt-out approach to organ donation. Everyone is assumed to be a donor, unless they expressly indicate that they wish to opt-out of the donation program. But almost no one does.

A simple difference in policy, from opting-in to opting-out of donation, dramatically increases the number of eligible donors. This seems like a relatively non-controversial use of precommitment and of behavioral economic methods, more generally. Thousands of additional lives are saved yearly in these countries. There's a clear benefit to their societies.

Most people report approving of organ donation. In fact, within the United States the number of people who support organ donation has historically been much larger than the number of eligible donors. So, the precommitment approach pushes them toward making a decision they'd prefer anyway. And, those people who don't wish to become organ donors can still decline participation, if they choose.

But, even this case raises ethical issues. Let's think about someone who is really against organ donation, who doesn't wish to participate, but because they are susceptible to all the same biases as the rest of us, they don't take any action to change the default. They end up being an organ donor—in a sense, against their wishes—because of their own inertia.

Now, there are obvious counterarguments. There's still an enormous societal benefit from increasing the pool of organ donors. And even this hypothetical person still could have opted out if they had just mustered the energy. So, that's hardly the most compelling case against an opt-out plan.

I do want to emphasize, however, that even the non-binding precommitment of an opt-out program involves ethical tradeoffs. Precommitment works. People stick with default options, perhaps because they really prefer that option, perhaps because of their own inertia, or perhaps because the default establishes a new social norm.

So, changing the organ donation program from opt-in to opt-out changes that program's mistakes. An opt-in program misses people who really prefer to participate but haven't enrolled, while an opt-out program includes people who would rather not participate but haven't withdrawn.

For organ donation, this tradeoff seems justified. Almost everyone benefits from the move to an opt-out program. But it isn't hard to imagine a circumstance in which a precommitment strategy might not be so benign, say a dubious investment vehicle, one where many people end up, by default, making decisions against their preferences.

So, I want you to think of precommitment as a tool, in fact, one of the two most effective tools for shaping our decisions. But like any tool, it can be applied toward a variety of purposes, and its very effectiveness means that we should be circumspect in its use.

We can easily use precommitment strategies in our everyday lives, and they don't have to be as extreme as lashing ourselves to a mast or cutting up our credit cards. Most of the time we use precommitment to avoid temptation, for which it is very effective. Indeed, the best approach to managing temptation is to avoid it in the first place.

Don't trust your future self to make good decisions. It'll be just as hard to skip dessert tomorrow as it is today. Help out your future self by precommitting. If you rarely have money at the end of each pay period to invest for the long term, force yourself to save money by an automatic payroll deduction. That's more likely to be successful than trusting in your future willpower.

And, avoid empty commitments. Just making a resolution isn't enough, and small steps toward a large goal can backfire. Make small commitments that are readily managed, and make them credible. You're better off if there are specific outcomes that depend on meeting your goals.

We can also use precommitment to improve our lives by giving into temptation, as strange as that may seem. Throughout this course, I've emphasized the idea of making good decisions, and I've discussed many examples where people fail to save for their future, or where they focus too much on an immediate reward. But, sometimes we need to live a little; some indulgence adds spice to life.

Suppose that I offer you a choice between $200 in cash and a gift certificate for $200 to a fancy restaurant in your town. What would you choose? When asked that sort of question, about a quarter of people prefer the gift certificate. That seems like a mistake because cash is more flexible. You could take your $200 and exchange it for that same gift certificate or for anything else you could imagine.

And, even more people choose the gift certificate or some similar luxury item when it is delayed farther in the future or when there's uncertainty, like when they register for a prize in a raffle drawing. This doesn't make sense. Why would people voluntarily give up the flexibility of cash for a very specific sort of luxury good? We can find the answer just by asking them. Of the people who choose the luxury good, nearly everyone reports that they wanted to force themselves to indulge. They purposely limited their future choices so that they will have the night out at the fancy restaurant, rather than devote the money to something more prosaic.

We know we'll enjoy a rare luxury. So, we give up flexibility in decision making, binding ourselves to a single course of action. And, we'll have a memorable experience, something with value far beyond what we're giving up. Think of precommitment as a tool to help plan and balance our lives, both to avoid unwanted temptations and to seek out desirable experiences.

In the next lecture, we'll explore the other key technique for making better decisions, and that's reframing the decision problem.

# Framing—Moving to a Different Perspective
## Lecture 23

In this lecture, you will learn about a second key tool, the first being precommitment, that changes the way you approach a decision: framing. This lecture will begin with some examples of framing to give you a sense of just how powerful it can be. Then, it will explore three types of frame—value frames, temporal frames, and goal frames—before ending with overall recommendations about how we can use framing to make better decisions.

**Framing**

- A framing effect arises when people make different choices based on how a decision problem is presented or interpreted. In framing, the core features of the decision problem don't change; people still have the same options and the same potential outcomes. But something changes in how people think about that decision problem, leading to different choices.

- There are multiple ways in which decisions can be framed. In economic decision making, frames can alter how we balance different factors, such as probability versus reward magnitude. In consumer choice, framing shapes what's important to us in our decisions—whether we prioritize the safety features or the engine performance of a new car. In addition, when we plan for the future, framing influences what goals we pursue—whether we seek to obtain a good outcome or avoid a bad outcome.

- In essence, a framing effect is a change in people's decisions when the same objective information is presented in two different ways. You might think that framing effects arise because of some idiosyncratic factors. Perhaps people aren't consistent in their choices when decisions involve hypothetical outcomes or small monetary stakes. Or perhaps people just aren't very sophisticated in how they use probability and magnitude information in their decisions. But framing effects aren't so easily dismissed.

**Value Frames**

- Framing effects can change what's important to us, whether outcomes seem good or bad. For example, if you look through the photographs of Olympic medal ceremonies, you'll see a consistent pattern. Again and again, the gold medalists seem very happy, the silver medalists seem neutral to unhappy, and the bronze medalists are beaming. It makes sense that the gold medalists are happy—they got the best outcome—but why are the bronze medalists happier than the silver medalists?

- Answering this question was the topic of a remarkable study by the psychologist Victoria Medvec and her colleagues. One possible explanation for this effect comes from the idea of reference dependence.

- This group of researchers examined the transcripts of interviews with the different medalists. The silver medalists were more likely to compare themselves to the gold medalist; they described how they almost won, how they could have been a gold medalist. The bronze medalists were more likely to compare themselves to those competitors who didn't win anything; they recognized that they could have done much worse, and they were happy to have at least won some medal.

- Silver and bronze medalists have different reference points. The silver medalists use the reference point of a gold medal, and they are disappointed—they regret not having done more. The bronze medalists use the reference point of no medal at all, and they are elated—they're satisfied with their performance.

- This is the typical effect, but there are exceptions. In general, the principle holds nevertheless: The same objective outcome can lead to disappointment or joy, depending on how it's framed.

- The way we frame something can even change our experiences, directly. Imagine that you are in the grocery store and see a package of ground beef that's labeled "90 percent lean." Immediately adjacent is a second package of ground beef from a different producer that is labeled "10 percent fat."

- The difference in labeling shouldn't affect consumers' attitudes or purchasing decisions. Those two labels just provide different frames through which the same information is presented. And this isn't an abstract or unfamiliar decision; it's a product for which shoppers have substantial experience and well-formed attitudes already.

- However, framing does affect consumer attitudes. Products described in the positive frame—like "90 percent lean"—are seen as higher quality and more desirable. In this case, emphasizing the leanness of the ground beef leads consumers to think that it will be less greasy, an important factor in their purchasing decisions.

- Does changing the descriptive frame alter how the product tastes? Yes. Participants in one experiment were first shown a label indicating either the leanness or the fat content of ground beef, and then they were given a small freshly cooked sample. Everyone sampled the same ground beef, so any differences in taste could only be attributed to what the label said.

**Framing meat as lean or fat changes the way people perceive the meat.**

- After they tasted the meat, people who had read labels indicating leanness rated the meat as leaner, of higher quality, and as less greasy—compared to people who had read about the fat content of the meat.

- Framing the same product in a different way actually changes how we experience that product. Specifically, it focuses our evaluation on particular attributes of the product, leading those attributes to dominate our judgments.

- As consumers, we should be attentive to such framing effects. We can mentally change the frame and change the desirability of a to-be-purchased product or our experiences after purchasing.

**Temporal Frames**
- Temporal framing is how the influence of time on our choices can change, depending on how a decision is framed. One such effect involves changing from a delay frame to an acceleration frame.

- Suppose that you have an investment—for example, a savings bond—that has now matured. If you withdraw it now, you'll receive 10,000 dollars, but if you allow it to remain invested for two more years, you'll receive 11,000 dollars.

- In decisions like this, people tend to be relatively impatient; they'd rather have less money now, instead of waiting for more money later. The decision scientist Elke Weber and her colleagues have argued that this impatience arises because people can easily bring to mind how they could use that money today.

- It's much harder to envision what you'll use money for in the future. You know that you'll need money for bills and expenses and trips, but those are all abstract needs, and they don't come to mind without prompting. So, money seems to be worth much less in the future than it is in the present.

- You can minimize this effect by changing the frame. Instead of thinking about your decision as a delay, think about it in terms of acceleration. You have an investment that will return 11,000 dollars in two years. You have the option of sacrificing 1,000 dollars of your investment to cash it in now. What do you do?

- This acceleration frame changes how people think. People report thinking more concrete thoughts about their future and about how they'll use the money. In turn, they become much more patient. They now know that they'll need the money in the future, and they don't want to take the sure loss of 1,000 dollars.

- Decision frames that call attention to our past also influence our decisions, even when they shouldn't. To be consistent over time, we should only make decisions based on the future benefits compared to the future costs. Past benefits and costs are just that—in the past. But they still influence our decisions.

**Goal Frames**

- Framing affects people's commitment to long-term goals. Goal framing differs from value framing and temporal framing in that it involves whether you continually take actions toward a goal, not whether you make a single decision.

- Suppose that you are an educator trying to encourage parents to teach their children good savings habits. The benefits of this program are straightforward: It helps their mathematical skills, helps them plan for the future, and teaches them basic economics—among many good features. So, how should those benefits be conveyed so that parents engage in the desired behavior?

- A positive frame could have the following hypothetical advice: Children whose parents teach them good savings habits by age eight are more likely to save enough money for retirement in adulthood. Alternatively, the same information could be presented in a negative frame: Children whose parents do not teach them good savings habits by age eight are less likely to save enough money for retirement in adulthood.

- Both frames have the same advice and are intended to encourage the same behavior—teaching children financial skills. But as a general guideline, negative frames are more effective. The negative outcome carries more weight than the positive outcome, especially if people see a credible link between their action and that negative outcome.

- Negative frames are more effective when specific actions lead to concrete outcomes, but they can be less effective when the link between actions and goals is much weaker. Without tangible links between one's own choices and the goal, a negative frame can encourage disengagement rather than action.

**Making Good Decisions**
- Of everything discussed in this course, the simple framing effect provides the most powerful tool for making good decisions. You can readily change how you approach your own decisions by just changing the frame. Nothing about the external environment or the decision itself needs to change; you just need to approach the same decision in a different way.

- But because framing effects are so powerful, and ubiquitous, they can influence our behavior even when we're not aware. Consumer marketing is rife with framing effects. Like in the example of the 90-percent-lean ground beef, our very experience with a product can be shaped by the way information is presented on a product label.

- There are some ways that we can inoculate ourselves against unwanted framing. The best approach is to obtain independent information, evaluating our options before we know how they are labeled. People aren't as influenced by frames when they've already experienced the substance of the decision.

- There's one approach to framing that almost always helps—or, at least, almost always gives you new insight into your decisions: taking another's perspective. When you face a challenging decision, step away from it for a moment. Imagine that a good friend was faced with a similar decision. What factors would you want your friend to consider? What's most important and what can be ignored?

What would you think of your friend if he or she made one choice or the other?

- When we think about decisions from another's perspective, we engage new cognitive processes, and we minimize the influence of our immediate emotional state. Thinking about a friend's decision won't always give you to the right choice, but it can be a good guide as to what's really important.

- Finally, changing your frame can just help you feel better about your decisions, your successes, and your failures.

## Suggested Reading

Loewenstein, "Frames of Mind in Intertemporal Choice."

Tversky and Kahneman, "The Framing of Decisions and the Psychology of Choice."

## Questions to Consider

1. What is mental accounting, and how might it contribute to the sunk-cost fallacy?

2. How might framing instructions differently change the decisions people make about retirement?

# Framing—Moving to a Different Perspective
## Lecture 23—Transcript

Welcome back. In the last lecture, we considered the first key tool for making better decisions: precommitment. That often involves making a binding choice now so that your future self won't make a bad decision. But sometimes the problem doesn't lie with your future self. So, you'll have to use another tool that changes the way you approach a decision. In today's lecture, I'll introduce that second key tool. It's called framing.

A framing effect arises when people make different choices based on how a decision problem is presented or interpreted. In framing, the core features of the decision problem don't change: People still have the same options and the same potential outcomes. But something changes in how people think about that decision problem, leading to different choices.

If an analogy helps, think about framing literally. Suppose that you are a museum curator hanging a valuable painting on the wall. People will come to see that painting, not the frame around it. If you asked them whether the frame matters, they'd probably say no, they haven't even noticed it.

But, the frame does matter. Different frames can emphasize different features of a painting, making it seem larger or smaller, more contemporary or more conservative. So, your task as a curator is to match the frame to the experience you desire for your visitors. You can't change the painting, but you can change its frame.

There are multiple ways in which decisions can be framed. In economic decision making, frames can alter how we balance different factors, like probability versus reward magnitude. In consumer choice, framing shapes what's important to us in our decisions—whether we prioritize the safety features or the engine performance of a new car. And, when we plan for the future, framing influences what goals we pursue—whether we seek to obtain a good outcome or avoid a bad outcome.

Because of the diversity of ways that framing influences our decisions, throughout this lecture I'll synthesize recommendations from throughout the course. I'll begin by providing some examples of framing to give you a sense of just how powerful it can be. I'll then explore three types of frames (value frames, temporal frames, and goal frames) before ending with overall recommendations about how we can use framing to make better decisions.

Let's start with a classic example of framing, which involves a single decision between a safe option and a risky option. Suppose that you are the leader of a disease response team preparing for this year's influenza outbreak. You expect something like 3,000 people to be infected with a potentially fatal form of influenza, and your team is preparing potential vaccines. The scientists on your team come to you with two candidate vaccines.

The first vaccine will work on any strain of influenza, but only partially. Your scientists are very confident that if you choose this vaccine, about 1,000 of those 3,000 people will survive. The second vaccine will work extremely well against one strain of influenza, but not as well against another more-common strain. Your scientists indicate that there would be a one in three chance that all 3,000 people will survive, but a two in three chance that none of those infected would survive.

I've presented this problem in what is called the survival or gain frame: All of the outcomes were described in positive terms, the number of survivors. When people hear the problem in the survival frame, they tend to pick the first, safer option, the one with a known number of survivors.

But, you can also present the problem in a more negative frame; you could emphasize the deaths from the disease. This is called the loss frame. Delivering the first vaccine will sentence 2,000 people to die, whereas the second vaccine has a one in three chance that no one will die.

These different frames don't change the raw facts of the decision. But they can have very large effects on behavior. In the original study by the behavioral economists Amos Tversky and Daniel Kahneman, in the gain frame about three-quarters of people chose the safe option. In the loss frame, however, three-quarters chose the risky option. That means that half of the people in the study flipped their choices between two mathematically equivalent decisions, based only on how the decision information was presented.

Similar biases can be shown when people make decisions about money. We can replace the numbers in the above example with dollar amounts, and replace surviving and dying with winning and losing money. And the same basic pattern holds. People are more risk-averse when trying to protect monetary gains than when trying to prevent monetary losses.

So, that's the basic idea of a framing effect. It's a change in people's decisions when the same objective information is presented in two different ways. Now, you might think that framing effects arise because of some idiosyncratic factors. Perhaps people aren't consistent in their choices when decisions involve hypothetical outcomes or small monetary stakes. Or perhaps people just aren't very sophisticated in how they use probability and magnitude information in their decisions. Let me convince you that framing effects aren't so easily dismissed.

Let's return to the idea of retirement planning, which I discussed in the previous lecture. Retirement decisions involve enormous stakes, both for individuals and for society. Within the United States, the Social Security program provides one of the most important sources of income during retirement: It is a defined monthly benefit that lasts until the end of life.

The amount of that benefit depends on what an individual paid in taxes during their working years, as based on their income and number of years working. But it also depends dramatically on the age of retirement. If the same person retires at the earliest possible date, usually 62 years of age, they are eligible for much less money per year than if they retire at the latest possible date, usually 70 years of age. How much less? The exact adjustment has been changed over the years. But for many individuals facing retirement, waiting could increase monthly payments by about 75 percent.

A group of economists studied how different ways of presenting that information could influence people's retirement decisions. So, they gave different surveys to a representative cross-section of Americans. Some surveys described the tradeoffs inherent in the Social Security program in much the same way that I just did, emphasizing that delaying benefits until age 70 increases your annual payments. This highlights the potential gains associated with a delay, like a gain frame in the previous example. After reading information presented in this gain frame, on average people report planning to retire at age 67.

Another survey took an opposite approach to explaining the same information. It calculated how long you'd need to live until you'd break even, that is, when would you earn more money overall by waiting. This emphasizes the potential losses associated with waiting; by delaying you forfeit money that you could have collected earlier. And, this loss frame pushes people toward earlier retirements. They now plan to retire around age 65 and a half.

Just changing the frame from gain to loss—from protecting your yearly income to forfeiting years of income—pushes people's planned retirement date more than a year earlier. That's a big deal. The effect of changing from a gain frame to a loss frame was greater than the effects associated with education levels and annual household income, even though those should affect one's decisions about the date of retirement, and framing effects should not. And these are potentially large stakes. Retiring too early can cost someone tens of thousands of dollars, while retiring too late can cost years of an enjoyable active lifestyle while one is still in good health.

Framing effects are hard to avoid, even among people who are sophisticated with numbers and have experience with decision biases. In a clever study, a group of researchers looked for framing effects among economics students registering for an academic conference, none of whom knew they were in an experiment. Like for many conferences, this conference had two registration fees: the fee for early registration before a deadline was $50 less than that for late registration after a deadline.

Half of the potential registrants received e-mail instructions that included the reminder "that the discounted conference fee for early registration is available until" July 10th. The other half received instructions with a reminder "that the conference fee will include a penalty for late registration after" July 10th. The actual charges for early and late registration were identical between the groups. This is a prototypic framing manipulation. A discount for early registration is exactly the same as a penalty for late registration. There's no objective difference in the discount and penalty frames.

But those frames still affect behavior. Of the students for whom early registration was described as a discount, 33 percent missed the deadline. But, when late registration was described as a penalty, only 7 percent missed the deadline. Changing the frame changes behavior, even among economists.

I want to move to the idea of value. Framing effects can change what's important to us, whether outcomes seem good or bad. I'll give you two examples from very different domains. In swimming, the 200-meter individual medley is one of the marquee events. It requires mastery of all four competition strokes, the endurance of a distance swimmer, and the finishing kick of a sprinter. In the 2008 Beijing Olympics, the three swimmers in the middle lanes were the Americans Michael Phelps and Ryan Lochte, and the Hungarian Lazlo Cseh. These three were the top of the field, and when the race ended, they all three earned Olympic medals: Phelps the gold, Cseh the silver, and Lochte the bronze. Phelps set a world record, and Cseh's time set a record for European swimmers.

In the official photograph of the medal stand, the gold-medalist Phelps stands at the center, beaming as he holds up his medal. Lochte stands to Phelps's left, holding his bronze medal with an even bigger smile on his face. And Cseh stands to Phelps's right, holding up his silver medal and looking despondent. Even though he just won a silver medal in one of swimming's premier events, even though he set a personal and European record, and even though he's the second-best swimmer in the whole world, his face is blank and he stares off into the distance, seeming closer to despair than joy.

This isn't an isolated case. If you look through the photographs of Olympic medal ceremonies, you'll see a consistent pattern. Again and again, the gold medalists seem very happy, the silver medalists seem neutral to unhappy, and the bronze medalists are beaming. It makes sense that the gold medalists are happy, they got the best outcome. But why are the bronze medalists happier than the silver medalists? Answering the question was the topic of a remarkable study by the psychologist Victoria Medvec and her colleagues.

They took videotapes of Olympic events and extracted footage of individual athletes right at the time the medalists learned the outcome of their events, that is, whether they finished first, second, and third. Then they had non-sports fans rate the emotions of each medalist. The ratings were consistent and clear: The bronze medalists were happier than the silver medalists. The researchers also studied video footage from the medal ceremonies, which typically are held a few minutes to a few hours after the conclusion of the event. Again, the bronze medalists were rated as happier.

One possible explanation for this effect comes from the idea of reference dependence, which I introduced in an early lecture. The same researchers examined the transcripts of interviews with the different medalists. The silver medalists were more likely to compare themselves to the gold medalist. They described how they almost won, how they could have been a gold medalist. The bronze medalists were more likely to compare themselves to those competitors who didn't win anything. They recognized that they could have done much worse, and they were happy to have at least won some medal.

Silver and bronze medalists have different reference points. The silver medalists use the reference point of a gold medal and they are disappointed; they regret not having done more. The bronze medalists use the reference point of no medal at all and they are elated; they're satisfied with their performance.

What I'm describing is the typical effect, but there are exceptions. Some silver medalists celebrate ecstatically, taking real joy when they do much better than they had expected. And, someone who expected gold but ended up with bronze could be disappointed despite their place among the worlds' best. But, the general principle holds nevertheless: The same objective outcome can lead to disappointment or joy depending on how it's framed.

The way we frame something can even change our experiences directly. Imagine that you are in the grocery store and you see a package of ground beef that's labeled 90-percent lean. Immediately adjacent is a second package of ground beef from a different producer. That second package is labeled 10-percent fat.

Now that difference in labeling (90-percent lean versus 10-percent fat) shouldn't affect consumers' attitudes or purchasing decisions. Those two labels just provide different frames through which the same information is presented. And, this isn't an abstract or unfamiliar decision; it's a product for which shoppers have substantial experience and well-formed attitudes already.

But, framing does affect consumer attitudes. Products described in the positive frame (like 90-percent lean) are seen as higher quality and more desirable. In this case, emphasizing the leanness of the ground beef leads consumers to think that it will be less greasy, which is an important factor in their purchasing decisions.

Let's take this a step further. Does changing the descriptive frame alter how the product tastes? Yes. Participants in one experiment were first shown a label indicating either the leanness or the fat content of ground beef, then they were given a small freshly cooked sample. Everyone sampled the same ground beef, so any differences in taste could only be attributed to what the label said. After they tasted the meat, people who had read labels indicating leanness rated the meat as leaner, of higher quality, and as less greasy, compared to people who had read about the fat content of the meat.

Framing the same product in a different way actually changes how we experience that product. Specifically, it focuses our evaluation on particular attributes of the product, leading those attributes to dominate our judgments. As consumers, we should be attentive to such framing effects. We can mentally change the frame and change the desirability of a to-be-purchased product or of our experiences after purchasing.

I'll next move to temporal framing: how the influence of time on our choices can change, depending on how a decision is framed. In the lecture on temporal discounting, I described one such effect: changing from a delay frame to an acceleration frame. I'll expand on that concept here.

Suppose that you have an investment, say a savings bond, that has now matured. If you withdraw it now, you'll receive $10,000. But, if you allow it to remain invested for two more years, you'll receive $11,000. I've chosen large values and long delays on purpose, so that this decision is a bit more realistic than the typical laboratory experiment.

In decisions like this, people tend to be relatively impatient; they'd rather have less money now, instead of waiting for more money later. The decision scientist Elke Weber and her colleagues have argued that this impatience arises because people can easily bring to mind how they could use that money, today. If I had an extra thousand dollars right now, I could pay bills, get a new computer, take that trip I've been putting off.

It's much harder to envision what you'll use money for in the future. You know that you'll need money for bills and expenses and trips, but those are all abstract needs, and they don't come to mind without prompting. So, money seems to be worth much less in the future than it is in the present.

So, how can you minimize this effect? Change the frame. Instead of thinking about your decision as a delay, think about it in terms of acceleration. You have an investment that will return $11,000 in two years. You have the option of sacrificing one thousand dollars of your investment to cash it in now. What do you do?

This acceleration frame changes how people think. People report thinking more concrete thoughts about their future and about how they'll use the money. In turn, they become much more patient. They now know that they'll need the money in the future, and they don't want to take the sure loss of $1,000.

Decision frames that call attention to our past also influence our decisions, even when they shouldn't. Suppose that you've spent $100 on a ticket to a play. The day before the play, you receive an invitation to a friend's party, and you know that you'd enjoy the party more than the play. But, you call your friend and decline, saying that you're going to a show that evening and you've already bought your ticket.

Most people understand this scenario. The final decision seems perfectly reasonable—you go to the show because you've already bought your ticket, and you don't want to waste your money. This seems like the right decision.

But there's actually an inconsistency here, it's called the sunk cost fallacy. You can understand this fallacy by thinking about some alternative scenarios. Suppose that you were simultaneously offered tickets to the play and invited to go to the party. If you preferred to go to the party, you'd turn down the tickets and just go.

So, the fact that you paid for the ticket in the past influences your decision today. The price of the ticket is what economists call a sunk cost, it's money that has already been spent. Sunk costs are endemic to government spending —politicians love to refer to what has already been spent when justifying an expensive program. But that money is already gone and shouldn't affect analyses of the viability of the program going forward. To be consistent over time, we should only make decisions based on the future benefits compared to the future costs. Past benefits and costs are just that: in the past. But, they still influence our decisions.

The behavioral economist Richard Thaler explains the sunk cost fallacy in terms of what he calls mental accounting. When we engage in a transaction (like buying a ticket to a play) we open a mental account for that purchase, and we close that account when the transaction is completed. So, if we buy tickets for a play and then don't go, it seems like we've lost the money in that account, and we don't think about the other opportunities that we've missed.

The key idea of mental accounting is that we tend to think about individual decisions, and we want to make each of those decisions pay off on its own. So, we let the past influence our present, which may be against our own interests. But we can adopt a different frame for our decisions. Don't think about whether you made a good decision when buying tickets for the play, that's in the past. Think about whether you want to go to the play or to the party, those are in your future. Excluding past events from your decision frame can help you avoid the sunk cost fallacy, and make better decisions about your future.

Finally, I want to discuss how framing affects people's commitment to long-term goals. Goal framing differs from what I've talked about so far (value framing and temporal framing) in that it involves whether you continually take actions toward a goal, not whether you make a single decision. Suppose that you are an educator trying to encourage parents to teach their children good savings habits. The benefits of this program are straightforward. It helps their mathematical skills, planning for the future, and teaches them basic economics. So, how should those benefits be conveyed, so that parents engage in the desired behavior?

A positive frame could have the following hypothetical advice: Children whose parents teach them good savings habits by age eight are more likely to save enough money for retirement in adulthood. Or, the same information could be presented in a negative frame: children whose parents do not teach them good savings habits by age eight are less likely to save enough money for retirement in adulthood. Both frames have the same advice and are intended to encourage the same behavior: teaching children financial skills. So the question is not what behavior the frame encourages, but how well it encourages that behavior.

As a general guideline, negative frames are more effective. The negative outcome carries more weight than positive outcome, especially if people see a credible link between their action and that negative outcome. The stronger effect of a negative frame is similar to the phenomenon of loss aversion I described in an early lecture.

But, I want to offer an important caveat. Negative frames are more effective when specific actions lead to concrete outcomes, but they can be less effective when the link between actions and goals is much weaker. If you are trying to encourage pro-environmental actions like minimizing one's carbon footprint, for example, negative frames may be ineffective. When you sacrifice your money or energy to help the environment, your own actions have negligible effects compared to the larger societal trends, and even those larger societal trends won't lead to negative personal consequences until some distant future date. So, without tangible links between one's own choices and the goal, a negative frame can encourage disengagement rather than action.

Of everything discussed in this course, the simple framing effect provides the most powerful tool for making good decisions. You can readily change how you approach your own decisions by just changing the frame. Nothing about the external environment nor the decision itself needs to change. You just need to approach the same decision in a different way.

But because framing effects are so powerful and so ubiquitous they can influence our behavior even when we're not aware. Consumer marketing is rife with framing effects. Like in the example of the 90-percent lean ground beef, our very experience with a product can be shaped by the way information is presented on a product label.

But, there are some ways that we can inoculate ourselves against unwanted framing. The best approach is to obtain independent information, evaluating our options before we know how they are labeled. In that study of framing and the taste of ground beef, there was one other condition that I've not yet told you about. Some participants tasted the ground beef first, then read about whether it was 90-percent lean or 10-percent fat. That initial experience greatly attenuated the framing effect: People aren't as influenced by frames when they've already experienced the, well, meat of the decision.

Throughout this lecture, I've described a number of different frames you can use in your own decisions: thinking about gains instead of losses, considering penalties instead of discounts, envisioning the future rather than the present, or the present instead of the past. All of these work, in specific circumstances. But there's one approach to framing that almost always helps, or at least almost always gives you new insight into your decisions. That's taking another's perspective. When you face a challenging decision step away from it for a moment. Imagine that a good friend was faced with a similar decision. What factors would you want your friend to consider? What's most important and what can be ignored? And, what would you think of your friend if they made one choice or the other?

When we think about decisions from another's perspective, we engage new cognitive processes and we minimize the influence of our immediate emotional state. Again, thinking about a friend's decision won't always give you to the right choice, but it can be a good guide as to what's really important.

Finally, changing your frame can just help you feel better about your decisions, your successes, and your failures. At the 2010 Vancouver Winter Games, the Canadian skier Jennifer Heil was visibly disappointed when she finished in second place. She had felt the pressure of her nation to be the first Canadian to win a gold medal on home soil. When interviewed after the race, her thoughts dwelled on her mistakes and the lost opportunity. A day later, she had changed her reference point. She now smiled and celebrated; she was no longer ashamed of losing gold, but justifiably proud of having won the silver medal. The next year, at the world championships, she won gold.

In the next and final lecture, I'll synthesize concepts from throughout the course. We'll explore how people and institutions use precommitment, framing, and all of the other tools of behavioral economics to shape decisions, and we'll consider the many practical and ethical issues this raises.

# Interventions, Nudges, and Decisions
## Lecture 24

Throughout this course, you have learned how people *should* make decisions and how they really *do* make decisions. The focus has been on you and your decisions. But in this lecture, you are going to take a different perspective, a larger perspective. You will think of yourself as someone interested in shaping other people's decisions. In this lecture, you will learn how you can use what you've learned about behavioral economics, psychology, and even neuroscience to influence what other people choose—perhaps for your own benefit, and perhaps for theirs.

## Information

- There are many different options available for shaping others' decisions, and there is no single approach that always pushes people toward good decisions. Sometimes institutional interventions like legislation or incentives will be necessary. Sometimes, although not often, information helps. And other times, the tools of behavioral economics like precommitment and framing can shape choices. The challenge for any policymaker, or parent, is knowing which tool works in which circumstances.

- In the realm of decision making, information is facts describing the outcomes that follow particular decisions. Giving people information about the outcomes of their potential decisions, especially in isolation, rarely helps them make better decisions. People mistrust information. They try to figure out what you're not telling them, and they mentally argue against the information provided.

- You also can't inoculate people against making bad decisions by telling them about their biases and the mistakes they'll make. Often, our biases affect us before we're even thinking of making a decision. We are more likely to seek out information consistent with our point of view—that's the confirmation bias.

- We don't necessarily even know when we're biased. For every effect described in this course, there are alternative explanations. We know that framing effects or ambiguity aversion exist—but not because we measure one person's behavior and see that they are influenced by a decision frame or ambiguity. We know that biases exist only when we look at groups of people; we can infer that the group shows framing effects, for example, even if we can't be sure about any one person.

- In addition, too often, our mistakes reflect failures of our will, not our knowledge. The problem of dieters isn't simply that they don't know what foods to avoid.

**Nudges**
- If incentives are too expensive and information is too ineffective, what's left? In recent years, behavioral economists and policy makers have begun working together to create policies that help people make better decisions.

- These policies aren't intended to limit choices—like legislation might—and they don't involve the introduction of new incentives. They introduce very small changes to the process of decision making, but those small changes can have large effects on decisions.

- The decision scientists Richard Thaler and Cass Sunstein use the term "nudge" to describe such policies: They're intended to give people a gentle push so that they start moving themselves in the right direction. If you want to nudge people, you should follow four basic steps.

    1. Identify some social issue that can be linked to poor decision making.

    2. Find a manipulation that changes what people can choose, the way outcomes are described, or the manner in which people make their decisions.

3. Introduce the manipulation, usually without telling people about it.

4. Track people's behavior and adapt your manipulation to reach the desired effect.

- Some nudges aren't really that controversial. When grocery stores place high-margin items at the end of aisles, that increases purchases of those items, but consumers don't stop shopping in protest.

**Architecture**
- People don't mind being nudged when the decision involves relatively low stakes and when their autonomy as independent decision makers isn't called into question. But nudges can be controversial and lead to resistance when the stakes are large and when people believe that they are giving up some freedom of choice.

- Suppose that you're now a human resources executive at a large multinational corporation. You have many thousands of employees, all of whom save for retirement through a defined-contributions plan like a 401(k). You want your employees to be well prepared for retirement, so your goals are completely aligned with those of your employees: They want their 401(k)s to grow, and you want their 401(k)s to grow.

- Your company implemented an opt-out 401(k) program a few years ago, and the program has had great effects on enrollment. Every new employee is automatically enrolled at a default three-percent contribution level, and very few of your employees ever drop out of that program.

- But things aren't perfect. Right now, your company allows employees to invest their 401(k) accounts in any of a half-dozen mutual fund companies, each with a dozen or more funds. And because of this diversity, many of your employees have suboptimal investment portfolios; they have large amounts of money in actively managed funds instead of index funds, or they have the wrong balance of stock and bond funds for their age.

- You know that your employees would be much better off, overall, if you simplified their options. Instead of allowing investments in any of a large set of diverse funds, which leads to inefficient portfolios, you could choose a single provider of target-retirement-date index funds. These are low-fee, balanced funds that change their allocation from more risky investments to more safe investments as a target retirement date nears.

- For the vast majority of Americans, investing one's retirement in a single such fund would be demonstrably better than how they currently invest. Most people, in the real world and in this hypothetical example, would become better off by simplifying their retirement savings and prioritizing target-retirement-date index funds. So, how can you nudge employees to change their approach to retirement investments to something that's almost certainly better for them?

### Paternalism

- By trying to shape their employees' retirement savings, the employer is in effect taking the sort of action that a parent would take with a child, helping them make a decision that's for their own good. As such, nudges have often been criticized as being paternalistic; they take away autonomy in a misguided attempt to make people better off.

- Let's consider the different nudges you might use—to

**Having enough money to support oneself into retirement is a major concern among many people.**

get a sense of whether the charge of paternalism is justified. You could transfer all existing employees' balances to an index fund connected to their own retirement date, and then require them to keep investing in those funds. This step is draconian, but it would indeed improve most employees' prospects for retirement and wouldn't hurt anyone that much. However, it raises the deepest ethical dilemma in philosophy: whether it's acceptable to help the greater number while also infringing on the rights of the few.

- This is the sort of paternalism that most people find unacceptable, but it's also not really a nudge. It cuts off choice options and, for exactly that reason, people won't support it. You need to find a nudge that improves outcomes for most people but doesn't seem to infringe on individual autonomy. You want a nudge that doesn't make choices for people but helps them make better choices.

- Based on your knowledge of endowment effects and precommitment, you know that people are often loath to change from some default option. So, you modify your opt-out program so that not only are all new employees automatically enrolled in the program, but they are also automatically enrolled in a target-retirement-date index fund appropriate for their age. After one month, they can change their fund distribution, or they can opt out of the program entirely.

- This sort of nudge is still paternalistic, but it doesn't preclude anyone from choosing a different investment strategy—it just starts people in a good default option. In addition, you know that many, many people will just stick with that option. The behavioral economist George Loewenstein and colleagues call this approach asymmetric paternalism: It helps people who would otherwise make bad decisions, but it doesn't impede the autonomy of people who want to actively pursue a different path.

- Selecting a good default option seems like a reasonable nudge because it helps people make better decisions, as judged against some external standard. But you could even go one step further.

You could try to nudge people so that they make better decisions, as judged against their own standards. Thaler and Sunstein describe such nudges as libertarian paternalism.

- So, as part of the mandatory employee orientation, you could have participants not only fill out the usual workplace safety forms, but you could also have them provide a sense of their retirement goals—to provide a measure of how their goals differ from those of others in the company. Then, you could structure their default plan to their specific goals.

- The same rules would apply as before; they can still opt out or change their investments at any time. But you've provided a starting point that's informed by their own stated preferences. Many people find this last option to provide the most acceptable balance between improving people's well-being and maintaining their autonomy.

- Not all nudges are this clean. In cases where there's conflict among people's preferences, like matching children to schools, there may be no way to structure a nudge or any other intervention without making some people worse off.

## Autonomy and Neuromarketing

- Understanding how we make decisions can give you powerful tools—tools that can change the way you make decisions or the way others make decisions. So, there's naturally going to be suspicion that the scientific study of decision making will lead to manipulations that aren't quite as benign as the nudges just described. This suspicion is particularly strong for the neuroscientific study of decision making.

- In recent years, there's been an explosion of interest in what's often called neuromarketing, the use of measurements of brain function and related body states in order to improve consumer advertising, branding, pricing, and product design.

- Proponents of neuromarketing—many of whom run companies selling neuromarketing services—argue that neuroscience can provide hidden knowledge about what influences people's purchasing decisions and that companies can use that knowledge to optimize their marketing.

- Neuromarketing has a real future, as a complement to traditional approaches. When behavioral economic methods are combined with neuroscience, researchers can gain access to processes of decision making that are often difficult or impossible to study otherwise. Knowing how people respond to advertisements without having to ask for their opinions would be extraordinarily valuable information for marketers and decision scientists alike.

- However, at present, neuromarketing engenders suspicion. Many consumers worry that the neuromarketers will indeed gain hidden knowledge and that those marketers will develop proprietary procedures for pushing some "buy button" in the brain, leading people to purchase things they don't want or need. Frankly, that's not a practical concern now or even in the distant future, but it still casts a shadow over this sort of research.

- There's an ethical issue here that keeps recurring in many guises: The scientific study of decision making allows us to be manipulated. Researchers and institutions will know more about our decisions than we will. We'll lose our autonomy. But knowledge can give us autonomy.

## Suggested Reading

Larrick and Soll, "Economics: The MPG Illusion."

Thaler and Sunstein, *Nudge*.

## Questions to Consider

1. Why aren't interventions that deliver information—such as those about the dangerous effects of drugs on the body—effective at changing people's behavior?

2. What are nudges? What sorts of nudges are justifiable, and what sorts are infringements on individual autonomy?

# Interventions, Nudges, and, Decisions
## Lecture 24—Transcript

We've covered quite a lot of ground in this course. We've discussed how people should make decisions, and how they really do make decisions. We've considered probability, time, things we want to gain, and things we don't want to lose. We've explored the limits of our rationality, and how we adopt strategies to deal with those limits. We've seen how we give to others when we don't need to, how we cooperate with others even when we don't know them, and how we punish others who fail to cooperate with us. We've examined when incentives work and when they backfire.

Throughout the entire course, I've emphasized steps you can take to make better decisions. I've tried to give you tools for decision making and the knowledge to use the right tool for the right decision. And, I've emphasized two of the most important tools: precommitment and framing. These key tools reliably change people's decisions, and they can be wielded in almost any situation.

To help you understand how decision making works, I've often asked you to envision some scenario (suppose that you are shopping for a new car or planning your retirement), and I've tried to walk you through circumstances in which you might make an unexpected decision. The focus has been on you and your decisions. But in today's lecture, I'm going to ask you to take a different perspective, a larger perspective. I'll want you to think of yourself as someone interested in shaping other people's decisions.

Perhaps you've been the leader of a charitable foundation or of a government agency. Or perhaps you've been a marketing executive or a small business owner. Perhaps you've been a parent trying to motivate two teenagers. In all of these cases and many others you've wanted to understand the decisions that other people made. And now as you finish this course, you want to know how you can use what you've learned about behavioral economics, about psychology, and even about neuroscience to influence what other people choose, perhaps for your own benefit, and perhaps for theirs.

I want to introduce the different options available for shaping others' decisions with a concrete example from a domain familiar to all of us. Suppose, for the moment, that you're the U.S. government policymaker tasked with decreasing gasoline consumption by automobiles. In a general sense, almost everyone agrees with this goal. We all want individually to spend less on gasoline, and we'd like for the collective use of gasoline to decrease for both economic and environmental reasons.

In principle, we'd be better off collectively if more Americans purchased more fuel-efficient cars. But to date, purely market-based solutions haven't worked. People have prioritized other features when purchasing cars, often even to the point of preferring features like car size and power that trade off inversely with fuel efficiency. So what are your options as a policymaker for shaping people's decisions?

One is legislation; you can mandate that manufacturers produce high-mileage automobiles. That happened in 2012, when legislation created new standards for the average fuel economy of a manufacturer's fleet of new cars. These standards were proposed to rise to more than 50 miles per gallon by the mid-2020s. In practice, legislation works, but it carries financial and political costs, and it also interferes with free markets.

Your second option involves incentives. You can give people an incentive to purchase more fuel-efficient cars through tax credits or similar. That would stimulate consumer demand for those cars, which would in turn change what's being produced. Incentives are expensive, though. When they were introduced to encourage the purchase of gasoline-electric hybrid vehicles, they cost the government billions of dollars in lost tax revenue.

A third option is information. You can give people information about the benefits of fuel-efficient cars, things like the money they'll save on gas, the advantages of those cars for the environment, and so forth. You can create fancy brochures and public service announcements. And, it won't help. Most of that information is already out there. Those same benefits are being promoted by manufacturers and car dealers, who have incentives to sell new cars. And, people tend to react negatively to unwanted information, if it seems like it comes from a biased source. They'll generate counterfactual thoughts like "hybrids may save money on gas, but they're less reliable," and the information can backfire.

A fourth option is precommitment. Precommitment works great when it can be enforced or when there are strong default behaviors, like when a company automatically enrolls employees into a retirement savings plan. But you can't use costly precommitment in this case—you can't ask people to precommit to purchasing a car. But you can use cheap precommitment. Marketing research indicates that just asking people about their intentions to purchase a fuel-efficient car makes those later purchases more likely. So, precommitment can help, but it doesn't scale up to the entire population. You can't influence every automobile purchasing decision by asking every American about their intention to purchase hybrids.

So, that leaves a fifth and final option: framing. You need to find some way to frame the automobile purchasing decision so that people use fuel efficiency information in the best way. For your purposes, you don't necessarily need everyone to purchase the same, optimally efficient car. You'd be happy if the overall efficiency across all cars improved.

It turns out that there's actually a straightforward way to do this. You can change the frame in which fuel efficiency information is presented, in a way that helps people make better future decisions. It's actually really easy—you just switch from miles per gallon to gallons per mile.

We traditionally have used miles per gallon, which is a measure of engine efficiency. Now miles per gallon does tell us something, but it can also mislead us in unexpected ways. Take a first pair of cars, one gets 50 miles per gallon and the other gets 100 miles per gallon. Is that a small difference in fuel usage or a big difference? It seems big, right? But consider a second pair of cars, one gets 14 miles per gallon and the other gets 20 miles per gallon. This seems like a meaningful difference in fuel usage, although it also seems to pale in comparison to the 50 mile per gallon difference in the first example.

Here's the surprising thing. The difference between 14 and 20 miles per gallon is twice as large as the difference between 50 and 100 miles per gallon. You heard me right; 14 to 20 is really big, but 50 to 100 is really small. Let me explain why. Suppose that you're planning to drive 100 miles. If you switch from a 50-miles-per-gallon car to a 100-miles-per-gallon car, you'll save 1 gallon. But switching from 14 miles per gallon to 20 miles per gallon saves you twice as much: 2 gallons.

The decision scientists Rick Larrick and Jack Soll showed that when people think about fuel efficiency or miles per gallon they get the tradeoffs exactly wrong. They overestimate the benefits of improving efficiency at the high end, and they underestimate the benefits at the low end. But, we can change the frame to emphasize not fuel efficiency but fuel consumption. When people see the same information expressed using a fuel consumption measure like gallons per hundred miles then they get the tradeoffs right, and they make decisions that better minimize overall fuel consumption.

I walked through this example in detail to underscore a take-home message. There's no single approach that always pushes people toward good decisions. Sometimes institutional interventions like legislation or incentives will be necessary. Sometimes, although not often, information helps. And other times, the tools of behavioral economics like precommitment and framing can shape choices. The challenge for any policymaker, like for any parent, is knowing which tool works in which circumstances.

Let's begin by talking about information, because that's the easiest to think about. By information, I mean facts describing the outcomes that follow particular decisions. If you want to discourage teenagers from using drugs like cocaine, you could tell them that chronic cocaine use impairs long-term memory, increases the risk of heart attack and stroke, and impairs daily decision making. You could tell them that cocaine users have financial difficulties and fewer close friends. And, those teenagers would simply ignore you.

Giving people information about the outcomes of their potential decisions, especially in isolation, rarely helps them make better decisions. People mistrust information. They try to figure out what you're not telling them, and they mentally argue against the information provided. Nor can we inoculate people against making bad decisions by telling them about their biases and the mistakes they'll make. Often our biases affect us before we're even thinking of making a decision. We are more likely to seek out information consistent with our point of view—that's the confirmation bias.

We don't necessarily even know when we're biased. For every single effect that I've described in this course, there are alternative explanations. We know that framing effects or ambiguity aversion exist but not because we measure one person's behavior and see that they are influenced by a decision frame or ambiguity. That person might be rejecting ambiguous gambles just because they are a very cautious decision maker, or because they really want to leave the experiment with enough money for lunch. We know that biases exist only when we look at groups of people. We can infer that the group shows framing effects, for example, even if we can't be sure about any one person. And, too often, our mistakes reflect failures of our will not our knowledge. Ask any dieter; their problem isn't simply that they don't know what foods to avoid.

So, if incentives are too expensive and information is too ineffective, what's left? In recent years, behavioral economists and policymakers have begun working together to create policies that help people make better decisions. These policies aren't intended to limit choices like legislation might, and they don't involve the introduction of new incentives. They introduce very small changes to the process of decision making, but those small changes can have large effects on decisions.

I'll borrow a word from the decision scientists Richard Thaler and Cass Sunstein and describe such policies as nudges. They're intended to give people a gentle push, so they start moving themselves in the right direction. If you want to nudge people, you should follow four basic steps.

First, you need to identify some social issue that can be linked to poor decision making. Second, find a manipulation that changes what people can choose, the way outcomes are described, or the manner in which people make their decisions. Again, I'll only consider some policy a nudge if it doesn't involve the introduction of meaningful incentives. Third, introduce the manipulation, usually without telling people about it. Giving people information often leads them to question that information, and we all react with mistrust when someone says, "This is for your own good." And, fourth, track people's behavior and adapt your manipulation to reach the desired effect.

Some nudges aren't really that controversial. Posting gallons per mile next to miles per gallon won't elicit revolts among either car shoppers or manufacturers. When grocery stores place high-margin items at the end of aisles, that increases purchases of those items, but consumers don't stop shopping in protest. People don't mind being nudged when the decision involves relatively low stakes and when their autonomy as independent decision makers isn't called into question.

But nudges can be controversial and lead to resistance when the stakes are large and when people believe that they are giving up some freedom of choice. Suppose that you're now a human resources executive at a large multinational corporation. You have many thousands of employees, all of whom save for retirement through a defined-contributions plan like a 401(k). You want your employees to be well prepared for retirement (your company takes pride in having a generous benefits package), and you know that employees are more productive when they are confident in their financial future. So, your goals are completely aligned with those of your employees: they want their 401(k)s to grow, and you want their 401(k)s to grow.

Your company implemented an opt-out 401(k) program a few years ago, in large part because of studies like those I introduced in the lecture on precommitment. And, your opt-out program has had great effects on enrollment. Every new employee is automatically enrolled at a default three-percent contribution level, and very few of your employees ever drop out of that program.

But things aren't perfect. Right now, your company allows employees to invest their 401(k) accounts in any of a half-dozen mutual fund companies, each with a dozen or more funds. And, because of this diversity, many of your employees have suboptimal investment portfolios. They have large amounts of money in actively managed funds instead of index funds, or they have the wrong balance of stock and bond funds for their age.

You know that your employees would be much better off, overall, if you simplified their options. Instead of allowing investments in any of a large set of diverse funds, which leads to inefficient portfolios, you could choose a single provider of target-retirement-date index funds. These are low-fee, balanced funds that change their allocation from more risky investments to more safe investments as a target retirement date nears.

I want to emphasize something: For the vast majority of Americans, investing one's retirement in a single such fund would be demonstrably better than how they currently invest. Most people in the real world and in this hypothetical example would become better off by simplifying their retirement savings and prioritizing target-retirement-date index funds.

So, how can you nudge employees to change their approach to retirement investments to something that's almost certainly better for them? I want to pause this example for just a moment and state this goal another way. By trying to shape their employees' retirement savings, the employer is saying in effect, "We care about you and your future. We know that this decision is very complex, and we don't think that you'll make a good decision on your own. And, so we want to make it easier for you by limiting your choices or by simplifying the process."

That's the sort of tone that a parent would take with a child, helping them make a decision that's for their own good. And, as such, nudges have often been criticized as being paternalistic. They take away autonomy in a misguided attempt to make people better off. So, let's go on with this example and consider the different nudges you might use to get a sense of whether the charge of paternalism is justified.

You could transfer all existing employees' balances to an index fund connected to their own retirement date, and then require them to keep investing in those funds. This step is draconian, but it would indeed improve most employees' prospects for retirement and wouldn't hurt anyone that much. But, it raises the deepest ethical dilemma in philosophy, whether it's acceptable to help the greater number while also infringing on the rights of the few. This is the sort of paternalism that most people find unacceptable, but it's also not really a nudge. It cuts off choice options, and for exactly that reason people won't support it. You need to find a nudge that improves outcomes for most people, but doesn't seem to infringe on individual autonomy. You want a nudge that doesn't make choices for people, but helps them make better choices.

Based on your knowledge of endowment effects and precommitment, you know that people are often loath to change from some default option. So, you modify your opt-out program so that not only are all new employees automatically enrolled in the program, but they are automatically enrolled in a target-retirement-date index fund appropriate for their age. After one month, they can change their fund distribution, or they can opt out of the program entirely.

This sort of nudge is still paternalistic, in a literal sense, but it doesn't preclude anyone from choosing a different investment strategy; it just starts people in a good default option. And, you know that many, many people will just stick with that option. I'll borrow a term introduced by the behavioral economist George Loewenstein and call this approach asymmetric paternalism. It helps people who would otherwise make bad decisions, but it doesn't impede the autonomy of people who want to actively pursue a different path.

Selecting a good default option seems like a reasonable nudge because it helps people make better decisions, as judged against some external standard. But you could even go one step further. You could try to nudge people so that they make better decisions, as judged against their own standards. Thaler and Sunstein describe such nudges as libertarian paternalism.

So, as part of the mandatory employee orientation, you could have participants not only fill out the usual workplace safety forms, you could also have them provide a sense of their retirement goals. That provides a measure of how their goals differ from those of others in the company—perhaps they seek to retire earlier, or they have a spouse who is much older or younger. And, then you could structure their default plan to their specific goals. The same rules would apply as before: they can still opt-out or change their investments at any time. But you've provided a starting point that's informed by their own stated preferences. Many people find this last option to provide the most acceptable balance between improving people's well-being and maintaining their autonomy.

Not all nudges are as clean as what I'm describing here. In cases where there's conflict among people's preferences, like matching children to schools, there may be no way to structure a nudge or any other intervention without making some people worse off. I'll return to this issue at the very end of this lecture.

Understanding how we make decisions can give you powerful tools, tools that can change the way you make decisions, or can change the way others make decisions. So, there's naturally going to be suspicion that the scientific study of decision making will lead to manipulations that aren't quite as benign as the nudges I've just described.

This suspicion is particularly strong for the neuroscientific study of decision making. Throughout this course, I've tried to introduce key findings from neuroscience where they help us understand decision-making behavior. I've emphasized that neuroscience doesn't replace the systematic study of behavior. Neuroscience complements research in economics and psychology. When it's done well, it provides insight into why we make certain decisions and how different decision biases are related.

But not all uses of neuroscience are so circumspect. In recent years, there's been an explosion of interest in what's often called neuromarketing, which is the use of measurements of brain function and related body states in order to improve consumer advertising, branding, pricing, and product design.

Proponents of neuromarketing, many of whom run companies selling neuromarketing services, argue that neuroscience can provide hidden knowledge about what influences people's purchasing decisions. They also argue that companies can use that knowledge to optimize their marketing. A typical approach might involve the following sort of experiment. A number of consumers come to corporate headquarters, but instead of participating in a focus group around a table, each is individually brought to a laboratory containing an electroencephalogram (or EEG). That's a device that can measure brain waves through electrodes placed on the head, allowing researchers to track how people perceive information and make decisions with millisecond-level precision. Then each person watches a series of commercials while their brain activity is recorded through the EEG, and afterward the neuromarketers try to decode the brain activity to identify which commercials evoked brain responses associated with purchasing intentions.

Now, you might readily wonder why bother with the trouble of hooking people up to an EEG machine and measuring their brain waves? You could instead just show them the commercial and then ask them about their purchasing intentions, afterward. Not exactly. Suppose that a commercial is 30 seconds long. That commercial might have 10 or more distinct scenes within it, each creating a somewhat different impression on the viewer. You can't ask people about each of those scenes at the end of the commercial because their memory won't be that precise. So, measuring consumers' intentions and attitudes while they watch the commercial might provide information that helps optimize its message. And, people don't always know or report their own intentions. They might be self-conscious about liking a product, or they want to seem sophisticated, or they may dislike the product in the focus group but remember it at the supermarket.

Neuromarketing has a real future, again, as a complement to traditional approaches. When behavioral economic methods are combined with neuroscience, researchers can gain access to processes of decision making that are often difficult or impossible to study otherwise. Knowing how people respond to advertisements without having to ask for their opinions would be extraordinarily valuable information for marketers and decision scientists alike.

But, at present, neuromarketing engenders suspicion. Many consumers worry that the neuromarketers will indeed gain hidden knowledge, and that those marketers will develop proprietary procedures for pushing some buy-button in the brain, leading people to purchase things they don't want or need. Frankly, that's not a practical concern now or even in the distant future, but it still casts a shadow over this sort of research. There's an ethical issue here that keeps recurring in many guises: the scientific study of decision making allows us to be manipulated. Researchers and institutions will know more about our decisions than we will. We'll lose our autonomy.

But knowledge can give us autonomy. Think of the deep themes of this course. We're not bad decision makers; we're good decision makers who have bounds on our rationality. We're constantly trying to find strategies that help us make good decisions right now. We simplify complex decisions to something manageable, isolating the most important features of a decision and discarding information that's less relevant. We use whatever we can to help make good decisions: our past history, the guidance of others, even our own emotions. And, as the most important themes of all. We have a number of tools that help us make good decisions, and our key challenge is matching the right tool to the right decision.

Knowledge about our own limitations doesn't make those limitations disappear. On the contrary, our knowledge highlights our limitations. It makes more aware of them, and it causes us to think of those limitations as tools that we can use, that we can wield to reach our goals.

Similarly, the rise of behavioral economics doesn't make traditional economics meaningless. Incentives still matter. Market forces matter. They often change behavior much faster than, say, any framing effect ever could. But, we can predict when incentives will fail and when they may even backfire. We can predict when market forces will fail because of correlated biases among participants or problems coordinating on a good outcome.

And when those failures happen, then knowledge about the decision making process provides a tool, a lever that can nudge behavior toward a better outcome. Behavioral economics isn't everything. But it's something. When applied to the right problem, it can make people's lives better.

As I end this course, I want you to reflect on how you've changed, how your new knowledge of decision making has altered how you approach decisions, or how you see the world around you. It's challenging to reflect on knowledge. Once you know something, you don't see the world in the same way as before. That knowledge colors how you interpret new information and face new decisions. This holds for us individually and for the policymakers and institutions who want to use behavioral economics. Once you know that opt-out plans increase retirement savings, then when you don't use an opt-out plan, you're still making a choice. Once you know that framing fuel usage as gallons per mile leads to better consumer decisions then when you use the traditional miles per gallon, you're still making a choice.

Our world isn't set up in a way that allows policymakers or institutions to structure decisions in a completely unbiased manner. Every way of presenting a decision introduces a different form of bias. Our world has structure that biases what we choose. And, every human carries all of the biases discussed in this course. But our biases give us a particular form of control. With a bit of knowledge, we can recognize how we'd naturally approach some decision, what tool we'd normally use, and we can put that tool away and pick up another one better suited for the task.

As individuals, we don't have much control over the world around us. We can't get rid of our limitations and biases. They're part of human nature. And, most importantly of all, we don't want to get rid of them. They give us power. We can approach the same problem from many different ways. We can simulate our future feelings through our emotions. We can envision how others would react. We can avoid calculating the cost–benefit tradeoffs within an impossibly large set of factors—and just walk into a new home, look around, and say, yes, this is the one.

All of those limitations and biases that you've encountered in this course aren't sources of concern. They're sources of pride. They make you into a very good decision maker, someone who's not perfect, but who can pare down a world of remarkable complexity and make a simple decision. And, that is an encouraging thought.

# Bibliography

Allon, G., A. Federgruen, and M. Pierson. "How Much Is a Reduction of Your Customers' Wait Worth? An Empirical Study of the Fast-Food Drive-Thru Industry Based on Structural Estimation Methods." *Manufacturing & Service Operations Management* 13 (2011): 489–507. This study demonstrates that fast-food patrons place a surprisingly high premium on their time, such that even very slight increases in waiting time can shift consumer behavior.

Beggs, A., and K. Graddy. "Anchoring Effects: Evidence from Art Auctions." *American Economic Review* 99 (2009): 1027–1039. This clever economic analysis shows that buyers do not account for prior market conditions when purchasing fine art, which leads to inflated prices for pieces that were previously sold in bull markets.

Bernstein, P. *Against the Gods: The Remarkable Story of Risk.* New York: Wiley, 1998. Bernstein illustrates much of the history of risk, from antecedents in probability theory to consequences for modern markets.

Bshary, R., and A. S. Grutter. "Image Scoring and Cooperation in a Cleaner Fish Mutualism." *Nature* 441 (2006): 975–978. This compelling short report illustrates mutual cooperation in an unlikely setting: cleaner fish working at a coral reef.

Camerer, C. *Behavioral Game Theory: Experiments in Strategic Interaction.* Princeton, NJ: Princeton University Press, 2003. This book provides a comprehensive introduction to the major classes of economic games and their empirical results.

———. "Prospect Theory in the Wild: Evidence from the Field." In *Choices, Values, and Frames*, edited by D. Kahneman and A. Tversky, 288–300. New York: Cambridge University Press, 2000. This article illustrates some key decision-making biases that are difficult to explain using traditional economic models.

Carmon, Z., and D. Ariely. "Focusing on the Forgone: How Value Can Appear So Different to Buyers and Sellers." *Journal of Consumer Research* 27 (2000): 360–370. By examining buying and selling prices for a rare commodity—Duke basketball tickets—this study shows that endowment effects can lead to striking market inefficiencies.

Carter, T. J., and T. Gilovich. "The Relative Relativity of Material and Experiential Purchases." *Journal of Personal and Social Psychology* 98 (2010): 146–159. This psychological article describes a set of studies all pointing toward a common conclusion: Experiences can be more valuable than material goods.

Fehr, E., and U. Fischbacher. "The Nature of Human Altruism." *Nature* 425 (2003): 785–791. This article considers how altruism—and prosocial behavior, more generally—depends on enforcement mechanisms and social norms.

Frank, R. H. *Passions within Reason: The Strategic Role of the Emotions*. New York: Norton, 1988. This thoughtful book describes how emotions can play a very important, adaptive role in decision making, particularly by providing a mechanism for precommitment.

Frey, B. S., and R. Jegen. "Motivation Crowding Theory." *Journal of Economic Surveys* 15 (2001): 589–611. This survey article describes many studies that collectively demonstrate how economic rewards can undermine intrinsic motivation to help others.

Gigerenzer, G., P. M. Todd, and T. A. R. Group. *Simple Heuristics That Make Us Smart*. New York: Oxford University Press, 1999. This edited collection provides a broad overview of "fast and frugal heuristics" models of decision making.

Gilovich, T. *How We Know What Isn't So: The Fallibility of Human Reason in Everyday Life*. New York: Free Press, 1991. This book provides a broad, interesting, and readable introduction to misperceptions in decision making.

Gilovich, T., R. Vallone, and A. Tversky. "The Hot Hand in Basketball: On the Misperception of Random Sequences." *Cognitive Psychology* 17 (1985): 295–314. This article demonstrates—in professional, amateur, and laboratory games—that the prior history of made and missed shots does not affect the accuracy of basketball players. That is, there is no "hot hand."

Gneezy, U., and A. Rustichini. "A Fine Is a Price." *Journal of Legal Studies* 29 (2000): 1–17. This simple but powerful study tracked parents who picked up their children from daycare. After introduction of economic incentives for on-time pickup, the proportion of late parents paradoxically increased.

Harbaugh, W. T., U. Mayr, and D. R. Burghart. "Neural Responses to Taxation and Voluntary Giving Reveal Motives for Charitable Donations." *Science* 316 (2007): 1622-1625. This neuroeconomic study shows how voluntary giving to charity engages brain systems for reward, consistent with warm-glow models of altruism.

Henrich, J., et al. "Markets, Religion, Community Size, and the Evolution of Fairness and Punishment." *Science* 327 (2010): 1480–1484. This anthropological article shows how societal demographic factors contribute to ideas of fairness in economic interactions.

Huber, J., J. W. Payne, and C. Puto. "Adding Asymmetrically Dominated Alternatives: Violations of Regularity and the Similarity Hypothesis." *Journal of Consumer Research* 9 (1982): 90–98. This article describes the phenomenon of asymmetric dominance, in which preferences between two options can be changed by the introduction of a third option that would never itself be chosen.

Johnson, E. J., and D. Goldstein. "Do Defaults Save Lives?" *Science* 302 (2003): 1338–1339. Decision scientists analyzed organ donation rates across a number of countries and showed that the countries that had opt-out policies (i.e., people were automatically organ donors but could choose otherwise) had markedly higher rates of donations.

Johnson, E. J., J. Hershey, J. Meszaros, and H. Kunreuther. "Framing, Probability Distortions, and Insurance Decisions." *Journal of Risk and*

*Uncertainty* 7 (1993): 35–51. This article shows that the vividness of a potential consequence, more than its true probability, shapes our willingness to purchase insurance.

Kahneman, D. *Thinking, Fast and Slow*. New York: Farrar, Straus and Giroux, 2011. This book, written by one of the founding figures of behavioral economics, outlines a psychological approach to judgment and decision making.

Kahneman, D., and A. Tversky. "Prospect Theory: An Analysis of Decision under Risk." *Econometrica* 47 (1979): 263–291. This article introduced prospect theory, which has become a central model within behavioral economics.

Kirby, K. N., and R. J. Herrnstein. "Preference Reversals Due to Myopic Discounting of Delayed Reward." *Psychological Science* 6 (1995): 83–89. This article shows how people switch their preferences from being more patient to more impulsive as a tempting reward becomes closer in time, as predicted by hyperbolic temporal discounting.

Koriat, A. "When Are Two Heads Better Than One and Why?" *Science* 336 (2012): 360–362. Under some specific conditions, group decisions can be worse than those made by individuals in isolation. This article shows that when a systematic bias exists in the population, more confident individuals are actually more likely to be wrong.

Knight, F. H. *Risk, Uncertainty, and Profit*. New York: Houghton Mifflin, 1921. This early book provides an economic perspective on how firms should deal with the unknown. It separates "risk" and "uncertainty" into distinct categories, presaging modern decision science.

Lakshminaryanan, V., M. K. Chen, and L. R. Santos. "Endowment Effect in Capuchin Monkeys." *Philosophical Transactions of the Royal Society B: Biological Sciences* 363 (2008): 3837–3844. This article shows that small, cute capuchin monkeys can learn to trade tokens for food rewards, while showing some of the same decision biases as humans.

Larrick, R. P., and J. B. Soll. "Economics: The MPG Illusion." *Science* 320 (2008): 1593–1594. This elegant study demonstrates that changing the way gasoline usage is reported—from miles per gallon to gallons per mile—can greatly improve the accuracy with which that information is used in economic decisions.

Loewenstein, G. "Frames of Mind in Intertemporal Choice." *Management Science* 34 (1988): 200–214. This study shows how a simple framing manipulation can make people more patient in their choices.

Loewenstein, G., T. Brennan, and K. G. Volpp. "Asymmetric Paternalism to Improve Health Behaviors." *JAMA* 298 (2007): 2415–2417. This editorial comment outlines how nudges should be used—or not used—to improve healthcare.

Mogilner, C., and J. Aaker. "The Time vs. Money Effect: Shifting Product Attitudes and Decisions through Personal Connection." *Journal of Consumer Research* 36 (2009): 277–291. This creative study demonstrates how people can be more motivated by experiences ("spending time") than by material goods ("saving money").

Morewedge, C. K., D. T. Gilbert, and T. D. Wilson. "The Least Likely of Times: How Remembering the Past Biases Forecasts of the Future." *Psychological Sciences* 16 (2005): 626–630. This study shows how people misremember events—they remember rare and extreme examples, not common and typical examples—and how that memory bias shapes subsequent judgment.

Payne, J. W., J. R. Bettman, and E. J. Johnson. *The Adaptive Decision Maker*. New York: Cambridge University Press, 1993. Authored by three leaders in judgment and decision-making research, this book argues that individuals possess a range of tools for decision making and can select different tools based on the decision problem.

Post, T., M. J. Van den Assem, G. Baltussen, and R. H. Thaler. "Deal or No Deal? Decision Making under Risk in a Large-Payoff Game Show." *American Economic Review* 98 (2008): 38–71. Post and colleagues subject the game show *Deal or No Deal* to economic analyses, not only reverse engineering the game itself but also assessing how the features of the game influence its players' behavior.

Rabin, M. "Risk Aversion and Expected-Utility Theory: A Calibration Theorem." *Econometrica* 68 (2000): 1281–1292. Rabin demonstrates, in this technical economic article, that individuals should not be risk averse when making decisions with small stakes—that implies massive risk aversion for large-stakes decisions.

Rangel, A., C. Camerer, and P. R. Montague. "A Framework for Studying the Neurobiology of Value-Based Decision Making." *Nature Reviews Neuroscience* 9 (2008): 545–556. This is a review by leaders in the field of neuroeconomics.

Reyna, V. F., and F. Farley. "Risk and Rationality in Adolescent Decision Making: Implications for Theory, Practice, and Public Policy." *Psychological Science* (2006): 1–44. This comprehensive review article describes what is known about the risky behavior of adolescents, including the counterintuitive notion that adolescents are more rational than adults in many circumstances.

Schelling, T. C. *The Strategy of Conflict*. Cambridge, MA: Harvard University Press, 1960. This masterwork by a Nobel Laureate economist illustrates how differing desires can be resolved through cooperation or conflict.

Sheehan, W. "Venus Spokes: An Explanation at Last?" *Sky & Telescope*, July 23, 2003. Available at http://www.skyandtelescope.com/news/3306251.html. This webpage describes the remarkable resolution to the hundred-year-old story of Percival Lowell's canals on Venus.

Simon, H. A. *Models of Man: Social and Rational*. New York: Wiley, 1957. A Nobel Laureate and polymath, Simon introduces the key ideas of bounded rationality in this book.

Surowiecki, J. *The Wisdom of Crowds*. New York: Anchor Books, 2005. This popularly aimed book provides an engaging overview of how decision quality can (sometimes) be improved by collecting information from large groups.

Taleb, N. N. *Fooled by Randomness: The Hidden Role of Chance in Life and in the Markets*. New York: Random House, 2004. A financial trader by vocation and a philosopher by avocation, Taleb describes how psychological biases lead traders (and everyone else) to see patterns where none exist.

Thaler, R. H., and C. R. Sunstein. *Nudge: Improving Decisions about Health, Wealth, and Happiness*. New Haven, CT: Yale University Press, 2008. This book describes a "paternalistic libertarian" approach to economic institutions. In it, the principles of behavioral economics provide the basis for interventions that can improve individuals' decision making without taking away their freedom of choice.

Tversky, A., and C. R. Fox. "Weighing Risk and Uncertainty." *Psychological Review* 102 (1995): 269–283. This article provides a technical but still accessible introduction to the core ideas of probability weighting.

Tversky, A., and D. Kahneman. "Judgment under Uncertainty: Heuristics and Biases." *Science* 185 (1974): 1124–1131. This seminal paper introduced the primary psychological heuristics that decision makers use to simplify complex choices.

———. "The Framing of Decisions and the Psychology of Choice." *Science* 211 (1981): 453–458. This paper introduced the idea of decision framing: how changes in the way that a decision is presented can exert substantial effects on choice.

Ubel, P. A. *Critical Decisions: How You and Your Doctor Can Make the Right Medical Choices Together*. New York: HarperOne, 2012. A physician and behavioral economist, Ubel describes a broad swath of work that illustrates the biases in medical decision making and how patients can work with their physicians to ameliorate those biases.

Vul, E., and H. Pashler. "Measuring the Crowd Within: Probabilistic Representations within Individuals." *Psychological Sciences* 19 (2008):

645–647. This brief empirical report describes a simple technique for improving one's own decisions, as inspired by the wisdom-of-crowds effect.

Weber, E. U., et al. "Asymmetric Discounting in Intertemporal Choice: A Query-Theory Account." *Psychological Sciences* 18 (2007): 516–523. This article demonstrates that people can become more patient in their choices if they envision the consequences of their decision for their future self.

Zweig, J. *Your Money and Your Brain: How the New Science of Neuroeconomics Can Help Make You Rich.* New York: Simon and Schuster, 2007. Zweig provides an engaging overview of the neuroscience of decision making; this is one of the rare popular finance books that remains relatively true to the original scientific studies.

# Notes

# Notes

# Notes

# Notes

# Notes

# Notes